CANADIAN POETS AND POETRY

CANADIAN POETS
AND POETRY

Chosen and Edited by
JOHN W. GARVIN, B. A.,
Editor of 'The Collected Poems of Isabella Valancy Crawford'

NEW YORK
FREDERICK A. STOKES COMPANY
PUBLISHERS

COPYRIGHT CANADA, 1916
McCLELLAND, GOODCHILD & STEWART, LIMITED
TORONTO

PRINTED IN CANADA

Editor's Foreword

ALMOST simultaneously with the Great War, has come a renaissance of Poetry, which is significant of that law of balance by which the heart turns instinctively from the terror and confusion of devastating human emotion, to the purity of a clearer and serener air.

Poetry, at its height, implies beauty and the driving force of passion. It implies also the austerity and emotional restraint which means spiritual strength, and it is, primarily, to the inherent strength of this Art which faces and pictures the truth in nature and human nature, that the people have turned in times past and will turn in times to come.

This volume contains brief but inclusive records of fifty men and women to whom song has come first. Many of their poems are indigenous to the soil,—vitally, healthfully Canadian; others are tinged with the legendary and mythical lore of older lands; but all are of Canada, inasmuch as the writers have lived in this country, and have been influenced by its history and atmosphere at a formative period of their lives. Among them, one ventures to think, there are world voices.

A recent reading of the published verse of Bliss Carman, has convinced me that he must soon be more widely recognized as a poet of preëminent genius. He is greater than some of more extended fame for the reason that his poetry expresses a nobler and more comprehensive philosophy of life and being. Bliss Carman has achieved more greatly than many others of this generation, because he has realized more fully than they that the Infinite Poet is constantly and eternally seeking media for expression, and that the function of a finite poet is to steadily improve the instrument, to keep it expectantly in tune, and to record the masterpieces.

It seems strange to look back upon the time—thirty-three years ago—when a successful Ontario educator felt justified in the statement that Canada had no national literature worthy of the name, and never would have until the country became an independent nation,—with no shackling colonial ties. At the very moment that such a declaration and prophecy was made, Roberts had begun his brilliant career as a writer,

[5]

Isabella Valancy Crawford was preparing for publication *Old Spookses' Pass, Malcolm's Katie, and Other Poems,* Charles Mair was thinking out the construction of his great drama, *Tecumseh,* and Lampman, Campbell, the two Scotts, Seranus and Bliss Carman were ambitiously fingering the chords. And to-day Canadians have no doubt of their national independence, are prouder than ever of their integral position in the British Empire, and have a school of verse, characterized by freshness, spontaneity, originality of theme and good artistry, that would reflect distinction on the literary genius of any civilized people.

The criticism that "most of the poetry of our day seems to have buried itself in obscurity," is not applicable to the verse of Canada. Even though much of it is highly imaginative and descriptive and sometimes profoundly reflective, the work of Canadian poets is exceptionally free of obscurity, or carelessness in artistic utterance. Love of Nature has been their chief source of inspiration; but themes based on love of humanity and man's kinship with the Infinite Life, have steadily gained of late in number and potency, and the Great War must necessarily arouse a more intense interest in human and divine relationships.

About thirty of the articles in this volume,— revised and improved for book publication—have appeared during the last three years in the *Public Health Journal,* of Toronto.

My thanks are due to the poets and the critics who have so graciously facilitated the preparation of this volume, and to the following owners of copyrights: the living poets included; Mrs. W. H. Drummond; McClelland, Goodchild & Stewart, Toronto; J. M. Dent & Sons, Toronto; S. B. Gundy, Toronto; The Globe Printing Company, Toronto; The Methodist Book and Publishing House, Toronto; Mitchell Kennerly, New York; Small, Maynard & Company, Boston; The Musson Book Company, Toronto; Sherman, French & Company, Boston; Little, Brown & Co., Boston; G. P. Putnam's Sons, New York and London; The Copp, Clark Co., Limited, Toronto; Morang & Co., Toronto; Canadian Magazine; Windsor Magazine; Atlantic Monthly; Metropolitan Magazine; University Magazine and Poetry.

Toronto, Canada,
　　November 1st, 1916.　　　　*John W. Garvin*

Contents

		PAGE
Editor's Foreword	. . . .	5
Charles Sangster	. . . .	9
Charles Mair	. . . .	19
Isabella Valancy Crawford	. . .	33
Charles G. D. Roberts	. . .	47
Archibald Lampman	. . . .	61
Frederick George Scott	. . .	75
Wilfred Campbell	. . . .	87
George Frederick Cameron	. . .	101
Bliss Carman	. . . .	109
S. Frances Harrison	. . .	123
Duncan Campbell Scott	. . .	133
E. Pauline Johnson	. . .	145
E. W. Thomson	. . . .	157
Ethelwyn Wetherald	. . .	167
William Henry Drummond	. . .	177
Jean Blewett	. . . .	189
Arthur Wentworth Hamilton Eaton	. .	197
Helena Coleman	. . . .	205
Thomas O'Hagan	. . . .	213
Elizabeth Roberts MacDonald	. .	221
Albert D. Watson	. . . .	227
Isabel Ecclestone Mackay	. . .	237
Tom McInnes	. . . .	247
Helen M. Merrill	. . . .	259

8 Contents

	PAGE
Dr. J. D. Logan	265
Annie Campbell Huestis	273
Alan Sullivan	281
Alma Frances McCollum	289
Peter McArthur	295
Marjorie L. C. Pickthall	305
Arthur Stringer	313
Katherine Hale	323
Robert Norwood	331
Marian Osborne	341
Albert E. S. Smythe	347
L. M. Montgomery	353
Robert W. Service	359
Florence Randal Livesay	371
Theodore Goodridge Roberts	377
Grace Blackburn	383
George A. Mackenzie	389
Gertude Bartlett	395
William E. Marshall	399
Norah M. Holland	407
Father Dollard	413
Laura E. McCully	421
Lloyd Roberts	429
Beatrice Redpath	437
Alfred Gordon	443
Virna Sheard	451
J. Edgar Middleton	459
Arthur S. Bourinot	463
Index	467

CANADIAN POETS

Charles Sangster

To him belongs the honour of being the first poet who made appreciative use of Canadian subjects in his poetical work. . . . . Though many defects may be found in his first volume, indicating undue haste in preparation and over-confidence on the part of the author, yet fine rhythm and spirit are often met with. . . . . This volume established his position as a poet of no common power, which was freely accorded him by writers in Britain, in the United States and in Canada. The lyric to 'The Isles in the St. Lawrence' is much admired, and also 'The Rapid'. . . . . The second volume is not open to the same objections. The poems are more highly finished and show greater skill and care in the poetic art. Mr. Sangster is at his best, perhaps, in his martial pieces, such as 'Brock,' 'Wolfe,' 'Song for Canada,' etc. . . . . He had a passionate love for nature; but his grand theme was love—the noblest of themes.

—Archibald MacMurchy, M.A., LL.D.

CHARLES SANGSTER was born at the Navy Yard, Point Frederick, Kingston, Ontario, on the 16th of July, 1822. He was the son of a joiner in the British Navy, and the grandson of a United Empire Loyalist, a Scotch soldier who had fought in the American Revolution.

Charles was but two years old when his father died; and when he was but fifteen years of age he retired from school to assist his mother in providing for the family.

He found work, first, in the naval laboratory at Fort Henry; and, second, in a subordinate position in the Ordnance Office, Kingston, which he held for several years.

It was during this period that he began to contribute both prose and verse to the public journals. In 1849, he was appointed editor of the *Courier* in Amherstburg, and went there to reside; but, the following year, resigned and returned to Kingston, where he joined the staff of the *Whig*. Subsequently, in 1864, the *Daily News* of the same city engaged his services.

It was during his journalistic career in the 'Limestone City' that he accomplished his best literary work. His first volume, *The St. Lawrence and the Saguenay, and Other Poems,* appeared in 1856, published by subscription; and his second, *Hesperus, and Other Poems and Lyrics,* in 1860.

When forty-six years of age he accepted a position in the Post-Office Department at Ottawa, where his poetic energy and ambition succumbed, apparently, to the incessant drudgery and to the hampering cares of ill-paid employment.

Sangster was a poet born, but his literary genius was handicapped by his elementary education and limited reading. For his opportunities, he achieved notably. He died in 1893.

Sonnet

I SAT within the temple of her heart,
   And watched the living Soul as it passed through,
Arrayed in pearly vestments, white and pure.
The calm, immortal presence made me start.
It searched through all the chambers of her mind
With one mild glance of love, and smiled to view
The fastnesses of feeling, strong, secure,
And safe from all surprise. It sits enshrined

And offers incense in her heart, as on
An altar sacred unto God. The dawn
Of an imperishable love passed through
The lattice of my senses, and I, too,
Did offer incense in that solemn place—
A woman's heart made pure and sanctified by grace.

Lyric to the Isles

HERE the spirit of Beauty keepeth
Jubilee for evermore;
Here the voice of Gladness leapeth,
  Echoing from shore to shore.
O'er the hidden watery valley,
  O'er each buried wood and glade,
Dances our delighted galley,
  Through the sunlight and the shade;
    Dances o'er the granite cells,
    Where the soul of Beauty dwells;

Here the flowers are ever springing,
  While the summer breezes blow;
Here the Hours are ever clinging,
  Loitering before they go;
Playing round each beauteous islet,
  Loath to leave the sunny shore,
Where, upon her couch of violet,
  Beauty sits for evermore;
    Sits and smiles by day and night,
    Hand in hand with pure Delight.

Here the spirit of Beauty dwelleth
  In each palpitating tree,
In each amber wave that welleth
  From its home beneath the sea;
In the moss upon the granite
  In each calm, secluded bay,
With the zephyr trains that fan it
  With their sweet breaths all the day—
    On the waters, on the shore,
    Beauty dwelleth evermore!

The Soldiers of the Plough

NO maiden dream, nor fancy theme,
  Brown Labour's muse would sing;
Her stately mien and russet sheen
  Demand a stronger wing.
Long ages since, the sage, the prince,
  The man of lordly brow,
All honour gave that army brave,
  The Soldiers of the Plough.
    Kind Heaven speed the plough,
      And bless the hands that guide it!
      God gives the seed—
      The bread we need,
    Man's labour must provide it.

In every land, the toiling hand
  Is blest as it deserves;
Not so the race who, in disgrace,
  From honest labour swerves.
From fairest bowers bring rarest flowers
  To deck the swarthy brow
Of him whose toil improves the soil,—
  The Soldier of the Plough.
    Kind Heaven speed the plough,
      And bless the hands that guide it!
      God gives the seed—
      The bread we need,
    Man's labour must provide it.

Blest is his lot, in hall or cot,
  Who lives as Nature wills,
Who pours his corn from Ceres' horn,
  And quaffs his native rills;
No breeze that sweeps trade's stormy deeps
  Can touch his golden prow.
Their foes are few, their lives are true,
  The Soldiers of the Plough.
    Kind Heaven speed the plough,
      And bless the hands that guide it!
      God gives the seed—
      The bread we need,
    Man's labour must provide it.

Harvest Hymn

GOD of the Harvest, Thou, whose sun
Has ripened all the golden grain,
We bless Thee for Thy bounteous store,
The cup of Plenty running o'er,
  The sunshine and the rain!

The year laughs out for very joy,
  Its silver treble echoing
Like a sweet anthem through the woods,
Till mellowed by the solitudes
  It folds its glossy wing.

But our united voices blend
  From day to day unweariedly;
Sure as the sun rolls up the morn,
Or twilight from the eve is born,
  Our song ascends to Thee.

Where'er the various-tinted woods,
  In all their autumn splendour dressed,
Impart their gold and purple dyes
To distant hills and farthest skies
  Along the crimson west:

Across the smooth, extended plain,
  By rushing stream and broad lagoon,
On shady height and sunny dale,
Wherever scuds the balmy gale
  Or gleams the autumn moon:

From inland seas of yellow grain,
  Where cheerful Labour, heaven-blest,
With willing hands and keen-edged scythe,
And accents musically blythe,
  Reveals its lordly crest:

From clover-fields and meadows wide,
  Where moves the richly-laden wain
To barns well-stored with new-made hay,
Or where the flail at early day
  Rolls out the ripened grain:

From meads and pastures on the hills
   And in the mountain valleys deep,
Alive with beeves and sweet-breathed kine
Of famous Ayr or Devon's line
   And shepherd-guarded sheep:

The spirits of the golden year,
   From crystal caves and grottoes dim,
From forest depths and mossy sward,
Myriad-tongued, with one accord
   Peal forth their harvest hymn.

The Rapid

ALL peacefully gliding,
   The waters dividing,
The indolent batteau moved slowly along,
   The rowers, light-hearted,
   From sorrow long parted,
Beguiled the dull moments with laughter and song:
'Hurrah for the rapid that merrily, merrily
   Gambols and leaps on its tortuous way!
Soon we will enter it, cheerily, cheerily,
   Pleased with its freshness, and wet with its spray.'

   More swiftly careering,
   The wild rapid nearing,
They dash down the stream like a terrified steed;
   The surges delight them,
   No terrors affright them,
Their voices keep pace with the quickening speed:
'Hurrah for the rapid that merrily, merrily
   Shivers its arrows against us in play!
Now we have entered it, cheerily, cheerily,
   Our spirits as light as its feathery spray.'

   Fast downward they're dashing,
   Each fearless eye flashing,
Though danger awaits them on every side.
   Yon rock—see it frowning!
   They strike—they are drowning!

But downward they speed with the merciless tide;
No voice cheers the rapid, that angrily, angrily
   Shivers their bark in its maddening play;
Gaily they entered it—heedlessly, recklessly,
   Mingling their lives with its treacherous spray!

The Wine of Song

WITHIN Fancy's halls I sit and quaff
   Rich draughts of the wine of Song,
     And I drink and drink
     To the very brink
   Of delirium wild and strong,
Till I lose all sense of the outer world
   And see not the human throng.

The lyral chords of each rising thought
   Are swept by a hand unseen,
     And I glide and glide
     With my music bride,
   Where few spiritless souls have been;
And I soar afar on wings of sound
   With my fair Æolian queen.

Deep, deeper still, from the springs of Thought
   I quaff till the fount is dry,
     And I climb and climb
     To a height sublime
   Up the stars of some lyric sky,
Where I seem to rise upon airs that melt
   Into song as they pass by.

Millennial rounds of bliss I live,
   Withdrawn from my cumb'rous clay,
     As I sweep and sweep
     Through infinite deep
   On deep of that starry spray;
Myself a sound on its world-wide round,
   A tone on its spheral way.

And wheresoe'er through the wondrous space
   My soul wings its noiseless flight,

On their astral rounds
Float divinest sounds,
Unseen, save by spirit-sight,
Obeying some wise, eternal law,
As fixed as the law of light.

But, oh, when my cup of dainty bliss
Is drained of the wine of Song,
How I fall and fall
At the sober call
Of the body that waiteth long
To hurry me back to its cares terrene,
And earth's spiritless human throng!

Brock

ONE voice, one people, one in heart
And soul and feeling and desire.
Re-light the smouldering martial fire
And sound the mute trumpet! Strike the lyre!
The hero dead cannot expire:
The dead still play their part.

Raise high the monumental stone!
A nation's fealty is theirs,
And we are the rejoicing heirs,
The honoured sons of sires whose cares
We take upon us unawares
As freely as our own.

We boast not of the victory,
But render homage, deep and just,
To his—to their—immortal dust,
Who proved so worthy of their trust;
No lofty pile nor sculptured bust
Can herald their degree.

No tongue can blazon forth their fame—
The cheers that stir the sacred hill
Are but mere promptings of the will
That conquered them, that conquers still;
And generations yet shall thrill
At Brock's remembered name.

Some souls are the Hesperides
    Heaven sends to guard the golden age,
    Illumining the historic page
    With record of their pilgrimage.
    True martyr, hero, poet, sage,—
And he was one of these.

Each in his lofty sphere, sublime,
    Sits crowned above the common throng:
    Wrestling with some pythonic wrong
    In prayer, in thunders, thought or song,
    Briareus-limbed, they sweep along,
The Typhons of the time.

The Plains of Abraham

I STOOD upon the Plain,
    That had trembled when the slain,
Hurled their proud defiant curses at the battle-hearted foe,
    When the steed dashed right and left
    Through the bloody gaps he cleft,
When the bridle-rein was broken, and the rider was laid low.

    What busy feet had trod
    Upon the very sod
Where I marshalled the battalions of my fancy to my aid!
    And I saw the combat dire,
    Heard the quick, incessant fire,
And the cannons' echoes startling the reverberating glade.

    I saw them one and all,
    The banners of the Gaul
In the thickest of the contest, round the resolute Montcalm;
    The well-attended Wolfe,
    Emerging from the gulf
Of the battle's fiery furnace, like the swelling of a psalm.

    I heard the chorus dire,
    That jarred along the lyre
On which the hymn of battle rung, like surgings of the wave
    When the storm, at blackest night,

Wakes the ocean in affright,
As it shouts its mighty pibroch o'er some shipwrecked vessel's
    grave.

I saw the broad claymore
Flash from its scabbard, o'er
The ranks that quailed and shuddered at the close and fierce
    attack;
When Victory gave the word,
Then Scotland drew the sword,
And with arm that never faltered drove the brave defenders
    back.

I saw two great chiefs die,
Their last breaths like the sigh
Of the zepher-sprite that wantons on the rosy lips of morn;
No envy-poisoned darts,
No rancour in their hearts,
To unfit them for their triumph over death's impending scorn.

And as I thought and gazed,
My soul, exultant, praised
The Power to whom each mighty act and victory are due,
For the saint-like Peace that smiled
Like a heaven-gifted child,
And for the air of quietude that steeped the distant view.

The sun looked down with pride,
And scattered far and wide
His beams of whitest glory till they flooded all the Plain;
The hills their veils withdrew,
Of white, and purplish blue,
And reposed all green and smiling 'neath the shower of golden
    rain.

Oh, rare, divinest life
Of Peace, compared with Strife!
Yours is the truest splendour, and the most enduring fame;
All the glory ever reaped
Where the fiends of battle leaped,
Is harsh discord to the music of your undertoned acclaim.

Charles Mair

*Charles Mair is the first of our poets of the nature school.
. . . . He might in many senses be called the first Canadian poet, as his first volume was published in 1868, one
year following Confederation. 'Dreamland' was a small volume
of one hundred and fifty pages, printed at the Citizen Printing
House in Ottawa. The author was then in his thirtieth
year. The thirty-three poems constitute the first attempt to
deal with Canadian nature, in the manner of Keats and the
other classic poets, and many of them in theme and treatment
are similar to the verse of Lampman and Roberts. . . . . .
And there are strong evidences in Mair's work that he influenced these poets to a great extent.*—WILFRED CAMPBELL, in
the Ottawa 'Journal.'

*Charles Mair and Isabella Valancy Crawford, whose
best work was written in the early 80's of last century,
were the first to raise the standard of Canadian poetry to
greatness, and it is doubtful if their work has since been out-
classed by that of any successor.*—'Public Health Journal.'

[19]

A S *Tecumseh*—a drama, native to the soil, and still without a successful rival—was published in 1886, and as the same author, by the publication in 1868 of *Dreamland and Other Poems,* originated our nature school of verse, it seems clear that the poetical work of Charles Mair has a significance in Canadian literature, not yet fully recognized.

Charles Mair, son of the late James Mair, a native of Scotland, one of the pioneers of the old square timber trade in the Ottawa valley, and Margaret (Holmes) Mair, was born in Lanark, Ontario, September, 1838. He was educated at the Perth Grammar School and at Queen's University, Kingston. In 1867, he returned to Queen's College and studied medicine. In the summer of 1868, he was called to Ottawa by the Hon. William McDougall, Minister of Public Works, to prepare a *précis* of available records in the Parliamentary Library, pertaining to the Hudson's Bay Company's territories and tenure. The following autumn, he was appointed paymaster of the first expedition sent to the North-West by the Canadian Government, its object being to open up an immigration route via the Lake of the Woods, and was requested to describe in the press, the prairie country and its inducement to settlers. His correspondence to the Toronto *Globe* and the Montreal *Gazette* was widely copied and was potent in influencing western immigration.

In Winnipeg, Sept. 8th, 1869, he married Elizabeth Louise, daughter of the late Augustus Mackenney, Amherstburg, Ont., and a niece of Sir John C. Schultz, K.C.M.G.

During the first Riel rebellion, 1869-70, Mr. Mair was imprisoned by the rebels, and until he escaped, his life was in serious danger, but his greatest distress was caused by the loss of valuable manuscripts which he had taken with him to the West, to revise and prepare for publication, and which his memory was unable to restore.

This loss and discouragement doubtless had its effect, for his next publication did not appear until 1886. In the meantime he was engaged in the fur trade at Portage la Prairie and later at Prince Albert until 1883, when he returned to Ontario and resided at Windsor. It was during the next two years that he had leisure to write his great drama.

In 1885, when the second Riel rebellion broke out, Mr. Mair promptly enlisted and served as quartermaster in the Governor General's Body Guard, commanded by Col. G. T. Denison. Afterwards he removed to Kelowna, B.C., of which he was one of the founders. Subsequently he joined the Immigration Service at Winnipeg, and several years later, took charge of the Lethbridge Immigration Office and Agency. Thence was removed to Coutts on the Boundary, and was afterwards transferred as relieving officer to Fort Steele, B.C., where he now resides.

The Last Bison, an original and virile poem of gripping interest, was written in 1890. In 1901, his collected poems, *Tecumseh, a drama, and Canadian Poems,* was published; and in 1908, there appeared in prose, his *Through the Mackenzie Basin,* an important work giving an account of the great Peace River Treaty of 1899, with the Indians of the North, who ceded a territory 800 miles by 400 in length and breadth. Mr. Mair was English Secretary to the Scrip Commission and gave a favourable account of the vast region, since confirmed by the extensive immigration into that country.

The Last Bison

EIGHT years have fled since, in the wilderness,
I drew the rein to rest my comrade there—
My supple, clean-limbed pony of the plains.
He was a runner of pure Indian blood,
Yet in his eye still gleamed the desert's fire,
And form and action both bespoke the Barb.
A wondrous creature is the Indian's horse;
Degenerate now, but from the 'Centaurs' drawn—
The apparitions which dissolved with fear
Montezuma's plumed Children of the Sun,
And throned rough Cortez in his realm of gold.

A gentle vale, with rippling aspens clad,
Yet open to the breeze, invited rest.
So there I lay, and watched the sun's fierce beams
Reverberate in wreathed ethereal flame;
Or gazed upon the leaves which buzzed o'erhead,
Like tiny wings in simulated flight.

2

Within the vale a lakelet, lashed with flowers,
Lay like a liquid eye among the hills,
Revealing in its depths the fulgent light
Of snowy cloud-land and cerulean skies.
And rising, falling, fading far around,
The homeless and unfurrowed prairies spread
In solitude and idleness eterne.

And all was silent save the rustling leaf,
The gadding insect, or the grebe's lone cry,
Or where Saskatchewan, with turbid moan,
Deep-sunken in the plain, his torrent poured.
Here Loneliness possessed her realm supreme,
Her prairies all about her, undeflowered,
Pulsing beneath the summer sun, and sweet
With virgin air and waters undefiled.
Inviolate still! Bright solitudes, with power
To charm the spirit-bruised, where ways are foul,
Into forgetfulness of chuckling wrong
And all the weary clangour of the world.

Yet, Sorrow, too, had here its kindred place,
As o'er my spirit swept the sense of change.
Here sympathy could sigh o'er man's decay;
For here, but yesterday, the warrior dwelt
Whose faded nation had for ages held,
In fealty to Nature, these domains.
Around me were the relics of his race:
The grassy circlets where his village stood,
Well-ruled by custom's immemorial law.
Along these slopes his happy offspring roved
In days gone by, and dusky mothers plied
Their summer tasks, or loitered in the shade.
Here the magician howled his demons up,
And here the lodge of council had its seat,
Once resonant with oratory wild.
All vanished! perished in the swelling sea
And stayless tide of an enroaching power
Whose civil fiat, man-devouring still,
Will leave, at last, no wilding on the earth
To wonder at or love!

With them had fled
The bison-breed which overflowed the plains,
And, undiminished, fed uncounted tribes.
Its vestiges were here—its wallows, paths,
And skulls and shining ribs and vertebrae:
Gray bones of monarchs from the herds, perchance,
Descended, by De Vaca first beheld,
Or Coronada, in mad quest of gold.
Here hosts had had their home; here had they roamed,
Endless and infinite—vast herds which seemed
Exhaustless as the sea. All vanished now!
Of that wild tumult not a hoof remained
To scour the countless paths where myriads trod.

Long had I lain 'twixt dreams and waking, thus,
Musing on change and mutability,
And endless evanescence, when a burst
Of sudden roaring filled the vale with sound.
Perplexed and startled, to my feet I sprang,
And in amazement from my covert gazed,
For, presently, into the valley came
A mighty bison, which, with stately tread
And gleaming eyes, descended to the shore.
Spell-bound I stood. Was this a living form,
Or but an image by the fancy drawn?
But no—he breathed! and from a wound blood flowed,
And trickled with the frothing from his lips.
Uneasily he gazed, yet saw me not,
Haply concealed; then, with a roar so loud
That all the echoes rent their valley-horns,
He stood and listened; but no voice replied!
Deeply he drank, then lashed his quivering flanks,
And roared again, and hearkened, but no sound,
No tongue congenial answered to his call—
He was the last survivor of his clan!

Huge was his frame! the famed Burdash, so grown
To that enormous bulk whose presence filled
The very vale with awe. His shining horns
Gleamed black amidst his fell of floating hair—
His neck and shoulders, of the lion's build,

Were framed to toss the world. Now stood he there
And stared, with head uplifted, at the skies,
Slow-yielding to his deep and mortal wound.
He seemed to pour his mighty spirit out
As thus he gazed, till my own spirit burned,
And teeming fancy, charmed and overwrought
By all the wildering glamour of the scene,
Gave to that glorious attitude a voice,
And, rapt, endowed the noble beast with song.

The Song

Here me, ye smokeless skies and grass-green earth,
   Since by your sufferance still I breathe and live!
Through you fond Nature gave me birth,
   And food and freedom—all she had to give.
Enough! I grew, and with my kindred ranged
Their realm stupendous, changeless and unchanged,
   Save by the toil of nations primitive,
Who throve on us, and loved our life-stream's roar,
And lived beside its wave, and camped upon its shore.

They loved us, and they wasted not. They slew,
   With pious hand, but for their daily need;
Not wantonly, but as the due
   Of stern necessity which Life doth breed.
Yea, even as earth gave us herbage meet,
So yielded we, in turn, our substance sweet
   To quit the claims of hunger, not of greed.
So stood it with us that what either did
Could not be on the earth foregone, nor Heaven forbid.

And, so companioned in the blameless strife
   Enjoined upon all creatures, small and great,
Our ways were venial, and our life
   Ended in fair fulfilment of our fate.
No gold to them by sordid hands was passed;
No greedy herdsman housed us from the blast;
   Ours was the liberty of regions rife
In winter's snow, in summer's fruits and flowers—
Ours were the virgin prairies, and their rapture ours!

So fared it with us both; yea, thus it stood
In all our wanderings from place to place,
Until the red man mixed his blood
With paler currents. Then arose a race—
The reckless hunters of the plains—who vied
In wanton slaughter for the tongue and hide,
To satisfy vain ends and longings base.
This grew; and yet we flourished, and our name
Prospered until the pale destroyer's concourse came.

Then fell a double terror on the plains,
The swift inspreading of destruction dire—
Strange men, who ravaged our domains
On every hand, and ringed us round with fire;
Pale enemies who slew with equal mirth
The harmless or the hurtful things of earth,
In dead fruition of their mad desire:
The ministers of mischief and of might,
Who yearn for havoc as the world's supreme delight.

So waned the myriads which had waxed before
When subject to the simple needs of men.
As yields to eating seas the shore,
So yielded our vast multitude, and then—
It scattered! Meagre bands, in wild dismay,
Were parted and, for shelter, fled away
To barren wastes, to mountain gorge and glen.
A respite brief from stern pursuit and care,
For still the spoiler sought, and still he slew us there.

Hear me, thou grass-green earth, ye smokeless skies,
Since by your sufferance still I breathe and live!
The charity which man denies
Ye still would tender to the fugitive!
I feel your mercy in my veins—at length
My heart revives, and strengthens with your strength—
Too late, too late, the courage ye would give!
Naught can avail these wounds, this failing breath,
This frame which feels, at last, the wily touch of death.

Here must the last of all his kindred fall;
Yet, midst these gathering shadows, ere I die—

Responsive to an inward call,
  My spirit fain would rise and prophesy.
I see our spoilers build their cities great
Upon our plains—I see their rich estate:
  The centuries in dim procession fly!
Long ages roll, and then at length is bared
The time when they who spared not are no longer spared.

Once more my vision sweeps the prairies wide,
  But now no peopled cities greet the sight;
All perished, now, their pomp and pride:
  In solitude the wild wind takes delight.
Naught but the vacant wilderness is seen,
And grassy mounds, where cities once had been.
  The earth smiles as of yore, the skies are bright,
Wild cattle graze and bellow on the plain,
And savage nations roam o'er native wilds again.

———

The burden ceased, and now, with head bowed down,
The bison smelt, then grinned into the air.
An awful anguish seized his giant frame,
Cold shudderings and indrawn gaspings deep—
The spasms of illimitable pain.
One stride he took, and sank upon his knees,
Glared stern defiance where I stood revealed,
Then swayed to earth, and, with convulsive groan,
Turned heavily upon his side, and died.

From 'Tecumseh'

LEFROY. This region is as lavish of its flowers
   As heaven of its primrose blooms by night.
This is the arum which within its root
Folds life and death; and this the prince's pine,
Fadeless as love and truth—the fairest form
That ever sun-shower washed with sudden rain.
This golden cradle is the moccasin flower,
Wherein the Indian hunter sees his hound;
And this dark chalice is the pitcher-plant,
Stored with the water of forgetfulness.
Whoever drinks of it, whose heart is pure,

Will sleep for aye 'neath foodful asphodel
And dream of endless love. I need it not.
I am awake, and yet I dream of love.
It is the hour of meeting, when the sun
Takes level glances at these mighty woods,
And Iena has never failed till now
To meet me here. What keeps her? Can it be
The Prophet? Ah, that villain has a thought,
Undreamt of by his simple followers,
Dark in his soul as midnight! If—but no—
He fears her though he hates.

What shall I do?
Rehearse to listening woods, or ask these oaks
What thoughts they have, what knowledge of the past?
They dwarf me with their greatness, but shall come
A meaner and a mightier than they,
And cut them down. Yet rather would I dwell
With them, with wildness and its stealthy forms—
Yea, rather with wild men, wild beasts and birds,
Than in the sordid town that here may rise.
For here I am a part of nature's self,
And not divorced from her like men who plod
The weary streets of care in search of gain.
And here I feel the friendship of the earth:
Not the soft cloying tenderness of hand
Which fain would satiate the hungry soul
With household honey combs and parloured sweets,
But the strong friendship of primeval things—
The rugged kindness of a giant heart,
And love that lasts.

I have a poem made
Which doth concern earth's injured majesty—
Be audience, ye still untroubled stems!

(Recites)

There was a time on this fair continent
When all things throve in spacious peacefulness.
The prosperous forests unmolested stood,
For where the stalwart oak grew there it lived
Long ages, and then died among its kind.

The hoary pines—those ancients of the earth—
Brimful of legends of the early world,
Stood thick on their own mountains unsubdued.
And all things else illumined by the sun,
Inland or by the lifted wave, had rest.
The passionate or calm pageants of the skies
No artist drew; but in the auburn west
Innumerable faces of fair cloud
Vanished in silent darkness with the day.
The prairie realm—vast ocean's paraphrase—
Rich in wild grasses numberless, and flowers
Unnamed save in mute nature's inventory,
No civilized barbarian trenched for gain.
And all that flowed was sweet and uncorrupt.
The rivers and their tributary streams,
Undammed, wound on forever, and gave up
Their lonely torrents to weird gulfs of sea,
And ocean wastes unshadowed by a sail.
And all the wild life of this western world
Knew not the fear of man; yet in those woods,
And by those plenteous streams and mighty lakes,
And on stupendous steppes of peerless plain,
And in the rocky gloom of canyons deep,
Screened by the stony ribs of mountains hoar
Which steeped their snowy peaks in purging cloud,
And down the continent where tropic suns
Warmed to her very heart the mother earth,
And in the congealed north where silence' self
Ached with intensity of stubborn frost,
There lived a soul more wild than barbarous:
A tameless soul—the sunburnt savage free—
Free, and untainted by the greed of gain:
Great nature's man content with nature's food.

But hark! I hear her footsteps in the leaves—
And so my poem ends.
                    —Scene II, Act I.
          . . . .

Tecumseh to General Harrison

TECUMSEH.   .   .   .

Once all this mighty continent was ours,
And the Great Spirit made it for our use.
He knew no boundaries, so had we peace
In the vast shelter of His handiwork,
And, happy here, we cared not whence we came.
We brought no evils thence—no treasured hate,
No greed of gold, no quarrels over God;
And so our broils, to narrow issues joined,
Were soon composed, and touched the ground of peace.
Our very ailments, rising from the earth,
And not from any foul abuse in us,
Drew back, and let age ripen to death's hand.
Thus flowed our lives until your people came,
Till from the East our matchless misery came!
Since then our tale is crowded with your crimes,
With broken faith, with plunder of reserves—
The sacred remnants of our wide domain—
With tamp'rings, and delirious feasts of fire,
The fruit of your thrice-cursèd stills of death
Which make our good men bad, our bad men worse,
Ay, blind them till they grope in open day
And stumble into miserable graves!
Oh, it is piteous, for none will hear!
There is no hand to help, no heart to feel,
No tongue to plead for us in all your land.
But every hand aims death, and every heart,
Ulcered with hate, resents our presence here;
And every tongue cries for our children's land
To expiate their crime of being born.
Oh, we have ever yielded in the past,
But we shall yield no more! Those plains are ours!
Those forests are our birth-right and our home!
Let not the Long-Knife build one cabin there—
Or fire from it will spread to every roof,
To compass you, and light your souls to death!
                              —Scene IV, Act II.

.   .   .   .

Enter General Brock and Lefroy

BROCK. You may be right, Lefroy, but, for my part,
I stand by old tradition and the past.
My father's God is wise enough for me,
And wise enough this gray world's wisest men.
    LEFROY. I tell you, Brock,
The world is wiser than its wisest men,
And shall outlive the wisdom of its gods,
Made after man's own liking. The crippled throne
No longer shelters the uneasy king,
And outworn sceptres and Imperial crowns
Now grow fantastic as an idiot's dream.
These perish with the kingly pastime, war,
And war's blind tool, the monster, Ignorance,
Both hateful in themselves, but this the worst.
One tyrant will remain—one impious fiend
Whose name is Gold—our earliest, latest foe.
Him must the earth destroy, ere man can rise,
Rightly self-made, to his high destiny,
Purged of his grossest faults: humane and kind;
Co-equal with his fellows and as free.
    BROCK. Lefroy, such thoughts let loose would wreck the
        world.
The kingly function is the soul of state,
The crown the emblem of authority,
And loyalty the symbol of all faith.
Omitting these, man's government decays—
His family falls into revolt and ruin.
But let us drop this bootless argument,
And tell me more of those unrivalled wastes
You and Tecumseh visited.
    LEFROY.   We left
The silent forest, and, day after day,
Great prairies swept beyond our aching sight
Into the measureless West; uncharted realms,
Voiceless and calm, save when tempestuous wind
Rolled the rank herbage into billows vast,
And rushing tides which never found a shore.
And tender clouds, and veils of morning mist,

Cast flying shadows, chased by flying light,
Into interminable wildernesses,
Flushed with fresh blooms, deep perfumed by the rose,
And murmurous with flower-fed bird and bee.
The deep-grooved bison-paths like furrows lay,
Turned by the cloven hoofs of thundering herds
Primeval, and still travelled as of yore.
And gloomy valleys opened at our feet,
Shagged with dusk cypresses and hoary pine;
The sunless gorges, rummaged by the wolf,
Which through long reaches of the prairie wound,
Then melted slowly into upland vales,
Lingering, far-stretched amongst the spreading hills.

BROCK. What charming solitudes! And life was there?
LEFROY. Yes, life was there, inexplicable life,
Still wasted by inexorable death!
There had the stately stag his battle-field—
Dying for mastery among his hinds.
There vainly sprung the affrighted antelope,
Beset by glittering eyes and hurrying feet.
The dancing grouse, at their insensate sport,
Heard not the stealthy footstep of the fox;
The gopher on his little earthwork stood,
With folded arms, unconscious of the fate
That wheeled in narrowing circles overhead;
And the poor mouse, on heedless nibbling bent,
Marked not the silent coiling of the snake.
At length we heard a deep and solemn sound—
Erupted moanings of the troubled earth
Trembling beneath innumerable feet.
A growing uproar blending in our ears,
With noise tumultuous as ocean's surge,
Of bellowings, fierce breath and battle shock,
And ardour of unconquerable herds.
A multitude whose trampling shook the plains,
With discord of harsh sound and rumblings deep,
As if the swift revolving earth had struck,
And from some adamantine peak recoiled,
Jarring. At length we topped a high-browed hill—
The last and loftiest of a file of such—

And, lo, before us lay the tameless stock,
Slow wending to the northward like a cloud!
A multitude in motion, dark and dense—
Far as eye could reach, and farther still,
In countless myriads stretched for many a league.
    BROCK. You fire me with the picture! What a scene!
    LEFROY. Nation on nation was invillaged there,
Skirting the flanks of that imbanded host;
With chieftains of strange speech and port of war,
Who, battled-armed, in weather-brawny bulk,
Roamed fierce and free in huge and wild content.
These gave Tecumseh greetings fair and kind,
Knowing the purpose havened in his soul.
And he, too, joined the chase as few men dare:
For I have seen him, leaping from his horse,
Mount a careering bull in foaming flight,
Urge it to fury o'er its burden strange,
Yet cling tenacious, with a grip of steel,
Then, by a knife-plunge, fetch it to its knees
In mid career and pangs of speedy death.
    BROCK. You rave, Lefroy, or saw this in a dream!
    LEFROY. No, no; 'tis true—I saw him do it, Brock!
Then would he seek the old, and with his spoils
Restore them to the bounty of their youth,
Cheering the crippled lodge with plenteous feasts,
And warmth of glossy robes, as soft as down,
Till withered cheeks ran o'er with feeble smiles,
And tongues, long silent, babbled of their prime.
    BROCK. This warrior's fabric is of perfect parts!
A worthy champion of his race—he heaps
Such giant obligations on our heads
As will outweigh repayment. It is late,
And rest must preface war's hot work to-morrow,
Else would I talk till morn. How still the night!
Here Peace has let her silvery tresses down
And falls asleep beside the lapping wave.
                  —Scene VI, Act IV.

Isabella Valancy Crawford

Let us to the work of this divinely dowered Isabella—this angelic mendicant, craving nothing of life but its finer gifts—this blessed gypsy of Canadian woods and streams. What a royal life she led! No pose to take, no reputation to sustain, no tendency to routine thinking or lassitude of the imaginative faculty to be struggled with . . . . not a single syllable out-breathing the 'vulgar luxury of despair.' Happy, happy poet! She, like every other genius, found in the ecstasy of expression at the full height of her nature a compensation that turned all outward trials into details not worth speaking of. . . . . She is purely a genius, not a craftswoman, and a genius who has patience enough to be an artist. She has in abundant measure that power of youth which persists in poets of every age—that capacity of seeing things for the first time, and with the rose and pearl of dawn upon them. . . . . —ETHELYWN WETHERALD in her Introduction to 'The Collected Poems.'

ISABELLA VALANCY CRAWFORD, one of the greatest of women poets, was born of cultured parents,—Stephen Dennis Crawford, M.D., and Sydney Scott—in Dublin, Ireland, on Christmas day, 1850.

In 1858, the family emigrated to Upper Canada and settled at Paisley, on the Saugeen river. Of these pioneer days in Bruce county, Maud Wheeler Wilson writes:

> The village was but just struggling out of the embrace of the forest, and it was here that the little Isabella, who had developed into a shy and studious child, blue-eyed and with a beautiful profile, beheld the practical results of those harbingers of civilization—the axe, the plough and the hammer—whose work she afterward depicted in *Malcolm's Katie.* . . . . Their children's education was conducted by both Dr. and Mrs. Crawford. The girls were carefully grounded in Latin, as well as in the English branches. They spoke French readily and were conversant with the good literature of the day, Isabella especially being an omnivorous reader, fondest of history and of verse, and claiming Dante as her favourite poet.

Good fortune did not accompany the Crawfords to the New World. In a few years, disease had taken nine of the twelve children, and a small medical practice had reduced the family to semi-poverty. In 1864, the remaining members moved to the village of Lakefield, the southern entrance to the beautiful Kawartha Lakes, in the county of Peterborough, and lived there about eight years. They then moved to the town of Peterborough, where the Doctor continued the practice of his profession, until his demise in 1875.

Prior to her sudden and premature death from heart failure, on February 12th, 1887, Miss Crawford and her mother had lived for nearly a decade in the city of Toronto,—most of the time in humble lodgings over a small corner grocery store on King St. Here this brilliant writer strove with tireless pen, to earn sufficient for their support. A small quarterly allowance was sent them regularly by Dr. John Irwin Crawford, of the Royal Navy, to whom his grateful niece dedicated her book of verse, *Old Spookses' Pass,* which she published at a financial loss in 1884.

In 1905, the editor of this volume, with the knowledge and consent of her brother, Mr. Stephen Crawford, collected, edited and published Miss Crawford's best poems, in a volume of over three hundred pages, together with a comprehensive and critical Introduction by Miss Wetherald.

Songs for the Soldiers

IF songs be sung let minstrels strike their harps
To large and joyous strains, all thunder-winged
To beat along vast shores. Ay, let their notes
Wild into eagles soaring toward the sun,
And voiced like bugles bursting through the dawn
When armies leap to life! Give them such breasts
As hold immortal fires, and they shall fly,
Swept with our little sphere through all the change
That waits a whirling world.
                            Joy's an immortal;
She hath a fiery fibre in her flesh
That will not droop or die; so let her chant
The pæans of the dead, where holy Grief
Hath, trembling, thrust the feeble mist aside
That veils her dead, and in the wondrous clasp
Of re-possession ceases to be Grief.
Joy's ample voice shall still roll over all,
And chronicle the heroes to young hearts
Who knew them not. . . . .
                            There's glory on the sword
That keeps its scabbard-sleep, unless the foe
Beat at the wall, then freely leaps to light
And thrusts to keep the sacred towers of Home
And the dear lines that map the nation out upon the world.

His Mother

IN the first dawn she lifted from her bed
The holy silver of her noble head,
And listened, listened, listened for his tread.

'Too soon, too soon!' she murmured, 'Yet I'll keep
My vigil longer—thou, O tender Sleep,
Art but the joy of those who wake and weep!

'Joy's self hath keen, wide eyes. O flesh of mine,
And mine own blood and bone, the very wine
Of my aged heart, I see thy dear eyes shine!

'I hear thy tread; thy light, loved footsteps run
Along the way, eager for that 'Well done!'
We'll weep and kiss to thee, my soldier son!

'Blest mother I—he lives! Yet had he died
Blest were I still,—I sent him on the tide
Of my full heart to save his nation's pride!'

'O God, if that I tremble so to-day,
Bowed with such blessings that I cannot pray
By speech—a mother prays, dear Lord, alway

'In some far fibre of her trembling mind!
I'll up—I thought I heard a bugle bind
Its silver with the silver of the wind.'

His Wife and Baby

IN the lone place of the leaves,
Where they touch the hanging eaves,
There sprang a spray of joyous song that sounded sweet and
    sturdy;
And the baby in the bed
Raised the shining of his head,
And pulled the mother's lids apart to wake and watch the birdie.

She kissed lip-dimples sweet,
The red soles of his feet,
The waving palms that patted hers as wind-blown blossoms
    wander;
He twined her tresses silk
Round his neck as white as milk—
'Now, baby, say what birdie sings upon his green spray yonder.'

'He sings a plenty things—
Just watch him wash his wings!
He says Papa will march to-day with drums home through the
    city.
Here, birdie, here's my cup.
You drink the milk all up;
I'll kiss you, birdie, now you're washed like baby clean and
    pretty.'

She rose; she sought the skies
With the twin joys of her eyes;
She sent the strong dove of her soul up through the dawning's
    glory;

She kissed upon her hand
The glowing golden band
That bound the fine scroll of her life and clasped her simple
    story.

His Sweetheart

SYLVIA'S lattices were dark—
    Roses made them narrow.
In the dawn there came a Spark,
    Armèd with an arrow:
Blithe he burst by dewy spray,
    Winged by bud and blossom,
All undaunted urged his way
    Straight to Sylvia's bosom.
'Sylvia! Sylvia! Sylvia!' he
    Like a bee kept humming,
'Wake, my sweeting'; waken thee,
    For thy Soldier's coming!'

Sylvia sleeping in the dawn,
    Dreams that Cupid's trill is
Roses singing on the lawn,
    Courting crested lilies.
Sylvia smiles and Sylvia sleeps,
    Sylvia weeps and slumbers;
Cupid to her pink ear creeps,
    Pipes his pretty numbers.
Sylvia dreams that bugles play,
    Hears a martial drumming;
Sylvia springs to meet the day
    With her Soldier coming.

Happy Sylvia, on thee wait
    All the gracious graces!
Venus mild her cestus plait
    Round thy lawns and laces!
Flora fling a flower most fair,
    Hope a rainbow lend thee!
All the nymphs to Cupid dear
    On this day befriend thee!
'Sylvia! Sylvia! Sylvia!' hear

How he keeps a-humming,
Laughing in her jewelled ear,
'Sweet, thy Soldier's coming!'

From ' Malcolm's Katie '

O LIGHT canoe, where dost thou glide?
   Below thee gleams no silvered tide,
But concave heaven's chiefest pride.

Above thee burns Eve's rosy bar;
Below thee throbs her darling star;
Deep 'neath thy keel her round worlds are.

Above, below—O sweet surprise
To gladden happy lover's eyes!
No earth, no wave—all jewelled skies.

. . . .

There came a morn the Moon of Falling Leaves
With her twin silver blades had only hung
Above the low set cedars of the swamp
For one brief quarter, when the Sun arose
Lusty with light and full of summer heat,
And, pointing with his arrows at the blue
Closed wigwam curtains of the sleeping Moon,
Laughed with the noise of arching cataracts,
And with the dove-like cooing of the woods,
And with the shrill cry of the diving loon,
And with the wash of saltless rounded seas,
And mocked the white Moon of the Falling Leaves:

"Esa! esa! shame upon you, Pale Face!
Shame upon you, Moon of Evil Witches!
Have you killed the happy, laughing Summer?
Have you slain the mother of the flowers
With your icy spells of might and magic?
Have you laid her dead within my arms?
Wrapped her, mocking, in a rainbow blanket?
Drowned her in the frost-mist of your anger?
She is gone a little way before me;
Gone an arrow's flight beyond my vision.

She will turn again and come to meet me
With the ghosts of all the stricken flowers,
In a blue smoke in her naked forests.
She will linger, kissing all the branches;
She will linger, touching all the places,
Bare and naked, with her golden fingers,
Saying, 'Sleep and dream of me, my children;
Dream of me, the mystic Indian Summer,—
I who, slain by the cold Moon of Terror,
Can return across the path of Spirits,
Bearing still my heart of love and fire,
Looking with my eyes of warmth and splendour,
Whispering lowly through your sleep of sunshine.
I, the laughing Summer, am not turnèd
Into dry dust, whirling on the prairies,
Into red clay, crushed beneath the snowdrifts.
I am still the mother of sweet flowers
Growing but an arrow's flight beyond you
In the Happy Hunting-Ground—the quiver
Of great Manitou, where all the arrows
He has shot from His great bow of Power,
With its clear, bright singing cord of Wisdom,
Are re-gathered, plumed again and brightened,
And shot out, re-barbed with Love and Wisdom;
Always shot, and evermore returning.
Sleep, my children, smiling in your heart-seeds
At the spirit words of Indian Summer.'
Thus, O Moon of Falling Leaves, I mock you!
Have you slain my gold-eyed squaw, the Summer?"

The mighty Morn strode laughing up the land,
And Max, the lab'rer and the lover, stood
Within the forest's edge beside a tree—
The mossy king of all the woody tribes—
Whose clattering branches rattled, shuddering,
As the bright axe cleaved moon-like through the air,
Waking the strange thunders, rousing echoes linked,
From the full lion-throated roar to sighs
Stealing on dove-wings through the distant aisles.
Swift fell the axe, swift followed roar on roar,

3

Till the bare woodland bellowed in its rage
As the first-slain slow toppled to his fall.
'O King of Desolation, art thou dead?'
Cried Max, and laughing, heart and lips, leaped on
The vast prone trunk. 'And have I slain a king?
Above his ashes will I build my house;
No slave beneath its pillars, but—a king!'

Max wrought alone but for a half-breed lad
With tough, lithe sinews, and deep Indian eyes
Lit with a Gallic sparkle. Max the lover found
The lab'rer's arms grow mightier day by day,
More iron-welded, as he slew the trees;
And with the constant yearning of his heart
Toward little Kate, part of a world away,
His young soul grew and showed a virile front,
Full-muscled and large-statured like his flesh.

Soon the great heaps of brush were builded high,
And, like a victor, Max made pause to clear
His battle-field high strewn with tangled dead.
Then roared the crackling mountains, and their fires
Met in high heaven, clasping flame with flame;
The thin winds swept a cosmos of red sparks
Across the bleak midnight sky; and the sun
Walked pale behind the resinous black smoke.

And Max cared little for the blotted sun,
And nothing for the startled, outshone stars;
For love, once set within a lover's breast,
Has its own sun, its own peculiar sky,
All one great daffodil, on which do lie
The sun, the moon, the stars, all seen at once
And never setting, but all shining straight
Into the faces of the trinity—
The one beloved, the lover, and sweet love.

       . . . .

    O Love builds on the azure sea,
      And Love builds on the golden sand,
    And Love builds on the rose-winged cloud,
      And sometimes Love builds on the land!

O if Love build on sparkling sea,
  And if Love build on golden strand,
And if Love build on rosy cloud,
  To Love these are the solid land!

O Love will build his lily walls,
  And Love his pearly roof will rear
On cloud, or land, or mist, or sea—
  Love's solid land is everywhere!

.   .   .   .

From his far wigwam sprang the strong North Wind
And rushed with war-cry down the steep ravines,
And wrestled with the giants of the woods;
And with his ice-club beat the swelling crests
Of the deep watercourses into death;
And with his chill foot froze the whirling leaves
Of dun and gold and fire in icy banks;
And smote the tall reeds to the hardened earth,
And sent his whistling arrows o'er the plains,
Scattering the lingering herds; and sudden paused,
When he had frozen all the running streams,
And hunted with his war-cry all the things
That breathed about the woods, or roamed the bleak,
Bare prairies swelling to the mournful sky.

"White squaw!" he shouted, troubled in his soul,
"I slew the dead, unplumed before; wrestled
With naked chiefs scalped of their leafy plumes;
I bound sick rivers in cold thongs of death,
And shot my arrows over swooning plains,
Bright with the paint of death, and lean and bare.
And all the braves of my loud tribe will mock
And point at me when our great chief, the Sun,
Relights his council fire in the Moon
Of Budding Leaves: 'Ugh, ugh! he is a brave!
He fights with squaws and takes the scalps of babes!'
And the least wind will blow his calumet,
Filled with the breath of smallest flowers, across
The war-paint on my face, and pointing with
His small, bright pipe, that never moved a spear

Of bearded rice, cry, 'Ugh! he slays the dead!'
O my white squaw, come from thy wigwam grey,
Spread thy white blanket on the twice-slain dead,
And hide them ere the waking of the Sun!"

High grew the snow beneath the low-hung sky,
And all was silent in the wilderness;
In trance of stillness Nature heard her God
Rebuilding her spent fires, and veiled her face
While the Great Worker brooded o'er his Work.

'Bite deep and wide, O Axe, the tree!
What doth thy bold voice promise me?'

'I promise thee all joyous things
That furnish forth the lives of kings;

'For every silver ringing blow
Cities and palaces shall grow.'

'Bite deep and wide, O Axe, the tree!
Tell wider prophecies to me.'

'When rust hath gnawed me deep and red,
A Nation strong shall lift his head.

'His crown the very heavens shall smite,
Æons shall build him in his might.'

'Bite deep and wide, O Axe, the tree!
Bright Seer, help on thy prophecy!'

Max smote the snow-weighed tree and lightly laughed,
'See, friend,' he cried to one that looked and smiled,
'My axe and I, we do immortal tasks;
We build up nations—this my axe and I.'

. . . .

Who curseth Sorrow knows her not at all.
Dark matrix she, from which the human soul
Has its last birth; whence it, with misty thews
Close knitted in her blackness, issues out
Strong for immortal toil up such great heights
As crown o'er crown rise through Eternity.
Without the loud, deep clamour of her wail,
The iron of her hands, the biting brine

Of her black tears, the sonl, but lightly built
Of indeterminate spirit, like a mist
Would lapse to chaos in soft, gilded dreams,
As mists fade in the gazing of the sun.
Sorrow, dark mother of the soul, arise!
Be crowned with spheres where thy blest children dwell,
Who, but for thee, were not. No lesser seat
Be thine, thou Helper of the Universe,
Than planet on planet piled—thou instrument
Close clasped within the great Creative Hand!

From 'The Helot'

WHO may quench the god-born fire
Pulsing at the soul's deep root?
Tyrant, grind it in the mire,
  Lo, it vivifies the brute!

Stings the chain-embruted clay,
  Senseless to his yoke-bound shame;
Goads him on to rend and slay,
  Knowing not the spurring flame!

Tyrant, changeless stand the gods,
  Nor their calm might yielded thee;
Not beneath thy chains and rods
  Dies man's god-gift, Liberty!

Bruteward lash thy Helots, hold
  Brain and soul and clay in gyves,
Coin their blood and sweat in gold,
  Build thy cities on their lives,—

Comes a day the spark divine
  Answers to the gods who gave;
Fierce the hot flames pant and shine
  In the bruised breast of the slave.

Changeless stand the gods!—nor he
  Knows he answers their behest,
Feels the might of their decree
  In the blind rage of his breast.

Tyrant, tremble when ye tread
  Down the servile Helot clods!

Under despot heel is bred
    The white anger of the gods.

Through the shackle-cankered dust,
    Through the gyved soul, foul and dark,
Force they, changeless gods and just,
    Up the bright, eternal spark,

Till, like lightnings vast and fierce,
    On the land its terror smites;
Till its flames the tyrant pierce,
    Till the dust the despot bites.

The Mother's Soul

WHEN the moon was horned the mother died,
    And the child pulled at her hand and knee,
And he rubbed her cheek and loudly cried:
    'O mother, arise, give bread to me!'
    But the pine tree bent its head,
    And the wind at the door-post said:
    'O child, thy mother is dead!'

The sun set his loom to weave the day;
    The frost bit sharp like a silent cur;
The child by her pillow paused in his play:
    'Mother, build up the sweet fire of fir!'
    But the fir tree shook its cones,
    And loud cried the pitiful stones:
    'Wolf Death has thy mother's bones!'

They bore the mother out on her bier;
    Their tears made warm her breast and shroud;
The smiling child at her head stood near;
    And the long, white tapers shook and bowed,
    And said with their tongues of gold,
    To the ice lumps of the grave mold:
    'How heavy are ye and cold!'

They buried the mother; to the feast
    They flocked with the beaks of unclean crows.
The wind came up from the red-eyed east
    And bore in its arms the chill, soft snows.
    They said to each other: 'Sere

Are the hearts the mother held dear;
Forgotten, her babe plays here!'

The child with the tender snowflakes played,
  And the wind on its fingers twined his hair;
And still by the tall, brown grave he stayed,
  Alone in the churchyard lean and bare.
    The sods on the high grave cried
    To the mother's white breast inside:
    'Lie still; in thy deep rest bide!'

Her breast lay still like a long-chilled stone,
  Her soul was out on the bleak, grey day;
She saw her child by the grave alone,
  With the sods and snow and wind at play.
    Said the sharp lips of the rush,
    'Red as thy roses, O bush,
    With anger the dead can blush!'

A butterfly to the child's breast flew,*
  Fluttered its wings on his sweet, round cheek,
Danced by his fingers, small, cold and blue.
  The sun strode down past the mountain peak.
    The butterfly whispered low
    To the child: 'Babe, follow me; know,
    Cold is the earth here below.'

The butterfly flew; followed the child,
  Lured by the snowy torch of its wings;
The wind sighed after them soft and wild
  Till the stars wedded night with golden rings;
    Till the frost upreared its head,
    And the ground to it groaned and said:
    'The feet of the child are lead!'

The child's head drooped to the brown, sere mold,
  On the crackling cones his white breast lay;
The butterfly touched the locks of gold,
  The soul of the child sprang from its clay.
    The moon to the pine tree stole,

*In Eastern Europe the soul of the deceased is said to hover, in the shape of a bird or butterfly, close to the body until after the burial.

And silver-lipped, said to its bole:
'How strong is the mother's soul!'
The wings of the butterfly grew out
To the mother's arms, long, soft and white;
She folded them warm her babe about,
She kissed his lips into berries bright,
She warmed his soul on her breast;
And the east called out to the west:
'Now the mother's soul will rest!'

Under the roof where the burial feast
Was heavy with meat and red with wine,
Each crossed himself as out of the east
A strange wind swept over oak and pine.
The trees to the home-roof said:
' 'Tis but the airy rush and tread
Of angels greeting thy dead.'

The Rose

THE Rose was given to man for this:
He, sudden seeing it in later years,
Should swift remember Love's first lingering kiss
And Grief's last lingering tears;

Or, being blind, should feel its yearning soul
Knit all its piercing perfume round his own,
Till he should see on memory's ample scroll
All roses he had known;

Or, being hard, perchance his finger-tips
Careless might touch the satin of its cup,
And he should feel a dead babe's budding lips
To his lips lifted up;

Or, being deaf and smitten with its star,
Should, on a sudden, almost hear a lark
Rush singing up—the nightingale afar
Sing through the dew-bright dark;

Or, sorrow-lost in paths that round and round
Circle old graves, its keen and vital breath
Should call to him within the yew's bleak bound
Of Life, and not of Death.

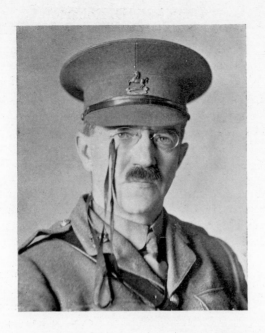

Charles G. D. Roberts

Mr. Roberts has tried a great variety of tones and themes in the course of his poetic career; no poet so many, that I know of. But the deepest thing in his poetic passion and experience is his poetry of nature description. Its basis is, in general, a pure æstheticism, for though it may occasionally be mingled with some fanciful train of thought or have appended to it a Wordsworthian moral, its value lies wholly in the gleaming and glancing surface which it brings before the reader's eye. This impressionistic nature poetry is the best part of his old Keatsian heritage for one thing, and it is part perhaps of his best days also, the days he describes in 'Tantramar Revisited,' long youthful days spent on the coast or amongst the farmsteads of New Brunswick, when he strove hardest to catch and to shape into some new line the vague, evasive, elemental beauty of nature. The power which he acquired then has never deserted him amongst all the transformations of spirit and literary ideals which he has experienced.—PROF. JAMES CAPPON, M.A.

[47]

THE Roberts family of Fredericton, New Brunswick, is Canada's most distinguished literary family. They are the sons, the daughter, and the grandsons of the late Rev. George Goodridge Roberts, M.A., LL.D., Rector of Fredericton and Canon of Christ Church Cathedral, and Emma Wetmore Bliss, daughter of the late Hon. G. P. Bliss, Attorney-General of New Brunswick.

Charles George Douglas Roberts, the eldest son, was born at Douglas, York County, N.B., January 10th, 1860. He was educated at the Fredericton Collegiate School, and at the University of New Brunswick (B.A., 1879, with honours in Mental and Moral Science, and Political Economy; M.A. in 1881; LL.D., honorary, in 1906).

In his twenty-first year, he married Miss Mary I. Fenety, daughter of the late George E. Fenety, Queen's Printer of N.B.

In 1883-4, Roberts was editor of *The Week*, Toronto, Ontario; in 1885-8, Professor of English and French Literature in King's College, Windsor, Nova Scotia; in 1888-95, Professor of English and Economics in the same College; in 1897-8, associate editor of *The Illustrated American,* New York. Since then, untrammelled by academic or editorial duties, he has devoted himself to the writing and publishing of many books, his fame steadily extending.

Before the close of the 19th century, he had written and published seven books of verse of notable quality; but in 1901 he issued a volume of poems selected from these, containing all that he wished to preserve, and of which the first poem is his imperishable threnody, 'Ave!'

No other writer known to me has more intimately associated his mind and spirit with every object and phase of nature. His poetic descriptions are vividly real, and exquisite in beauty of expression, whilst his animal stories in felicitous literary English, in accuracy of particulars, in intensity of dramatic interest, are beyond criticism.

Dr. Roberts enlisted in September, 1914, as a trooper in the Legion of Frontiersmen. Since then he has been promoted to a Captaincy in the King's Liverpool Regiment. For some months he has been training cadets, etc., in England and Wales. Captain Roberts' family,—wife, daughter and sons— are living in Ottawa, Canada.

I N the original copy, the following poems were included in full in the next twelve pages, in this order: 'The Solitary Woodsman,' 'Kinship,' 'The Succour of Gluscâp,' 'Two Spheres,' 'Earth's Complines,' 'Introductory,' 'The Flight of the Geese,' 'The Furrow,' 'The Sower,' 'The Mowing,' 'Where the Cattle Come to Drink,' 'The Pumpkins in the Corn' and 'A Nocturne of Consecration.'

Captain Roberts cabled from England his consent, but we have been unable to procure from his Boston publisher, who claims ownership of copyright, permission for their inclusion. However, we are fortunate in being able to give the reader a number of this popular author's more recent poems, and copious extracts from the scholarly, comprehensive and thorough critique on *Roberts and the Influences of His Time* which was published in 1905, by James Cappon, M.A., Professor of English Language and Literature, Queen's University.

Since the biographical data on the preceding page were printed, the Editor has secured this interesting extract from a letter written by Roberts, in May, 1907:

For the first fourteen years of my life—a formative period which influenced my future more than any other—I lived in the village of Westcock, below Sackville, in Westmoreland county at the mouth of the Tantramar river. There my home was the old Westcock Parsonage, of which I have given a very minute and precise description in chapter III of my latest novel, *The Heart That Knows*. The opening chapter describes the local scenery and those wonderful Tantramar marshes in particular. My father and mother are studied in the characters of the Rev. G. G. Goodridge and Mrs. Goodridge.

In February, 1904, *The National Monthly* published a special article by Arthur Stringer on Charles G. D. Roberts, "The Father of Canadian Poetry." This title has been frequently accorded him since and it is deserved, if it be understood to mean that Roberts influenced more than any other writer the remarkable group of poets who were born in the years, 61-2, of last century, and many of their successors. But the evidence is conclusive that Charles Mair and Isabella Valancy Crawford preceded him in the writing and publishing of great verse, whether in the interpretation and description of nature or of human life.

Cambrai and Marne

BEFORE our trenches at Cambrai
We saw their columns cringe away.
We saw their masses melt and reel
Before our line of leaping steel.

A handful to their storming hordes,
We scourged them with the scourge of swords,
And still, the more we slew, the more
Came up for every slain a score.

Between the hedges and the town
The cursing squadrons we rode down;
To stay them we outpoured our blood
Between the beetfields and the wood.

In that red hell of shrieking shell
Unfaltering our gunners fell;
They fell, or ere that day was done,
Beside the last unshattered gun.

But still we held them, like a wall
On which the breakers vainly fall—
Till came the word, and we obeyed,
Reluctant, bleeding, undismayed.

Our feet, astonished, learned retreat;
Our souls rejected still defeat;
Unbroken still, a lion at bay,
We drew back grimly from Cambrai.

In blood and sweat, with slaughter spent,
They thought us beaten as we went,
Till suddenly we turned, and smote
The shout of triumph in their throat.

At last, at last we turned and stood—
And Marne's fair water ran with blood;
We stood by trench and steel and gun,
For now the indignant flight was done.

We ploughed their shaken ranks with fire,
We trod their masses into mire;
Our sabres drove through their retreat
As drives the whirlwind through young wheat.

At last, at last we drove them back
Along their drenched and smoking track;
We hurled them back, in blood and flame,
The reeking ways by which they came.

By cumbered road and desperate ford
How fled their shamed and harassed horde!
Shout, Sons of Freemen, for the day
When Marne so well avenged Cambrai!
                    —*Westminster Gazette.*

Wayfarer of Earth

UP, heart of mine,
    Thou wayfarer of Earth!
Of seed divine,
Be mindful of thy birth.
Though the flesh faint
Through long-endured constraint
Of nights and days,
Lift up thy praise
To Life, that set thee in such strenuous ways,
And left thee not
To drowse and rot
In some thick-perfumed and luxurious plot.

Strong, strong is Earth,
With vigour for thy feet,
To make thy wayfaring
Tireless and fleet.
And good is Earth—
But Earth not all thy good,
O thou with seed of suns
And star-fire in thy blood.

And though thou feel
The slow clog of the hours
Leaden upon thy heel,

Put forth thy powers.
Thine the deep sky,
The unpreëmpted blue,
The haste of storm,
The hush of dew.
Thine, thine the free
Exalt of star and tree,
The reinless run
Of wind and sun,
The vagrance of the sea!
—*The Craftsman.*

Monition

A FAINT wind, blowing from World's End,
    Made strange the city street,
A strange sound mingled in the fall
    Of the familiar feet.

Something unseen whirled with the leaves
    To tap on door and sill.
Something unknown went whispering by
    Even when the wind was still.

And men looked up with startled eyes,
    And hurried on their way,
As if they had been called, and told
    How brief their day.   —*Century.*

At the Gates of Spring

WITH April here,
    And first thin green on the awakening bough,
What wonderful things and dear,
My tired heart to cheer,
At last appear!
Colours of dream afloat on cloud and tree,
So far, so clear,
A spell, a mystery;
And joys that thrill and sing,
New come on mating wing,
The wistfulness and ardour of the spring—
And Thou!
     —*The Smart Set.*

All Night the Lone Cicada

ALL night the lone cicada
Kept shrilling through the rain—
A voice of joy undaunted
  By unforgotten pain.

Down from the wind-blown branches
  Rang out the high refrain,
By tumult undisheartened,
  By storm assailed in vain.

To looming vasts of mountain
  And shadowy deeps of plain,
The ephemeral, brave defiance
  Adventured not in vain.

Till to the faltering spirit
  And to the weary brain,
From loss and fear and failure,
  My joy returned again.   *—Century.*

Hilltop Song

WHEN the lights come out in the cottages
  Along the shores at eve,
And across the darkening water
  The last pale colours leave;

And up from the rock-ridged pasture slopes
  The sheep-bell tinklings steal,
And the folds are shut, and the shepherds
  Turn to their quiet meal;

And even here, on the unfenced height,
  No journeying wind goes by,
But the earth-sweet smells and the home-sweet sounds
  Mount, like prayer, to the sky;

Then from the door of my opened heart
  Old blindness and pride are driven,
Till I know how high is the humble,
  The dear earth how close to heaven.
        —McClure's Magazine.

O Earth, Sufficing all our Needs

O EARTH, sufficing all our needs, O you
    With room for body and for spirit, too,
How patient while your children vex their souls
    Devising alien heavens beyond your blue!

Dear dwelling of the immortal and unseen,
    How obstinate in my blindness have I been,
Not comprehending what your tender calls,
    Veiled promises and reassurance, mean!

Not far and cold the way that they have gone,
    Who thro' your sundering darkness have withdrawn:
Almost within our hand-reach they remain
    Who pass beyond the sequence of the dawn.

Not far and strange the heavens, but very near,
    Your children's hearts unknowingly hold dear.
At times we almost catch the door swung wide—
    An unforgotten voice almost we hear.

I am the heir of heaven—and you are just.
    You, you alone I know, and you I trust.
Tho' I seek God beyond the farthest star,
    Here shall I find Him, in your deathless dust.

                                    —*The Craftsman.*

Extracts from Professor Cappon's Critique
Early Poems—The School of Keats

It is natural for a young poet to begin by following some established tradition in his art, and Roberts started with one of the highest.
The direct influence of Keats had almost ceased to be felt in English
poetry when the Canadian poet revived it in its purest form for his
countrymen. His early poems hardly disguise the fact that they are
imitations of Keats, and belong to that new world of Arcadia which
the English poet had created. That poetic world which Crabbe and
Wordsworth, with their naturalism, thought they had banished; that
land where the departed gods and heroes of Hellas still live, where
the steps of Pan are still heard in the forest, and Thetis glides with
silvery feet over the waves, had been revived for us by the poet of

Endymion, and its green bowers had allured a good many poetic aspirants into them, amongst whom Roberts may be counted as the latest, perhaps the last. For the poetry of to-day is looking for its material in another region where the forms of life are more robust and actual and the atmosphere more electrical than they are in the old legendary world of Arcadia.

From a philosophic point of view, there was nothing very complete in Keats' reconstruction of the Greek mythology. But he gave it all that poetry needs to make a new world of, a new sky, a new earth and new seas enchanting as those of fairyland; he filled its landscape with green wealth and aerial minstrelsy and every harmonious form of beauty in shape or sound or colour. But, more than all, he created the language in which alone this new world could be fitly described, a new language of idyllic description, a language of the subtlest, impression-istic power which could render the shapes of things seen in this dreamland with a visionary distinctness altogether unique. Its move-ment and cadence, too, were unique, natural as those of a man talking to himself, yet quaint and captivating as voices from the cave of the Sibyl:

> 'Twas a lay
> More subtle-cadenced, more forest wild
> Than Dryope's lone lulling of her child;
> And nothing since has floated on the air
> So mournful strange.

If Southey had been able to discover a similar language for his Domdaniels and Padalons his grandiose epics would not be where they now are, but that would be saying that Southey had a poetic genius which he had not. The line of Keats was a marvellous creation, and made him the indispensable master for all the idyllic poets who came after him. He had the master's secret of making everything which he touched new. His Apollos and Naiads had nothing to do with the fossilized mythology of the eighteenth century poets; you never thought of comparing them; you never thought of his "leaden-eyed despairs" in connection with the deliberate personifications of Collins or Gray, no more than you thought of the stiff framework of the eighteenth century couplet in reading his fluent verse.

Of course there was something in his style which remains inimitable and his own. The imaginative felicity of his phrase, the passionate simplicity of his cry, the entire naturalness of his movement, no one could repeat these. But there was also something which could be more or less easily imitated, and this became the possession of a whole school and even part of the universal language of poetry. That large, elusive epithet, that new reach of synecdoche, those novel compounds, that richly blazoned phrase in general, with delicate luxury and efflorescence, were readily appropriated by the æsthetic schools of poetry. Phrases like "argent revelry," "warm-cloistered hours," "tall oaks branch-charmed by the earnest stars," set the mould for a new

and finely sensuous impressionism in descriptive poetry. The critics
of *Blackwood* and the *Quarterly* might sniff at first at the new poesy
as the sickly affectation of the Cockney School, but it could not long
be neglected by young poets seeking to learn the secrets of colour and
rhythm in their art. The youthful Tennyson quietly drew some of his
finest threads for his own loom, and Rossetti, with the whole æsthetic
school, shows everywhere the influence of Keats' line. To most of
them he was more even than Shelley, for he taught them more, though
the other, with the star-domed grandeur of his universe, and his Titanic
passion and conflict, might be the greater inspiration to them. William
Rossetti says of his famous brother that he "truly preferred" Keats to
Shelley, "though not without some compunctious visitings now and
then."

As to Wordsworth's influence, it is not surprising that there is little
or no trace of it in the early work of Roberts, though it was just the
time when the reputation of the sage and singer of Rydal Mount was
in its second bloom with the public, owing mainly to the fine and
discriminating criticism of Arnold. But the young poets of the
æsthetic school disliked Wordsworth. They hated the plain texture of
his style and its want of colour. It might, however, have been well for
Roberts if he had come under the influence of Wordsworth's simplicity
and candour at this formative period of his life.

But, for better or worse, the school of Keats was that in which
Mr. Roberts received his training. He simply lives at this period in
that green world of neo-classical idyllism which Keats had created.
The style of the master, his colour, his rhythmical movement, his
manner of treating his subject, are reproduced with the interesting but
somewhat deceptive similitude which a copy always gives of a great
original . . . in the stanzas of the *Ariadne* almost every epithet
and every verb recall something which is familiar to us in the manner
of the master:

[*Part of the "Ode to Drowsihood" is here quoted.*]

That poetry is steeped in the rich Tyrian dye of Keats' fancy, and
the luxury of sense impression which is so marked in the work of the
master is the too exclusive quality of the disciple's. For after all there
is an ethical element in the poetry of Keats which Roberts does not
reproduce so well, an insistence on the spirituality and the healthful-
ness of beauty which runs through all the work of the English poet
and gives its special flavour to many of his finest passages. It is the
ascetic element needed to complete the chord in Keats, without which
his poetry would be rather overpowering in its sensuous richness.
Every one knows the opening lines of Endymion, and the fine outburst
in *The Ode to a Grecian Urn:*

> Heard melodies are sweet, but those unheard
>   Are sweeter; therefore, ye soft pipes play on;
> Not to the sensual ear, but, more endeared,
>   Pipe to the spirit ditties of no tone.

Poetry of Nature—Tantramar Revisited

The training which Roberts received in the school of Keats was mainly that of a nature poet. The underlying reality in the neo-classical idyll was its beautiful, if rather fanciful, treatment of nature, which was based, just as that of the ancient idyll had been, on a free selection of all fine pastoral images untrammeled by conditions of climate or locality. The poet might revel in any combination of scenery which his imagination suggested as long as he could give the whole the harmony which here took the place of reality. The oceans might be as serene and the Arcadian hunting ranges as wild as he liked:

> With muffled roarings through the clouded night,
> And heavy splashings through the misty pools.

Of course he had chosen the school because it gave a splendid form to his own natural instincts as a poet. His real power, his original impulse towards poetry, lies nearly altogether in the region of nature description, and it was a short and natural step for him to take from the fanciful delineations of Nature in *Orion* and *Actæon* to the description of actual Canadian scenes. But it involved in his case a decided change in the forms of poetic composition. The grand framework of epic and idyllic narrative which he could use when he had that shadowy Arcadian mythology to fill it with the shapes of life, was laid aside . . . It was a change which had already taken place very generally in the poetry of our time, as part of that return to nature and simplicity of form which had begun with Wordsworth. Our new singers seem no longer willing to support the weight of those grand forms of stanzaic verse which the great poets of the Italian Renaissance and all those who followed their traditions loved so well. The sonnet, with its well-established paces, is about the only great traditional form in use now.

It is a kind of light lyrical and descriptive verse which is the most characteristic form of Roberts' productivity at this period:

[*Quotations from "Birch and Paddle" and from "Aylesford Lake" follow.*]

The Solitary Woodsman, a little idyll of Canadian life which haunts the mind after you have read it, as true poetry will, may be noticed here, although it was published at a later time in *The Book of the Native* (1897). The Woodsman represents nearly all that Roberts has given us in the way of human portraiture, and even his personality, it must be admitted, is of the faintest. But there is a beautiful simplicity and naturalness about the poem:

[*Four stanzas quoted here.*]

It needed only a touch more to make that solitary woodsman as universal and popular a portrait as Longfellow's *Village Blacksmith,* a touch more of personal detail and moral characterization. A contemplative delicacy of feeling for nature is the chief characteristic of the poems of this class and they are best when they remain simply descriptive. . . .

4

Amongst all these varieties of the Canadian idyll, the one which leaves the strongest impression on the mind of originality in tone and treatment is *Tantramar Revisited*. Here Roberts' classical taste in style again asserted itself, though in the not very pure form of the modern hexameter. Longfellow had given the measure popular currency on this continent in his *Evangeline,* and Mathew Arnold had lately been directing the attention of literary circles to its possibilities. Both he and the poet Clough had done something to rescue it from the monotonous softness of Longfellow's movement and give it more strength and variety. Roberts, who has never quite lost his first love for the grand style, was quick to profit by the lesson, and uses this high but somewhat artificial form as a mould in which to pour his tenderest memories of the scenes familiar to his youth on the coast of New Brunswick. There is no direct picture of life in the poem, not a single human figure, but the landscape is powerfully painted in large, distant, softened traits, the true colour of elegiac reminiscence. Of direct elegiac reflection the poet has been sparing, perhaps wisely, but what there is has a sincerity which shows how deeply he felt his subject.

[*Twenty-eight lines of quotation follow.*]

In spite of the exotic character of the verse, which after all is a bar to the highest qualities of expression, something of the visionary eye and depth of feeling with which the poet looks on those scenes of his boyhood gets into every line. The poem is a true whole also and speaks in a subtle way to the heart. Perhaps he has lavished the resources of his style a little too freely on that description of the empty net reels. Its luxuriance is rather overpowering. . . .

Songs of the Common Day—A Sonnet Sequence

. . . It was a happy inspiration which made him think of putting his poetic impressions of Canadian pastoral life and scenery together in the form of a sonnet sequence. . . .

The Sonnet Sequence is a poetic form which unites a certain harmony of effect with entire independence in the treatment of each member of the series. It is a succession of short efforts with a continuity of aim which is capable of producing in the end something of the effect of a great whole. It has the authority of great literary traditions from Petrarch to Wordsworth and it seems to be nearly the only grand form of composition which the poetry of to-day can attempt with success. In this form then Mr. Roberts describes for us the general aspects of life and nature as one might see them at some Canadian farmstead, near the coast of New Brunswick, I suppose,—spring pastures and summer pools, burnt lands and clearings, fir forests and the winter stillness of the woods, mingled with descriptions of the common occupations of farm life, milking time and mowing, the potato harvest, bringing home the cattle and the like, all in a kind of sequence from spring sowing to midwinter thaw.

The poet, I need hardly say, finds a splendid field here for the impressionistic glance and vision. Look at this description of a September afternoon:

[*Quotation from "In September."*]

Or at this, from the sonnet *Where the Cattle Come to Drink:*

[*Second quatrain of the octave quoted.*]

If these passages were found in Wordsworth, say in the series of sonnets on the Duddon, they would be quoted by everyone as fine and subtle renderings of the moods of nature. Another striking example of Roberts' gift in this direction is to be found in the last sonnet of the series, *The Flight of the Geese.* I shall quote it in full:

. . . . . .

The purest might find fault with the strong lyrism of that sonnet and with inelegances like that thrice repeated overflow from two final words of the same structure, but it is a splendid piece of imaginative impressionism and a fine example of Roberts' power of style in this field.

Many of these sonnets have a luxuriance of style and fancy, particularly in the direction of what Ruskin has called the Pathetic Fallacy, which is perhaps excessive for this poetic form with its small compass; but some of them also show a new plainness of style and treatment indicating that realistic influences from Wordsworth are beginning to work on Roberts. Sometimes there is even a kind of roughness in the manner of giving details, as in the following from *The Potato Harvest:*

[*The sestet quoted in full.*]

The Furrow and *In an Old Barn* are also, in part at least, examples of this closer, more realistic treatment. Here, too, I may notice *The Sower,* the poet's popular masterpiece, which hits the golden mean between austerity and luxuriance of style:

[*The Sower is given in full.*]

The selection and treatment of materials in that sonnet are perfect. It is equally free from unleavened realism of detail and from impressionistic finery, from those overfeathered shafts of phrase which hang so heavy on the thought in sonnets like *The Summer Pool* and *A Vesper Sonnet.* The traits are select, harmonious and firmly drawn, with a wise economy of stroke. The manner in which the eye is conducted from the solitary field to the distant horizon, where lies that world of men for whom the sower works, and then concentrated again on the scene of the sower's labour and his movements, is a good illustration of the simplicity and naturalness of a perfect piece of art. The closing thought is noble and true to the subject, reflecting itself powerfully back on the previous details in a way which gives them new significance.

Technically Mr. Roberts' sonnets generally show something of the structural freedom and something also of the looseness of conception which are characteristic of American sonnets. The rhyme system as a rule is the pure Petrarchan, but as often as not he entirely disregards the division of thought in the two quatrains of the octave. Sometimes the poise and counterpoise of thought between the octave and sestet is strongly marked, the first containing the descriptive part and the second the moral which the poet appends to it. At other times the division is but faintly felt, though it often exists in a form which is virtually a new type of sonnet structure. In this type the octave gives the general outline of a landscape and is followed by a sestet which gives a more particular description of some characteristic or significant object in it. This is the structural character of *The Herring Weir, The Oat Threshing, The Sower, The Flight of the Geese,* and other sonnets. In this way the old function of the sestet in summing up or pointing the significance of the octave is revived in a new form, and when the object thus selected for particular treatment is significant enough, and its connection with the description in the octave evident and inevitable, this arrangement makes an excellent type of sonnet. It is part of the perfection of *The Sower* that the connection between the landscape described in the octave and the object described in the sestet is of this natural, inevitable kind. But *The Sower* perhaps, owes something of the selectness and harmony of its details to the fact that the subject is one which has been worked over by more than one great mind in the sister arts of painting and engraving. It is a curious example of the relation which may occasionally exist between poetry and the other fine arts, and Roberts may be counted fortunate in having furnished a perfect literary expression for a conception on which Dürer and Millet had laboured.

On the whole this sonnet sequence may be considered as the most important poetic work Mr. Roberts has so far produced. It represents in its highest form what is most original in him, that in which his experience is deeper than that of other men. It gives the fairest scope, too, for that impressionistic painting of nature in which he is a master. The general tone of these sonnets is that of a pensive melancholy such as arises naturally enough from the contemplation of quiet pastoral morns and eves. Grey Corot-like pictures they mostly are, often a little huddled and indistinct or indeterminate in their outlines but delicately tinted and suffused with a true Canadian atmosphere of light and space and wide, pale, clear horizons. It is an atmosphere which keeps the colour tone of the landscape low, or at least cool, with nothing of tropical luxuriance about it, the bloom of the golden-rod, of the clover, the buttercups and the great purple patches of fire-weed in the woods being tempered by the cold clear lustre of a northern sky and the pale verdure of the marshes. The general features of nature in eastern Canada are faithfully reflected in these sonnets, sometimes in exquisite bits of verse. . . . .

Archibald Lampman

Lampman is Canada's greatest nature poet. . . . . It is to the exquisite felicity of his nature poems that he owes his reputation both in this country and abroad. . . . . Never was there a more genuine lover of nature for her own sake. He was not under the spell alone of her sublimer aspects. Indeed, the mountains he had never seen, and the sea but rarely, and in later life. He loved nature as Thoreau loved her—in all her moods. The very thorns and burs were dear to him, and it was this gentle sympathy which he felt for the unobtrusive beauties which we too commonly fail to see, or, seeing, fail to understand that imparted to his poetry its peculiar charm. . . . . If landscape is, as has been said, 'a state of the soul,' no other Canadian poet has so adequately rendered the spiritual significance which nature gains from the reflection of human emotions. . . . . His message to his generation is the promise of consolation which nature accords to her devotees.—Prof. Pelham Edgar, Ph.D., in the 'Globe Magazine.'

ARCHIBALD LAMPMAN, the beloved poet, was born on Sunday morning, Nov. 17th, 1861, in the village of Morpeth, Ont., where his father, the Rev. Archibald Lampman, was rector of Trinity Church. He was of Dutch descent, and the father of each of his parents was a United Empire Loyalist.

Lampman dedicated his third volume of verse, *Alcyone,* as follows: "To the memory of my father, himself a poet, who first instructed me in the art of verse"; and we are told by his biographer that there had been poets and scientists on his mother's side of the house.

When Archibald had entered his sixth year, the family left Morpeth, resided for a time at Perrytown, near Port Hope, and in October, 1867, moved to Gore's Landing, a small community on the shore of Rice Lake. Here, in the midst of beautiful surroundings, they dwelt for seven years, the most impressionable years of the poet's life.

Unfortunately, in November, 1868, the boy was stricken with rheumatic fever, induced by a damp rectory. He suffered acutely for months, and in consequence was lame for four years. It was probably due to this illness that in youth and in manhood he never enjoyed robust health.

The future poet was educated at home until nearly nine years of age, when he entered the school of a notable schoolmaster, Mr. F. W. Barron, M.A., of Cambridge, formerly Principal of Upper Canada College. Here he was thoroughly grounded in Latin and Greek. When thirteen years old, he attended the Cobourg Collegiate Institute for a year, and then went to Trinity College School, Port Hope, to prepare for attendance at Trinity College, Toronto. During his two years in Port Hope, he was noted as a prize-winner. In September, 1879, he entered Trinity College, Toronto, where, by the help of scholarships won, he completed his course, graduating with honours in classics in 1882. After graduation, he taught for a few months in the Orangeville High School, and then accepted permanent employment in the Post-Office Department at Ottawa.

In 1887, Lampman married Maud, the youngest daughter of Dr. Edward Playter, of Toronto, and during their twelve years of happiness, several children were born to them.

In 1888, our poet published his first book of verse, *Among the Millet,* which extended his fame and encouraged him to greater effort. Five years later was issued his second book, *Lyrics of Earth,* which won for him additional laurels. His third, *Alcyone,* was on the press when he was stricken by the brief illness which resulted in his death, two days later, on the 10th of February, 1899.

Archibald Lampman was slight of form and of middle height. He was quiet and undemonstrative in manner, but had a fascinating personality. Sincerity and high ideals characterized his life and work.

In 1900, his three books, with additional poems, and with an excellent memoir from the pen of Mr. Duncan Campbell Scott, were published in one large volume of nearly five hundred pages,—his enduring monument.

April in the Hills

TO-DAY the world is wide and fair
With sunny fields of lucid air,
And waters dancing everywhere;
   The snow is almost gone;
The noon is builded high with light,
And over heaven's liquid height,
In steady fleets serene and white,
   The happy clouds go on.

The channels run, the bare earth steams,
And every hollow rings and gleams
With jetting falls and dashing streams;
   The rivers burst and fill;
The fields are full of little lakes,
And when the romping wind awakes
The water ruffles blue and shakes,
   And the pines roar on the hill.

The crows go by, a noisy throng;
About the meadows all day long,
The shore-lark drops his brittle song;
   And up the leafless tree

The nut-hatch runs, and nods, and clings;
The bluebird dips with flashing wings,
The robin flutes, the sparrow sings,
    And the swallows float and flee.

I break the spirit's cloudy bands,
A wanderer in enchanted lands,
I feel the sun upon my hands;
    And far from care and strife
The broad earth bids me forth. I rise
With lifted brow and upward eyes.
I bathe my spirit in blue skies,
    And taste the springs of life.

I feel the tumult of new birth;
I waken with the wakening earth;
I match the bluebird in her mirth;
    And wild with wind and sun,
A treasurer of immortal days,
I roam the glorious world with praise,
The hillsides and the woodland ways,
    Till earth and I are one.

The Truth

FRIEND, though thy soul should burn thee, yet be still
    Thoughts were not meant for strife, nor tongues for swords,
He that sees clear is gentlest of his words,
And that's not truth that hath the heart to kill.
The whole world's thought shall not one truth fulfil.
Dull in our age, and passionate in youth,
No mind of man hath found the perfect truth,
Nor shalt thou find it; therefore, friend, be still.

Watch and be still, nor hearken to the fool,
The babbler of consistency and rule:
Wisest is he, who, never quite secure,
Changes his thoughts for better day by day:
To-morrow some new light will shine, be sure,
And thou shalt see thy thought another way.

Morning on the Lievre

FAR above us where a jay
    Screams his matins to the day,
Capped with gold and amethyst,
Like a vapour from the forge
Of a giant somewhere hid,
Out of hearing of the clang
Of his hammer, skirts of mist
Slowly up the woody gorge
Lift and hang.

Softly as a cloud we go,
Sky above and sky below,
Down the river; and the dip
Of the paddles scarcely breaks,
With the little silvery drip
Of the water as it shakes
From the blades, the crystal deep
Of the silence of the morn,
Of the forest yet asleep;
And the river reaches borne
In a mirror, purple gray,
Sheer away
To the misty line of light,
Where the forest and the stream
In the shadow meet and plight,
Like a dream.

From amid a stretch of reeds,
Where the lazy river sucks
All the water as it bleeds
From a little curling creek,
And the muskrats peer and sneak
In around the sunken wrecks
Of a tree that swept the skies
Long ago,
On a sudden seven ducks
With a splashy rustle rise,
Stretching out their seven necks,

One before, and two behind,
And the others all arow,
And as steady as the wind
With a swivelling whistle go,
Through the purple shadow led,
Till we only hear their whir
In behind a rocky spur,
Just ahead.

Heat

FROM plains that reel to southward, dim,
  The road runs by me white and bare;
Up the steep hill it seems to swim
  Beyond, and melt into the glare.
Upward half-way, or it may be
  Nearer the summit, slowly steals
A hay-cart, moving dustily
  With idly clacking wheels.

By his cart's side the wagoner
  Is slouching slowly at his ease,
Half-hidden in the windless blur
  Of white dust puffing to his knees.
This wagon on the height above,
  From sky to sky on either hand,
Is the sole thing that seems to move
  In all the heat-held land.

Beyond me in the fields the sun
  Soaks in the grass and hath his will;
I count the marguerites one by one;
  Even the buttercups are still.
On the brook yonder not a breath
  Disturbs the spider or the midge.
The water-bugs draw close beneath
  The cool gloom of the bridge.

Where the far elm-tree shadows flood
  Dark patches in the burning grass,
The cows, each with her peaceful cud,
  Lie waiting for the heat to pass.

From somewhere on the slope near by
  Into the pale depth of the noon
A wandering thrush slides leisurely
  His thin revolving tune.

In intervals of dreams I hear
  The cricket from the droughty ground;
The grasshoppers spin into mine ear
  A small innumerable sound.
I lift mine eyes sometimes to gaze:
  The burning sky-line blinds my sight:
The woods far off are blue with haze:
  The hills are drenched in light.

And yet to me not this or that
  Is always sharp or always sweet;
In the sloped shadow of my hat
  I lean at rest, and drain the heat;
Nay more, I think some blessèd power
  Hath brought me wandering idly here:
In the full furnace of this hour
  My thoughts grow keen and clear.

A January Morning

THE glittering roofs are still with frost; each worn
  Black chimney builds into the quiet sky
Its curling pile to crumble silently.
Far out to the westward on the edge of morn,
The slender misty city towers up-borne
Glimmer faint rose against the pallid blue;
And yonder on those northern hills, the hue
Of amethyst, hang fleeces dull as horn.

And here behind me come the woodmen's sleighs
With shouts and clamorous squeakings; might and main
Up the steep slope the horses stamp and strain,
Urged on by hoarse-tongued drivers—cheeks ablaze,
Iced beards and frozen eyelids—team by team,
With frost-fringed flanks, and nostrils jetting steam.

After Rain

FOR three whole days across the sky,
   In sullen packs that loomed and broke,
With flying fringes dim as smoke,
The columns of the rain went by;
At every hour the wind awoke;
   The darkness passed upon the plain;
   The great drops rattled at the pane.

Now piped the wind, or far aloof
Fell to a sough remote and dull;
And all night long with rush and lull
The rain kept drumming on the roof:
I heard till ear and sense were full
   The clash or silence of the leaves,
   The gurgle in the creaking eaves.

But when the fourth day came—at noon,
The darkness and the rain were by;
The sunward roofs were steaming dry;
And all the world was flecked and strewn
With shadows from a fleecy sky.
   The haymakers were forth and gone,
   And every rillet laughed and shone.

Then, too, on me that loved so well
The world, despairing in her blight,
Uplifted with her least delight,
On me, as on the earth, there fell
New happiness of mirth and might;
   I strode the valleys pied and still;
   I climbed upon the breezy hill.

I watched the gray hawk wheel and drop,
Sole shadow on the shining world;
I saw the mountains clothed and curled,
With forest ruffling to the top;
I saw the river's length unfurled,
   Pale silver down the fruited plain,
   Grown great and stately with the rain.

Through miles of shadow and soft heat,
Where field and fallow, fence and tree,
Were all one world of greenery,
I heard the robin ringing sweet,
The sparrow piping silverly,
    The thrushes at the forest's hem;
    And as I went I sang with them.

Winter Evening

TO-NIGHT the very horses springing by
    Toss gold from whitened nostrils. In a dream
The streets that narrow to the westward gleam
Like rows of golden palaces; and high
From all the crowded chimneys tower and die
A thousand aureoles. Down in the west
The brimming plains beneath the sunset rest,
One burning sea of gold. Soon, soon shall fly

The glorious vision, and the hours shall feel
A mightier master; soon from height to height,
With silence and the sharp unpitying stars,
Stern creeping frosts, and winds that touch like steel,
Out of the depth beyond the eastern bars,
Glittering and still shall come the awful night.

In March

THE sun falls warm: the southern winds awake:
    The air seethes upwards with a steamy shiver:
Each dip of the road is now a crystal lake,
And every rut a little dancing river.
Through great soft clouds that sunder overhead
The deep sky breaks as pearly blue as summer:
Out of a cleft beside the river's bed
Flaps the black crow, the first demure newcomer.

The last seared drifts are eating fast away
With glassy tinkle into glittering laces:
Dogs lie asleep, and little children play
With tops and marbles in the sun-bare places;
And I that stroll with many a thoughtful pause
Almost forget that winter ever was.

The Railway Station

THE darkness brings no quiet here, the light
    No waking: ever on my blinded brain
The flare of lights, the rush, and cry, and strain,
The engine's scream, the hiss and thunder smite:
I see the hurrying crowds, the clasp, the flight,
Faces that touch, eyes that are dim with pain.
I see the hoarse wheels turn, and the great train
Move labouring out into the bourneless night.

So many souls within its dim recesses,
So many bright, so many mournful eyes:
Mine eyes that watch grow fixed with dreams and guesses;
What threads of life, what hidden histories,
What sweet or passionate dreams and dark distresses,
What unknown thoughts, what various agonies!

War

BY the Nile, the sacred river,
    I can see the captive hordes,
Strain beneath the lash and quiver
    At the long papyrus cords,
While in granite rapt and solemn,
Rising over roof and column,
    Amen-hotep dreams, or Ramses,
        Lord of Lords.

I can hear the trumpets waken
    For a victory old and far—
Carchemish or Kadesh taken—
    I can see the conqueror's car
Bearing down some Hittite valley,
Where the bowmen break and sally,
    Sargina or Esarhaddon,
        Grim with war!

From the mountain streams that sweeten
    Indus, to the Spanish foam,
I can feel the broad earth beaten
    By the serried tramp of Rome;

Through whatever foes environ
Onward with the might of iron—
   Veni, vidi; veni vici—
      Crashing home!

I can see the kings grow pallid
  With astonished fear and hate,
As the hosts of Amr or Khaled
  On their cities fall like fate;
Like the heat-wind from its prison
In the desert burst and risen—
   La ilaha illah 'llahu—
      God is great!

I can hear the iron rattle,
  I can see the arrows sting
In some far-off northern battle,
  Where the long swords sweep and swing;
I can hear the scalds declaiming,
I can see their eyeballs flaming,
   Gathered in a frenzied circle
      Round the king.

I can hear the horn of Uri
  Roaring in the hills enorm;
Kindled at its brazen fury,
  I can see the clansmen form;
In the dawn in misty masses,
Pouring from the silent passes
   Over Granson or Morgarten
      Like the storm.

On the lurid anvil ringing
  To some slow fantastic plan,
I can hear the sword-smith singing
  In the heart of old Japan—
Till the cunning blade grows tragic
With his malice and his magic—
   Tenka tairan! Tenka tairan!
      War to man!

Where a northern river charges
  From a wild and moonlit glade,

From the murky forest marges,
  Round a broken palisade,
I can see the red men leaping,
See the sword of Daulac sweeping,
  And the ghostly forms of heroes
    Fall and fade.

I can feel the modern thunder
  Of the cannon beat and blaze,
When the lines of men go under
  On your proudest battle-days;
Through the roar I hear the lifting
Of the bloody chorus drifting
  Round the burning mill at Valmy—
    Marseillaise!

I can see the ocean rippled
  With the driving shot like rain,
While the hulls are crushed and crippled,
  And the guns are piled with slain;
O'er the blackened broad sea-meadow
Drifts a tall and titan shadow,
  And the cannon of Trafalgar
    Startle Spain.

Still the tides of fight are booming,
  And the barren blood is spilt;
Still the banners are up-looming,
  And the hands are on the hilt;
But the old world waxes wiser,
From behind the bolted visor
  It descries at last the horror
    And the guilt.

Yet the eyes are dim, nor wholly
  Open to the golden gleam,
And the brute surrenders slowly
  To the godhead and the dream.
From his cage of bar and girder,
Still at moments mad with murder,
  Leaps the tiger, and his demon
    Rules supreme.

One more war with fire and famine
   Gathers—I can hear its cries—
And the years of might and Mammon
   Perish in a world's demise;
When the strength of man is shattered,
And the powers of earth are scattered,
   From beneath the ghastly ruin
      Peace shall rise!

April Night

HOW deep the April night is in its noon,
  The hopeful, solemn, many-murmured night!
The earth lies hushed with expectation; bright
Above the world's dark border burns the moon,
Yellow and large; from forest floorways, strewn
With flowers, and fields that tingle with new birth,
The moist smell of the unimprisoned earth
Come up, a sigh, a haunting promise. Soon,

Ah, soon, the teeming triumph! At my feet
The river with its stately sweep and wheel
Moves on slow-motioned, luminous, gray like steel.
From fields far off whose watery hollows gleam,
Aye with blown throats that make the long hours sweet,
The sleepless toads are murmuring in their dreams.

The Largest Life

I

I LIE upon my bed and hear and see.
  The moon is rising through the glistening trees;
And momently a great and sombre breeze,
With a vast voice returning fitfully,
Comes like a deep-toned grief, and stirs in me,
Somehow, by some inexplicable art,
A sense of my soul's strangeness, and its part
In the dark march of human destiny.
What am I, then, and what are they that pass
Yonder, and love and laugh, and mourn and weep?
What shall they know of me, or I, alas!

Of them? Little. At times, as if from sleep,
We waken to this yearning passionate mood,
And tremble at our spiritual solitude.

II

Nay, never once to feel we are alone,
While the great human heart around us lies:
To make the smile on other lips our own,
To live upon the light in others' eyes:
To breathe without a doubt the limped air
Of that most perfect love that knows no pain:
To say—I love you—only, and not care
Whether the love come back to us again:
Divinest self-forgetfulness, at first
A task, and then a tonic, then a need;
To greet with open hands the best and worst,
And only for another's wound to bleed:
This is to see the beauty that God meant,
Wrapped round with life, ineffably content.

III

There is a beauty at the goal of life,
A beauty growing since the world began,
Through every age and race, through lapse and strife
Till the great human soul complete her span.
Beneath the waves of storm that lash and burn,
The currents of blind passion that appall,
To listen and keep watch till we discern
The tide of sovereign truth that guides it all;
So to address our spirits to the height,
And so attune them to the valiant whole,
That the great light be clearer for our light,
And the great soul the stronger for our soul:
To have done this is to have lived, though fame
Remember us with no familiar name.

Frederick George Scott

Frederick George Scott's poetry has followed three or four well-defined lines of thought. He has reflected in turn the academic subjects of a library, the majesty of nature, the tender love of his fellowmen, and the vision and enthusiasm of an Imperialist. His work in any one field would attract attention; taken in mass it marks him as a sturdy, developing interpreter of his country and of his times. Whether he writes of 'Samson' and 'Thor,' of the 'Little River,' or whether he expands his soul in a 'Hymn of Empire,' his lines are marked by imagination, melody, sympathy and often wistfulness. Living on the edge of the shadow-flecked Laurentians, he constantly draws inspiration from them, and more than any other has made articulate their lonely beauties. His pastoral relations with a city flock give colour and tenderness to not a few of his poems of human relationships. His ardent love of the Empire gives rein to his restless, roving thoughts and has finally drawn him to the battle-front as a chaplain. . .—M. O. HAMMOND, of 'The Globe,' Toronto.

FREDERICK GEORGE SCOTT, "The Poet of the Laurentians," has this supreme gift as a writer: the art of expressing noble, beautiful and often profound thoughts, in simple, appropriate words which all who read can understand. His poems uplift the spirit and enrich the heart.

He was born in Montreal, April 7th, 1861, son of the late Dr. William Edward Scott, for nearly forty years Professor of Anatomy, in McGill University, and Elizabeth Sproston. Both parents were of English birth.

He was educated at the Montreal High School, at Bishop's College, Lennoxville (B.A., 1881; M.A., 1884; D.C.L., honorary, 1902), and at King's College, London, England.

Ordained deacon, 1884, and priest, 1886, his subsequent clerical career is indicated by the following: curate at Coggeshall, Essex, England, 1886-7; Rector of Drummondville, P.Q., 1887-96; curate, St. Mathews, Quebec, 1896-9, and then Rector; Canon, Holy Trinity Cathedral, Quebec, 1906, and ever since; Provincial Superior, Confraternity of the Blessed Sacrament.

As an author, Canon Scott has won distinction by these publications: *The Soul's Quest, and Other Poems,* 1888; *Elton Hazlewood,* 1892; *My Lattice, and Other Poems,* 1894; *The Unnamed Lake, and Other Poems,* 1897; *Poems Old and New,* 1900; *The Hymn of Empire, and Other Poems,* 1906; *The Key of Life, a Mystery Play,* 1907; *Collected Poems,* 1910.

At a special meeting of the Royal Society of Canada,—of which he was elected a Fellow in 1900,—held during the Quebec Tercentenary, he read an ode, *Canada,* written for the occasion.

His marriage to Amy, eldest daughter of the late George Brooks, of Barnet, England, took place in April, 1887. Of this union there are six children living, five boys and one girl. The two eldest sons are practising lawyers in Montreal.

This hero-poet at the Front—he is Major and Senior Chaplain of the 1st Canadian Division—is more than an eminent writer of verse and an impressive preacher, he is as the *Montreal Star* has said:

A man of liberal culture and wide sympathies, a patriot whose heart has thrilled with the truth of the larger life, political, social and religious, a man of strong courage born of reverent unquestioning faith.

The Feud

I HEAR a cry from the Sansard cave,
  O mother, will no one hearken?
A cry of the lost, will no one save?
A cry of the dead, though the oceans rave,
And the scream of a gull as he wheels o'er a grave,
  While the shadows darken and darken.'

'Oh, hush thee, child, for the night is wet,
  And the cloud-caves split asunder,
With lightning in a jagged fret,
Like the gleam of a salmon in the net,
When the rocks are rich in the red sunset,
  And the stream rolls down in thunder.'

'Mother, O mother, a pain at my heart,
  A pang like the pang of dying.'
'Oh, hush thee, child, for the wild birds dart
Up and down, and close and part,
Wheeling round where the black cliffs start,
  And the foam at their feet is flying.'

'O mother, a strife like the black clouds' strife,
  And a peace that cometh after.'
'Hush, child, for peace is the end of life,
And the heart of a maiden finds peace as a wife,
But the sky and the cliffs and the ocean are rife
  With the storm and thunder's laughter.'

'Come in, my sons, come in and rest,
  For the shadows darken and darken,
And your sister is pale as the white swan's breast,
And her eyes are fixed and her lips are pressed
In the death of a name ye might have guessed,
  Had ye twain been here to hearken.'

'Hush, mother, a corpse lies on the sand,
  And the spray is round it driven,
It lies on its face, and one white hand
Points through the mist on the belt of strand
To where the cliffs of Sansard stand,
  And the ocean's strength is riven.'

5

'Was it God, my sons, who laid him there?
  Or the sea that left him sleeping?'
'Nay, mother, our dirks where his heart was bare,
As swift as the rain through the teeth of the air;
And the foam-fingers play in the Saxon's hair,
  While the tides are round him creeping.'

'Oh, curses on you, hand and head,
  Like the rains in this wild weather,
The guilt of blood is swift and dread,
Your sister's face is cold and dead,
Ye may not part whom God would wed
  And love hath knit together.'

Samson

PLUNGED in night, I sit alone
  Eyeless on this dungeon stone,
Naked, shaggy, and unkempt,
Dreaming dreams no soul hath dreamt.

Rats and vermin round my feet
Play unharmed, companions sweet;
Spiders weave me overhead
Silken curtains for my bed.

Day by day the mould I smell
Of this fungus-blistered cell;
Nightly in my haunted sleep
O'er my face the lizards creep.

Gyves of iron scrape and burn
Wrists and ankles when I turn,
And my collared neck is raw
With the teeth of brass that gnaw.

God of Israel, canst Thou see
All my fierce captivity?
Do Thy sinews feel my pains?
Hearest Thou the clanking chains?

Thou who madest me so fair,
Strong and buoyant as the air,
Tall and noble as a tree,
With the passions of the sea,

Swift as horse upon my feet,
Fierce as lion in my heat,
Rending, like a wisp of hay,
All that dared withstand my way,

Canst Thou see me through the gloom
Of this subterranean tomb,—
Blinded tiger in his den,
Once the lord and prince of men?

Clay was I; the potter Thou
With Thy thumb-nail smooth'dst my brow,
Roll'dst the spittle-moistened sands
Into limbs between Thy hands.

Thou didst pour into my blood
Fury of the fire and flood,
And upon the boundless skies
Thou didst first unclose my eyes.

And my breath of life was flame,
God-like from the source it came,
Whirling round like furious wind,
Thoughts upgathered in the mind.

Strong Thou mad'st me, till at length
All my weakness was my strength;
Tortured am I, blind and wrecked,
For a faulty architect.

From the woman at my side,
Was I woman-like to hide
What she asked me, as if fear
Could my iron heart come near?

Nay, I scorned and scorn again
Cowards who their tongues restrain;
Cared I no more for Thy laws
Than a wind of scattered straws.

When the earth quaked at my name
And my blood was all aflame,
Who was I to lie, and cheat
Her who clung about my feet?

From Thy open nostrils blow
Wind and tempest, rain and snow;
Dost Thou curse them on their course,
For the fury of their force?

Tortured am I, wracked and bowed,
But the soul within is proud;
Dungeon fetters cannot still
Forces of the tameless will.

Israel's God, come down and see
All my fierce captivity;
Let Thy sinews feel my pains,
With Thy fingers lift my chains,

Then, with thunder loud and wild,
Comfort Thou Thy rebel child,
And with lightning split in twain
Loveless heart and sightless brain.

Give me splendour in my death—
Not this sickening dungeon breath,
Creeping down my blood like slime,
Till it wastes me in my prime.

Give me back for one blind hour,
Half my former rage and power,
And some giant crisis send,
Meet to prove a hero's end.

Then, O God, Thy mercy show—
Crush him in the overthrow
At whose life they scorn and point,
By its greatness out of joint.

Dawn

THE immortal spirit hath no bars
  To circumscribe its dwelling place;
My soul hath pastured with the stars
  Upon the meadow-lands of space.

My mind and ear at times have caught,
  From realms beyond our mortal reach,

The utterance of Eternal Thought
Of which all nature is the speech.

And high above the seas and lands,
On peaks just tipped with morning light,
My dauntless spirit mutely stands
With eagle wings outspread for flight.

The River

WHY hurry, little river,
Why hurry to the sea?
There is nothing there to do
But to sink into the blue
And all forgotten be.
There is nothing on that shore
But the tides for evermore,
And the faint and far-off line
Where the winds across the brine
For ever, ever roam
And never find a home.

Why hurry, little river,
From the mountains and the mead,
Where the graceful elms are sleeping
And the quiet cattle feed?
The loving shadows cool
The deep and restful pool;
And every tribute stream
Brings its own sweet woodland dream
Of the mighty woods that sleep
Where the sighs of earth are deep,
And the silent skies look down
On the savage mountain's frown.

Oh, linger, little river,
Your banks are all so fair,
Each morning is a hymn of praise,
Each evening is a prayer.
All day the sunbeams glitter
On your shallows and your bars,
And at night the dear God stills you
With the music of the stars.

The Storm

O GRIP the earth, ye forest trees,
 Grip well the earth to-night,
The Storm-God rides across the seas
 To greet the morning light.

All clouds that wander through the skies
 Are tangled in his net,
The frightened stars have shut their eyes,
 The breakers fume and fret.

The birds that cheer the woods all day
 Now tremble in their nests,
The giant branches round them sway,
 The wild wind never rests.

The squirrel and the cunning fox
 Have hurried to their holes,
Far off, like distant earthquake shocks,
 The muffled thunder rolls.

In scores of hidden woodland dells,
 Where no rough winds can harm,
The timid wild-flowers toss their bells
 In reasonless alarm.

Only the mountains rear their forms,
 Silent and grim and bold;
To them the voices of the storms
 Are as a tale re-told.

They saw the stars in heaven hung,
 They heard the great Sea's birth,
They know the ancient pain that wrung
 The entrails of the Earth.

Sprung from great Nature's royal lines,
 They share her deep repose,—
Their rugged shoulders robed in pines,
 Their foreheads crowned with snows.

But now there comes a lightning flash,
 And now on hill and plain
The charging clouds in fury dash,
 And blind the world with rain.

In the Winter Woods

WINTER forests mutely standing
  Naked on your bed of snow,
Wide your knotted arms expanding
  To the biting winds that blow,
Nought ye heed of storm or stress,
Stubborn, silent, passionless.

Buried is each woodland treasure,
  Gone the leaves and mossy rills,
Gone the birds that filled with pleasure
  All the valleys and the hills;
Ye alone of all that host
Stand like soldiers at your post.

Grand old trees, the words ye mutter,
  Nodding in the frosty wind,
Wake some thoughts I cannot utter,
  But which haunt the heart and mind,
With a meaning, strange and deep,
As of visions seen in sleep.

Something in my inmost thinking
  Tells me I am one with you,
For a subtle bond is linking
  Nature's offspring through and through,
And your spirit like a flood
Stirs the pulses of my blood.

While I linger here and listen
  To the crackling boughs above,
Hung with icicles that glisten
  As if kindling into love,
Human heart and soul unite
With your majesty and might.

Horizontal, rich with glory,
  Through the boughs the red sun's rays
Clothe you as some grand life-story
  Robes an aged man with praise,
When, before his setting sun,
Men recount what he has done.

But the light is swiftly fading,
  And the wind is icy cold,
And a mist the moon is shading,
  Pallid in the western gold;
In the night-winds still ye nod,
Sentinels of Nature's God.

Now with laggard steps returning
  To the world from whence I came,
Leave I all the great West burning
  With the day that died in flame,
And the stars, with silver ray,
Light me on my homeward way.

The Unnamed Lake

IT sleeps among the thousand hills
  Where no man ever trod,
And only nature's music fills
  The silences of God.

Great mountains tower above its shore,
  Green rushes fringe its brim,
And o'er its breast for evermore
  The wanton breezes skim.

Dark clouds that intercept the sun
  Go there in Spring to weep,
And there, when Autumn days are done,
  White mists lie down to sleep.

Sunrise and sunset crown with gold
  The pinks of ageless stone,
Her winds have thundered from of old
  And storms have set their throne.

No echoes of the world afar
  Disturb it night or day,
The sun and shadow, moon and star
  Pass and repass for aye.

'Twas in the grey of early dawn,
  When first the lake we spied,
And fragments of a cloud were drawn
  Half down the mountain side.

Along the shore a heron flew,
  And from a speck on high,
That hovered in the deepening blue,
  We heard the fish-hawk's cry.

Among the cloud-capt solitudes,
  No sound the silence broke,
Save when, in whispers down the woods,
  The guardian mountains spoke.

Through tangled brush and dewy brake,
  Returning whence we came,
We passed in silence, and the lake
  We left without a name.

The Burden of Time

BEFORE the seas and mountains were brought forth,
  I reigned. I hung the universe in space,
I capped earth's poles with ice to South and North,
  And set the moving tides their bounds and place.

I smoothed the granite mountains with my hand,
  My fingers gave the continents their form;
I rent the heavens and loosed upon the land
  The fury of the whirlwind and the storm.

I stretched the dark sea like a nether sky
  Fronting the stars between the ice-clad zones;
I gave the deep his thunder; the Most High
  Knows well the voice that shakes His mountain thrones.

I trod the ocean caverns black as night,
  And silent as the bounds of outer space,
And where great peaks rose darkly towards the light
  I planted life to root and grow apace.

Then through a stillness deeper than the grave's,
  The coral spires rose slowly one by one,
Until the white shafts pierced the upper waves
  And shone like silver in the tropic sun.

I ploughed with glaciers down the mountain glen,
  And graved the iron shore with stream and tide;

I gave the bird her nest, the lion his den,
  The snake long jungle-grass wherein to hide.

In lonely gorge and over hill and plain,
  I sowed the giant forests of the world;
The great earth like a human heart in pain
  Has quivered with the meteors I have hurled.

I plunged whole continents beneath the deep,
  And left them sepulchred a million years;
I called, and lo, the drowned lands rose from sleep,
  Sundering the waters of the hemispheres.

I am the lord and arbiter of man—
  I hold and crush between my finger-tips
Wild hordes that drive the desert caravan,
  Great nations that go down to sea in ships.

In sovereign scorn I tread the races down,
  As each its puny destiny fulfils,
On plain and island, or where huge cliffs frown,
  Wrapt in the deep thought of the ancient hills.

The wild sea searches vainly round the land
  For those proud fleets my arm has swept away;
Vainly the wind along the desert sand
  Calls the great names of kings who once held sway.

Yea, Nineveh and Babylon the great
  Are fallen—like ripe ears at harvest-tide;
I set my heel upon their pomp and state,
  The people's serfdom and the monarch's pride.

One doom waits all—art, speech, law, gods, and men,
  Forests and mountains, stars and shining sun,—
The hand that made them shall unmake again,
  I curse them and they wither one by one.

Waste altars, tombs, dead cities where men trod,
  Shall roll through space upon the darkened globe,
Till I myself be overthrown, and God
  Cast off creation like an outworn robe.

Wilfred Campbell

It is just because Campbell has always made man and the larger, greater interests of man, the prevailing note of his poetic work, and is doing it more than ever before, that he is to be placed in the very front of our Canadian singers. . . . . . The majesty and grandeur of nature appeals to the poet, but there is always attached thereto the larger human interest. . . . His exquisite nature poems are as worthy of being read as any that Wordsworth wrote. . . . .'The Bereavement of the Fields,' the beautiful tribute to the memory of Archibald Lampman, worthily takes its place beside the other greater elegies of the English language. In technique and melody it ranks very high . . . . . .The well known poem, 'The Mother,' has justly been praised as one of the finest poems in all English literature. —PROF. L. E. HORNING, M.A., PH.D., in 'Globe Magazine.'

His poetry not only touches the deepest thought and feeling of humanity, but goes into the sacred and tragic places, where the great dramatic moments of life are known.—Toronto 'Saturday Night.'

WILFRED CAMPBELL, one of the most distinguished of our native writers, is a poet and novelist by inherited right. Through his father, the Rev. Thomas Swaniston Campbell, a descendant of the first Lord Campbell, of the House of Argyll, he is of the same stock as the poet, Thomas Campbell, and as the novelist, Henry Fielding.

His maternal grandfather was the late Major Francis Wright of the Royal Horse Guards.

He was born in Berlin, Ontario, June 1st, 1861, and was educated at the local High School, at University College, Toronto, and at Cambridge, Massachusetts. The honorary degree, LL.D., was conferred on him, in 1906, by the University of Aberdeen.

He was married in 1884 to Mary Louisa, only child of the late David Mark Dibble, M.D., of Woodstock, Ontario.

Dr. Campbell was ordained a clergyman of the Episcopal Church in 1885, and undertook parish work in New England. Three years later he returned to Canada and became Rector of St. Stephen, New Brunswick. In 1891, he retired from the ministry to devote his life chiefly to literary effort, and entered the civil service at Ottawa. For some years he has been associated with Dr. Doughty in the Dominion Archives Bureau.

In 1905, the best of Campbell's lyrics and sonnets were published in a substantial volume entitled, *The Collected Poems of Wilfred Campbell*. At the same time appeared *The Collected Poems of Isabella Valancy Crawford*, and such a notable coincidence aroused much interest in Canadian literary circles.

There is another coincidence of singular interest pertaining to these poets: each has written a remarkable poem on an identical theme,— *the soul of a mother returning from the grave for her child.*

In 1908, Campbell's *Poetical Tragedies:* "Mordred," "Daulac," "Morning" and "Hildebrand," were issued in a handsome volume, and his *Sagas of Vaster Britain,* a notable selection of his verse, in 1914.

The historical novels of this author, *Ian of the Orcades* (1906) and *A Beautiful Rebel* (1909), should be more widely read, and several other volumes of historical importance. Indeed his literary achievements are being added to yearly with a will and energy indomitable and purposeful.

England

ENGLAND, England, England,
Girdled by ocean and skies,
And the power of a world, and the heart of a race,
  And a hope that never dies.

England, England, England,
  Wherever a true heart beats,
Wherever the rivers of commerce flow,
Wherever the bugles of conquest blow,
Wherever the glories of liberty grow,
  'Tis the name that the world repeats.

And ye, who dwell in the shadow
  Of the century-sculptured piles,
Where sleep our century-honoured dead,
Whilst the great world thunders overhead,
  And far out, miles on miles,
Beyond the smoke of the mighty town,
  The blue Thames dimples and smiles;
Not yours alone the glory of old,
  Of the splendid thousand years,
Of Britain's might and Britain's right
  And the brunt of British spears.
Not yours alone, for the great world round,
  Ready to dare and do,
Scot and Celt and Norman and Dane,
With the Northman's sinew and heart and brain,
And the Northman's courage for blessing or bane,
  Are England's heroes too.

North and south and east and west,
  Wherever their triumphs be,
Their glory goes home to the ocean-girt isle,
Where the heather blooms and the roses smile,
  With the green isle under her lee.
And if ever the smoke of an alien gun
  Should threaten her iron repose,
Shoulder to shoulder against the world,
  Face to face with her foes,

Scot, and Celt and Saxon are one
  Where the glory of England goes.

And we of the newer and vaster West,
  Where the great war-banners are furled,
And commerce hurries her teeming hosts,
And the cannon are silent along our coasts,
Saxon and Gaul, Canadians claim
A part in the glory and pride and aim
  Of the Empire that girdles the world.

England, England, England,
  Wherever the daring heart
By Arctic floe or torrid strand
  Thy heroes play their part;
For as long as conquest holds the earth,
  Or commerce sweeps the sea,
By orient jungle or western plain
  Will the Saxon spirit be:
And whatever the people that dwell beneath,
  Or whatever the alien tongue,
Over the freedom and peace of the world
  Is the flag of England flung,
Till the last great freedom is found,
  And the last great truth be taught,
Till the last great deed be done,
  And the last great battle is fought;
Till the last great fighter is slain in the last great fight,
  And the war-wolf is dead in his den—
England, breeder of hope and valour and might,
  Iron mother of men.

Yea, England, England, England,
  Till honour and valour are dead,
Till the world's great cannons rust,
Till the world's great hopes are dust,
  Till faith and freedom be fled,
Till wisdom and justice have passed
To sleep with those who sleep in the many-chambered vast,
Till glory and knowledge are charnelled dust in dust,
To all that is best in the world's unrest,

In heart and mind you are wed.
While out from the Indian jungle
To the far Canadian snows,
Over the East and over the West,
  Over the worst and over the best,
The flag of the world to its winds unfurled,
  The blood-red ensign blows.

The Children of the Foam

OUT forever and forever,
  Where our tresses glint and shiver
    On the icy moonlit air;
Come we from a land of gloaming,
Children lost, forever homing,
  Never, never reaching there;
Ride we, ride we, ever faster,
Driven by our demon master,
  The wild wind in his despair.
Ride we, ride we, ever home,
Wan, white children of the foam.

In the wild October dawning,
When the heaven's angry awning
  Leans to lakeward, bleak and drear;
And along the black, wet ledges,
Under icy, caverned edges,
  Breaks the lake in maddened fear;
And the woods in shore are moaning;
Then you hear our weird intoning,
  Mad, late children of the year;
Ride we, ride we, ever home,
Lost, white children of the foam.

All grey day, the black sky under,
Where the beaches moan and thunder,
  Where the breakers spume and comb,
You may hear our riding, riding,
You may hear our voices chiding,
  Under glimmer, under gloam;
Like a far-off infant wailing,

You may hear our hailing, hailing,
  For the voices of our home;
Ride we, ride we, ever home,
Haunted children of the foam.

And at midnight, when the glimmer
Of the moon grows dank and dimmer,
  Then we lift our gleaming eyes;
Then you see our white arms tossing,
Our wan breasts the moon embossing,
  Under gloom of lake and skies;
You may hear our mournful chanting,
And our voices haunting, haunting,
  Through the night's mad melodies;
Riding, riding, ever home,
Wild, white children of the foam.

There, forever and forever,
Will no demon-hate dissever
  Peace and sleep and rest and dream:
There is neither fear nor fret there
When the tired children get there,
  Only dews and pallid beam
Fall in gentle peace and sadness
Over long surcease of madness,
  From hushed skies that gleam and gleam,
In the longed-for, sought-for home
Of the children of the foam.

There the streets are hushed and restful,
And of dreams is every breast full,
  With the sleep that tired eyes wear;
There the city hath long quiet
From the madness and the riot,
  From the failing hearts of care;
Balm of peacefulness ingliding,
Dream we through our riding, riding,
  As we homeward, homeward fare;
Riding, riding, ever home,
Wild, white children of the foam.

Under pallid moonlight beaming,
Under stars of midnight gleaming,
  And the ebon arch of night;
Round the rosy edge of morning,
You may hear our distant horning,
  You may mark our phantom flight;
Riding, riding, ever faster,
Driven by our demon master,
  Under darkness, under light;
Ride we, ride we, ever home,
Wild, white children of the foam.

The Dreamers

THEY lingered on the middle heights
  Betwixt the brown earth and the heaven;
They whispered, 'We are not the night's,
  But pallid children of the even.'

They muttered, 'We are not the day's,
  For the old struggle and endeavour,
The rugged and unquiet ways
  Are dead and driven past for ever.'

They dreamed upon the cricket's tune,
  The winds that stirred the withered grasses:
But never saw the blood-red moon
  That lit the spectre mountain-passes.

They sat and marked the brooklet steal
  In smoke-mist o'er its silvered surges:
But marked not, with its peal on peal,
  The storm that swept the granite gorges.

They dreamed the shimmer and the shade,
  And sought in pools for haunted faces:
Nor heard again the cannonade
  In dreams from earth's old battle-places.

They spake, 'The ages all are dead,
  The strife, the struggle, and the glory;
We are the silences that wed
  Betwixt the story and the story.

'We are the little winds that moan
  Between the woodlands and the meadows;
We are the ghosted leaves, wind-blown
  Across the gust-light and the shadows.'

Then came a soul across those lands
  Whose face was all one glad, rapt wonder,
And spake: 'The skies are ribbed with bands
  Of fire, and heaven all racked with thunder.

'Climb up and see the glory spread,
  High over cliff and 'scarpment yawning:
The night is past, the dark is dead,
  Behold the triumph of the dawning!'

Then laughed they with a wistful scorn,
  'You are a ghost, a long-dead vision;
You passed by ages ere was born
  This twilight of the days elysian.

'There is no hope, there is no strife,
  But only haunted hearts that hunger
About a dead, scarce-dreamed-of life,
  Old ages when the earth was younger.'

Then came by one in mad distress,
  'Haste, haste below, where strong arms weaken,
The fighting ones grow less and less!
  Great cities of the world are taken!

'Dread evil rolls by like a flood,
  Men's bones beneath his surges whiten,
Go where the ages mark in blood
  The footsteps that their days enlighten.'

Still they but heard, discordant mirth,
  The thin winds through the dead stalks rattle,
While out from far-off haunts of earth
  There smote the mighty sound of battle.

Now there was heard an awful cry,
  Despair that rended heaven asunder,
White pauses when a cause would die,
  Where love was lost and souls went under,

The while these feebly dreamed and talked
  Betwixt the brown earth and the heaven,
Faint ghosts of men who breathed and walked,
  But deader than the dead ones even.

And out there on the middle height
  They sought in pools for haunted faces,
Nor heard the cry across the night
  That swept from earth's dread battle-places.

Stella Flammarum

An Ode to Halley's Comet

STRANGE wanderer out of the deeps,
  Whence, journeying, come you?
From what far, unsunned sleeps
  Did fate foredoom you,
Returning for ever again,
  Through the surgings of man,
A flaming, awesome portent of dread
  Down the centuries' span?

Riddle! from the dark unwrung
  By all earth's sages;—
God's fiery torch from His hand outflung,
  To flame through the ages;
Thou Satan of planets eterne,
  'Mid angry path,
Chained, in circlings vast, to burn
  Out ancient wrath.

By what dread hand first loosed
  From fires eternal?
With majesties dire infused
  Of force supernal,
Takest thy headlong way
  O'er the highways of space?
O wonderful, blossoming flower of fear
  On the sky's far face!

What secret of destiny's will
  In thy wild burning?

What portent dire of humanity's ill
　　In thy returning?
Or art thou brand of love
　　In masking of bale?
And bringest thou ever some mystical surcease
　　For all who wail?

Perchance, O Visitor dread,
　　Thou hast thine appointed
Task, thou bolt of the vast outsped!
　　With God's anointed,
Performest some endless toil
　　In the universe wide,
Feeding or cursing some infinite need
　　Where the vast worlds ride.

Once, only once, thy face
　　Will I view in this breathing;
Just for a space thy majesty trace
　　'Mid earth's mad seething;
Ere I go hence to my place,
　　As thou to thy deeps,
Thou flambent core of a universe dread,
　　Where all else sleeps.

But thou and man's spirit are one,
　　Thou poet! thou flaming
Soul of the dauntless sun,
　　Past all reclaiming!
One in that red unrest,
　　That yearning, that surge,
That mounting surf of the infinite dream,
　　O'er eternity's verge.

The Mother
I

IT was April, blossoming spring,
They buried me, when the birds did sing;

Earth, in clammy wedging earth,
They banked my bed with a black, damp girth.

Under the damp and under the mould,
I kenned my breasts were clammy and cold.

Out from the red beams, slanting and bright,
I kenned my cheeks were sunken and white.

I was a dream, and the world was a dream,
And yet I kenned all things that seem.

I was a dream, and the world was a dream,
But you cannot bury a red sunbeam.

For though in the under-grave's doom-night
I lay all silent and stark and white,

Yet over my head I seemed to know
The murmurous moods of wind and snow,

The snows that wasted, the winds that blew,
The rays that slanted, the clouds that drew

The water-ghosts up from lakes below,
And the little flower-souls in earth that grow.

Under earth, in the grave's stark night,
I felt the stars and the moon's pale light.

I felt the winds of ocean and land
That whispered the blossoms soft and bland.

Though they had buried me dark and low,
My soul with the season's seemed to grow.

II

From throes of pain they buried me low,
For death had finished a mother's woe.

But under the sod, in the grave's dread doom,
I dreamed of my baby in glimmer and gloom.

I dreamed of my babe, and I kenned that his rest
Was broken in wailings on my dead breast.

I dreamed that a rose-leaf hand did cling;
Oh, you cannot bury a mother in spring!

When the winds are soft and the blossoms are red
She could not sleep in her cold earth-bed.

I dreamed of my babe for a day and a night,
And then I rose in my grave-clothes white.

I rose like a flower from my damp earth-bed
To the world of sorrowing overhead.

Men would have called me a thing of harm,
But dreams of my babe made me rosy and warm.

I felt my breasts swell under my shroud;
No star shone white, no winds were loud;

But I stole me past the graveyard wall,
For the voice of my baby seemed to call;

And I kenned me a voice, though my lips were dumb:
Hush, baby, hush! for mother is come.

I passed the streets to my husband's home;
The chamber stairs in a dream I clomb;

I heard the sound of each sleeper's breath,
Light waves that break on the shores of death.

I listened a space at my chamber door,
Then stole like a moon-ray over its floor.

My babe was asleep on a stranger's arm,
'O baby, my baby, the grave is so warm,

'Though dark and so deep, for mother is there!
O come with me from the pain and care!

'O come with me from the anguish of earth,
Where the bed is banked with a blossoming girth,

'Where the pillow is soft and the rest is long,
And mother will croon you a slumber-song—

'A slumber-song that will charm your eyes
To a sleep that never in earth-song lies!

'The loves of earth your being can spare,
But never the grave, for mother is there.'

I nestled him soft to my throbbing breast,
And stole me back to my long, long rest.

And here I lie with him under the stars,
Dead to earth, its peace and its wars;

Dead to its hates, its hopes, and its harms,
So long as he cradles up soft in my arms.

And heaven may open its shimmering doors,
And saints make music on pearly floors,

And hell may yawn to its infinite sea,
But they never can take my baby from me.

For so much a part of my soul he hath grown
That God doth know of it high on His throne.

And here I lie with him under the flowers
That sun-winds rock through the billowy hours,

With the night-airs that steal from the murmuring sea,
Bringing sweet peace to my baby and me.

The Last Prayer

MASTER of life, the day is done;
My sun of life is sinking low;
I watch the hours slip one by one
    And hark the night-wind and the snow.

And must Thou shut the morning out,
    And dim the eye that loved to see;
Silence the melody and rout,
    And seal the joys of earth for me?

And must Thou banish all the hope,
    The large horizon's eagle-swim,
The splendour of the far-off slope
    That ran about the world's great rim,

That rose with morning's crimson rays
    And grew to noonday's gloried dome,
Melting to even's purple haze
    When all the hopes of earth went home?

Yea, Master of this ruined house,
  The mortgage closed, outruns the lease;
Long since is hushed the gay carouse,
  And now the windowed lights must cease.

The doors all barred, the shutters up,
  Dismantled, empty, wall and floor,
And now for one grim eve to sup
  With Death, the bailiff, at the door.

Yea, I will take the gloomward road
  Where fast the Arctic nights set in,
To reach the bourne of that abode
  Which Thou hast kept for all my kin.

And all life's splendid joys forego,
  Walled in with night and senseless stone,
If at the last my heart might know
  Through all the dark one joy alone.

Yea, Thou mayst quench the latest spark
  Of life's weird day's expectancy,
Roll down the thunders of the dark
  And close the light of life for me;

Melt all the splendid blue above
  And let these magic wonders die,
If Thou wilt only leave me, Love,
  And Love's heart-brother, Memory.

Though all the hopes of every race
  Crumbled in one red crucible,
And melted, mingled into space,
  Yet, Master, Thou wert merciful.

George Frederick Cameron

It seems strange to me that you have not thought of using any of the work of the late Mr. Cameron of Kingston, who was most certainly the poet of most genuine and fervid poetic energy that this country has yet produced. There are half a dozen things of his that I would not give for all that the rest of us have written. I can get a better effect upon people by reading them some of Cameron's poems, than those of any other Canadian writer; and that I have always found is the true test. . . . . If I were making a selection, I would put them in this order:—The poem without title, 'Standing on Tiptoe,' 'The Way Of The World,' 'I Am Young,' 'What Matters It,' 'To The West Wind,' 'An Answer,' 'Wisdom,' 'Amor Finis,' 'In After Days.' . . . . That first poem I would include in any selection of English masterpieces however restricted, and the second one, 'Standing On Tiptoe,' is almost as fine.—ARCHIBALD LAMPMAN, in letters to a Canadian anthologist, 1892.

G EORGE FREDERICK CAMERON was born at New Glasgow, Nova Scotia, September 24th, 1854,—the eldest son of James Grant Cameron and Jessie Sutherland. He was educated at the local High School, where he read Virgil and Cicero in the original and devoted much time to poetry, and at the Boston University of Law. His family had moved to Boston in 1869. After graduation he entered a law office, but gave considerable attention to literary work, contributing to a number of journals. In 1882, he entered Queen's University, Kingston, Ontario, and the following year had the distinction to win the prize for the best original poem.

In March, 1883, Mr. Cameron became editor of the Kingston *News,* and in the following August, married Ella, the eldest daughter of Mr. Billings Amey, of Millhaven. He continued in his editorial position until a few weeks before his untimely death from heart failure, September 17th, 1885. For two years he had suffered much from insomnia. His young wife and their daughter survived him.

In 1887, Charles J. Cameron, M.A., edited and published a volume of his brother's poems, of about 300 pages, entitled *Lyrics on Freedom, Love and Death,* and which, he says in his Preface, "represents about one fourth of his life work."

The unique interest attaching to such a spontaneous and emphatic expression of opinion by Lampman, has induced the editor to quote the poems only that he mentioned and to record no other critical judgment.

A H, me! the mighty love that I have borne
  To thee, sweet song! A perilous gift was it
My mother gave me that September morn
  When sorrow, song, and life were at one altar lit.

A gift more perilous than the priest's: his lore
  Is all of books and to his books extends;
And what they see and know he knows—no more,
  And with their knowing all his knowing ends.

A gift more perilous than the painter's: he
  In his divinest moments only sees
The inhumanities of colour, we
  Feel each and all the inhumanities.

Standing on Tiptoe

STANDING on tiptoe ever since my youth
   Striving to grasp the future just above,
I hold at length the only future—Truth,
   And Truth is Love.

I feel as one who being awhile confined
   Sees drop to dust about him all his bars:—
The clay grows less, and, leaving it, the mind
   Dwells with the stars.

The Way of the World

WE sneer and we laugh with the lip—the most of us do it,
   Whenever a brother goes down like a weed with the tide;
We point with the finger and say—Oh, we knew it! we knew it!
   But, see! we are better than he was, and we will abide.

He walked in the way of his will—the way of desire,
   In the Appian way of his will without ever a bend;
He walked in it long, but it led him at last to the mire,—
   But we who are stronger will stand and endure to the end.

His thoughts were all visions—all fabulous visions of flowers,
   Of bird and of song and of soul which is only a song;
His eyes looked all at the stars in the firmament, ours
   Were fixed on the earth at our feet, so we stand and are
      strong.

He hated the sight and the sound and the sob of the city;
   He sought for his peace in the wood and the musical wave;
He fell, and we pity him never, and why should we pity—
   Yea, why should we mourn for him—we who still stand, who
      are brave?

Thus speak we and think not, we censure unheeding, unknow-
      ing,—
   Unkindly and blindly we utter the words of the brain;
We see not the goal of our brother, we see but his going,
   And sneer at his fall if he fall, and laugh at his pain.

Ah, me! the sight of the sod on the coffin lid,
   And the sound, and the sob, and the sigh of it as it falls!
Ah, me! the beautiful face forever hid
   By four wild walls!

You hold it a matter for self-gratulation and praise
   To have thrust to the dust to have trod on a heart that was
      true,—
To have ruined it there in the beauty and bloom of its days?
Very well! There is somewhere a Nemesis waiting for you.

I Am Young

I AM young, and men
   Who long ago have passed their prime
Would fain have what I have again,—
   Youth, and it may be—time.

To gain these, and make
   Life's end what it may not be now,
Monarchs of thought and song would shake
   The laurels from their brow.

And each king of earth,
   Whose life we deem a holiday,
For this would give his kingship's worth
   Most joyously away!

What Matters It?

WHAT reck we of the creeds of men?—
   We see them—we shall see again.
What reck we of the tempest's shock?
What reck we where our anchor lock?
   On golden marl or mould—
In salt-sea flower or riven rock—
   What matter—so it hold?

What matters it the spot we fill
   On Earth's green sod when all is said?—
When feet and hands and heart are still
   And all our pulses quieted?
When hate or love can kill nor thrill,—
   When we are done with life and dead?

So we be haunted night nor day
  By any sin that we have sinned,
What matter where we dream away
  The ages?—In the isles of Ind,
In Tybee, Cuba, or Cathay,
  Or in some world of winter wind?

It may be I would wish to sleep
  Beneath the wan, white stars of June,
And hear the southern breezes creep
  Between me and the mellow moon;
But so I do not wake to weep
  At any night or any moon,

And so the generous gods allow
  Repose and peace from evil dreams,
It matters little where or how
  My couch is spread:—by moving streams,
Or on some eminent mountain's brow
  Kist by the morn's or sunset's beams.

For we shall rest; the brain that planned,
  That thought or wrought or well or ill,
At gaze like Joshua's moon shall stand,
  Not working any work or will,
While eye and lip and heart and hand
  Shall all be still—shall all be still!

To the West Wind

WEST wind, come from the west land
    Fair and far!
Come from the fields of the best land
  Upon our star!

Come, and go to my sister
  Over the sea:
Tell her how much I have missed her,
  Tell her for me!

Odours of lilies and roses—
  Set them astir;
Cull them from gardens and closes,—
  Give them to her!

Say I have loved her, and love her:
    Say that I prize
Few on the earth here above her,
    Few in the skies!

Bring her, if worth the bringing,
    A brother's kiss:
Should she ask for a song of his singing,
    Give her this!

An Answer

'CAN it be good to die?' you question, friend;
    'Can it be good to die, and move along
Still circling round and round, unknowing end,
    Still circling round and round amid the throng
Of golden orbs attended by their moons—
    To catch the intonation of their song
As on they flash, and scatter nights, and noons,
    To worlds like ours, where things like us belong?'

To *me* 'tis idle saying, 'He is dead.'
    Or, 'Now he sleepeth and shall wake no more;
The little flickering, fluttering life is fled,
    Forever fled, and all that *was* is o'er.'
I have a faith—that life and death are *one,*
    That each depends upon the self-same thread,
And that the seen and unseen rivers run
    To one calm sea, from one clear fountain head.

I have a faith—that man's most potent mind
    May cross the willow-shaded stream nor sink;
I have a faith—when he has left behind
    His earthly vesture on the river's brink,
When all his little fears are torn away,
    His soul may beat a pathway through the tide,
And, disencumbered of its coward-clay,
    Emerge immortal on the sunnier side.

So, say:—It must be good to die, my friend!
    It must be good and more than good, I deem;
'Tis all the replication I may send—
    For deeper swimming seek a deeper stream.

It must be good or reason is a cheat,
  It must be good or life is all a lie,
It must be good and more then living sweet,
  It must be good—*or man would never die.*

Wisdom

WISDOM immortal from immortal Jove
    Shadows more beauty with her virgin brows
Than is between the pleasant breasts of Love
Who makes at will and breaks her random vows,
And hath a name all earthly names above:
The noblest are her offspring; she controls
The times and seasons—yea, all things that are—
The heads and hands of men, their hearts and souls,
And all that moves upon our mother star,
And all that pauses twixt the peaceful poles.
Nor is she dark and distant, coy and cold,—
But all in all to all who seek her shrine
In utter truth, like to that king of old
Who wooed and won—yet by no right divine.

Amoris Finis

AND now I go with the departing sun:
    My day is dead and all my work is done.
No more for me the pleasant moon shall rise
  To show the splendour in my dear one's eyes;
No more the stars shall see us meet; we part
  Without a hope, or hope of hope, at heart;
For Love lies dead, and at his altar, lo,
  Stands in his room, self-crowned and crested,—*Woe!*

In After Days

I WILL accomplish that and this,
    And make myself a thorn to Things—
    Lords, councillors and tyrant kings—
Who sit upon their thrones and kiss

The rod of Fortune; and are crowned
  The sovereign masters of the earth
  To scatter blight and death and dearth
Wherever mortal man is found.

I will do this and that, and break
  The backbone of their large conceit,
  And loose the sandals from their feet,
And show 'tis holy ground they shake.

So sang I in my earlier days,
  Ere I had learned to look abroad
  And see that more than monarchs trod
Upon the form I fain would raise.

Ere I, in looking toward the land
  That broke a triple diadem,
  That grasped at Freedom's garment hem,
Had seen her, sword and torch in hand,

A freedom-fool: ere I had grown
  To know that Love is freedom's strength—
  France taught the world that truth at length!—
And Peace her chief foundation stone.

Since then, I temper so my song
  That it may never speak for blood;
  May never say that ill is good;
Or say that right may spring from wrong:

Yet am what I have ever been—
  A friend of Freedom, staunch and true,
  Who hate a tyrant, be he—you—
A people,—sultan, czar, or queen!

And then the Freedom-haters came
  And questioned of my former song,
  If *now* I held it right, or wrong:
And still my answer was the same:—

The good still moveth towards the good:
  The ill still moveth towards the ill:
  But who affirmeth that we will
Not form a nobler brotherhood

When communists, fanatics, those
  Who howl their '*vives*' to Freedom's name
  And yet betray her unto shame,
Are dead and coffined with her foes.

Bliss Carman

Carman is before everything else a nature poet, but he is not a nature poet alone. . . . . Carman's genius has its limits—it rarely, and scarcely ever with success, displays itself in themes dealing with the social life of man—but within its own compass its strength and versatility are undeniable. The imagination of the poet, which would seem extremely sensitive to the influence of his environment, is wide-reaching and full of colour; his fancy is fine and delicate; his diction is cultured and 'magical'; and he possesses a gift of melodious versification such as perhaps no other transatlantic writer, with the exception of Poe, has as yet exhibited. Canadian in his youthful gaiety and love of adventure, New England in his practical idealism and freedom from dogma, and more Latin than anything else in his passionate love of the beautiful, Bliss Carman is not only a singer of whom the Dominion has every reason to be proud, but one of the most original and captivating poets of the present century.—H. D. C. LEE, Docteur De L'Université De Rennes, in *Bliss Carman: A Study in Canadian Poetry*, 1912.

BLISS CARMAN 'has the rare and vital individuality of genius.' He was brought up in the beautiful valley of the St. John river, New Brunswick, and as in the case of his distinguished cousin, Charles G. D. Roberts, his early quest of beauty intensified later into a craving. He has ever felt his kinship with the trees, the flowers, and the furtive wild things, and has regarded himself and every other manifestation of the Infinite Spirit, as a vagrant seeking to attain to perfection. For him 'God lurks as potency in all things.'

After pointing out that Carman's philosophic thought had probably been influenced more by Robert Browning than by anyone else, Dr. Lee sums up his later philosophy in these three principles:

Love is the Lord of Life, the revealer of the purpose of creation. This divine energy can only be transmitted to the soul through the media of the senses and in proportion as the senses are perfect. The ideals awakened in the soul by Love can only be adequately realized with the help of reason.

William Bliss Carman, of United Empire Loyalist descent, was born at Fredericton, N.B., April 15th, 1861,—son of William Carman, a barrister, at one time a prominent Government official, and Sophia Bliss, an elder sister of the mother of Roberts. He was tutored at home prior to entering the Collegiate School, in Fredericton, where he came under the influence of a cultured man of letters and an ardent lover of open-air life,—Dr. George R. Parkin. To this educationist of world-wide repute, Carman has gratefully acknowledged his debt, in a dedicatory preface to *The Kinship of Nature*. In 1878, he won the School medal for Greek and Latin, and passed into the University of New Brunswick (B. A., and Gold Medalist, 1881; M.A., 1884; LL.D., honorary, 1906). He had taken high honours in both classics and mathematics, and in the academic year, 1882-3, he pursued these subjects, together with philosophy, in a postgraduate course at the University of Edinburgh. Returning to Canada, he had difficulty, apparently, in choosing a profession, as he successively taught school, studied law, and practised civil engineering, before, in 1886, he resolved to take postgraduate work in Harvard University.

From 1890 to 1892, he was on the editorial staff of the

Independent, New York, and later was similarly connected with *Current Literature.* He was one of the founders of the *Chap-Book.* But tiring of the editorial chair, he soon became an independent man of letters.

Since he first attracted wide attention with his *Low Tide on Grand Pré* (1893), Carman has published many books of poems of rare quality, and four volumes of illuminating essays. *April Airs,* daintily issued by Small, Maynard and Company, Boston, in the spring of 1916, contains his latest lyrics. They are exquisite indeed, with deep, rich tones and great beauty of expression.

Earth Voices

I

I HEARD the spring wind whisper
Above the brushwood fire,
'The world is made forever
Of transport and desire.

'I am the breath of being,
The primal urge of things;
I am the whirl of star dust,
I am the lift of wings.

'I am the splendid impulse
That comes before the thought,
The joy and exaltation
Wherein the life is caught.

'Across the sleeping furrows
I call the buried seed,
And blade and bud and blossom
Awaken at my need.

'Within the dying ashes
I blow the sacred spark,
And make the hearts of lovers
To leap against the dark.'

II

I heard the spring light whisper
Above the dancing stream,

'The world is made forever
In likeness of a dream.

'I am the law of planets,
I am the guide of man;
The evening and the morning
Are fashioned to my plan.

'I tint the dawn with crimson,
I tinge the sea with blue;
My track is in the desert,
My trail is in the dew.

'I paint the hills with colour,
And in my magic dome
I light the star of evening
To steer the traveller home.

'Within the house of being,
I feed the lamp of truth
With tales of ancient wisdom
And prophecies of youth.'

III

I heard the spring rain murmur
Above the roadside flower,
'The world is made forever
In melody and power.

'I keep the rhythmic measure
That marks the steps of time,
And all my toil is fashioned
To symmetry and rhyme.

'I plough the untilled upland,
I ripe the seeding grass,
And fill the leafy forest
With music as I pass.

'I hew the raw rough granite
To loveliness of line,
And when my work is finished,
Behold, it is divine!

'I am the master-builder
In whom the ages trust.
I lift the lost perfection
To blossom from the dust.'

IV

Then Earth to them made answer,
As with a slow refrain
Born of the blended voices
Of wind and sun and rain,

'This is the law of being
That links the threefold chain:
The life we give to beauty
Returns to us again.'

A Mountain Gateway

I KNOW a vale where I would go one day,
When June comes back and all the world once more
Is glad with summer. Deep in shade it lies
A mighty cleft between the bosoming hills,
A cool dim gateway to the mountains' heart.

On either side the wooded slopes come down,
Hemlock and beech and chestnut. Here and there
Through the deep forest laurel spreads and gleams,
Pink-white as Daphne in her loveliness.
Among the sunlit shadows I can see
That still perfection from the world withdrawn,
As if the wood-gods had arrested there
Immortal beauty in her breathless flight.

The road winds in from the broad river-lands,
Luring the happy traveller turn by turn
Up to the lofty mountains of the sky.
And as he marches with uplifted face,
Far overhead against the arching blue
Gray ledges overhang from dizzy heights,
Scarred by a thousand winters and untamed.

And where the road runs in the valley's foot,
Through the dark woods a mountain stream comes down,

Singing and dancing all its youth away
Among the boulders and the shallow runs,
Where sunbeams pierce and mossy tree trunks hang
Drenched all day long with murmuring sound and spray.

There light of heart and footfree, I would go
Up to my home among the lasting hills.
Nearing the day's end, I would leave the road,
Turn to the left and take the steeper trail
That climbs among the hemlocks, and at last
In my own cabin doorway sit me down,
Companioned in that leafy solitude
By the wood ghosts of twilight and of peace,
While evening passes to absolve the day
And leave the tranquil mountains to the stars.

And in that sweet seclusion I should hear,
Among the cool-leafed beeches in the dusk,
The calm-voiced thrushes at their twilight hymn.
So undistraught, so rapturous, so pure,
They well might be, in wisdom and in joy,
The seraphs singing at the birth of time
The unworn ritual of eternal things.

Garden Shadows

WHEN the dawn winds whisper
    To the standing corn,
And the rose of morning
From the dark is born,
All my shadowy garden
Seems to grow aware
Of a fragrant presence,
Half expected there.

In the golden shimmer
Of the burning noon,
When the birds are silent
And the poppies swoon,
Once more I behold her
Smile and turn her face,
With its infinite regard,
Its immortal grace.

When the twilight silvers
Every nodding flower,
When the new moon hallows
The first evening hour,
Is it not her footfall
Down the garden walks,
Where the drowsy blossoms
Slumber on their stalks?

In the starry quiet,
When the soul is free,
And a vernal message
Stirs the lilac tree,
Surely I have felt her
Pass and brush my cheek,
With the eloquence of love
That does not need to speak!

The Tent of Noon

BEHOLD, now, where the pageant of the high June
Halts in the glowing noon!
The trailing shadows rest on plain and hill;
The bannered hosts are still,
While over forest crown and mountain head
The azure tent is spread.

The song is hushed in every woodland throat;
Moveless the lilies float;
Even the ancient ever-murmuring sea
Sighs only fitfully;
The cattle drowse in the field-corner's shade;
Peace on the world is laid.

It is the hour when Nature's caravan,
That bears the pilgrim Man
Across the desert of uncharted time
To his far hope sublime,
Rests in the green oasis of the year,
As if the end drew near.

Ah, traveller, hast thou naught of thanks or praise
For these fleet halcyon days?—

7

No courage to uplift thee from despair
Born with the breath of prayer?
Then turn thee to the lilied field once more!
God stands in His tent door.

Spring's Saraband

OVER the hills of April
With soft winds hand in hand,
Impassionate and dreamy-eyed,
Spring leads her saraband.
Her garments float and gather
And swirl along the plain,
Her headgear is the golden sun,
Her cloak the silver rain.

With colour and with music,
With perfumes and with pomp,
By meadowland and upland,
Through pasture, wood, and swamp,
With promise and enchantment
Leading her mystic mime,
She comes to lure the world anew
With joy as old as time.

Quick lifts the marshy chorus
To transport, trill on trill;
There's not a rod of stony ground
Unanswering on the hill.
The brooks and little rivers
Dance down their wild ravines,
And children in the city squares
Keep time, to tambourines.

The blue bird in the orchard
Is lyrical for her,
The starling with his meadow pipe
Sets all the wood astir,
The hooded white spring-beauties
Are curtsying in the breeze,
The blue hepaticas are out
Under the chestnut trees.

The maple buds make glamour
Vibernum waves its bloom,
The daffodils and tulips
Are risen from the tomb.
The lances of narcissus
Have pierced the wintry mold;
The commonplace seems paradise
To veils of greening gold.

O hark, hear thou the summons,
Put every grief away,
When all the motley masques of earth
Are glad upon a day.
Alack, that any mortal
Should less than gladness bring
Into the choral joy that sounds
The saraband of spring!

Low Tide on Grand-Pré

THE sun goes down, and over all
These barren reaches by the tide
Such unelusive glories fall,
I almost dream they yet will bide
Until the coming of the tide.

And yet I know that not for us,
By any ecstasy of dream,
He lingers to keep luminous
A little while the grievous stream,
Which frets, uncomforted of dream—

A grievous stream, that to and fro,
Athrough the fields of Acadie
Goes wandering, as if to know
Why one belovèd face should be
So long from home and Acadie.

Was it a year or lives ago
We took the grasses in our hands,
And caught the summer flying low
Over the waving meadow lands,
And held it there between our hands?

The while the river at our feet—
A drowsy inland meadow stream—
At set of sun the after-heat
Made running gold, and in the gleam
We freed our birch upon the stream.

There down along the elms at dusk
We lifted dripping blade to drift,
Through twilight scented fine like musk,
Where night and gloom awhile uplift,
Nor sunder soul and soul adrift.

And that we took into our hands—
Spirit of life or subtler thing—
Breathed on us there, and loosed the bands
Of death, and taught us, whispering,
The secret of some wonder-thing.

Then all your face grew light, and seemed
To hold the shadow of the sun;
The evening faltered, and I deemed
That time was ripe, and years had done
Their wheeling underneath the sun.

So all desire and all regret,
And fear and memory, were naught;
One to remember or forget
The keen delight our hands had caught;
Morrow and yesterday were naught.

The night has fallen, and the tide. . .
Now and again comes drifting home,
Across these aching barrens wide,
A sigh like driven wind or foam:
In grief the flood is bursting home.

Threnody for a Poet

NOT in the ancient abbey,
    Nor in the city ground,
Not in the lonely mountains,
Nor in the blue profound,
Lay him to rest when his time is come
And the smiling mortal lips are dumb;

But here in the decent quiet
Under the whispering pines,
Where the dogwood breaks in blossom
And the peaceful sunlight shines,
Where wild birds sing and ferns unfold,
When spring comes back in her green and gold.

And when that mortal likeness
Has been dissolved by fire,
Say not above the ashes,
'Here ends a man's desire.'
For every year when the bluebirds sing,
He shall be part of the lyric spring.

Then dreamful-hearted lovers
Shall hear in wind and rain
The cadence of his music,
The rhythm of his refrain,
For he was a blade of the April sod
That bowed and blew with the whisper of God.

At the Making of Man

FIRST all the host of Raphael
In liveries of gold,
Lifted the chorus on whose rhythm
The spinning spheres are rolled,—
The Seraphs of the morning calm
Whose hearts are never cold.

He shall be born a spirit,
Part of the soul that yearns,
The core of vital gladness
That suffers and discerns,
The stir that breaks the budding sheath
When the green spring returns,—

The gist of power and patience
Hid in the plasmic clay,
The calm behind the senses,
The passionate essay
To make his wise and lovely dream
Immortal on a day.

The soft Aprilian ardours
That warm the waiting loam
Shall whisper in his pulses
To bid him overcome,
And he shall learn the wonder-cry
Beneath the azure dome.

And though all-dying nature
Should teach him to deplore,
The ruddy fires of autumn
Shall lure him but the more
To pass from joy to stronger joy,
As through an open door.

He shall have hope and honour,
Proud trust and courage stark,
To hold him to his purpose
Through the unlighted dark,
And love that sees the moon's full orb
In the first silver arc.

And he shall live by kindness
And the heart's certitude,
Which moves without misgiving
In ways not understood,
Sure only of the vast event,—
The large and simple good.

Then Gabriel's host in silver gear
And vesture twilight blue,
The spirits of immortal mind,
The warders of the true,
Took up the theme that gives the world
Significance anew.

He shall be born to reason,
And have the primal need
To understand and follow
Wherever truth may lead,—
To grow in wisdom like a tree
Unfolding from a seed.

A watcher by the sheepfolds,
With wonder in his eyes,
He shall behold the seasons,
And mark the planets rise,
Till all the marching firmament
Shall rouse his vast surmise.

Beyond the sweep of vision,
Or utmost reach of sound,
This cunning fire-maker,
This tiller of the ground,
Shall learn the secrets of the suns
And fathom the profound.

For he must prove all being,
Sane, beauteous, benign,
And at the heart of nature
Discover the divine,—
Himself the type and symbol
Of the eternal trine.

He shall perceive the kindling
Of knowledge, far and dim,
As of the fire that brightens
Below the dark sea-rim,
When ray by ray the splendid sun
Floats to the world's wide brim.

And out of primal instinct,
The lore of lair and den,
He shall emerge to question
How, wherefore, whence, and when,
Till the last frontier of the truth
Shall lie within his ken.

Then Michael's scarlet-suited host
Took up the word and sang;
As though a trumpet had been loosed
In heaven, the arches rang;
For these were they who feel the thrill
Of beauty like a pang.

He shall be framed and balanced
For loveliness and power,
Lithe as the supple creatures,
And coloured as a flower,
Sustained by the all-feeding earth,
Nurtured by wind and shower,

To stand within the vortex
Where surging forces play,
A poised and pliant figure
Immutable as they,
Till time and space and energy
Surrender to his sway.

He shall be free to journey
Over the teeming earth,
An insatiable seeker,
A wanderer from his birth,
Clothed in the fragile veil of sense,
With fortitude for girth.

His hands shall have dominion
Of all created things,
To fashion in the likeness
Of his imaginings,
To make his will and thought survive
Unto a thousand springs.

The world shall be his province,
The princedom of his skill;
The tides shall wear his harness,
The winds obey his will;
Till neither flood, nor fire, nor frost,
Shall work to do him ill.

A creature fit to carry
The pure creative fire,
Whatever truth inform him,
Whatever good inspire,
He shall make lovely in all things
To the end of his desire.

S. Frances Harrison

(Seranus)

Nature has done much for Mrs. Harrison, in giving her a quick and ready wit, a profoundly sympathetic nature, an unusual power of entering into the thoughts and sentiments of others, besides a very high poetic endowment. . . . . It is necessary to mention that Mrs. Harrison is of British stock, and a native of Toronto. We do not mean that there are not abundant evidences of this origin in her writings; but those who rise from the perusal of her principal volume of poems will find it difficult to believe that she has no Gallic strain in her constitution. It may perhaps be sufficient explanation for this phenomenon, the delicate perception of every shade of French thought and feeling, that the young artist was removed to Lower Canada when only a girl of fifteen, and there became conscious of all the rich material which lay around her, ready to be worked up into living pictures. . . . . Five pages from 'Pine, Rose and Fleur De Lis' are included in Stedman's splendid 'Victorian Anthology,' a high and just tribute from the foremost critic of America.—REV. WILLIAM CLARK, D.C.L., in 'The Magazine of Poetry,' 1896.

S. FRANCES HARRISON is one of our greater poets whose work has not yet had the recognition in Canada it merits. For unique originality and interest, her pen pictures, in villanelle form, of French-Canadian character and life, stand in almost as distinctive a class as Dr. Drummond's *habitant* poems, and like the latter they were produced from first-hand knowledge.

Susie Frances Riley was born in Toronto, February 24th, 1859, and is of Irish-Canadian extraction, her father being the late John Byron Riley, for many years proprietor of the 'Revere House,' King St. West. She was educated in a private school for girls, and later, for two years, in Montreal. In her twenty-first year, she married Mr. J. W. F. Harrison, of Bristol, England, a professional musician, at that time organist of St. George's Church, Montreal. In those days, and later, Mrs. Harrison was well known as a professional pianist and vocalist, and indeed her proficiency as a musician has since had expression in compositions of worth. In 1883, while living in Ottawa, where her husband was musical director of the Ottawa Ladies College and organist and choirmaster of Christ Church Cathedral, she wrote and composed a *Song of Welcome* for the initial public appearance of the Marquis of Lansdowne; and she has since composed many songs, and an entire opera, words and music.

In 1887, Mr. and Mrs. Harrison moved to Toronto, where the former had become organist and choirmaster of the Church of St. Simon, the Apostle. It was about this time that 'Seranus' began her literary career in earnest, and since then her contributions have appeared in many of the leading periodicals and journals. The following are her book publications: *Crowded Out and Other Sketches,* 1886; *Canadian Birthday Book,* 1887; *Pine, Rose and Fleur De Lis,* 1891; *The Forest of Bourg-Marie,* a novel, 1898; *In Northern Skies and Other Poems,* 1912; and *Ringfield,* a novel, 1914.

Crowded Out and Other Sketches has special significance, as 'it was in point of time the first attempt to put Muskoka, and the feeling and landscape of Lower Canada, before our people in an artistic way.'

Mr. and Mrs. Harrison have a son and a daughter.

From 'Down the River'
Gatineau Point

A HALF-BREED, slim, and sallow of face,
  Alphonse lies full length on his raft,
The hardy son of a hybrid race.

Lithe and long, with the Indian grace,
  Versed in the varied Indian craft,
A half-breed, slim, and sallow of face,

He nurses within mad currents that chase—
  The swift, the sluggish—a foreign graft,
This hardy son of a hybrid race.

What southern airs, what snows embrace
  Within his breast—soft airs that waft
The half-breed—slim, and sallow of face,

Far from the Gatineau's foaming base!
  And what strong potion hath he quaffed,
This hardy son of a hybrid race,

That upon this sun-baked blistered place
  He sleeps, with his hand on the burning haft,
A Metis—slim and sallow of face,
  The hardy son òf a hybrid race!

The Voyageur

LIKE the swarthy son of some tropic shore
  He sleeps, with his olive bosom bared,
He sleeps—in his earrings of brassy ore.

Like a tawny tiger whom hot hours bore,
  When all night long he has growled and glared
At the swarthy son of some tropic shore,

Like a fierce-eyed blossom with heart of gore
  That too long in the sun-flushed fields has flared,
He sleeps—in his earrings of brassy ore,

And his scarlet sash that he gaily wore
  To tempt Madelon—who his heart has snared,
Like the swarthy son of some tropic shore.

That dusky form might a queen adore—
  Prenez garde, Madelon, for a season spared,
He sleeps—in his earrings of brassy ore.

For a season only. What may be in store
  For Madelon? She who has never cared! . . .
Like the swarthy son of some tropic shore
He sleeps—in his earrings of brassy ore.

Danger

WELL! Let him sleep! Time enough to awake
  When sunset ushers a kind release,
When cooling shadows the raft overtake.

For Madelon's heart will never break
  For Alphonse, but for Verrier, *fils,*
So—let him sleep! Time enough to awake

When Verrier, dressed for Madelon's sake
  In his best, is up the river a piece,
When cooling shadows the raft overtake.

A Carmen—she—whose eyelashes make
  Havoc with all—old Boucher's niece—
So—let him sleep! Time enough to awake,

For a desperate thing is a bad heart-ache,
  And one that may not entirely cease
When cooling shadows the raft overtake.

If they met, who knows—a spring, a shake,
  A jack-knife, deadly as Malay crease—
Hush! Let him sleep! Time enough to awake
When cooling shadows the raft overtake.

Les Chantiers

FOR know, my girl, there is always the axe
  Ready at hand in this latitude,
And how it stings and bites and hacks

When Alphonse the sturdy trees attacks!
  So fear, child, to cross him, or play the prude,
For know, my girl, there is always the axe.

See! It shines even now as his hands relax
  Their grip with a dread desire imbued,
And how it stings and bites and hacks,

And how it rips and cuts and cracks—
  Perhaps—in his brain as the foe is pursued!
For know, my girl, there is always the axe.

The giant boles in the forest tracks
  Stagger, soul-smitten, when afar it is viewed,
And how it stings and bites and hacks!

Then how, Madelon, should its fearful thwacks
  A slender lad like your own elude?
For know, my girl, there is always the axe,
And how it stings! and bites! and hacks!

Petite Ste. Rosalie

FATHER Couture loves a fricassee,
  Served with a sip of home-made wine,
He is the Curé, so jolly and free,

And lives in Petite Ste. Rosalie.
  On Easter Sunday when one must dine,
Father Couture loves a fricassee.

No stern ascetic, no stoic is he,
  Preaching a rigid right divine.
He is the Curé, so jolly and free,

That while he maintains his dignity,
  When Lent is past and the weather is fine,
Father Couture loves a fricassee.

He kills his chicken himself—*on dit,*
  And who is there dare the deed malign?
He is the Curé, so jolly and free.

Open and courteous, fond of a fee,
  The village deity, bland and benign,
Father Couture loves a fricassee,
He's a sensible Curé, so jolly and free!

St. Jean B'ptiste

'TIS the day of the blessed St. Jean B'ptiste,
  And the streets are full of the folk awaiting
The favourite French-Canadian feast.

One knows by the bells which have never ceased,
  Since early morn reverberating,
'Tis the day of the blessed St. Jean B'ptiste.

Welcome it! Joyeux, the portly priest!
  Welcome it! Nun at your iron grating!
The favourite French-Canadian feast.

Welcome it! Antoine, one of the least
  Of the earth's meek little ones, meditating
On the day of the blessed St. Jean B'ptiste,

And the jostling crowd that has swift increased
  Behind him, before him, celebrating
The favourite French-Canadian feast.

He is clothed in the skin of some savage beast.
  Who cares if he be near suffocating?
'Tis the day of the blessed St. Jean B'ptiste,
The favourite French-Canadian feast.

II

Poor little Antoine! He does not mind.
  It is all for the Church, for a grand good cause,
The nuns are so sweet and the priests so kind.

The martyr spirit is fast enshrined
  In the tiny form that the ox-cart draws,
Poor little Antoine, he does not mind.

Poor little soul, for the cords that bind
  Are stronger than ardour for fame or applause—
The nuns are so sweet and the priests so kind.

And after the fête a feast is designed—
  Locusts and honey are both in the clause—
Brave little Antoine! He does not mind

The heat, nor the hungry demon twined
  Around his vitals that tears and gnaws,
The nuns are so sweet and the priests so kind.

The dust is flying. The streets are lined
  With the panting crowd that prays for a pause.
Poor little Antoine! He does not mind!
The nuns are *so sweet* and the priests *so kind*.

Catharine Plouffe

THIS grey-haired spinster, Catharine Plouffe—
    Observe her, a contrast to convent chits,
At her spinning wheel, in the room in the roof.

Yet there are those who believe that the hoof
  Of a horse is nightly heard as she knits—
This grey-haired spinster, Catharine Plouffe—

Stockings of fabulous warp and woof,
    And that old Benedict's black pipe she permits
At her spinning wheel, in the room in the roof,

For thirty years. So the gossip. A proof
  Of her constant heart? Nay. No one twits
This grey-haired spinster, Catharine Plouffe;

The neighbours respect her, but hold aloof,
    Admiring her back as she steadily sits
At her spinning wheel, in her room in the roof.

Will they ever marry? Just ask her. Pouf!
  She would like you to know she's not lost her wits—
This grey-haired spinster, Catharine Plouffe,
At her spinning wheel, in her room in the roof.

Benedict Brosse

HALE, and though sixty, without a stoop,
    What does old Benedict want with a wife?
Can he not make his own pea soup?

Better than most men—never droop
  In the August noons when storms are rife?
Hale, and though sixty, without a stoop,

Supreme in the barn, the kitchen, the coop,
  Can he not use both broom and knife?
Can he not make his own pea soup?

Yet Widow Gouin in command of the troop
  Of gossips, can tell of the spinsters' strife.
Hale, and though sixty, without a stoop,

There's a dozen would jump through the golden hoop,
   For he's rich, and hardy for his time of life,—
Can he not make his own pea soup?

But Benedict's wise and the village group
   He ignores, while he smokes and plays on his fife.
Hale, and though sixty, without a stoop,
Can he not make his own pea soup?

II

As for Catharine—now, she's a woman of sense,
   Though hard to win, so Benedict thinks,
Though hard to please and near with the pence.

Down to the Widow Rose Archambault's fence
   Her property runs and Benedict winks—
As for Catharine—now, she's a woman of sense.

At times he has wished to drop all pretense
   And ask her—she's fond of a bunch of pinks,
Though hard to please and near with the pence,

But he never progresses—the best evidence
   That from *medias res* our Benedict shrinks.
As for Catharine—now, she's a woman of sense,

A woman of rarest intelligence;
   She manages well, is as close as the Sphinx,
Though hard to please and near with the pence.

Still, that is a virtue at St. Clements.
   Look at Rose Archambault, the improvident minx!
As for Catharine—now, *she's* a woman of sense,
Though hard to please and near with the pence.

In March

HERE on the wide waste lands,
   Take—child—these trembling hands,
Though my life be as blank and waste,
My days as surely ungraced
By glimmer of green on the rim
Of a sunless wilderness dim,
As the wet fields barren and brown,
As the fork of each sterile limb
Shorn of its lustrous crown.

See—how vacant and flat
The landscape—empty and dull,
Scared by an ominous lull
Into a trance—we have sat
This hour on the edge of a broken, a grey snake-fence,
And nothing that lives has flown,
Or crept, or leapt, or been blown
To our feet or past our faces—
So desolate, child—the place is!
It strikes, does it not, a chill,
Like that other upon the hill,
We felt one bleak October?
See—the grey woods still sober
Ere it be wild with glee,
With growth, with an ecstasy,
A fruition born of desire.
The marigold's yellow fire
Doth not yet in the sun burn to leap, to aspire;
Its myriad spotted spears
No erythronium rears;
We cannot see
Anemone,
Or heart-lobed brown hepatica;
There doth not fly,
Low under sky,
One kingfisher—dipping and darting
From reedy shallows where reds are starting,
Pale pink tips that shall burst into bloom,
Not in one night's mid-April gloom,
But inch by inch, till ripening tint,
And feathery plume and emerald glint
Proclaim the waters are open.

All this will come,
The panting hum
Of the life that will stir,
Glance and glide, and whistle and whir,
Chatter and crow, and perch and pry,
Crawl and leap and dart and fly,
Things of feather and things of fur,

Under the blue of an April sky.
Shall speak, the dumb,
Shall leap, the numb,
All this will come,
It never misses,
Failure, yet—
Never was set
In the sure spring's calendar,
Wherefore—-Pet—
Give me one of your springtime kisses!
While you plant some hope in my cold man's breast—
Ah! How welcome the strange flower-guest—
Water it softly with maiden tears,
Go to it early—and late—with fears;
Guard it, and watch it, and give it time
For the holy dews to moisten the rime—
Make of it some green gracious thing,
Such as the heavens shall make of the spring!

. . . . .

The trees and the houses are darkling,
No lamps yet are sparkling
  Along the ravine;
A wild wind rises, the waters are fretting,
  No moon nor star in the sky can be seen.

But if I can bring her with thinking
The thoughts that are linking
  Her life unto mine:
Then blow wild wind! And chafe, proud river!
  At least a Star in my heart shall shine.

. . . . .

Had I not met her, great had been my loss,
  Had I not loved her, pain I had been spared.
So this life goes, and lovers bear the cross,
  Burden borne willingly, if only it be shared.

Had I not met her, Song had passed me by,
  Had I not loved her, Fame had been more sure.
So this life goes, we laugh, and then we sigh,
  While we believe 'tis blessed to endure.

Duncan Campbell Scott

He is above everything a poet of climate and atmosphere, employing with a nimble, graphic touch the clear, pure, transparent colours of a richly-furnished palette. He leaves unrecorded no single phase in the pageant of the northern year, from the odorous heat of June to the ice-bound silence of December. His work abounds in magically luminous phrases and stanzas. . . . . Mr. Scott is particularly happy in the phrases suggested to him by the songs of birds. . . . . Though it must not be understood that his talent is merely descriptive. There is a philosophic and also a romantic strain in it. . . . . There is scarcely a poem of Mr. Scott's from which one could not cull some memorable descriptive passage. . . . . As a rule Mr. Scott's workmanship is careful and highly finished. He is before everything a colourist. He paints in lines of a peculiar and vivid translucency. But he is also a metrist of no mean skill, and an imaginative thinker of no common capacity.—WILLIAM ARCHER, in 'Poets of the Younger Generation.'

SINCE the publication, in 1910, of this critique by William Archer, the distinguished English critic, observers of the poetry of Duncan Campbell Scott have found it steadily growing in imaginative and philosophic as well as in human qualities. His latest work, *Lines in Memory of Edmund Morris,* a poem of nearly three hundred lines, published for private distribution, is so original, tender and beautiful that it is destined to live among the best in Canadian literature.

Mr. Scott was born in Ottawa, Canada, August 2nd, 1862, and was educated in the public schools of his native city, and at Stanstead Wesleyan Academy. He is of English and Scottish origin, son of the late Rev. William Scott of the Methodist ministry and Janet McCallum.

In 1894, he was married to Miss Belle W. Botsford, a well-known violinist, daughter of Mr. George W. Botsford, of Greenfield, Massachusetts.

In 1880, Mr. Scott entered the Canadian Civil Service at Ottawa, in the Department of Indian Affairs, and ever since has been an official of this Department. Repeated promotion rewarded his industry and efficiency until, in 1913, he became Deputy Superintendent General. This appointment, in his youth, has been fortunate, in another sense, for his associations with the Redmen have inspired and coloured a number of his most original poems.

The following are the names and dates of Mr. Scott's most notable publications: *The Magic House and Other Poems,* 1893; *In the Village of Viger,* 1896; *Labour and the Angel,* 1898; *New World Lyrics and Ballads,* 1905; *John Graves Simcoe,* 1905, "Makers of Canada" series, edited by him and Prof. Pelham Edgar, Ph.D.; *Via Borealis,* 1906, Wm. Tyrrell & Co., Toronto; *Lines in Memory of Edmund Morris,* 1915; and *Lundy's Lane and Other Poems,* 1916, McClelland, Goodchild and Stewart, Toronto.

In 1903, he was elected Vice-President of the Canadian Society of Authors, and in 1911, Honorary Secretary of the Royal Society of Canada.

In the *Christmas Globe* contest of 1908, Mr. Scott won with "The Battle of Lundy's Lane," the prize of one hundred dollars, offered for the best poem on a Canadian historical theme.

At the Cedars

YOU had two girls—Baptiste—
One is Virginie—
Hold hard—Baptiste!
Listen to me.
The whole drive was jammed
In that bend at the Cedars,
The rapids were dammed
With the logs tight rammed
And crammed; you might know.
The Devil had clinched them below.

We worked three days—not a budge,
'She's as tight as a wedge, on the ledge,'
Says our foreman;
'Mon Dieu! boys, look here,
We must get this thing clear.'

He cursed at the men
And we went for it then;
With our cant-dogs arow,
We just gave he-yo-ho;
When she gave a big shove
From above.

The gang yelled and tore
For the shore,
The logs gave a grind
Like a wolf's jaws behind,
And as quick as a flash
With a shove and a crash,
They were down in a mash,
But I and ten more,
All but Isaac Dufour,
Were ashore.

He leaped on a log in the front of the rush,
And shot out from the bind
While the jam roared behind;
As he floated along

8

He balanced his pole
And tossed us a song.
But just as we cheered,
Up darted a log from the bottom,
Leaped thirty feet square and fair,
And came down on his own.

He went up like a block
With the shock,
And when he was there
In the air,
Kissed his hand to the land;
When he dropped
My heart stopped,
For the first logs had caught him
And crushed him;
When he rose in his place
There was blood on his face.

There were some girls, Baptiste,
Picking berries on the hillside,
Where the river curls, Baptiste,
You know—on the still side.
One was down by the water,
She saw Isaac
Fall back.

She did not scream, Baptiste,
She launched her canoe;
It did seem, Baptiste,
That she wanted to die too,
For before you could think
The birch cracked like a shell
In that rush of hell,
And I saw them both sink—

Baptiste!—
He had two girls,
One is Virginie,
What God calls the other
Is not known to me.

The Forgers

IN the smithy it began:
Let's make something for a man!
Hear the bellows belch and roar,
Splashing light on roof and floor:
From their nest the feathery sparks
Fly like little golden larks:
Hear each forger's taunting yell,
Tell—tell—tell—tell—
Tell us what we make, my master!
Hear the tenor hammers sound,
Ring-a-round, ring-a-round;
Hear the treble hammers sing,
Ding-a-ring, ding-a-ring;
Hear the forger's taunting yell,
Tell—tell—tell—tell!
Though the guess be right or wrong
You must wear it all life long!
How it glows as it grows,
Ding-a-ring-a-derry-down,
Into something—is't a crown?
Hear them half in death with laughter,
Shaking soot from roof and rafter;
Tell—tell—tell—tell—
Ding-a-ring, ding-a-ring,
See them round the royal thing,
See it fade to ruby rose,
As it glows and grows,
Guess, they shout, *for worse or better:*
Not a crown!
Is't a fetter?
Hear them shout demonic mirth:
Here's a guesser something worth;
Make it solid, round, and fine,
Fashioned on a cunning plan,
For the riddle-reader Man;
Ho—ho—ho—ho!
Hear the bellows heave and blow:

Heat dries up their tears of mirth;
Let the marvel come to birth,
Though his guess be right or wrong
He must wear it—all life long!
Sullen flakes of golden fire
Fawn about the dimming choir,
They're a dusky pack of thieves
Shaking rubies from their sleeves,
Hear them wield their vaunting yell,
Tell—tell—tell—tell!
Forging faster—taunting faster—
Guess, my master—Guess, my master!
Grows the enigmatic thing!
Ruddy joyance—Deep disaster?
Ding-a-ring, ding-a-ring,
Ding-a-ring-a-derry-down!
Is't a fetter—Is't a crown?

The Voice and the Dusk

THE slender moon and one pale star,
  A rose leaf and a silver bee
From some god's garden blown afar,
  Go down the gold deep tranquilly.

Within the south there rolls and grows
  A mighty town with tower and spire,
From a cloud bastion masked with rose
  The lightning flashes diamond fire.

The purple martin darts about
  The purlieus of the iris fen;
The king-bird rushes up and out,
  He screams and whirls and screams again.

A thrush is hidden in a maze
  Of cedar buds and tamarac bloom,
He throws his rapid flexile phrase,
  A flash of emeralds in the gloom.

A voice is singing from the hill
  A happy love of long ago;

Ah! tender voice, be still, be still,
   ' 'Tis sometimes better not to know.'

The rapture from the amber height
   Floats tremblingly along the plain,
Where in the reeds with fairy light
   The lingering fireflies gleam again.

Buried in dingles more remote,
   Or drifted from some ferny rise,
The swooning of the golden throat
   Drops in the mellow dusk and dies.

A soft wind passes lightly drawn,
   A wave leaps silverly and stirs
The rustling sedge, and then is gone
   Down the black cavern in the firs.

The Sea by the Wood

I DWELL in the sea that is wild and deep,
   But afar in a shadow still,
I can see the trees that gather and sleep
   In the wood upon the hill.

The deeps are green as an emerald's face,
   The caves are crystal calm,
But I wish the sea were a little trace
   Of moisture in God's palm.

The waves are weary of hiding pearls,
   Are aweary of smothering gold,
They would all be air that sweeps and swirls
   In the branches manifold.

They are weary of laving the seaman's eyes
   With their passion prayer unsaid,
They are weary of sobs and the sudden sighs
   And movements of the dead.

All the sea is haunted with human lips
   Ashen and sere and gray,
You can hear the sails of the sunken ships
   Stir and shiver and sway

In the weary solitude;
  If mine were the will of God, the main
Should melt away in the rustling wood
  Like a mist that follows the rain.

But I dwell in the sea that is wild and deep
  And afar in the shadow still,
I can see the trees that gather and sleep
  In the wood upon the hill.

The Wood by the Sea

I DWELL in the wood that is dark and kind
  But afar off tolls the main,
Afar, far off I hear the wind,
  And the roving of the rain.

The shade is dark as a palmer's hood,
  The air with balm is bland:
But I wish the trees that breathe in the wood
  Were ashes in God's hand.

The pines are weary of holding nests,
  Are aweary of casting shade;
Wearily smoulder the resin crests
  In the pungent gloom of the glade.

Weary are all the birds of sleep,
  The nests are weary of wings,
The whole wood yearns to the swaying deep,
  The mother of restful things.

The wood is very old and still,
  So still when the dead cones fall,
Near in the vale or away on the hill,
  You can hear them one and all.

And their falling wearies me;
  If mine were the will of God,—oh, then
The wood should tramp to the sounding sea,
  Like a marching army of men!

But I dwell in the wood that is dark and kind,
  Afar off tolls the main;
Afar, far off I hear the wind
  And the roving of the rain.

The Builder

WHEN the deep cunning architect
　Had the great minster planned,
They worked in faith for twice two hundred years
And reared the building grand;
War came and famine and they did not falter,
But held his line,
And filled the space divine
With carvings meet for the soul's eye;
And not alone the chantry and thereby
The snowy altar,
But in every part
They carved the minster after his own heart,
And made the humblest places fair,
Even the dimmest cloister-way and stair,
With vineyard tendrils,
With ocean-seeming shells,
With filmy weeds from sea,
With bell-flowers delicate and bells,
All done minute with excellent tracery.
Come, O my soul,
And let me build thee like the minster fair,
Deep based and large as air,
And full of hidden graces wrought
In faith and infinite thought,
Till all thy dimmest ways,
Shall gleam with little vines and fruits of praise,
So that one day
The consummate Architect
Who planned the souls that we are set to build,
May pause and say:
How curiously wrought is this!
The builder followed well My thought, My chart,
And worked for Me, not for the world's wild heart;
Here are the outward virtues true!
But see how all the inner parts are filled
With singular bliss:
Set it aside
I shall come here again at eventide.

The Half-Breed Girl

SHE is free of the trap and the paddle,
   The portage and the trail,
But something behind her savage life
   Shines like a fragile veil.

Her dreams are undiscovered,
   Shadows trouble her breast,
When the time for resting cometh
   Then least is she at rest.

Oft in the morns of winter,
   When she visits the rabbit snares,
An appearance floats in the crystal air
   Beyond the balsam firs.

Oft in the summer mornings
   When she strips the nets of fish,
The smell of the dripping net-twine
   Gives to her heart a wish.

But she cannot learn the meaning
   Of the shadows in her soul,
The lights that break and gather,
   The clouds that part and roll.

The reek of rock-built cities,
   Where her fathers dwelt of yore,
The gleam of loch and shealing,
   The mist on the moor.

Frail traces of kindred kindness,
   Of feud by hill and strand,
The heritage of an age-long life
   In a legendary land.

She wakes in the stifling wigwam,
   Where the air is heavy and wild,
She fears for something or nothing
   With the heart of a frightened child.

She sees the stars turn slowly
   Past the tangle of the poles,

Through the smoke of the dying embers,
  Like the eyes of dead souls.

Her heart is shaken with longing
  For the strange, still years,
For what she knows and knows not,
  For the wells of ancient tears.

A voice calls from the rapids,
  Deep, careless and free,
A voice that is larger than her life
  Or than her death shall be.

She covers her face with her blanket,
  Her fierce soul hates her breath,
As it cries with a sudden passion
  For life or death.

From 'Lines in Memory of Edmund Morris'

HERE, Morris, on the plains that we have loved,
  Think of the death of Akoose, fleet of foot,
Who, in his prime, a herd of antelope
From sunrise, without rest, a hundred miles
Drove through rank prairie, loping like a wolf,
Tired them and slew them, ere the sun went down.
Akoose, in his old age, blind from the smoke
Of tepees and the sharp snow light, alone
With his great grandchildren, withered and spent,
Crept in the warm sun along a rope
Stretched for his guidance. Once when sharp autumn
Made membranes of thin ice upon the sloughs,
He caught a pony on a quick return
Of prowess, and, all his instincts cleared and quickened,
He mounted, sensed the north and bore away
To the Last Mountain Lake where in his youth
He shot the sand-hill-cranes with his flint arrows.
And for these hours in all the varied pomp
Of pagan fancy and free dreams of foray
And crude adventure, he ranged on entranced,
Until the sun blazed level with the prairie,
Then paused, faltered and slid from off his pony.

In a little bluff of poplars, hid in the bracken,
He lay down; the populace of leaves
In the lithe poplars whispered together and trembled,
Fluttered before a sunset of gold smoke,
With interspaces, green as sea water,
And calm as the deep water of the sea.

There Akoose lay, silent amid the bracken,
Gathered at last with the Algonquin Chieftains.
Then the tenebrous sunset was blown out,
And all the smoky gold turned into cloud wrack.
Akoose slept forever amid the poplars,
Swathed by the wind from the far-off Red Deer
Where dinosaurs sleep, clamped in their rocky tombs.
Who shall count the time that lies between
The sleep of Akoose and the dinosaurs?
Innumerable time, that yet is like the breath
Of the long wind that creeps upon the prairie
And dies away with the shadows at sundown.

.   .   .   .   .   .

What we may think, who brood upon the theme,
Is, when the old world, tired of spinning, has fallen
Asleep, and all the forms, that carried the fire
Of life, are cold upon her marble heart—
Like ashes on the altar—just as she stops,
That something will escape of soul or essence,—
The sum of life, to kindle otherwhere:
Just as the fruit of a high sunny garden,
Grown mellow with autumnal sun and rain,
Shrivelled with ripeness, splits to the rich heart,
And looses a gold kernel to the mould,
So the old world, hanging long in the sun,
And deep enriched with effort and with love,
Shall, in the motions of maturity,
Wither and part, and the kernel of it all
Escape, a lovely wraith of spirit, to latitudes
Where the appearance, throated like a bird,
Winged with fire and bodied all with passion,
Shall flame with presage, not of tears, but joy.

E. Pauline Johnson

(Tekahionwake)

Since 1889, I have been following her career with a glow of admiration and sympathy. I have been delighted to find that this success of hers had no damaging effect upon the grand simplicity of her nature. Up to the day of her death her passionate sympathy with the aborigines of Canada never flagged. . . . . Her death is not only a great loss to those who knew and loved her: it is a great loss to Canadian literature and to the Canadian nation. I must think that she will hold a memorable place among poets in virtue of her descent and also in virtue of the work she has left behind, small as the quantity of that work is. I believe that Canada will, in future times, cherish her memory more and more, for of all Canadian poets she was the most distinctly a daughter of the soil, inasmuch as she inherited the blood of the great primeval race now so rapidly vanishing, and of the greater race that has supplanted it.—THEODORE WATTS-DUNTON.

EMILY PAULINE JOHNSON (Tekahionwake) was born at 'Chiefswood' on her father's estate, in the Reserve near Brantford, Ontario, in 1862. She was the youngest of four children, and early showed a marked tendency towards the reading and the writing of rhymes.

Her father was the late G. H. M. Johnson (Onwanonsyshon), Head Chief of the Six Nations Indians, and a descendant of one of the fifty noble families of Hiawatha's Confederation, founded four centuries ago. Her mother was Emily S. Howells, of Bristol, England.

Pauline's education in school lore was meagre,—a nursery governess for two years, attendance at an Indian day school, near her home, for three years, and two finishing years at the Brantford Central School—but her education in the School of Nature was extensive, and that with her voracious reading— of poetry particularly—and retentive memory, richly stored her naturally keen mind.

As a poet and recitalist, Miss Johnson won her first distinction of note in 1892, when she took part, in Toronto, in an unique entertainment of Canadian literature, read or recited by the authors themselves. Miss Johnson's contribution was 'A Cry From an Indian Wife,' which presented the Redman's view of the North-West Rebellion, and won for the author the only encore of the evening. The next day the Toronto press so eulogized her performance and spread her fame, that another entertainment was quickly arranged for, to be given, two weeks later, entirely by herself. Her best known poem, 'The Song My Paddle Sings,' was written for this occasion. There followed a series of recitals throughout Canada, in the hope that their financial success would be such as to enable the poet to go to England and submit her poems to a London publisher. In two years this object was attained, and *The White Wampum* appeared. It was received with enthusiasm by the critics and the public generally. Pauline Johnson had 'arrived,' and as a poet and entertainer she was henceforth in demand in the British Isles, as well as in Canada and the United States.

In 1903, her second book of verse, *Canadian Born,* was published and the entire edition was sold out within a year.

Miss Johnson continued her recitals for sixteen years, when failing health compelled her to retire. She located in Vancouver, B.C., where she lived until her death in 1913.

An edition of collected verse, entitled *Flint and Feather,* with an introduction by the English critic, the late Theodore Watts-Dunton, was published in 1912. Besides this notable volume which has run into several editions, she has left behind *Legends of Vancouver,* issued in 1911, and a series of entertaining tales for boys.

Canadians have long been proud of Pauline Johnson, and as the years pass, their love of her and their pride in her achievement will continue to increase. The editor of this volume met her on the train while she was en route for England, in 1906; and her beauty and charm of person, her delightful conversation, her warmth of heart and sympathetic interest in others, have persisted in his memory with a steadfast radiance.

In the Shadows

I AM sailing to the leeward,
Where the current runs to seaward
   Soft and slow,
Where the sleeping river grasses
Brush my paddle as it passes
   To and fro.

On the shore the heat is shaking
All the golden sands awaking
   In the cove;
And the quaint sandpiper, winging
O'er the shallows, ceases singing
   When I move.

On the water's idle pillow
Sleeps the overhanging willow,
   Green and cool;
Where the rushes lift their burnished
Oval heads from out the tarnished
   Emerald pool.

Where the very silence slumbers,
Water lilies grow in numbers,
　　Pure and pale;
All the morning they have rested,
Amber crowned, and pearly crested,
　　Fair and frail.

Here, impossible romances,
Indefinable sweet fancies,
　　Cluster round;
But they do not mar the sweetness
Of this still September fleetness
　　With a sound.

I can scarce discern the meeting
Of the shore and stream retreating,
　　So remote;
For the laggard river, dozing,
Only wakes from its reposing
　　Where I float.

Where the river mists are rising,
All the foliage baptizing
　　With their spray;
There the sun gleams far and faintly,
With a shadow soft and saintly,
　　In its ray.

And the perfume of some burning
Far-off brushwood, ever turning
　　To exhale
All its smoky fragrance dying,
In the arms of evening lying,
　　Where I sail.

My canoe is growing lazy,
In the atmosphere so hazy,
　　While I dream;
Half in slumber I am guiding,
Eastward indistinctly gliding
　　Down the stream.

As Red Men Die

CAPTIVE! Is there a hell to him like this?
A taunt more galling than the Huron's hiss?
He—proud and scornful, he—who laughed at law,
He—scion of the deadly Iroquois,
He—the bloodthirsty, he—the Mohawk chief,
He—who despises pain and sneers at grief,
Here in the hated Huron's vicious clutch,
That even captive he disdains to touch!

Captive! But *never* conquered; Mohawk brave
Stoops not to be to *any* man a slave;
Least, to the puny tribe his soul abhors,
The tribe whose wigwams sprinkle Simcoe's shores.
With scowling brow he stands and courage high,
Watching with haughty and defiant eye
His captors, as they counsel o'er his fate,
Or strive his boldness to intimidate.
Then flung they unto him the choice:

                    'Wilt thou
Walk o'er the bed of fire that waits thee now—
Walk with uncovered feet upon the coals,
Until thou reach the ghostly Land of Souls,
And, with thy Mohawk death-song please our ear?
Or wilt thou with the women rest thee here?'
His eyes flash like an eagle's, and his hands
Clench at the insult. Like a god he stands.
'Prepare the fire!' he scornfully demands.

He knoweth not that this same jeering band
Will bite the dust—will lick the Mohawk's hand;
Will kneel and cower at the Mohawk's feet;
Will shrink when Mohawk war drums wildly beat.
His death will be avenged with hideous hate
By Iroquois, swift to annihilate
His vile detested captors, that now flaunt
Their war clubs in his face with sneer and taunt,
Not thinking, soon that reeking, red and raw,
Their scalps will deck the belts of Iroquois.

The path of coals outstretches, white with heat,
A forest fir's length—ready for his feet.
Unflinching as a rock he steps along
The burning mass, and sings his wild war song;
Sings, as he sang when once he used to roam
Throughout the forests of his southern home,
Where, down the Genesee, the water roars,
Where gentle Mohawk purls between its shores,
Songs, that of exploit and of prowess tell;
Songs of the Iroquois invincible.

Up the long trail of fire he boasting goes,
Dancing a war dance to defy his foes.
His flesh is scorched, his muscles burn and shrink,
But still he dances to death's awful brink.
The eagle plume that crests his haughty head
Will *never* droop until his heart be dead.
Slower and slower yet his footstep swings,
Wilder and wilder still his death-song rings,
Fiercer and fiercer through the forest bounds
His voice that leaps to Happier Hunting Grounds.
One savage yell—

　　　　　Then loyal to his race,
He bends to death—but *never* to disgrace.

The Song My Paddle Sings

WEST wind, blow from your prairie nest,
　　Blow from the mountains, blow from the west.
The sail is idle, the sailor too;
O wind of the west, we wait for you!
Blow, blow,
I have wooed you so,
But never a favour you bestow.
You rock your cradle the hills between,
But scorn to notice my white lateen.

I stow the sail, unship the mast;
I wooed you long but my wooing's past;
My paddle will lull you into rest.

O drowsy wind of the drowsy west,
Sleep, Sleep,
By your mountain steep,
Or down where the prairie grasses sweep!
Now fold in slumber your laggard wings,
For soft is the song my paddle sings.

August is laughing across the sky,
Laughing while paddle, canoe and I,
Drift, drift,
Where the hills uplift
On either side of the current swift.

The river rolls in its rocky bed;
My paddle is plying its way ahead;
Dip, dip,
While the waters flip
In foam as over their breast we slip.

And oh, the river runs swifter now,
The eddies circle about my bow!
Swirl, swirl!
How the ripples curl
In many a dangerous pool awhirl!

And forward far the rapids roar,
Fretting their margin for evermore.
Dash, dash,
With a mighty crash,
They seethe, and boil, and bound, and splash.

Be strong, O paddle! be brave, canoe!
The reckless waves you must plunge into.
Reel, reel,
On your trembling keel,—
But never a fear my craft will feel.

We've raced the rapid, we're far ahead;
The river slips through its silent bed.
Sway, sway,
As the bubbles spray
And fall in tinkling tunes away.

And up on the hills against the sky,
A fir tree rocking its lullaby,
Swings, swings,
Its emerald wings,
Swelling the song that my paddle sings.

The Lost Lagoon

IT is dusk on the Lost Lagoon,
And we two dreaming the dusk away,
Beneath the drift of a twilight grey,
Beneath the drowse of an ending day,
And the curve of a golden moon.

It is dark in the Lost Lagoon,
And gone are the depths of haunting blue,
The grouping gulls, and the old canoe,
The singing firs, and the dusk and—you,
And gone is the golden moon.

O lure of the Lost Lagoon!—
I dream to-night that my paddle blurs
The purple shade where the seaweed stirs,
I hear the call of the singing firs
In the hush of the golden moon.

The Pilot of the Plains

'FALSE,' they said, 'thy Pale-face lover, from the land of
        waking morn;
Rise and wed thy Redskin wooer, nobler warrior ne'er was
        born;
Cease thy watching, cease thy dreaming,
    Show the white thine Indian scorn.'

Thus they taunted her, declaring, 'He remembers naught of
        thee:
Likely some white maid he wooeth, far beyond the inland sea.'
But she answered ever kindly,
    'He will come again to me,'

Till the dusk of Indian summer crept athwart the western
        skies;
But a deeper dusk was burning in her dark and dreaming eyes,

As she scanned the rolling prairie,
   Where the foothills fall and rise.

Till the autumn came and vanished, till the season of the rains,
Till the western world lay fettered in midwinter's crystal
     chains,
Still she listened for his coming,
   Still she watched the distant plains.

Then a night with nor'land tempest, nor'land snows a-swirl-
     ing fast,
Out upon the pathless prairie came the Pale-face through
     the blast,
Calling, calling, 'Yakonwita,
   I am coming, love, at last.'

Hovered night above, about him, dark its wings and cold and
     dread;
Never unto trail or tepee were his straying footsteps led;
Till benumbed, he sank, and pillowed
   On the drifting snows his head,

Saying, 'O my Yakonwita, call me, call me, be my guide
To the lodge beyond the prairie—for I vowed ere winter died
I would come again, belovèd;
   I would claim my Indian bride!'

'Yakonwita, Yakonwita,' O the dreariness that strains
Through the voice that calling, quivers, till a whisper but
     remains!
'Yakonwita, Yakonwita,
   I am lost upon the plains!'

But the Silent Spirit hushed him, lulled him as he cried anew,
'Save me, save me, O belovèd, I am Pale, but I am true!
Yakonwita, Yakonwita,
   I am dying, love, for you!'

Leagues afar, across the prairie, she had risen from her bed,
Roused her kinsmen from their slumber: 'He has come to-
     night,' she said.
'I can hear him calling, calling,
   But his voice is as the dead.

9

Listen !' and they sate all silent, while the tempest louder grew,
And a spirit-voice called faintly, 'I am dying, love, for you.'
Then they wailed, 'O Yakonwita,
　　He was Pale, but he was true !'

Wrapped she then her ermine round her, stepped without the
　　tepee door,
Saying, 'I must follow, follow, though he call for evermore,
Yakonwita, Yakonwita,'
　　And they never saw her more.

Late at night, say Indian hunters, when the starlight clouds
　　or wanes,
Far away they see a maiden, misty as the autumn rains,
Guiding with her lamp of moonlight
　　Hunters lost upon the plains.

The Songster

MUSIC, music with throb and swing,
Of a plaintive note, and long;
'Tis a note no human throat could sing,
No harp with its dulcet golden string,—
Nor lute, nor lyre with liquid ring,
　　Is sweet as the robin's song.

He sings for love of the season
　　When the days grow warm and long,
For the beautiful God-sent reason
　　That his breast was born for song.

Calling, calling so fresh and clear,
　　Through the song-sweet days of May;
Warbling there, and whistling here,
He swells his voice on the drinking ear,
On the great, wide, pulsing atmosphere
　　Till his music drowns the day.

He sings for love of the season
　　When the days grow warm and long,
For the beautiful God-sent reason
　　That his breast was born for song.

The Riders of the Plains
(The Royal North-West Mounted Police)

WHO is it lacks the knowledge? Who are the curs that
    dare
To whine and sneer that they do not fear the whelps in the
    Lion's lair?
But we of the North will answer, while life in the North
    remains,
Let the curs beware lest the whelps they dare are the Riders
    of the Plains;
For these are the kind whose muscle makes the power of the
    Lion's jaw,
And they keep the peace of our people and the honour of
    British law.

A women has painted a picture,—'tis a neat little bit of art
The critics aver, and it roused up for her the love of the big
    British heart.
'Tis a sketch of an English bulldog that tigers would scarce
    attack;
And round and about and beneath him is painted the Union
    Jack,
With its blaze of colour, and courage, its daring in every fold,
And underneath is the title, 'What we have we'll hold.'
'Tis a picture plain as a mirror, but the reflex it contains
Is the counterpart of the life and heart of the Riders of the
    Plains;
For like to that flag and that motto, and the power of that
    bulldog's jaw,
They keep the peace of our people and the honour of British
    law.

These are the fearless fighters, whose life in the open lies,
Who never fail on the prairie trail 'neath the Territorial skies,
Who have laughed in the face of the bullets and the edge of
    the rebels' steel,
Who have set their ban on the lawless man with his crime be-
    neath their heel;
These are the men who battle the blizzards, the suns, the rains,

These are the famed that the North has named, 'The Riders of
the Plains,'
And theirs is the might and the meaning and the strength of
the bulldog's jaw,
While they keep the peace of the people and the honour of
British law.

These are the men of action, who need not the world's renown,
For their valour is known to England's throne as a gem in the
British crown;
These are the men who face the front, with courage the world
may scan,
The men who are feared by the felon, but are loved by the
honest man;
These are the marrow, the pith, the cream, the best that the
blood contains,
Who have cast their days in the valiant ways of the Riders
of the Plains;
And theirs is the kind whose muscle makes the power of old
England's jaw,
And they keep the peace of her people and the honour of
British law.

Then down with the cur that questions,—let him slink to his
craven den,
For he daren't deny our hot reply as to 'who are our mounted
men.'
He shall honour them east and westward, he shall honour them
south and north,
He shall bare his head to that coat of red wherever that red
rides forth.
'Tis well that he knows the fibre that the great North-West
contains,
The North-West pride in her men that ride on the Territorial
plains,—
For such as these are the muscles and the teeth in the Lion's
jaw,
And they keep the peace of our people and the honour of
British law.

E. W. Thomson

The name of E. W. Thomson is a household word among Canadian literary men, and stands for a skilled craftsman in both prose and verse. . . . . The dramatic and thoughtful power of his stanzas, his finished workmanship, the gentleness and breadth of his love for humanity, all stamp his work as that of an artist of whom Canadians have good reason to be proud, and of the first rank of our litterateurs.—W. D. LIGHTHALL, F.R.S.L., in 'The Witness.'

Here is a poet, manly, fresh, independent, a democratic lover of man. . . . . He has technique, but can hide it and get an effect of life and originality thereby. He has heart and brains and imagination. He is daringly vernacular in his speech, which is all the better, for it reminds us that the proper idiom of poetry is drawn from the people, not the drawing-room. He is a realist, not in diction alone, but in his liking for plain realities and persons. But he is equally an idealist, because he sees the beauty which hides in common things, and believes in the spirit which aspires from clod to star.—PROF. RICHARD E. BURTON, PH.D., in 'The Bellman.'

EDWARD WILLIAM THOMSON was born in Toronto township, county of Peel, Ontario, February 12th, 1849. His father was William Thomson, grandson of Archibald Thomson, the first settler in Scarboro. His grandfather Edward William Thomson, was present at the taking of Detroit, and served with distinction under Brock at Queenston Heights; and was afterwards well known in Upper Canada as Col. E. W. Thomson of the Legislative Council, and as the one successful opponent of William Lyon Mackenzie in an election for the Legislature. The mother of the present E. W. Thomson was Margaret Hamilton Foley, sister of the Hon. M. H. Foley, twice Postmaster-General of the united Canadas.

The future poet was educated at the Brantford Grammar School, and at the Trinity College Grammar School at Weston; but when about fourteen years of age, he was sent to an uncle and aunt in Philadelphia and given a position in a wholesale mercantile house as 'office junior.' Finding this employment very uncongenial, he enlisted in the Union army, in October, 1864, as a trooper in the 3rd Pennsylvania Cavalry. This corps was engaged twice at Hatcher's Run, and was with Grant when he took Petersburgh. Discharged in August, 1865, he returned to the parental home at Chippewa, Ontario. In June, 1866, when the Fenians raided Upper Canada, young Thomson promptly enlisted in the Queen's Own, and was in action at the Ridgeway fight. The following year he entered the profession of Civil Engineering, and in 1872 was registered a Provincial Land Surveyor. He practised his profession until December, 1878, when at the invitation of the Hon. George Brown, he joined the staff of *The Globe,* Toronto, as an editorial writer. Four years later the Manitoba boom attracted him, and he practised surveying for two or three years in Winnipeg. In 1885, he rejoined *The Globe* staff, but retired again in 1891, because of his opposition to the Liberal policy of Unrestricted Reciprocity. Shortly afterwards he was invited to join the staff of the *Youth's Companion.* He accepted and remained for eleven years.

Since 1903, he has lived in Ottawa, employed as a newspaper correspondent and engaged in literary work. *The Many-Mansioned House and Other Poems* was issued in 1909. His poems, like his short stories, are lucid, vital, original.

Thunderchild's Lament

WHEN the years grew worse, and the tribe longed sore
      For a kinsman bred to the white man's lore,
To the Mission School they sent forth me
From the hunting life and the skin tepee.

In the Mission School eight years I wrought
Till my heart grew strange to its boyhood's thought,
Then the white men sent me forth from their ways
To the Blackfoot lodge and the roving days.

'He tells of their God,' said the Chiefs when I spake,
'But naught of the magic our foemen make,
'T is a Blackfoot heart with a white man's fear,
And all skill forgot that could help him here.'

For the Mission Priest had bent my will
From the art to steal and the mind to kill,
Then out from the life I had learned sent me
To the hungry plain and the dim tepee.

When the moon of March was great and round,
No meat for my father's teeth I found;
When the moon of March was curved and thin,
No meat for his life could my hunting win.

Wide went the tracks of my snowshoe mesh,
Deep was the white, and it still fell fresh
Far in the foothills, far on the plain,
Where I searched for the elk and the grouse in vain.

In the Lodge lay my father, grim in the smoke,
His eyes pierced mine as the gray dawn broke,
He gnawed on the edge of the buffalo hide,
And I must be accurst if my father died.

He spoke with wail: 'In the famine year
When my father starved as I starve here,
Was my heart like the squaw's who has fear to slay
'Mongst the herds of the white man far away?'

From the Mission School they sent forth me
To the gaunt, wild life of the dark tepee;

With the fear to steal, and the dread to kill,
And the love of Christ they had bent my will.

But my father gnawed on the buffalo hide;—
Toward the sunrise trod my snowshoe stride,
Straight to the white man's herd it led,
Till the sun sank down at my back in red.

Next dawn was bleak when I slew the steer,
I ate of the raw, and it gave me cheer;
So I set my feet in the track once more,
With my father's life in the meat I bore.

Far strode the herder, fast on my trail;
Noon was high when I heard his hail;
I fled in fear, but my feet moved slow,
For the load I shouldered sank them low.

Then I heard no sound but the creak and clack
Of his snowshoes treading my snowshoe track,
And I saw never help in plain or sky
Save that he should die or my father die.

The Mission Priest had broke my will
With the curse on him who blood would spill,
But my father starved in the black tepee,
And the cry of his starving shrieked to me.

The white world reeled to its cloudy rim,
The plain reeled red as I knelt by him,—
Oh, the spot in the snow, how it pulsed and grew,
How it cried from the mid-white up to the blue!

For the Mission Priest had sent forth me
To the wants and deeds of the wild tepee,
Yet the fear of God's strong curse fulfilled,
Cried with the blood that would not be stilled.

They found me not while the year was green
And the rose blew sweet where the stain had been,
They found me not when the fall-flowers flare,
But the red in the snow was ever there.

To the Jail I fled from the safe tepee,
And the Mission Priest will send forth me,

A Blackfoot soul cleansed white from stain—
Yet never the red spot fades from the plain.

It glares in my eyes when sunbeams fall
Through the iron grate of my stone-gray wall,
And I see, through starlight, foxes go
To track and to taste of the ruddy snow.

The Mandan Priest

THEY call me now the *Indian* Priest,
  Their fathers' fathers did not so,
The very Mandan name hath ceased
From speech since fifty years ago;
I am so old my fingers fail
My trembling rosary beads to tell,
Yet all my years do not avail
My Mandan memories to quell.

The whole flat world I've seen how changed
Within my lifetime's hundred years;
O'er plains where herding buffalo ranged
Came strange new grass with white men's steers,
The lowing cattle passed as dreams,
Their pastures reared a farmer race,
Now city windows flash their gleams
Nigh our old Monastery's place.

The Prior gives to me no more
Even a task of inward praise,
The Brethren bear me through our door
To bask me here on summer days;
I am so old I cannot kneel,
I cannot hear, I cannot see,
Often I wonder if I feel
The very sunbeams warming me.

Yet do I watch the Mandan dogs
And Mandan ponies slain for meat
That year the squaws chewed snakes and frogs
That babes might tug a living teat,
And Mandan braves, in daylight dance,

Gashed side and arm and painted breast,
Praying The Manitou might trance
No more the buffalo from their quest.

A circled plain all horse-high grassed
Our mounting scouts beheld at dawn,
They saw naught else though far they passed
Apart before the sun was gone;
Each night's ride back through starlit lanes
They saw the tepee sparks ascend,
And hoped, and sniffed, and knew their pains
Of famine had not yet an end.

Alone within his magic tent
The new-made Midi wrought the spell   .
That soothed Life's Master to relent
In years the Old remembered well.
He cried,—'The Mission Priests have wreaked
Some curse that balks the Ancient Art!'
'Thou useless Fool,' the war-chief shrieked,
And sped the knife-thrust to his heart.

With that, *What comes?* my mother screamed—
How quick the squatted braves arose!
Far in the south the tallest deemed
He saw the flight of up-scared crows;
Above the horse-high grass came slow
A lifted Cross, a tonsured head,—
And what the meaning none could know
Until the black-robed rider said:—

'Mandans, I bear our Mission's word,—
Your children, brought to us, shall eat.'
Scarce had the fierce young War-chief heard
Ere fell the Blackrobe from his seat;
The Chief held high the reeking knife,
He frowned about the Woman's Ring,
And yet my mother's face took life
Anew in pondering the thing.

She stole at night the dead Priest's scrip,
His meagre wallet's hard-baked food,

His crucifix, his waist-rope strip
All blackened with his martyr blood;
Through dark, day-hidden, hand in hand,
We traced his trail for ninety mile,
She starved herself that I might stand,
She spoke me comfort all the while:—

'So shalt thou live, my little son,
The white men's magic shalt thou learn,
And when the hungry moons are run,
Be sure thy mother shall return;
Oh, sweet my joy when, come again,
I find thy Mandan heart untamed,
As fits a warrior of the plain,
That I, thy mother, be not shamed.'

She left me while the black-robed men
Blest and beseeched her sore to stay;
No voice hath told my heart since then
How fared my mother's backward way.
Years, *years* within the Mission School,
By love, by prayer they gained my heart;
It held me to Our Order's rule,
From all the Mandan life apart.

From tribe to tribe, through sixty years,
The Mandan Priest for Christ he wrought,
And many an Indian heart to tears,
And many a soul to God he brought;
Yet do I hear my mother's voice
Soft lingering round her little son,
And, O dear Lord, dost *Thou* rejoice
In all my mother's child hath done?

The Canadian Rossignol
(In May)

WHEN furrowed fields of shaded brown,
   And emerald meadows spread between,
And belfries towering from the town,
   All blent in wavering mists are seen;

When quickening woods with freshening hue
  Along Mount Royal rolling swell,
When winds caress and May is new,
  Oh, then my shy bird sings so well!

Because the bloodroots flock so white,
  And blossoms scent the wooing air,
And mounds with trillium flags are dight,
  And dells with violets frail and rare;
Because such velvet leaves unclose,
  And new-born rills all chiming ring,
And blue the sun-kissed river flows,
  My timid bird is forced to sing.

A joyful flourish lifted clear,
  Four notes, then fails the frolic song,
And memories of a sweeter year
  The wistful cadences prolong;—
'*A sweeter year—Oh, heart too sore!—*
  I cannot sing!'—So ends the lay.
Long silence. Then awakes once more
  His song, ecstatic with the May.

The Canadian Rossignol

(In June)

PRONE where maples widely spread
  I watch the far blue overhead,
Where little pillowy clouds arise
From naught to die before my eyes;
Within the shade a pleasant rout
Of dallying zephyrs steal about;
Lazily as moves the day
Odours float and faint away
From roses yellow, red, and white,
That prank yon garden with delight;
Round which the locust blossoms swing,
And some late lilacs droop for spring.
Anon swells up a dubious breeze,
Stirring the half-reluctant trees,

Then, rising to a mimic gale,
Ruffles the massy oaks to pale,
Till spent its sudden force, once more
The zephyrs come that went before;
Now silvery poplars shivering stand,
And languid lindens waver bland,
Hemlock traceries scarcely stir,
All the pines of summer purr.
Hovering butterflies I see,
Full of business shoots the bee,
Straight from the valley is his flight
Where crowding marbles solemn white
Show through the trees and mutely tell
How there the low-laid loved rest well.
Half hid in the grasses there
Red breast thrushes jump and stare,
Sparrows flutter up like leaves
Tossed upon the wind in sheaves,
Curve-winged swallows slant and slide
O'er the graves that stretch so wide,
Steady crows go labouring by—
Ha! the Rossignol is nigh!

Rossignol, why will you sing,
Though lost the lovely world of spring?
'T was well that then your roulades rang
Of joy, despite of every pang;
But now the sweet, the bliss is gone—
   Nay, now the summer joy is on,
   And lo, the foliage and the bloom,
   The fuller life, the bluer room,
   'T was this the sweet spring promised me.
Oh, bird, and can you sing so free,
Though never yet the roaming wind
Could leave earth's countless graves behind?
And will you sing when summer goes
And leaves turn brown and dies the rose?
   Oh, then how brave shall Autumn dress
   The maple out with gorgeousness!
   And red-cheeked apples deck the green,

And corn wave tall its yellow sheen.
But, bird, bethink you well, I pray,
Then marches winter on his way.
 Ah, winter—yes, ah yes—but still,
 Hark! sweetly chimes the summer rill,
 And joy is here and life is strong,
 And love still calls upon my song.
No, Rossignol, sing not that strain,
Triumphant 'spite of all the pain,—
She cannot hear you, Rossignol,
She does not pause and flush, your thrall,
She does not raise that slender hand
And, poised, lips parted, understand
What you are telling of the years,
Her brown eyes soft with happy tears,
She does not hear a note of all,
Ah, Rossignol! ah, Rossignol!
 But skies are blue, and flowers bloom,
 And roses breathe the old perfume,
 And here the murmuring of the trees
 In all of lovelier mysteries—
And maybe now she hears thy song
Pouring the summer rills along,
Listens with joy that still to me
Remain the summer time and thee.

From 'Peter Ottawa'

COUNT up the dead by fever, shot and shell,
Count up the cripples, count all tears that fell,
Count up the orphan children of the strife,
Count the long-yearning heart of parent, wife,
Count the vast treasure, count the labour's waste
Count all the cost of passion's headlong haste,
And then you'll know what *solid* nations pay
When common impulse sweeps good sense away,
Flushing the millions madly all at once
With *Wisdom down, and up the truculent dunce.*

Ethelwyn Wetherald

'The Last Robin' is an attractive volume, showing in the cover design the songster most closely associated with the spring, whose ecstatic chant so nearly assimilates the poet's own gift of overflowing, uplifting melody. . . . . . The salient quality of Miss Wetherald's work is its freshness of feeling, a perennial freshness, renewable as spring. This has a setting of harmonious form, for the poet's ear is delicately attuned to the value of words, both as to the sound and the meaning. . . . . Dealing for the most part with the familiar objects of nature and of life, she remains the poet, as well in the level regions of her subjects as in the elevated. . . . . Now and again she has attained the supreme elevation, as in her lovely poems, 'Earth's Silences', 'The Patient Earth', 'The Wind of Death' and 'The Little Noon'. . . . . The sonnets are an important part of the volume, and, to some minds, will represent the most important part. Miss Wetherald's sonnets are flowing in expression and harmonious in thought; some are beautiful.—PHAROS, *in 'The Globe.'*

AGNES ETHELWYN WETHERALD was born of English-Quaker parents at Rockwood, Ontario, April 26th, 1857. Her father was the late Rev. William Wetherald, who founded the Rockwood Academy about the middle of the last century, and was its principal for some years. He was a lover of good English, spoken and written, and his talented daughter has owed much to his careful teaching. He was the teacher whom the late James J. Hill, the railway magnate, had held in such grateful remembrance.

Additional education was received by Miss Wetherald at the Friends' Boarding School, Union Springs, N.Y., and at Pickering College.

Miss Wetherald began the writing of poetry later in life than most poets and her first book of verse, *The House of the Trees and Other Poems,* did not appear until 1895. This book at once gave her high rank among women poets.

Prior to this, she had collaborated with G. Mercer Adam in writing and publishing a novel, *An Algonquin Maiden,* and had conducted the Woman's Department in *The Globe,* Toronto, under the *nom de plume,* 'Bel Thistlewaite.'

In 1902, appeared her second volume of verse, *Tangled in Stars,* and, in 1904, her third volume, *The Radiant Road.*

In the autumn of 1907, a collection of Miss Wetherald's best poems was issued, entitled, *The Last Robin: Lyrics and Sonnets.* It was warmly welcomed generally, by reviewers and lovers of poetry. The many exquisite gems therein so appealed to Earl Grey, the then Governor-General of Canada, that he wrote a personal letter of appreciation to the author, and purchased twenty-five copies of the first edition for distribution among his friends.

For years Miss Wetherald has resided on the homestead farm, near the village of Fenwick, in Pelham Township, Welland county, Ontario, and there in the midst of a large orchard and other rural charms, has dreamed, and visioned, and sung, pouring out her soul in rare, sweet songs, with the naturalness of a bird. And like a bird she has a nest in a large willow tree, cunningly contrived by a nature-loving brother, where her muse broods contentedly, intertwining her spirit with every aspect of the beautiful environment.

The House of the Trees

OPE your doors and take me in,
  Spirit of the wood;
Wash me clean of dust and din,
  Clothe me in your mood.

Take me from the noisy light
  To the sunless peace,
Where at midday standeth Night,
  Signing Toil's release.

All your dusky twilight stores
  To my senses give;
Take me in and lock the doors,
  Show me how to live.

Lift your leafy roof for me,
  Part your yielding walls,
Let me wander lingeringly
  Through your scented halls.

Ope your doors and take me in,
  Spirit of the wood;
Take me—make me next of kin
  To your leafy brood.

The Screech-Owl

HEARING the strange night-piercing sound
  Of woe that strove to sing,
I followed where it hid, and found
  A small soft-throated thing,
A feathered handful of gray grief,
Perched by the year's last leaf.

And heeding not that in the sky
  The lamps of peace were lit,
It sent abroad that sobbing cry,
  And sad hearts echoed it.
O hush, poor grief, so gray, so wild,
God still is with His child!

My Orders

MY orders are to fight;
Then if I bleed, or fail,
Or strongly win, what matters it?
God only doth prevail.

The servant craveth naught
Except to serve with might.
I was not told to win or lose,—
My orders are to fight.

If One Might Live

IF one might live ten years among the leaves,
Ten—only ten—of all a life's long day,
Who would not choose a childhood 'neath the eaves
Low-sloping to some slender footpath way?

With the young grass about his childish feet,
And the young lambs within his ungrown arms,
And every steamlet side a pleasure seat
Within the wide day's treasure-house of charms.

To learn to speak while young birds learned to sing,
To learn to run e'en as they learned to fly;
With unworn heart against the breast of spring,
To watch the moments smile as they went by.

Enroofed with apple buds afar to roam,
Or clover-cradled on the murmurous sod,
To drowse within the blessed fields of home,
So near to earth—so very near to God.

How could it matter—all the after strife,
The heat, the haste, the inward hurt, the strain,
When the young loveliness and sweet of life
Came flood-like back again and yet again?

When best begins it liveth through the worst;
O happy soul, beloved of Memory,
Whose youth was joined to beauty as at first
The morning stars were wed to harmony!

Legacies

UNTO my friends I give my thoughts,
  Unto my God my soul,
Unto my foe I leave my love—
  These are of life the whole.

Nay, there is something—a trifle—left;
  Who shall receive this dower?
See, Earth Mother, a handful of dust—
  Turn it into a flower.

The Hay Field

WITH slender arms outstretching in the sun
  The grass lies dead;
The wind walks tenderly and stirs not one
  Frail fallen head.

Of baby creepings through the April day
  Where streamlets wend,
Of child-like dancing on the breeze of May,
  This is the end.

No more these tiny forms are bathed in dew,
  No more they reach
To hold with leaves that shade them from the blue
  A whispered speech.

No more they part their arms and wreathe them close
  Again, to shield
Some love-full little nest—a dainty house
  Hid in a field.

For them no more the splendour of the storm,
  The fair delights
Of moon and star-shine, glimmering faint and warm
  On summer nights.

Their little lives they yield in summer death,
  And frequently
Across the field bereaved their dying breath
  Is brought to me.

The Followers

ONE day I caught up with my angel, she
  Who calls me bell-like from a sky-touched tower.
'Twas in my roof-room, at the stillest hour
Of a still, sunless day, when suddenly
A flood of deep unreasoned ecstasy
  Lifted my heart, that had begun to cower,
  And wrapped it in a flame of living power.
My leader said, 'Arise and follow me.'

Then as I followed gladly I beheld
  How all men baffled, burdened, crossed or curst,
    Clutch at an angel's hem, if near or far;
One not-to-be-resisted voice, deep-belled,
  Speaks to them, and of those we call the worst,
    Lo, each poor blackened brow strains to a Star!

The Wind of Death

THE wind of death, that softly blows
  The last warm petal from the rose,
The last dry leaf from off the tree,
To-night has come to breathe on me.

There was a time I learned to hate
  As weaker mortals learn to love;
The passion held me fixed as fate,
Burned in my veins early and late;
  But now a wind falls from above—

The wind of death, that silently
Enshroudeth friend and enemy.

There was a time my soul was thrilled
  By keen ambition's whip and spur;
My master forced me where he willed,
And with his power my life was filled;
  But now the old-time pulses stir

How faintly in the wind of death,
That bloweth lightly as a breath.

And once, but once, at Love's dear feet
  I yielded strength and life and heart;
His look turned bitter into sweet,
His smile made all the world complete;
  The wind blows loves like leaves apart—

The wind of death, that tenderly
Is blowing 'twixt my love and me.

O wind of death, that darkly blows
Each separate ship of human woes
Far out on a mysterious sea,
I turn, I turn my face to thee!

The Indigo Bird

WHEN I see,
    High on the tip-top twig of a tree,
Something blue by the breezes stirred,
But so far up that the blue is blurred,
So far up no green leaf flies
'Twixt its blue and the blue of the skies,
Then I know, ere a note be heard,
That is naught but the Indigo bird.

Blue on the branch and blue in the sky,
And naught between but the breezes high,
And naught so blue by the breezes stirred
As the deep, deep blue of the Indigo bird.

When I hear
A song like a bird laugh, blithe and clear,
As though of some airy jest he had heard
The last and the most delightful word;
A laugh as fresh in the August haze
As it was in the full-voiced April days;
Then I know that my heart is stirred
By the laugh-like song of the Indigo bird.

Joy on the branch and joy in the sky,
And naught between but the breezes high;
And naught so glad on the breezes heard
As the gay, gay note of the Indigo bird.

At Waking

WHEN I shall go to sleep and wake again
　　At dawning in another world than this,
What will atone to me for all I miss?
The light melodious footsteps of the rain,
The press of leaves against my window-pane,
　The sunset wistfulness and morning bliss,
　The moon's enchantment, and the twilight kiss
Of winds that wander with me through the lane.

Will not my soul remember evermore
　The earthly winter's hunger for the spring,
　　The wet sweet cheek of April, and the rush
Of roses through the summer's open door;
　The feelings that the scented woodlands bring
　　At evening with the singing of the thrush?

The Song Sparrow's Nest

HERE where tumultuous vines
　　Shadow the porch at the west,
Leaf with tendril entwines
　Under a song sparrow's nest.

She in her pendulous nook
　Sways with the warm wind tide,
I with a pen or a book
　Rock as soft at her side.

Comrades with nothing to say,
　Neither of us intrudes,
But through the lingering day
　Each of us sits and broods.

Not upon hate and fear,
　Not upon grief or doubt,
Not upon spite or sneer,
　These we could never hatch out.

She broods on wonderful things:
　Quickening life that belongs
To a heart and a voice and wings,
　But—I'm not so sure of my songs!

Then in the summer night,
  When I awake with a start,
I think of the nest at the height—
  The leafy height of my heart;

I think of the mother love,
  Of the patient wings close furled,
Of the sky that broods above,
  Of the Love that broods on the world.

Earth's Silences

HOW dear to hearts by hurtful noises scarred
    The stillness of the many-leavèd trees,
The quiet of green hills, the million-starred
  Tranquility of night, the endless seas
Of silence in deep wilds, where nature broods
In large, serene, uninterrupted moods.

Oh, but to work as orchards work—bring forth
  Pink bloom, green bud, red fruit and yellow leaf,
As noiselessly as gold proclaims its worth,
  Or as the pale blade turns to russet sheaf,
Or splendid sun goes down the glowing west,
Still as forgotten memories in the breast.

How without panting effort, painful word,
  Comes the enchanting miracle of snow,
Making a sleeping ocean. None have heard
  Its waves, its surf, its foam, its overflow;
For unto every heart, all hot and wild,
It seems to say, 'Oh, hush thee! hush, my child!'

Mother and Child

I SAW a mother holding
    Her play-worn baby son,
Her pliant arms enfolding
    The drooping little one.

Her lips were made of sweetness,
    And sweet the eyes above;
With infantile completeness
    He yielded to her love.

And I who saw the heaving
   Of breast to dimpling cheek,
Have felt, within, the weaving
   Of thoughts I cannot speak;

Have felt myself the nestling,
   All strengthless, love-enisled;
Have felt myself the mother
   Abrood above her child.

Prodigal Yet

MUCK of the sty, reek of the trough,
   Blackened my brow where all might see,
Yet while I was a great way off
   My Father ran with compassion for me.

He put on my hand a ring of gold,
   (There's no escape from a ring, they say)
He put on my neck a chain to hold
   My passionate spirit from breaking away.

He put on my feet the shoes that miss
   No chance to tread in the narrow path;
He pressed on my lips the burning kiss
   That scorches deeper than fires of wrath.

He filled my body with meat and wine,
   He flooded my heart with love's white light;
Yet deep in the mire, with sensual swine,
   I long—God help me!— to wallow to-night.

Muck of the sty, reek of the trough,
   Blacken my soul where none may see.
Father, I yet am a long way off—
   Come quickly, Lord! Have compassion on me!

Pluck

THANK God for pluck—unknown to slaves—
   The self ne'er of its Self bereft,
Who, when the right arm's shattered, waves
   The good flag with the left.

William Henry Drummond

In the great family of modern poets, of which he is undoubt-
edly a member, Dr. Drummond takes the same place that
would be accorded in the family of artists to the master of
'genre': that is to say, he depicts with rare fidelity and affec-
tion a certain type, makes it completely his own and then
presents us with the finished picture. The habitant on his
little farm, the voyageur on wild river ways and the coureurs
de bois are all immortalized in songs that for humour, pathos
and picturesqueness it would be hard to excel. They are in-
herently native to the only section of Canada that can conscien-
tiously be called 'quaint,' and will always remain among our
valuable historic and human documents.—KATHERINE HALE.

I incline to think Drummond was never a bookish man.
. . . . He was plainly the kind of man to be fascinated by
any novel phase of the wild and vagabondish . . . . his
eye was ever alert for racial idiosyncrasy. . . . . Among
the poets of the British Empire, he holds a place unique.
—NEIL MUNRO, in his Appreciation of Drummond.

[177]

D R. WILLIAM HENRY DRUMMOND, *the poet of the habitant,* was born in the village of Mohill, County Leitrim, Ireland, on the 13th of April, 1854. Shortly afterwards, his father, an officer in the Royal Irish Constabulary, moved to the village of Tawley, on the Bay of Donegal. It was in this village that the future poet's education began.

While he was still a boy, the family emigrated to Canada, where the father in a few months died, leaving but limited means for the support of his wife and children.

William Henry soon found it necessary to leave school, to earn what he could to help provide for the family. Having learned telegraphy, he was employed at Borde à Plouffe, a small village on the Rivière des Prairies, near Montreal. It was here that he first observed the speech and the customs of the *habitant,* whom, with the kindliest intent, he has so faithfully portrayed.

In time, the family exchequer permitted him to attend the High School in Montreal, later, McGill University, and finally, Bishop's College, where he graduated in medicine in 1884. Dr. Drummond practised his profession for four years in the district about Brome, and then returned to the City of Montreal, where he continued to reside until his lamented death in 1907.

In 1894, he married Miss May Harvey, of Savannah la Mar, Jamaica. In Mrs. Drummond's memoir of her husband, she relates that he read with many misgivings, one of his earliest poems, 'Le Vieux Temps,' at a dinner of the Shakespeare Club, of Montreal, and further says:

This was the beginning of a long series of triumphs of a like nature, triumphs which owed little to elocutionary art, much to the natural gift of a voice rare alike in strength, quality and variety of tone, but, most of all to the fact that the characters he delineated were not mere creations of a vivid imagination. They were portraits tenderly drawn by the master hand of a true artist, and one who knew and loved the originals.

The Habitant and other French-Canadian Poems was published in 1898, and the popularity of the book was such as to bring the poet fame, and a substantial income in royalties. It was followed by *Johnnie Courteau and other Poems* in 1901; by *Phil-o'-Rum's Canoe and Madeleine Vercheres* in 1903;

and by *The Voyageur and other Poems* in 1905. His unpublished poems were edited and issued with the afore-mentioned
memoir, by his wife, in 1909; and, in 1912, a complete and
beautiful edition of his works, in one volume, was published
by G. T. Putnam's Sons, of New York.

For several years he was Professor of Medical Jurisprudence
in his Alma Mater. In 1902, the University of Toronto conferred on him the degree of LL.D. Subsequently he was
elected Fellow of the Royal Society of Literature of England,
and, later, of the Royal Society of Canada.

Much of the last two years of his life, Dr. Drummond spent
in the Cobalt district, where he had mining interests. There
he was stricken with cerebral hemorrhage and died in the
morning of April 6th, 1907. Probably no other Canadian poet
has been so widely mourned.

The Wreck of the 'Julie Plante'
A Legend of Lac St. Pierre

ON wan dark night on Lac St. Pierre,
De win' she blow, blow, blow,
An' de crew of de wood scow *Julie Plante*
Got scar't an' run below—
For de win' she blow lak hurricane,
Bimeby she blow some more,
An' de scow bus' up on Lac St. Pierre
Wan arpent from de shore.

De captinne walk on de fronte deck,
An' walk de hin' deck too—
He call de crew from up de hole,
He call de cook also.
De cook she's name was Rosie,
She come from Montreal,
Was chambre maid on lumber barge,
On de Grande Lachine Canal.

De win' she blow from nor'-eas'-wes',
De sout' win' she blow too,
W'en Rosie cry, 'Mon cher captinne,
Mon cher, w'at I shall do?'

Den de captinne t'row de beeg ankerre,
  But still de scow she dreef,
De crew he can't pass on de shore,
  Becos he los' hees skeef.

De night was dark lak wan black cat,
  De wave run high an' fas',
W'en de captinne tak' de Rosie girl
  An' tie her to de mas'.
Den he also tak' de life preserve,
  An' jomp off on de lak',
An' say, 'Good-bye, ma Rosie dear,
  I do drown for your sak'.'

Nex' morning very early
  'Bout ha'f pas' two-t'ree-four—
De captinne—scow—an' de poor Rosie
  Was corpses on de shore,
For de win' she blow lak hurricane,
  Bimeby she blow some more,
An' de scow bus' up on Lac St. Pierre,
  Wan arpent from de shore.

MORAL

Now all good wood scow sailor man,
  Tak' warning by dat storm,
An' go an' marry some nice French girl
  An' leev on wan beeg farm.
De win' can blow lak hurricane,
  An' s'pose she blow some more,
You can't get drown on Lac St. Pierre
  So long you stay on shore.

Little Bateese

YOU bad leetle boy, not moche you care
  How busy you're kipin' your poor gran'pere
Tryin' to stop you ev'ry day
Chasin' de hen aroun' de hay—
W'y don't you geev' dem a chance to lay?
    Leetle Bateese!

Off on de fiel' you foller de plough
Den w'en you're tire you scare de cow
Sickin' de dog till dey jomp de wall
So de milk ain't good for not'ing at all—
An' you're only five an' a half dis fall,
          Leetle Bateese!

Too sleepy for sayin' de prayer to-night?
Never min', I s'pose it'll be all right
Say dem to-morrow—ah! dere he go!
Fas' asleep in a minute or so—
And he'll stay lak dat till de rooster crow,
          Leetle Bateese!

Den wake us up right away toute suite
Lookin' for somet'ing more to eat,
Makin' me t'ink of dem long leg crane
Soon as dey swaller, dey start again,
I wonder your stomach don't get no pain,
          Leetle Bateese!

But see heem now lyin' dere in bed,
Look at de arm onderneat' hees head;
If he grow lak dat till he's twenty year
I bet he'll be stronger dan Louis Cyr
An' beat all de voyageurs leevin' here,
          Leetle Bateese!

Jus' feel de muscle along hees back,
Won't geev' heem moche bodder for carry pack
On de long portage, any size canoe,
Dere's not many t'ing dat boy won't do,
For he's got double-joint on hees body too,
          Leetle Bateese!

But leetle Bateese! please don't forget
We rader you're stayin' de small boy yet,
So chase de chicken an' mak' dem scare,
An' do w'at you lak wit' your old gran'pere
For w'en you're beeg feller he won't be dere—
          Leetle Bateese!

Johnnie Courteau

JOHNNIE COURTEAU of de mountain,
Johnnie Courteau of de hill,
Dat was de boy can shoot de gun,
Dat was de boy can jomp an' run,
An' it's not very offen you ketch heem still,
　　Johnnie Courteau!

Ax dem along de reever,
Ax dem along de shore,
Who was de mos' bes' fightin' man
From Managance to Shaw-in-i-gan,
De place w'ere de great beeg rapide roar?
　　Johnnie Courteau!

Sam' t'ing on ev'ry shaintee
Up on de Mekinac,
Who was de man can walk de log,
W'en w'ole of de reever she's black wit' fog,
An' carry de beeges' load on hees back?
　　Johnnie Courteau!

On de rapide you want to see heem
If de raf' she's swingin' roun',
An' he's yellin', 'Hooraw, Bateese! good man!'
W'y de oar come double on hees han'
W'en he's makin' dat raf' go flyin' down,
　　Johnnie Courteau!

An' Tête de Boule chief can tole you
De feller w'at save hees life,
W'en big moose ketch heem up a tree,
Who's shootin' dat moose on de head, sapree!
An' den run off wit' hees Injun wife?
　　Johnnie Courteau!

An' he only have pike pole wit' heem
On Lac a la Tortue
W'en he meet de bear comin' down de hill,
But de bear very soon is get hees fill!
An' he sole dat skin for ten dollar too,
　　Johnnie Courteau!

Oh, he never was scare for no'ting
Lak de ole coureurs de bois,
But w'en he's gettin' hees winter pay
De bes' t'ing sure is kip out de way,
For he's goin' right off on de Hip Hooraw!
　　　　Johnnie Courteau!

Den pullin' hees sash aroun' heem
He dance on hees botte sauvage
An' shout, 'All aboar' if you want to fight!'
Wall! you never can see de finer sight
W'en he go lak dat on de w'ole village!
　　　　Johnnie Courteau!

But Johnnie Courteau get marry
On Philomene Beaurepaire,
She's nice leetle girl was run de school
On w'at you call parish of Sainte Ursule
An' he see her off on de pique-nique dere,
　　　　Johnnie Courteau!

Den somet'ing come over Johnnie
W'en he marry on Philomene,
For he stay on de farm de w'ole year roun',
He chop de wood an' he plough de groun'
An' he's quieter feller was never seen,
　　　　Johnnie Courteau!

An' ev'ry wan feel astonish,
From La Tuque to Shaw-in-i-gan,
W'en day hear de news was goin' aroun',
Along on de reever up an' down,
How wan leetle woman boss dat beeg man,
　　　　Johnnie Courteau!

He never come out on de evening
No matter de hard we try,
'Cos he stay on de kitchen an' sing hees song,

　　　'A la claire fontaine,
　　　M'en allant promener,
　　　J'ai trouvé l'eau si belle
　　　Que je m'y suis baigner!

Lui y'a longtemps que je t'aime
Jamais je ne t'oublierai.'

Rockin' de cradle de w'ole night long
Till baby's asleep on de sweet bimeby,
Johnnie Courteau!

An' de house, wall! I wish you see it,
De place she's so nice an' clean,
Mus' wipe your foot on de outside door,
You're dead man sure if you spit on de floor,
An' he never say not'ing on Philomene,
Johnnie Courteau!

An' Philomene watch de monee
An' put it all safe away
On very good place; I dunno w'ere,
But anyhow nobody see it dere,
So she's buyin' new farm de noder day,
MADAME Courteau!

De Nice Leetle Canadienne

YOU can pass on de worl' w'erever you lak,
Tak' de steamboat for go Angleterre,
Tak' car on de State, an' den you come back,
An' go all de place, I don't care—
Ma frien', dat's a fack, I know you will say,
W'en you come on dis contree again,
Dere's no girl can touch, w'at we see ev'ry day,
De nice leetle Canadienne.

Don't matter how poor dat girl she may be,
Her dress is so neat an' so clean,
Mos' ev'rywan t'ink it was mak' on Paree,
An' she wear it, wall! jus' lak de Queen.
Den come for fin' out she is mak' it herse'f,
For she ain't got moche monee for spen',
But all de sam' tam, she was never get lef',
Dat nice leetle Canadienne.

W'en 'un vrai Canayen' is mak' it mariée,
You t'ink he go leev on beeg flat

An' bodder hese'f all de tam, night an' day,
   Wit' housemaid, an' cook, an' all dat?
Not moche, ma dear frien', he tak' de maison,
   Cos' only nine dollar or ten,
W'ere he leev lak blood rooster, an' save de l'argent,
   Wit' hees nice leetle Canadienne.

I marry ma famme w'en I'm jus' twenty year,
   An' now we got fine familee,
Dat skip roun' de place lak leetle small deer,
   No smarter crowd you never see—
An' I t'ink as I watch dem all chasin' about,
   Four boy an' six girl, she mak' ten,
Dat's help mebbe kip it, de stock from run out,
   Of de nice leetle Canadienne.

O she's quick, an' she's smart, an' got plaintee heart,
   If you know correc' way go about,
An' if you don' know, she soon tole you so,
   Den tak' de firs' chance an' get out;
But if she love you, I spik it for true,
   She will mak' it more beautiful den,
An' sun on de sky can't shine lak de eye
   Of dat nice leetle Canadienne.

Madeleine Vercheres

I'VE told you many a tale, my child, of the old heroic days
Of Indian wars and massacres, of villages ablaze
With savage torch, from Ville Marie to the Mission of Trois
      Rivieres
But never have I told you yet, of Madeleine Vercheres.

Summer had come with its blossoms, and gaily the robin sang
And deep in the forest arches the axe of the woodman rang,
Again in the waving meadows, the sun-browned farmers met
And out on the green St. Lawrence, the fisherman spread his
      net.

And so through the pleasant season, till the days of October
      came
When children wrought with their parents, and even the old
      and lame

With tottering frames and footsteps, their feeble labours lent
At the gathering of the harvest, le bon Dieu himself had sent.

For news there was none of battle, from the forts on the
Richelieu
To the gates of the ancient city, where the flag of King Louis
flew,
All peaceful the skies hung over the seigneurie of Vercheres,
Like the calm that so often cometh, ere the hurricane rends
the air.

And never a thought of danger had the Seigneur sailing away,
To join the soldiers of Carignan, where down at Quebec they
lay,
But smiled on his little daughter, the maiden Madeleine,
And a necklet of jewels promised her, when home he should
come again.

And ever the days passed swiftly, and careless the workmen
grew
For the months they seemed a hundred, since the last war-bugle
blew.
Ah! little they dreamt on their pillows, the farmers of Vercheres,
That the wolves of the southern forest had scented the harvest
fair.

Like ravens they quickly gather, like tigers they watch their
prey.
Poor people! with hearts so happy, they sang as they toiled
away,
Till the murderous eyeballs glistened, and the tomahawk
leaped out
And the banks of the green St. Lawrence echoed the savage
shout.

'O mother of Christ have pity,' shrieked the women in despair
'This is no time for praying,' cried the young Madeleine
Vercheres,
'Aux armes! aux armes! les Iroquois! quick to your arms and
guns,
Fight for your God and country and the lives of the innocent
ones.'

And she sped like a deer of the mountain, when beagles press
    close behind
And the feet that would follow after, must be swift as the
    prairie wind.
Alas! for the men and women, and little ones that day
For the road it was long and weary, and the fort it was far
    away.

But the fawn had outstripped the hunters, and the palisades
    drew near,
And soon from the inner gateway the war-bugle rang out clear;
Gallant and clear it sounded, with never a note of despair,
'Twas a soldier of France's challenge, from the young Made-
    leine Vercheres.

'And this is my little garrison, my brothers Louis and Paul?
With soldier's two—and a cripple? may the Virgin pray for us
    all.
But we've powder and guns in plenty, and we'll fight to the
    latest breath
And if need be for God and country, die a brave soldier's death.

Load all the carabines quickly, and whenever you sight the foe
Fire from the upper turret, and the loopholes down below.
Keep up the fire, brave soldiers, though the fight may be fierce
    and long
And they'll think our little garrison is more than a hundred
    strong.'

So spake the maiden Madeleine, and she roused the Norman
    blood
That seemed for a moment sleeping, and sent it like a flood
Through every heart around her, and they fought the red
    Iroquois
As fought in the old time battles, the soldiers of Carignan.

And they say the black clouds gathered, and a tempest swept
    the sky
And the roar of the thunder mingled with the forest tiger's cry,
But still the garrison fought on, while the lightning's jagged
    spear

Tore a hole in the night's dark curtain, and showed them a
    foeman near.

And the sun rose up in the morning, and the colour of blood
    was he,
Gazing down from the heavens on the little company.
'Behold! my friends!' cried the maiden, ''tis a warning lest
    we forget,
Though the night saw us do our duty, our work is not finished
    yet.'

And six days followed each other, and feeble her limbs became
Yet the maid never sought her pillow, and the flash of the
    carabines' flame
Illumined the powder-smoked faces, aye, even when hope seem-
    ed gone
And she only smiled on her comrades, and told them to fight,
    fight on.

And she blew a blast on the bugle, and lo! from the forest
    black,
Merrily, merrily ringing, an answer came pealing back.
Oh! pleasant and sweet it sounded, borne on the morning air,
For it heralded fifty soldiers, with gallant De la Monniere.

And when he beheld the maiden, the soldier of Carignan,
And looked on the little garrison that fought the red Iroquois
And held their own in the battle, for six long weary days,
He stood for a moment speechless, and marvelled at woman's
    ways.

Then he beckoned the men behind him and steadily they
    advance,
And, with carabines uplifted, the veterans of France
Saluted the brave young Captain so timidly standing there
And they fired a volley in honour of Madeleine Vercheres.

And this, my dear, is the story of the maiden Madeleine.
God grant that we in Canada may never see again
Such cruel wars and massacres, in waking or in dream,
As our fathers and mothers saw, my child, in the days of the
    old regime.

Jean Blewett

*Mrs Blewett is a woman's poet. She deals with homely sub-
jects in a homely way. She does not attempt wild flights of
rhapsody or deep philosophical problems. It is an everyday
sort of poetry, simple in theme and treatment, unpretentious,
domestic, kindly, humorous and natural. . . . . Perhaps
it is because of this very simplicity of theme and treatment
that Mrs. Blewett's writings, both in prose and poetry, are so
popular among a very large class of the Canadian public.
. . . . In sentiment and in morals her poems are wholesome and, to use a feminine adjective, 'sweet'. . . . .
Mrs. Blewett is perhaps the most conspicuous example in
Canada of the class of writers who try to bring the plain
people into touch with the highest ideals that are frequently
most effectively taught in verse. Her lessons are of self-
denial, and of the power of love to mould men and women.
—'Globe Magazine.'*

J EAN BLEWETT was born at Scotia, Lake Erie, Ontario, November 4th, 1872. Her parents, John and Janet (MacIntyre) McKishnie, were both natives of Argyllshire. She was educated at the local public school and at the St. Thomas College giate Institute. In 1889 she married Mr. Bassett Blewett, a native of Cornwall, England.

Through her mother she is related to Duncan Ban MacIntyre, the famous Gaelic poet.

While still in her teens, Mrs. Blewett's poems, short stories and articles in the public press and in magazines began to attract attention; and, in 1890, she published a novel, *Out of the Depths. Heart Songs,* a collection of her verse, appeared in 1897, and at once became popular; and *The Cornflower and Other Poems,* issued in 1906, increased the author's fame and popularity. One of her poems, 'Spring' captured the prize of six hundred dollars, offered for the best poem on this trite subject, by the Chicago *Times-Herald.*

In 1915, Mary Josephine Trotter contributed an interesting article on Jean Blewett to *Everywoman's World,* from which is quoted:

A BARD OF THE COMMON THINGS

Jean Blewett has neither refused to grow up, nor has she required to 'think back' to experience joy as quick as childhood's in the springing blade and the spreading leaf, and also in the realm of human nature. All this I know from her voice and her expression as she showed me the view from the window in her bedroom, in which she has been a prisoner since November.

Prisoner? The word is not à propos exactly. Not even the pangs of physical suffering have been able to bind the imagination of a woman profoundly in love with life and able to put her passion into writing. For months Mrs. Blewett has been busy on a novel, having for its setting the Peace River country in which wild and romantic district she camped with her husband and son for weeks last summer.

She was married early—at sixteen—and the first verses she ever wrote and for which she was paid by *Frank Leslie's Monthly,* were a lullaby to her own baby. . . . .

Jean Blewett is one of a literary family. Her brother, Mr. Archibald McKishnie, is frequently a contributor to Canadian publications, and a younger sister is winning success as a journalist in Detroit, Michigan.

For years Mrs. Blewett has been a special writer for the *Globe* and other household publications, so that her name has become familiar to a very large and appreciative public. She delights to write of 'the common things,' would rather be sympathetic than startling.

. . . .

Chore Time

WHEN I'm at gran'dad's on the farm,
  I hear along 'bout six o'clock,
Just when I'm feelin' snug an' warm,
  'Ho, Bobby, come and feed your stock.'

I jump and get into my clothes;
  It's dark as pitch, an' shivers run
All up my back. Now, I suppose
  Not many boys would think this fun.

But when we get out to the barn
  The greedy pigs begin to squeal,
An' I throw in the yellow corn,
  A bushel basket to the meal.

Then I begin to warm right up,
  I whistle 'Yankee Doodle' through,
An' wrastle with the collie pup—
  And sometimes gran'dad whistles too.

The cow-shed door, it makes a din
  Each time we swing it open wide;
I run an' flash the lantern in,
  There stand the shorthorns side by side.

Their breathin' makes a sort of cloud
  Above their heads—there's no frost here.
'My beauties,' gran'dad says out loud,
  'You'll get your breakfasts, never fear.'

When up I climb into the loft
  To fill their racks with clover hay,
Their eyes, all sleepy like and soft,
  A heap of nice things seem to say.

The red ox shakes his curly head,
  An' turns on me a solemn face;
I know he's awful glad his shed
  Is such a warm and smelly place.

An' last of all the stable big,
  With harness hanging on each door,—

I always want to dance a jig
 On that old musty, dusty floor.

It seems so good to be alive,
 An' tendin' to the sturdy grays,
The sorrels, and old Prince,—that's five—
 An' Lightfoot with her coaxing ways.

My gran'dad tells me she is mine,
 An' I'm that proud! I braid her mane,
An' smooth her sides until they shine,
 An' do my best to make her vain.

When we have measured oats for all,
 Have slapped the grays upon the flanks,
An' tried to pat the sorrels tall,
 An' heard them whinny out their thanks,

We know it's breakfast time, and go
 Out past the yellow stacks of straw,
Across the creek that used to flow,
 But won't flow now until a thaw.

Behind the trees the sky is pink,
 The snow drifts by in fat white flakes,
My gran'dad says: 'Well, Bob, I think
 There comes a smell of buckwheat cakes.'

For He Was Scotch, and So Was She

THEY were a couple well content
 With what they earned and what they spent,
Cared not a whit for style's decree—
For he was Scotch, and so was she.

And oh, they loved to talk of Burns—
Dear blithesome, tender Bobby Burns!
They never wearied of his song,
He never sang a note too strong.
One little fault could neither see—
For he was Scotch, and so was she.

They loved to read of men who stood
And gave for country life and blood,

Who held their faith so grand a thing
They scorned to yield it to a king.
Ah, proud of such they well might be—
For he was Scotch, and so was she.

From neighbours' broils they kept away;
No liking for such things had they,
And oh, each had a canny mind,
And could be deaf, and dumb, and blind.
With words or pence was neither free—
For he was Scotch, and so was she.

I would not have you think this pair
Went on in weather always fair,
For well you know in married life
Will come, sometimes, the jar and strife;
They couldn't always just agree—
For he was Scotch, and so was she.

But near of heart they ever kept,
Until at close of life they slept;
Just this to say when all was past,
They loved each other to the last.
They're loving yet, in heaven, maybe—
For he was Scotch, and so was she.

The Passage

O SOUL on God's high seas! the way is strange and long,
    Yet fling your pennons out, and spread your canvas
        strong;
For though to mortal eyes so small a craft you seem,
The highest star in heaven doth lend you guiding gleam.

O soul on God's high seas! look to your course with care,
Fear most when winds are kind and skies are blue and fair.
Your helm must sway at touch of no hand save your own—
The soul that sails on God's high seas must sail alone.

O soul on God's high seas! sail on with steady aim,
Unmoved by wind of praise, untouched by seas of blame.
Beyond the lonely ways, beyond the guiding star,
There stretches out the strand and golden harbour bar.

11

Quebec

QUEBEC, the gray old city on the hill,
Lies with a golden glory on her head,
Dreaming throughout this hour so fair, so still,
Of other days and her belovèd dead.
The doves are nesting in the cannons grim,
The flowers bloom where once did run a tide
Of crimson when the moon rose pale and dim
Above a field of battle stretching wide.

Methinks within her wakes a mighty glow
Of pride in ancient times, her stirring past,
The strife, the valour of the long ago
Feels at her heart-strings. Strong and tall, and vast
She lies, touched with the sunset's golden grace,
A wondrous softness on her gray old face.

What Time the Morning Stars Arise

[Lieutenant Reginald Warneford, while patrolling the skies over
Belgium in his aeroplane at 3 o'clock in the morning of June 7th,
1915, destroyed a German armed Zeppelin, containing twenty-eight
men. The young aviator won instant fame by his heroic act. He
received the Victoria Cross from King George and the Legion of
Honour from France.]

ABOVE him spreads the purple sky,
Beneath him spreads the ether sea,
And everywhere about him lie
    Dim ports of space, and mystery.

Ho, lonely Admiral of the Fleet!
    What of the night? What of the night?
'Methinks I hear,' he says, 'the beat
    Of great wings rising for the flight.'

Ho, Admiral neighbouring with the stars
    Above the old world's stress and din!
With Jupiter and lordly Mars—
    'Ah, yonder sweeps a Zeppelin!

'A bird with menace in its breath,
    A thing of peril, spoil and strife,

The little children done to death,
  The helpless old bereft of life.

'The moan of stricken motherhood,
  The cowardice beyond our ken,
The cruelty that fires the blood,
  And shocks the souls of honest men.

'These call for vengeance—mine the chase.'
  He guides his craft—elate and strong.
Up, up, through purple seas of space,
  While in his heart there grows a song.

'Ho, little ship of mine that soars
  Twixt earth and sky, be ours to-day
To free our harassed seas and shores
  Of yonder evil bird of prey!'

The gallant venture is his own,
  No friend to caution, pray, or aid,
But strong is he who fights alone,
  Of loss and failure unafraid.

He rises higher, higher still,
Till poised above the startled foe—
It is a fight to stir and thrill
  And set the dullest breast aglow.

Old Britain hath her battles won
  On fields that are a nation's pride,
And oh the deeds of daring done
  Upon her waters deep and wide!

But warfare waged on solid land,
  Or on the sea, can scarce compare
With this engagement, fierce, yet grand,
  This duel to the death in air.

He wins! he wins in sea of space!
  Why prate we now of other wars
Since he has won his name and place
  By deathless valour 'mong the stars?

No more that Zeppelin will mock,
  No more will sound her song of hate;

With bursting bomb, and fire, and shock,
  She hurtles downward to her fate.

A touch of rose in eastern skies,
  A little breeze that calls and sings,
Look yonder where our hero flies,
  Like homing bird on eager wings.

He sees the white mists softly curl,
  He sees the moon drift pale and wan,
Sees Venus climb the stairs of pearl
  To hold her court of Love at dawn.

The Usurer

FATE says, and flaunts her stores of gold,
  'I'll loan you happiness untold.
What is it you desire of me?'
A perfect hour in which to be
In love with life, and glad, and good,
The bliss of being understood,
Amid life's cares a little space
To feast your eyes upon a face,
The whispered word, the love-filled tone,
The warmth of lips that meet your own,
    To-day of Fate you borrow;
      In hunger of the heart, and pain,
      In loneliness, and longing vain,
    You pay the debt to-morrow!

Prince, let grim Fate take what she will
Of treasures rare, of joys that thrill,
Enact the cruel usurer's part,
Leave empty arms and hungry heart,
Take what she can of love and trust,
Take all life's gladness, if she must,
Take meeting smile and parting kiss—
The benediction and the bliss.
    What then? The fairest thing of all
    Is ours, O Prince, beyond recall—
    Not even Fate would dare to seize
    Our store of golden memories.

Arthur Wentworth Hamilton Eaton

*These verses are direct, unstrained, natural, and always
simple in form and motive. There is much easy melody,
much tenderness of mood, much faithful and effective description. In the 'Acadian Legends' Mr. Eaton may be said
to revive that pleasant art that has long been in disuse, the
art of telling a not very striking story in verse, and adding
an evasive grace which persuades one that the tale was worth
telling. The 'Lyrics' are human and wholesome, almost without exception, and improve on close acquaintance.*—Charles
G. D. Roberts, in 'St. John Progress.'

*Mr. Eaton's 'Acadian Legends' are characterized by melo-
dy, pathos, a strong feeling for nature, and refined taste.
The spirit of Evangeline's country has been absorbed by the
poet, who celebrates the Gaspereau and all the region round
about with a tender melancholy fitted to the scene and its
associations. He has caught the old world atmosphere which
surrounds and mellows that beautiful land, and has given to
his verse a softness and repose which are in perfect keeping
with the subject.*—'New York Tribune.'

ARTHUR WENTWORTH HAMILTON EATON, M.A., D.C.L., poet, priest, educator and historian, was born at Kentville, Nova Scotia, the eldest son of William Eaton, a descendant of a Puritan family and at one time Inspector of Schools for his county, and Anna Augusta Willoughby Hamilton, of New England Puritan stock.

His higher education was received at Dalhousie College, Halifax, and at Harvard University where he graduated in arts with the class of 1880. [Of this class, Theodore Roosevelt was a member.] The honorary degree, D.C.L., was conferred on him in 1905, by King's College University, in recognition of his literary achievements and high scholastic attainments.

Ordained deacon of the Protestant Episcopal Church, in 1884, and priest the next year, he was, for a time, incumbent of the parish of Chestnut Hill, Boston.

In 1888, Dr. Eaton's first notable work, *The Heart of the Creeds: Historical Religion in the Light of Modern Thought,* was published. This was followed, in 1889, by his first book of verse, *Acadian Legends and Lyrics,* so favourably reviewed by the critics. His third publication, *The Church of England in Nova Scotia, and the Tory Clergy of the Revolution,* a permanently valuable historical work, was issued in 1891. His historical researches have resulted also in a number of authoritative genealogical and family monographs, in the *History of King's County, N.S.: Heart of the Acadian Land,* and in an important *History of Halifax, Nova Scotia,* now being published in instalments, in 'Americana.' Two other volumes of verse appeared in 1905,—*Acadian Ballads, and De Soto's Last Dream,* and *Poems of the Christian Year*—and, in 1907, was published *The Lotus of the Nile and Other Poems.*

As Professor of English Literature, for years, in a New York college, Dr. Eaton gained a wide reputation as an educator.

Dr. Eaton has made an enviable record as a Canadian litterateur. His Legends and Ballads must continue to hold their distinctive place in Canadian verse, whilst his historical writings must ever increase in value and importance.

The Phantom Light of the Baie des Chaleurs

'TIS the laughter of pines that swing and sway
    Where the breeze from the land meets the breeze from
        the bay;
'Tis the silvery foam of the silver tide
In ripples that reach to the forest side;
'Tis the fisherman's boat, in a track of sheen
Plying through tangled seaweed green,
    O'er the Baie des Chaleurs.

Who has not heard of the phantom light
That over the moaning waves, at night,
Dances and drifts in endless play,
Close to the shore, then far away,
Fierce as the flame in sunset skies,
Cold as the winter light that lies
    On the Baie des Chaleurs.

They tell us that many a year ago,
From lands where the palm and the olive grow,
Where vines with their purple clusters creep
Over the hillsides gray and steep,
A knight in his doublet, slashed with gold,
Famed, in that chivalrous time of old,
For valorous deeds and courage rare,
Sailed with a princess wondrous fair
    To the Baie des Chaleurs.

That a pirate crew from some isle of the sea,
A murderous band as e'er could be,
With a shadowy sail, and a flag of night,
That flaunted and flew in heaven's sight,
Swept in the wake of the lovers there,
And sank the ship and its freight so fair
    In the Baie des Chaleurs.

Strange is the tale that the fishermen tell,—
They say that a ball of fire fell
Straight from the sky, with crash and roar,
Lighting the bay from shore to shore;
That the ship, with a shudder and a groan,
Sank through the waves to the caverns lone
    Of the Baie des Chaleurs.

That was the last of the pirate crew;
But many a night a black flag flew
From the mast of a spectre vessel, sailed
By a spectre band that wept and wailed
For the wreck they had wrought on the sea, on the land,
For the innocent blood they had spilt on the sand
    Of the Baie des Chaleurs.

This is the tale of the phantom light
That fills the mariner's heart, at night,
With dread as it gleams o'er his path on the bay,
Now by the shore, then far away,
Fierce as the flame in sunset skies,
Cold as the winter moon that lies
    On the Baie des Chaleurs.

The Lotus of the Nile

PROUD, languid lily of the sacred Nile,
  'Tis strange to see thee on our western wave,
Far from those sandy shores that mile on mile,
  Papyrus-plumed, stretch silent as the grave.

O'er limpid pool, and wide, palm-sheltered bay,
  And round deep-dreaming isles, thy leaves expand,
Where Alexandrian barges plough their way,
  Full-freighted, to the ancient Theban land.

On Karnak's lofty columns thou wert seen,
  And spacious Luxor's temple-palace walls,
Each royal Pharaoh's emeralded queen
  Chose thee to deck her glittering banquet halls;

Yet thou art blossoming on this fairy lake
  As regally, amidst these common things,
As on the shores where Nile's brown ripples break,
  As in the ivory halls of Egypt's kings.

Thy grace meets every passer's curious eyes,
  But he whose thought has ranged through faiths of old
Gazing at thee feels lofty temples rise
  About him, sees long lines of priests, white-stoled,

That chant strange music as they slowly pace
  Dim-columned aisles; hears trembling overhead
Echoes that lose themselves in that vast space,
  Of Egypt's solemn ritual for the dead.

Ay, deeper thoughts than these, though undefined,
  Start in the reflective soul at sight of thee,
For this majestic orient faith enshrined
  Man's yearning hope of immortality.
And thou didst symbolize the deathless power
  That under all decaying forms lies hid,
The old world worshipped thee, O Lotus flower,
  Then carved its sphinx and reared its pyramid!

I Watch the Ships

I WATCH the ships by town and lea
  With sails full set glide out to sea,
Till by the distant lighthouse rock
The breakers beat with roar and shock,
And crisp foam whitening all the decks;
While deep below lie ocean's wrecks,
        What careth she!

I stand beside the beaten quay
And look while laden ships from sea
Come proudly home upon the tide
Like conquering kings, at eventide;
Or from fierce fights with wintry gales
Steal harbourward with tattered sails,
        O cruel sea!

I pass the ancient moss-grown pier
Where men have waited year by year
For ships that ne'er again shall glide
By town and lea on favouring tide,
Strong ships that struggled till the gales
Of winter hid their shrouds and sails
        In ocean drear.

With sails full set young spirits glide
From harbour, on a sea untried,
To breast the waves and bear the shocks
Beyond the guarded lighthouse rocks,
To strive with tempests many a year;
Strong souls, indeed, if they can bear
        Life's wind and tide!

I watch beside the beaten quay
The surf bring back all joyously

To anchor by the sheltered shore
Some laden deep with precious ore,
Or spices won from perfumed sands
Of rich, luxuriant tropic lands,—
    O kindly sea!

But some come back on wintry gales
With broken spars and shattered sails
And fling to shore a feeble rope;
While many a loving heart in hope
Waits on for ships that nevermore
Shall anchor by a friendly shore,
    O sad, sad sea!

L'ile Sainte Croix

The first French Settlement in America was made here in 1604.

WITH tangled brushwood overgrown,
    And here and there a lofty pine,
    Around whose form strange creepers twine,
And crags that mock the wild sea's moan,

And little bays where no ships come,
    Though many a white sail passes by,
    And many a drifting cloud on high
Looks down and shames the sleeping foam,

Unconscious on the waves it lies,
    While midst the golden reeds and sedge
    That, southward, line the water's edge,
The thrush sings her shrill melodies.

No human dwelling now is seen
    Upon its rude, unfertile slopes,
    Though many a summer traveller gropes
For ruins midst the tangled green,

And seeks upon the northern shore
    The graves of that adventurous band
    That followed to the Acadian land
Champlain, De Monts, and Poutrincourt.

There stood the ancient fort that sent
    Fierce cannon echoes through the wold,
    There waved the Bourbon flag that told
The mastery of a continent;

There through the pines the echoing wail
    Of ghostly winds was heard at eve,
    And hoarse, deep sounds like those that heave
The breasts of stricken warriors pale.

There Huguenots and cassocked priests,
    And noble-born and sons of toil,
    Together worked the barren soil,
And shared each other's frugal feasts,

And dreamed beneath the yellow moon
    Of golden reapings that should be,
    Conjuring from the sailless sea
A glad, prophetic harvest-tune,

Till stealthy winter through the reeds
    Crept, crystal-footed, to the shore,
    And to the little hamlet bore
His hidden freight of deathly seeds.

Spring came at last, and o'er the waves
    The welcome sail of Pontgravé,
    But half the number silent lay,
Death's pale first-fruits, in western graves.

Sing on, wild sea, your sad refrain
    For all the gallant sons of France,
    Whose songs and sufferings enhance
The witchery of the western main,

Keep kindly watch before the strand
    Where lie in hidden mounds, secure,
    The men De Monts and Poutrincourt
First led to the Acadian land.

By the Bridge

WITH subtlest mimicry of wave and tide,
    Of ocean storm, and current setting free,
Here by the bridge the river deep and wide,
Swaying the reeds along its muddy marge,
Speeds to the wharf the dusky coaling-barge
And dreams itself a commerce-quickening sea.

Wide sedge-rimmed meadows westward meet the eye,
Brown, silty, sere, where driftwood from the mills
Is thrown, as Spring's full flood sweeps by,

And weeds grow rank as on the wild salt-marsh,
And lonely cries of sea-gulls, loud and harsh,
Pierce evening's silence to the echoing hills.

The scene, with all its varied, voiceless moods,
My eyes have looked upon so many years
That like my mother's songs, or the deep woods
In whose mysterious shade I used to play,
Weaving sweet fancies all the summer day,
It has strange power to waken joy or tears.

I love the lights that fringe the farther shore,
Great golden fireflies by a silver mere;
Mysterious torches they, that o'er and o'er
Recall to mind the dear souls gone, not set
Cold-gleaming crystals in God's coronet,
But gems that light our way with ruddy cheer.

Sometimes inverted in the wave they seem
Like orient palace-roofs and towers aflame
With rubies, or those sapphire walls that gleam
Amidst the visions of the holy Seer,
Who by the blue Ægean, with vision clear,
Saw splendours in the heavens he might not name.

When all the river lies encloaked in mist
So far away those trembling orbs of light
They symbol memories fair that still persist,
With glow or glimmer, of the shrouded years
Before we left, for laughter, cries and tears,
That world serene where souls are born in light.

I cannot watch unmoved the sunset here,
When swift volcanic fires of liquid gold
Alight on hills of purple haze appear,
And clouds, deep-crimsoned in the day's decline,
Like snowy festal-garments splashed with wine,
Lie careless, resting fleecy fold on fold.

So deep the meanings in these changing moods
Of earth and heaven, that I who reverent stand
Before a flower, and in the sombre woods
Hear speech that silences the common creeds,
Stand lost in wonder, like a man who reads
Immortal prophecies none can understand.

Helena Coleman

The poet's claim to fame depends very largely on his or her mastery of outward form or technique, on skill in phrasing, in emphasis and in sonority of verse. Measured by such canons of taste, we have no hesitation in saying that Miss Coleman's style singles her out at once from the latter-day lamp-poetry magazine versifiers. Her command of rhythm is very pleasing, and because of her love of Latinized English, reaches a certain degree of opulence which cannot fail to give any lover of cadence great delight. Yet in spite of her love for colour and sonority our new poet is at all times eminently clear. . . . .
Miss Coleman has much in common with Mathew Arnold. Just as he did, she knows how to combine concreteness of colour, with a certain noble simplicity and restraint of style, and like Arnold, she likes best of all to devote her thought to the deep things of the soul. . . . . . She knows life in its sadness, gladness and beauty, and sings of it in relation to Nature and to God.—PROF. W. T. ALLISON, M.A., PH.D., in the 'Canadian Magazine.'

A S Miss Coleman's poems appeared for years in the *Atlantic Monthly* and other periodicals, under a nom de plume, a few intimate friends only knew the real name and personality of the author, prior to 1906. In that year appeared her *Songs and Sonnets,* published under the auspices of the Tennyson Club, Toronto.

It was recognized at once that Canada had a new poet of distinctive merit; and the first edition was soon followed by a second. The critics invariably ranked the forty-four sonnets in the book as work of high quality,—spontaneous, rhythmic, noble; and indeed this form of verse seems to suit most adequately the finer instincts of her genius. The lyrics quoted are also beautiful.

A daughter of the Rev. Francis Coleman, a Methodist clergyman, and his wife, Emmeline Maria Adams, she is a descendant through her mother of John Quincy Adams, sixth President of the United States, and the reputed author of the "Monroe Doctrine." She is the only sister of the well-known geologist, Prof. A. P. Coleman, Ph.D., F.R.S.

Miss Coleman is a Canadian by birth and education and a resident of Toronto. She travels quite extensively—was in Germany when the Great War began—but in the summer months is found most frequently at Pinehurst, her lovely island and cottage in the Thousand Islands, where the fresh air and the beauty of nature renew her health and inspiration; and where, as a gracious hostess, she entertains congenial friends.

More Lovely Grows the Earth

M ORE lovely grows the earth as we grow old,
More tenderness is in the dawning spring,
More bronze upon the blackbird's burnished wing;
And richer is the autumn cloth-of-gold;
A deeper meaning, too, the years unfold,
Until to waiting hearts each living thing
For very love its bounty seems to bring,
Intreating us with beauty to behold.

Or is it that with years we grow more wise
And reverent to the mystery profound—

Withheld from careless or indifferent eyes—
That broods in simple things the world around,
More conscious of the Love that glorifies
The common ways and makes them holy ground?

To a Bluebell

I WATCH thy little bells of blue,
  So delicate of form and hue,
And when I see them swing and sway
I listen for the chimes to play;
But dull has grown the mortal ear,
And I can never, never hear
The dainty tunes, but only guess
Their music from thy loveliness.

Dost thou announce the day new-born,
And ring the changes of the morn,
And summon for an early mass
The little peoples of the grass,
That they may give fresh meed of praise
For sun and rain and summer days?
Dost thou the moon's late rising tell,
And sound at eve a curfew bell?

When drowsy bees go loitering,
And butterflies are on the wing,
Dost beat the merry music out,
And swell the rhythm of the rout?
Dost ever some faint message sound
For all the wee folk of the ground,
Of those far mysteries that lie
Beyond their ken in earth and sky?

Keep thou thy silence, fairy bell,
Thou art no less a miracle;
No less a rapture thou dost bring
Because we cannot hear thee ring;
For they who give attentive ear
Must catch thy silvery cadence clear,
And know a joy no language tells,
When in the heart there sings and swells
The music of thy magic bells.

Indian Summer

OF all Earth's varied, lovely moods,
The loveliest is when she broods
Among her dreaming solitudes
    On Indian Summer days;
When on the hill the aster pales,
And Summer's stress of passion fails,
And Autumn looks through misty veils
    Along her leafy ways.

How deep the tenderness that yearns
Within the silent wood that turns
From green to gold, and slowly burns
    As by some inward fire!
How dear the sense that all things wild
Have been at last by love beguiled
To join one chorus, reconciled
    In satisfied desire!

The changing hillside, wrapped in dreams
With softest opalescent gleams,
Like some ethereal vision seems,
    Outlined against the sky;
The fields that gave the harvest gold—
Afar before our eyes unrolled
In purple distance, fold on fold—
    Lovely and tranquil lie.

We linger by the crimson vine,
Steeped to the heart with fragrant wine,
And where the rowan-berries shine,
    And gentians lift their blue;
We stay to hear the wind that grieves
Among the oak's crisp russet leaves,
And watch the moving light, that weaves
    Quaint patterns, peering through.

The fires that in the maples glow,
The rapture that the beeches know,
The smoke-wraiths drifting to and fro,
    Each season more endears;

Vague longings in the heart arise,
A dimming mist comes to the eyes
That is not sadness, though it lies
    Close to the place of tears.

We share the ecstasy profound
That broods in everything around,
And by the wilderness are crowned—
    Its silent worship know.
O when our Indian Summer days
Divide the parting of the ways,
May we, too, linger here in praise
    Awhile before we go!

Prairie Winds

I LOVE all things that God has made
    That show His ordered care and might,
But most, I think, I love the wind
    That blows at night.

It holds so much of mystery,
    Like that in mine own restless heart—
Brother to me and well-beloved,
    O Wind, thou art!

Across these unresisting plains
    It sweeps at times with force sublime,
And always like the wraith it seems
    Of happier clime.

For in the South its home has been,
    A sun-kissed, warm and fertile land,
Where Nature pours her treasure from
    Unstinting hand.

Through fields of rustling corn it came
    And acres broad of bearded wheat,
Past hillsides clad with evergreen
    And orchards sweet.

It rifled scent from clover fields
    Where harvesters have been at work,

And ruffled little running brooks
  Where mosses lurk.

It bears the note of piping frogs,
  The stir of tender, untried wings—
Of lowing kine, and homely sounds
  Of barnyard things.

O barren land! what dost thou dream
  Beneath these surging winds that bear
The echoes of a life which thou
  Canst never share?

Dost thou not long to break thy calm—
  To know that living, sweet unrest?
And feel the tread of busy feet
  Upon thy breast?

To hear thy children's laughter voiced
  In myriad tongues, and know that when
Their day is done within thy breast
  They'll sleep again?

O silent land! the winds that blow
  Within men's hearts and fan the fire
Of hidden hopes and show the soul
  Its own desire,

Have come to me from distant shores
  And borne in broken whisperings
A tale that thrilled me like a tide
  From rising springs.

The full-pressed wine of life my lips
  Have never tasted, yet is known,
My heart, though held in bondage, leaps
  To claim its own.

I know my lawful heritage,
  Although I stand on alien ground;
I know what kingship is, although
  I go uncrowned.

At night when inner tempests blow,
   And sleep forsakes my weary eye,
I love to hear the wind without
   Go storming by.

It speaks my own wild native tongue
   And gives me courage to withstand,
As if a comrade came to me
   And took my hand.

I love all things that God has made
   In earth or sea or heavens bright,
But most I love the prairie winds
   That blow at night.

Enlargement

AROUND us unaware the solemn night
   Had hung its shadowy mantle, while we sought
To find each other by the roads of thought;
I felt thy orbit nearing, and a light
Streamed suddenly across my inner sight,
Effulgent, incommunicable, fraught
With some constraining tenderness that caught
My quickened spirit to its utmost height.

And lo! I saw as with the eyes of two,
In that swift moment when thy soul touched mine,
The walls of being widened, and I drew
Near to the portal of a nameless shrine,
A sudden blinding rapture pierced me through,
And in that instant earth became divine.

Day and Night

WHEN in the affluent splendour of the day,
   To heaven's cloudless blue I lift my eyes,
Thrilled with the beauty that around me lies,
My heart goes up on wings of ecstasy;
But when Orion and the Milky Way
Reveal the story of the midnight skies,
And all the starry hosts of space arise—
Mutely I bow in reverence to pray.

And so with life; the daylight of success
Rounds earth and pleasure to a perfect sphere,
But in the night of trial and distress
The quickened soul to vaster realms draws near,
And o'er the borders of our consciousness
Foretokens of the Infinite appear.

Beyond the Violet Rays

BEYOND the violet rays we do not know
What colours lie, what fields of light abound,
Or what undreamed effulgence may surround
Our dreaming consciousness above, below;
Nor is it far that finite sense can go
Along the subtle passages of sound,
The finer tonal waves are too profound
For mortal ears to catch their ebb and flow.

But there are moments when upon us steal
Monitions of far wider realms that lie
Beyond our spirit borders, and we feel
That fine, ethereal joys we cannot name,
In some vast orbit circling, sweeping by,
Touch us in passing as with wings of flame.

As Day Begins to Wane

ENCOMPASSED by a thousand nameless fears,
I see life's little day begin to wane,
And hear the well-loved voices call in vain
Across the narrowing margin of my years;
And as the Valley of the Shadow nears,
Such yearning tides of tenderness and pain
Sweep over me that I can scarce restrain
The gathering flood of ineffectual tears.

Yet there are moments when the shadows bring
No sense of parting or approaching night,
But, rather, all my soul seems broadening
Before the dawn of unimagined light—
As if within the heart a folded wing
Were making ready for a wider flight.

Thomas O'Hagan

Of the merits of the poems it is only necessary to say that while most of the poetry of our day seems to have buried itself in obscurity, Mr. O'Hagan's poems come freely from the thought and imagination . . . . and can be understood by any person of intelligence, who is fond of poetry and believes that it springs from the heart . . . . and the best wishes of all will be that the immortality which we all so ardently crave, may crown his efforts to endow mankind with sweetest and purest sentiments.—HON. JUSTICE LONGLEY, D.C.L., LL.D.

Tenderness, piety, friendship, filial affection, love that conquers death and lasts beyond the grave, the call of the 'Settlement,' loyalty to the college that has been the poet's Alma Mater: all these we have in Dr. O'Hagan's volume, 'In the Heart of the Meadow,' and not often in recent years have they been more poetically or more gracefully phrased.—P. J. LENNOX, LITT.D., Washington, D.C.

THOMAS O'HAGAN, the youngest son of John and Bridget (O'Reilly) O'Hagan, natives of County Kerry, Ireland, was born in 'the Gore of Toronto,' on the 6th of March, 1855, and was a babe in arms, when his parents, three brothers, a sister and himself, moved into the wilderness of the county of Bruce, Ontario. They located in the township of Elderslie, three miles from the village of Paisley. The other settlers were mostly Highland Scotch, and Thomas as a lad learned to speak quite fluently not only the Gaelic tongue of his neighbours, but also the Keltic Irish, which was spoken freely by his parents. He attended the public school of the settlement where the teachers were Scotch, and where he applied himself with such diligence and ability that he won a Second Class Teacher's Certificate at the early age of sixteen.

Few Canadians have devoted so much time to academic study as Dr. O'Hagan. After graduating from St. Michael's College, a prize winner in Latin and English, he entered the Ottawa University and graduated B.A., in 1882, with honours in English, Latin, French and German. Three years later the same University conferred on him the degree of M.A. In 1889, he received the degree of Ph.D. from Syracuse University; and in subsequent years took postgraduate work at Cornell, Columbia, Chicago, Louvain, Grenoble and Fribourg Universities. In September, 1914, Laval University, Montreal, conferred on him the honorary degree of Litt.D.

During his young manhood he taught for some years in Separate Schools and High Schools of Ontario.

Dr. O'Hagan is widely known as a scholarly and popular lecturer on many literary themes.

Recently (1910-13), he was Chief Editor and Director of the *New World,* Chicago, but is now resident in Toronto.

The following is a list of Dr. O'Hagan's books of verse: *A Gate of Flowers,* 1887; *In Dreamland and Other Poems,* 1893; *Songs of the Settlement,* 1899; *In the heart of the Meadow,* 1914; and *Songs of Heroic Days,* 1916. He has also published several volumes of interesting and instructive essays: *Studies in Poetry; Canadian Essays; Essays Literary, Critical and Historical; Chats by the Fireside;* and, in 1916, *Essays of Catholic Life.*

An Idyl of the Farm

O THERE'S joy in every sphere of life from cottage unto
  throne,
But the sweetest smiles of nature beam upon the farm alone;
And in memory I go back to the days of long ago,
When the teamster shouted 'Haw, Buck!' 'Gee!' 'G'lang!'
    and 'Whoa!'

I see out in the logging-field the heroes of our land,
With their strong and sturdy faces, each with handspike in
    his hand;
With shoulders strong as Hercules, they feared no giant foe,
As the teamster shouted 'Haw, Buck!' 'Gee!' 'G'lang!' and
    'Whoa!'

The logging-bees are over, and the woodlands all are cleared,
The face that then was young and fair is silvered o'er with
    beard;
The handspike now holds not the place it did long years ago,
When the teamster shouted 'Haw, Buck!' 'Gee!' 'G'lang!' and
    'Whoa!'

On meadow land and orchard field there rests a glory round,
Sweet as the memory of the dead that haunts some holy
    ground;
And yet there's wanting to my heart some joy of long ago,
When the teamster shouted 'Haw, Buck!' 'Gee!' 'G'lang!'
    and 'Whoa!'

Demosthenes had silvery tongue, and Cicero knew Greek,
The Gracchi brothers loved old Rome and always helped the
    weak;
But there's not a Grecian hero, nor Roman high or low,
Whose heart spake braver patriot words than 'Gee!' 'G'lang!'
    and 'Whoa!'

They wore no coat of armour, the boys in twilight days—
They sang no classic music, but the old 'Come all ye' lays;
For armed with axe and handspike, each giant tree their foe,
They rallied to the battle-cry of 'Gee!' 'G'lang!' and 'Whoa!'

12

And so they smote the forest down, and rolled the logs in
    heaps,
And brought our country to the front in mighty strides and
    leaps;
And left upon the altar of each home wherein you go,
Some fragrance of the flowers that bloom through 'Gee!'
    'G'lang!' and 'Whoa!'

The Old Brindle Cow

OF all old memories that cluster round my heart,
    With their root in my boyhood days,
The quaintest is linked to the old brindle cow
    With sly and mysterious ways.
She'd linger round the lot near the old potato patch,
    A sentinel by night and by day,
Watching for the hour when all eyes were asleep,
    To start on her predatory way.

The old brush fence she would scorn in her course,
    With turnips and cabbage just beyond,
And corn that was blooming through the halo of the night—
    What a banquet so choice and so fond!
But when the stars of morn were paling in the sky
    The old brindle cow would take the cue,
And dressing up her line she'd retreat beyond the fence,
    For the old cow knew just what to do.

What breed did you say? Why the very best blood
    That could flow in a democratic cow;
No herd-book could tell of the glory in her horns
    Or whence came her pedigree or how:
She was Jersey in her milk and Durham in her build,
    And Ayrshire when she happened in a row,
But when it came to storming the old 'slash' fence
    She was simply the old brindle cow.

It seems but a day since I drove her to the gate
    To yield up her rich and creamy prize;
For her theft at midnight hour she would yield a double dower,
    With peace of conscience lurking in her eyes.

But she's gone—disappeared with the ripened years of time,
  Whose memories my heart enthrall e'en now;
And I never hear a bell tinkling through the forest dell
  But I think of that old brindle cow.

The Dance at McDougall's

IN a little log house near the rim of the forest
  With its windows of sunlight, its threshold of stone,
Lived Donald McDougall, the quaintest of Scotchmen,
  And Janet his wife, in their shanty, alone:
By day the birds sang them a chorus of welcome,
  At night they saw Scotland again in their dreams;
They toiled full of hope 'mid the sunshine of friendship,
  Their hearts leaping onward like troutlets in streams,
          In the little log home of McDougall's.

At evening the boys and the girls would all gather
  To dance and to court 'neath McDougall's rooftree;
They were wild as the tide that rushes up Solway
  When lashed by the tempests that sweep the dark sea:
There Malcolm and Flora and Angus and Katie
  With laughter-timed paces came tripping along,
And Pat, whose gay heart had been nursed in Old Erin,
  Would link each Scotch reel with a good Irish song,
          Down at the dance at McDougall's.

For the night was as day at McDougall's log shanty,
  The blaze on the hearth shed its halo around,
While the feet that tripped lightly the reel 'Tullagorum,'
  Pattered each measure with 'ooch!' and with bound;
No 'Lancers' nor 'Jerseys' were danced at McDougall's,
  Nor the latest waltz-step found a place on the floor,
But reels and strathspeys and the liveliest hornpipes
  Shook the room to its centre from fireplace to door,
          In the little log house at McDougall's.

Gone now is the light in McDougall's log shanty,
  The blaze on the hearth long has sunk into gloom,
And Donald and Janet who dreamed of 'Auld Scotia'
  Are dreaming of Heaven in the dust of the tomb.

While the boys and the girls—the 'balachs' and 'calahs'—
  Who toiled during day and danced through the night,
Live again in bright dreams of Memory's morning
  When their hearts beat to music of life, love and light,
       Down at the dance at McDougall's.

The Song My Mother Sings

O SWEET unto my heart is the song my mother sings
  As eventide is brooding on its dark and noiseless wings;
Every note is charged with memory—every memory bright
    with rays
Of the golden hours of promise in the lap of chidhood's days;
The orchard blooms anew and each blossom scents the way,
And I feel again the breath of eve among the new-mown hay;
While through the halls of memory in happy notes there rings
All the life-joy of the past in the song my mother sings.

I have listened to the dreamy notes of Chopin and of Liszt,
As they dripped and drooped about my heart and filled my
    eyes with mist;
I have wept strong tears of pathos 'neath the spell of Verdi's
    power,
As I heard the tenor voice of grief from out the donjon tower;
And Gounod's oratorios are full of notes sublime
That stir the heart with rapture through the sacred pulse of
    time;
But all the music of the past and the wealth that memory brings
Seem as nothing when I listen to the song my mother sings.

It's a song of love and triumph, it's a song of toil and care;
It is filled with chords of pathos and it's set in notes of prayer;
It is bright with dreams and visions of the days that are to be,
And as strong in faith's devotion as the heart-beat of the sea;
It is linked in mystic measure to sweet voices from above,
And is starred with ripest blessing through a mother's sacred
    love;
Oh, sweet and strong and tender are the memories that it
    brings,
As I list in joy and rapture to the song my mother sings.

Ripened Fruit

I KNOW not what my heart hath lost;
  I cannot strike the chords of old;
The breath that charmed my morning life
  Hath chilled each leaf within the wold.

The swallows twitter in the sky,
  But bare the nest within the eaves;
The fledglings of my care are gone,
  And left me but the rustling leaves.

And yet, I know my life hath strength,
  And firmer hope and sweeter prayer,
For leaves that murmur on the ground
  Have now for me a double care.

I see in them the hope of spring,
  That erst did plan the autumn day;
I see in them each gift of man
  Grow strong in years, then turn to clay.

Not all is lost—the fruit remains
  That ripened through the summer's ray;
The nurslings of the nest are gone,
  Yet hear we still their warbling lay.

The glory of the summer sky
  May change to tints of autumn hue;
But faith that sheds its amber light
  Will lend our heaven a tender blue.

O altar of eternal youth!
  O faith that beckons from afar,
Give to our lives a blossomed fruit—
  Give to our morns an evening star!

The Bugle Call

DO you hear the call of our Mother
  From over the sea, from over the sea?
The call to her children in every land;
To her sons on Afric's far-stretched veldt;
To her dark-skinned children on India's shore,
Whose souls are nourished on Aryan lore;
To her sons of the Northland where frosty stars

Glitter and shine like a helmet of Mars;
   Do you hear the call of our Mother?

Do you hear the call of our Mother
   From over the sea, from over the sea?
The call to Australia's legions strong,
That move with the might and stealth of a wave;
To the men of the camp and men of the field,
Whose courage has taught them never to yield;
To the men whose counsel has saved the State
And thwarted the plans of impending fate;
   Do you hear the call of our Mother?

Do you hear the call of our Mother
   From over the sea, from over the sea?
To the little cot on the wind-swept hill;
To the lordly hall in the city street;
To her sons who toil in the forest deep
Or bind the sheaves where the reapers reap;
To her children scattered far East and West;
To her sons who joy in her Freedom Blest;
   Do you hear the call of our Mother?

The Chrism of Kings

IN the morn of the world, at the day break of time,
When kingdoms were few and empires unknown,
God searched for a Ruler to sceptre the land,
   And gather the harvest from the seed He had sown.
He found a young shepherd boy watching his flock
   Where the mountains looked down on deep meadows of
      green;
He hailed the young shepherd boy king of the land
   And anointed his brow with a Chrism unseen.

He placed in his frail hands the sceptre of power,
   And taught his young heart all the wisdom of love;
He gave him the vision of prophet and priest,
   And dowered him with counsel and light from above.
But alas! came a day when the shepherd forgot
   And heaped on his realm all the woes that war brings,
And bartering his purple for the greed of his heart
   He lost both the sceptre and Chrism of Kings.

Elizabeth Roberts MacDonald

The old Rectory of Fredericton, N.B., has been aptly called 'A Nest of Singing Birds,' for it was there that the four brothers and one sister of the famous Roberts' family were fledglings; it was there they tried their eager wings in many flights of imagination, and piped their new and tuneful songs.

Elizabeth Roberts was born in the Rectory of Westcock, N.B., February 17th, 1864, and was educated at the Collegiate School, Fredericton, and at the New Brunswick University. She taught for a time in the School for the Blind, Halifax, N.S. Poems of hers have appeared in the 'Century,' the 'Independent,' 'Outing' and other prominent magazines, and in 1906, her book, 'Dream Verses and Others,' was published. She has the instinctive knowledge and love of nature and the exquisite fancy and touch, so characteristic of this family.

Mrs. MacDonald is the author also of 'Our Little Canadian Cousin,' a popular child's story, and has written many charming essays and short stories.—The Editor.

[221]

MRS. C. F. FRASER has written beautifully in *East and West* of the old Fredericton Rectory and its happy, brilliant inmates, of which I quote:

The gift in which so many have thus happily participated is in great degree a matter of happy inheritance. 'Dear Rector Roberts'—for so, irrespective of creed, a whole town styled him—was a cultivated, scholarly gentleman of old English descent. So devoted was he to his chosen work of service to others, so companionable was he with all his helpful goodness, so constant was he to his vision of the ideal, that it was truly said of him when he was laid to rest, that his whole life had been a veritable path of light. The maiden name of his widow, Emma Wetmore Bliss, is suggestive of a fine loyalist stock which has given scholars, lawyers and judges to succeeding generations. Wise, gracious, purposeful, ambitious always for the best efforts of her children, and patient as only mothers can be, she entered as wholly as did her husband into the literary pursuits of her gifted offspring.

Of winter evenings the favourite gathering place was about the great centre table in the sitting-room, where the young people were wont to read aloud for each other's amusement or edification the rhymes or stories which the day had called forth. Spirited discussions frequently arose, but the utmost good humour prevailed and final decisions on most questions were sought and accepted from the father's store of wit and erudition, or from the quiet mother seemingly so fully occupied with the contents of her great mending basket. Bright brains sharpened bright brains, and thus, all unconsciously, the informal gathering gave a training which no school or carefully planned course of study could have achieved. . . . . . In summer weather the great old-fashioned garden, haunt of all fragrant and time-forgotten flowers, was the favourite meeting place. There, in and about the hammocks, with their cousin, Bliss Carman, extending his great length on the turf below, and shaggy Nestor, wisest and most understanding of household dogs, wandering about from one to another for a friendly word or pat, and a score of half-tamed wild birds fluttering and twittering in the trees above, the young people did indeed see visions and dream dreams. It is of this scented garden that Elizabeth, the sister, who though too fragile to companion her stirring brothers in the active sports in which they delighted, and yet their leader when the elysian pastures were to be attained, sings so beautifully in her book, *Dream Verses and Others.*

Staff Sergeant S. A. R. MacDonald, husband of Elizabeth Roberts, is in charge of the Dispensary of the Canadian Special Hospital at Ramsgate, England. Of this marriage, the eldest of two sons, Cuthbert Goodridge, is already contributing to magazines.

IN the original copy, the following poems from *Dream Verses and Others* were included by consent of the author: 'Voices,' 'The Spell of the Forest,' 'The House Among the Firs,' 'The Fire of the Frost,' 'White Magic,' 'The Signal-Smokes' and 'Dreamhurst.' But as permission to use them could not be procured from her Boston publisher, Mrs. Mac-Donald kindly sent us these new poems for insertion:

The Whispering Poplars

I HEAR the whispering poplars
  In the hollow by my door;
They sound like fairy waters
  Beside a magic shore,
They sound like long-lost secrets
  Of childhood's golden lore,—
The murmuring, nodding poplars
  In the hollow by my door.

All night they talk together
  Beneath the silent sky;
The mountains crouch beyond them,
  The blue lake sleeps near by,—
But still the silver, sibilant
  Small voices laugh and sigh,
Talking all night together
  Beneath the silent sky.

Flood-Tide

WHEN the sea sobs by lonely shores,
  Bleak shores, with shattered boulders strown,
When the dark wind my soul implores
  And claims me for its own,—

How weak, how frail the bars that part
  This hour from unforgotten years;
The dykes of time are down; my heart
  Is swept with love and tears.

Mountain-Ash

ALL the hills are dark,
  Sombre clouds afloat;
Sunlight, not a spark,
  Birdsong, not a note;
Only, through the blight,
Facing winter's night,
  Flaunts the mountain-ash
Scarlet berries bright.

Like a flame of love,
  Like a lilt of song
Lifted sheer above
  Cares that press and throng,
Through the darkling day,—
Scarlet set in grey—
  Splendid mountain-ash
Gleams along the way.

March Wind

THE dark Spring storm swept up
  From some forgotten shore,
The rain beat on my window
  The same tune o'er and o'er,
And the wind, the maker of poets,
  Sobbed at my door.

'Give me thy heart,' he cried,
  'To blow from sea to sea,
To fill with lonely fear,
  To taunt with bitter glee;
Give me thy heart; I'll give
  My song to thee.'

Now nay, but Love forbid!
  What comes my heart must bear,
But forth on sorrow's trail
  In truth it shall not fare,
Nor would I learn the song
  Hope may not share.

But all night long the wind
  Sobbed, and would not forget
Its burden of by-gone years,
  Sadness, and vain regret,—
O longing heart, what goal
  For thee is set?

Harvest

RICH days there are when wisdom, love, and dream
Leave their high heaven and close beside us keep,
With comrade-steps, from dawn to happy sleep;
When golden lights on paths familiar gleam,
And life's strong river leaps, a singing stream,
Through countless wonders toward a mystic deep;
When every field has gold for thought to reap,
And faint and far life's wintry troubles seem,

This wheat of gladness garner, oh my heart;
With songs of gladness bring the harvest home
And under sheltering eaves its bounty store,—
Then, when the snows drift deep about your door
And grey wolf-winds through desolate woodlands roam,
To all who need, the magic hoard impart.

Reassurance

NOW lucent splendours, amethyst and gold
And clearest emerald, flood the western sky,
Though all day long dark clouds were heaped on high
And angry winds went racing, icy-cold;
But calm has come with sunset, and behold
Where late the pageantry of storm went by,
What dream-bright majesties of colour lie
Across the solemn depths of space unrolled.

All beautiful things the heart of man can dream,
Deep joy unfaltering, love fulfilled that fears
No parting evermore nor any tears,
Youth's dear desires like beacon-lights that gleam,—
When sunset's luminous miracle appears
How sure, how close those heights of gladness seem!

The Shepherd

AMONG the hills of night my thoughts
Go wandering lost and lorn;
No rest they find, or gleam of light
To solace them till morn;
Stumbling they fare, and know not where
Safe pasturage to win;
O Shepherd Sleep, across the steep
Go out and call them in!

An errant flock, they follow far
By bitter pools of tears,
Lured on by Memory's lonely voice
And tracked by stealthy fears;
But wanderings cease, doubt sinks in peace,
If once the fold they win;
O Shepherd Sleep, across the steep
Go out and call them in!

A Madrigal

SPRING went by with laughter
Down the greening hills,
Singing lyric snatches,
Crowned with daffodils;
Now, by breath of roses
As the soft day closes
Know that April's promise
June fulfills.

Youth goes by with gladness
Faery woodlands through,
Led by starry visions,
Fed with honey-dew;
Life, who dost forever
Urge the high endeavor,
Grant that all the dreaming
Time brings true!

Albert D. Watson

There is no rhetorical aping of a style above his degree, but the honest and genuine expression in language always dignified, frequently distinguished, and at times most felicitous of thoughts, which, to a large extent didactic, are yet illumined with the creative power of life itself. . . . . 'His word was a white light,' he says, in speaking of 'The Crusader,' in a line which may be the most eloquent in the book, and it may be applied to Dr. Watson's own work. His word is a white light, and its purity is lacking neither in warmth nor strength. . . . . But the greater part of the volume is given to a group of biographical sketches in monologue form, entitled 'The Immortals,' where twenty-six of the great ones of earth who have appealed to Dr. Watson's imagination and sympathies, are made to summarize their life and times by a flash-like glimpse. That there is really notable work here is unquestionable, and the catholic sympathies of the poet are evident in the widely varying subjects chosen.—ALBERT E. STAFFORD, in the 'Sunday World,' Toronto.

[227]

POETIC genius is necessarily innate—it cannot be acquired. But given the genius, assiduous effort can greatly develop the beauty, strength and music of its expression. This can be seen clearly by a comparison of Dr. Albert D. Watson's first and second books of verse. *The Wing of the Wild-Bird* was published in 1908, and while it contains a few poems of merit, the work as a whole is not notable. Five years later appeared his *Love and the Universe, the Immortals and Other Poems,* a book of such value that it placed him at once among the greater poets of Canada.

Albert Durrant Watson, M.D.; L.R.C.P.(Edin.) was born in Dixie, county of Peel, Ontario, the 8th of January, 1859, —the youngest son of the late William Youle and Mary A. (Aldred) Watson. His maternal grandfather fought in Wellington's cavalry in the Peninsula and at Waterloo.

Dr. Watson was educated at the Toronto Normal School, and at Victoria and Edinburgh Universities, and for more than thirty years has practised his profession in the city of Toronto. During this period, he has found time also for much public service in connection with important official positions, and is now President of the Royal Astronomical Society of Canada, and Treasurer of the Social Service Department of the Methodist Church.

In September, 1885, Dr. Watson was married to Sarah, a daughter of the late Samuel Clare, of Toronto. Mrs. Watson is interested in sculpture and has developed artistically in clay-modelling.

Two prose works of merit have added to the reputation of this author,—*The Sovereignty of Ideals,* published in 1904, and *The Sovereignty of Character: Lessons from the Life of Jesus,* in 1906. The latter, one of the noblest of readable books, was republished in 1914, in London, England.

A third prose work, *Three Comrades of Jesus,* will be issued before the close of 1916.

His national hymn, written, in 1915, for the melody, 'O Canada' together with five other selections from his sacred poems, are included in the new Methodist Hymnal.

Dr. and Mrs. Watson have three sons and two daughters. One son is in the Imperial Transport Service,—aircraft defence.

Dream-Valley

I KNOW a vale where the oriole swings
    Her nest to the breeze and the sky,
The iris opens her petal wings
    And a brooklet ripples by;
In the far blue is a cloud-drift,
    And the witch-tree dresses,
With a rare charm in the warm light,
    Her long dream-tresses.

But yestermorn—or was it a dream?
    When daisies were drinking the dew,
I wandered down by the little stream,
    And who was there but you?
Though nature smiled with the old joy
    To the boldest comer,
It was your voice and the wild-bird's
    Were the soul of summer.

When bowed with the toils of many years,
    I would rest, if it be Love's will,
In a vale where the bird songs to my ears
    Come floating across the hill,
With the sweet breath of the June air
    And the purple clover,
And the lone dream of the old love,
    And the blue skies over.

From 'Love and the Universe'

THE voiceless symphony of moor and highland,
    The rainbow on the mist,
The white moon-shield above the slumber-island,
    The mirror-lake, star-kist,
The life of budding leaf and spray and branches,
    The dew upon the sod,
The roar of downward-rushing avalanches,
    Are eloquent of God.

My eye sweeps far-extended plains of vision
    And golden seas of light;

Upon my ear fall cadences elysian,
  Like music in the night;
But all the glories to my sense appealing
  Can no such raptures win
As come with majesty and joy of healing
  From love and light within.

How shall the Universe its own creation,
  Life of its life, destroy?
How bring to nothingness of desolation
  The soul of its own joy?
The echo of itself, not merely fashioned
  Of clay, God's outer part,
But fibre of His being, love-impassioned,
  The glory of His heart!

Drive on, then, Winds of God, drive on forever
  Across the shoreless sea;
The soul's a boundless deep, exhausted never
  By full discovery.
The atmosphere and storms, the roll of ocean,
  The paths by planets trod,
Are time-expressions of a Soul's emotion,
  Are will and thought of God.
In storm or calm, that soundless ocean sweeping
  Is still the sailor's goal;
The destiny of every man is leaping
  To birth in his own soul.

Breeze and Billow

A FAIR blue sky,
   A far blue sea,
Breeze o'er the billows blowing!
The deeps of night o'er the waters free,
With mute appeal to the soul of me
In billows and breezes flowing;

The stars that watch
While sunbeams sleep,
Breeze o'er the billows blowing!

The soft-winged zephyrs that move the deep
And rock my barque in a dreamy sweep;
The moonlight softly glowing;

The glint of wave,
The gleam of star,
Breeze o'er the billows blowing!
The surf-line music on beach and bar,
The voice of nature near and far,
The night into morning growing;

And I afloat
With canvas free,
Breeze o'er the billows blowing!
At one with the heart of eternity,
The fair blue sky and the far blue sea,—
And the breeze o'er the billows blowing.

The Comet

SPECTRAL, mysterious, flame-like thing
Cleaving the western night,
Waking from chrysalis-dream to fling
Out of thy spirit's long chastening
Far-flashing streams of light,

Tell us thy thought of the things that are;
How doth the morning sing?
What hast thou seen in the worlds afar?
Tell us thy dream, O thou silvery star,
Bird with the white-flame wing.

What though the glow of thy fading ray
Dim and elusive seem,
Constant thou art to the sun's bright sway
Faithful and true in thy tireless way,
True in thy spectral gleam.

Rising anew from thine ancient pyre,
Vapour and dust thy frame,
Still art thou Psyche, the soul's desire,
Wingless, save when from reefs of fire
Mounting in shaft of flame.

The Sacrament

THE World was builded out of flame and storm.
The oak, blast-beaten on the hills, stands forth,
Stalwart and strong. The ore is broken, crushed
And sifted in the fiery crucible;
The remnant is pure gold. Brave hearts must dare
The billowy surge beneath the stern white stars
To net the finny harvests of the sea.
No boon is won, but some true hero dies.

Therefore is every gift a sacrament,
And every service is a holy thing,—
Not unto him whose filthy pence unearned
The treasure buys, but to the one who takes
The gift with reverence from that unknown
Who went forth brave and strong, came broken back,
But won for us a rare and priceless pearl.

The Lily

EMBLEM of beauty and sorrow,
Twine with each wistful to-morrow
The past with its memories teeming
And all its dear innocent dreaming.
    Go thou, O Lily, and o'er her cast
The drifting breath of the wind-swept hills;
Sing her the music of forest rills;
    Whisper a dream of the sacred past;
Lie on her heart till the angels wake
Her deathless love for the old time's sake.

    Still to that love I am turning
    Though beyond reach of my yearning;
        And never the vision shall vanish
        Nor time nor eternity banish
    That dream so splendid of love and tears
    That still transfigures the lonely years.

Go, Lily, go with my love and lie
Close to her heart and never die;

To her with my love I bequeath you,
Fair as the glow of the golden sky
When twilight falls and the breezes sigh,
  Sweet as the bosom beneath you,
Pure as the dew on the glistening sod,
White as the snowflake, perfect as God.

God and Man

GOD is eternity, the sky, the sea,
  The consciousness of universal space,
  The source of energy and living grace,
Of life and light, of love and destiny,
God is that deep, ethereal ocean, free,
  Whose billows keep their wide unbarriered place
  Amid the stars that move before His face
In robes of hurricane and harmony.

A light that twinkles in a distant star,
  A wave of ocean surging on the shore,
  One substance with the sea; a wing to soar
Forever onward to the peaks afar,
  A soul to love, a mind to learn God's plan,
  A child of the eternal—such is man.

A Prayer

O THOU whose finger-tips,
    From out the unveiled universe around,
  Can touch my human lips
With harmonies beyond the range of sound;

  Whose living word,
All vital truth revealing,
  My soul hath stirred
To raptures holy, comforting and healing;

  Beneath, around, above,
Breathe on me atmospheres
  Of universal Love—
The music of the timeless years;

Upon my soul,
Pour vast eternities of might,
Up through my being roll
Deep seas of light
To urge me onward to the Goal,
The Infinite, the Whole.

From ' The Hills of Life '

ERE yet the dawn
Pushed rosy fingers up the arch of day
And smiled its promise to the voiceless prime,
Love sat and patterns wove at life's great loom.

He flung the suns into the soundless arch,
Appointed them their courses in the deep,
To keep His great time-harmonies, and blaze
As beacons in the ebon fields of night.
Love balanced them and held them firm and true,
Poised 'twixt attractive and repulsive drift
Amid the throngs of heaven. What though this power
Was ever known to us as gravity,
Its first and last celestial name is Love.

Love spake the word omnipotent, and lo!
Upon the distant and mid deep, the earth
Was flung, robed in blue skies and summer lands,
Green-garlanded with leaves and bright with flowers,
While songsters fluttered in the rosy skies.
But sometimes, moaning through the dark-leaved pines,
Or sobbing down the lonely shores of time,
Or wailing in the tempest-arch of night,
Love moved unresting and unsatisfied.
The faces of the hills in beauty smiled,
The night's deep vault blazed with configured stars,
Fair nature throbbed through all her frame of light,
And everywhere was Love's fine energy;

But fields and forests, flowers and firmaments
Had not attained to understand the throb
And thrill of life, so Love made human hearts
That mightily could feel and understand;

Made them his constant home, centre and sweep,
Channel and instrument of life and truth,
The word of God on earth, Love's other self,
The high ambassadors of truth and light;
And Love was free where Life was wholly true.

Cromwell

SAY not to me:
'Cromwell, thou diest.' Save thy timid breath.
Do not the wild winds noise it o'er the world?
Shall he alone who made God's word his guide
And put the yoke of England on the seas
Not know the face of death when all God's foes
Whisper and say: 'The Lord Protector dies'?

Suppose ye he will tremble, gasp, turn pale,
At hint of death, which he so often dared?
Life's shuttle drifts across the web of time,
And if posterity see but one strand
Of purpose fair, or trace amid the woof
One feeble pattern to some worthy end,
Life was not vain. My sword my spokesman was;
It speaks no more, yet all the world doth know
It curbed the pride of kings.

                    Play not the role
Of simulated tears, but draw ye near,
For there are some words still Cromwell would say,
Even though his word be silent. Nearer still,
Lest nature's furious voice baffle your ears
With roaring winds and thunders pierced with fire.
The toils of state—these do not matter much;
But that the people love not righteousness,
Know not reality, bowing their souls
To musty precedents—that matters much.
That warders of the realm would still with words
The groans that from the battle's whirlwind call,
With paper promises and inky lies
Would heal the hurt of England, matters more.
That they whose thought doth show no real fact;
Whose words show something other than their thought;

13

Whose office, tricked with gaudy trappings, struts
So loud with blare of brass they cannot hear
The voice of God; so big with littleness,
They cannot see the lawful rights of man—
That matters all.

                  This too remember well—
I learned it late: None but a tyrant makes
That good prevail that is not in men's hearts,
And tyranny is questionable good.
Therefore must all men learn by liberty,
And with what pain their doings on them bring.

Give these my words to those who care to hear;
My thanks to you that ye report them true,
And for your patience now. I cannot hear
Your words, nor can I more, so stand apart,
That, undistracted by the storms of state
Or any human presence, I may come
Before the King of kings in hope and faith
For pardon of my sins.

Usury

HEIR to the wealth of all the storied past,
    A thousand generations pour their life
      Into this heart of mine;
'Twere base indeed if these should be the last,
  Life's standard bearing in some noble strife,
    To advance the battle line.

Let life grow richer by its cost to me,
  Till hope, too strong for dream of weak despair,
    Seize each momentous goal;
No monster of chimeric mystery,
  Or fabled horror with its deathful stare,
    Palsy my dauntless soul.

Lord of this heritage of life and hope,
  Dowered with what gifts the ages could achieve
    By dint of toil and tears,
I, in my turn, with some new problem cope,
  And gratefully the sure solution leave
    For all the coming years.

Isabel Ecclestone Mackay

Mrs. Isabel Ecclestone Mackay is one of the cleverest writers we have. She is a Vancouver lady, one whose work both in prose and verse is finding a high place in the United States and in England. In prose she displays a keen, analytical mind, a genius for new ideas, and a style that is easy and convincing. In poetry she has a philosophic turn, an artful and subtle conception of a circumstance. On the other hand, as a writer in a beautiful lyrical style, she has few superiors in these days.—'Canadian Magazine.'

It is perhaps not too much to say that no other Canadian writer is producing work equal in strength, beauty and balance, to that of Mrs. Mackay.—'Toronto Daily News,'—editorially.

Mrs. Mackay has a sensitive ear for the music of words and an instinctive feeling for rhythm. She has both imagination and humour, and a keen appreciation of the wonderful and the beautiful.—JOHN MARKEY, editor of the 'Sentinel-Review,' Woodstock, Ontario.

TO her teachers and classmates, in the Woodstock schools, she was known as 'Bell MacPherson,' and many remember vividly her eager, glowing face,—her warm, sensitive heart. She was so ready to work, so ambitious to achieve, so happy to have pleased. These qualities, together with the natural tendency to write, have given her the proud position she holds to-day. There has been another strong motive force in her career, since her marriage,—*her love of children.* 'There is nothing so sweet as a baby,' she will tell you, and indeed the Madonna passion has inspired and coloured much of her prose, and not a little of her verse.

Isabel Ecclestone Mackay was born in Woodstock, Ontario, November 25th, 1875,—a daughter of Donald McLeod MacPherson, a native of Scotland, and his wife, Priscilla Ecclestone, of England. She was educated in the local public schools and Collegiate Institute. In April, 1895, she married Mr. P. J. Mackay, Court Stenographer, and is now the mother of three interesting daughters,—Phyllis, Margaret, and Janet Priscilla.

Mrs. Mackay's work has appeared in *Cassel's, Harper's, Scribners', Independent, McClure's, St. Nicholas, Youth's Companion, Red Book, Life, Ainslee's, Smart Set, Metropolitan, Canadian Magazine,* and other periodicals of note. In 1904, she published a book of verse, *Between the Lights,* but most of her magazine verse, since, has been of much higher quality, —in originality of thought, constructive imagination, and artistic expression. Her two poems, 'Marguerite de Roberval,' and 'The Passing of Cadieux'—each of which won for the author, $100.00, in the *Globe's* prize-poem competitions—stand out for their excellence of treatment of those historic themes. Serial stories of merit from her pen have appeared in the *Canadian Courier* and the *Canadian Home Journal,* and in 1912, Cassell & Co. brought out, *The House of Windows,* a novel, of which *The Anthenæum* said: 'Possesses a charm of fresh straightforwardness; the pictures of life are vivid and well drawn'; and the London *Times:* 'An enjoyable tale, of much fresh, wholesome sentiment'.

Mrs. Mackay has recently completed a new novel, '*Yesterday's Servant,*' which will be published soon. A second volume of her poems may also be looked for at an early date.

The Mother

LAST night he lay within my arm,
　So small, so warm, a mystery
　To which God only held the key—
But mine to keep from fear and harm!

Ah! He was all my own, last night,
　With soft, persuasive, baby eyes,
　So wondering and yet so wise,
And hands that held my finger tight.

Why was it that he could not stay—
　Too rare a gift? Yet who could hold
　A treasure with securer fold
Than I, to whom love taught the way?

As with a flood of golden light
　The first sun tipped earth's golden rim,
　So all my world grew bright with him
And with his going fell the night—

O God, is there an angel arm
　More strong, more tender than the rest?
　Lay Thou my baby on his breast,
To keep him safe from fear and harm!

Out of Babylon

THEIR looks for me are bitter,
　And bitter is their word—
I may not glance behind unseen,
　I may not sigh unheard!

So fare we forth from Babylon,
　Along the road of stone;
And none looks back to Babylon
　Save I—save I alone!

My mother's eyes are glory-filled,
　Save when they fall on me;
The shining of my father's face
　I tremble when I see.

For they were slaves in Babylon,
　And now they're walking free—

They leave their chains in Babylon,
    I bear my chains with me!

At night a sound of singing
    The vast encampment fills;
'Jerusalem! Jerusalem!'
    It sweeps the nearing hills—

But no one sings of Babylon,—
    Their home of yesterday—
And no one prays for Babylon,
    And I—I dare not pray!

Last night the Prophet saw me,
    And while he held me there
The holy fire within his eyes
    Burned all my secret bare.

'What! Sigh you so for Babylon?'
    (I turned away my face)
'Here's one who turns to Babylon,
    Heart-traitor to her race!'

I follow and I follow,
    My heart upon the rack!
I follow to Jerusalem—
    The long road stretches back

To Babylon, to Babylon!
    And every step I take
Bears farther off from Babylon
    A heart that cannot break!

Marguerite de Roberval

O THE long days and nights! The days that bring
    No sunshine that my shrinking soul can bear,
The nights that soothe not. All the airs of France,
Soft and sun-steeped, that once were breath of life,
Now stir no magic in me. I could weep—
Yet can I never weep—to see the land
That is my land no more! For where the soul
Doth dwell and the heart linger, there
Alone can be the native land, and I have left

Behind me one small spot of barren earth
That is my hold on heav'n!

     You bid me tell
My story? That were hard. I have no art
And all my words have long been lost amid
The greater silences. The birds—they knew
My grief, nor did I feel the need of speech
To make my woe articulate to the wind!
If my tale halts, know 'tis the want of words
And not the want of truth.

       'Twas long, you say?
Yes, yet at first it seemed not long. We watched
The ship recede, nor vexed them with a prayer.
Was not his arm about me? Did he not
Stoop low to whisper in my tingling ear?
The little Demon-island was our world,
So all the world was ours—no brighter sphere
That swung into our ken in purple heaven
Was half so fair a world! We were content.
Was he not mine? And I (he whispered this)
The only woman on love's continent!
How can I tell my story? Would you care
To hear of those first days? I cannot speak
Of them—they lie asleep so soft within
My heart a word would wake them? I'll not speak that word!

      There came at last a golden day
When in my arms I held mine own first-born,
And my new world held three. And then I knew,
Mid joy so great, a passion of despair!
I knew our isle was barren, girt with foam
And torn with awful storm. I knew the cold,
The bitter, cruel cold! My tender babe,
What love could keep him warm? Beside my couch
Pale famine knelt with outstretched, greedy hand,
To snatch my treasure from me. Ah, I knew,
I knew what fear was then!

     We fought it back,
That ghost of chill despair. He whom I loved

Fought bravely, as a man must fight who sees
His wife and child defenceless. But I knew—
E'en from the first—the unequal strife would prove
Too long, the fear too keen! It wore his strength
And in his eyes there grew the look of one
Who grapples time, and will not let it go,
Yet feels it slipping, slipping—

        Ah, my dear!
I saw you die, and could not help or save—
Knowing myself to be the awful care
That weighed thee to thy grave!

        The world held two
Now—one so frail and small, and one made strong
By love and weak by fear. That little life!
It trembled in my arms like some small flame
Of candle in a stealthy draught that blows
And blows again—one never knows from whence,
Yet feareth always—till at last, at last,
A darkness falls! So came the dark to me—
And it was night indeed!

        Beside my love
I laid my lovely babe. And all fear fled;
For where joy is there only can fear be.
They fear not who have nothing left to fear!

    .   .   .   .   .

So that is all my tale. I lived, I live
And shall live on, no doubt. The changeful sky
Is blue in France, and I am young—think you
I am still young! Though joy has come and passed
And I am gazing after with dull eyes!

One day there came a sail. It drew near
And found me on my island, all alone—
That island that had once held all the world—
They succoured me and bought me back again
To sunny France, and here I falter through
This halting tale of mine. And now 'tis told
I pray you speak of it no more!

If I would sleep o' nights my ears must close
To that sad sound of waves upon the beach,

To that sad sound of wind that waileth so!
To visions of the sun upon the sea
And green, grass-covered mounds, bleak, bleak, but still
With early flowers clustering here and there!

[When the Sieur de Roberval, appointed Viceroy of Canada by
Francis I., sailed for his new possessions, he took with him his niece,
the lovely and high-spirited Marguerite de Roberval. A cavalier of
Picardy, who loved her, but was too poor to ask her hand in marriage,
joined the company as a volunteer, but on the voyage out the affection
of the young people was discovered by de Roberval, who was so
enraged that he devised a terrible punishment. Near Newfoundland
was a solitary island, called the Isle of Demons, because of the
strange wailings of the wind over the rocks, and here Marguerite
was abandoned. Her lover, however, succeeded in escaping his guards,
and swam to shore. They built such shelter as they could, and this is
the first European family home of which we know in Canada. After
some years Marguerite was rescued by a fishing boat and restored to
France, but not until both husband and child were dead. The poem
contains her story, told by herself, upon her arrival in France.—
Author's Note.]

The Passing of Cadieux

THAT man is brave who at the nod of fate
   Will lay his life a willing offering down,
That they who loved him may know length of days;
May stay awhile upon this pleasant earth
Drinking its gladness and its vigour in,
Though he himself lie silent evermore,
Dead to the gentle calling of the Spring,
Dead to the warmth of Summer; wrapt in dream
So deep, so far, that never dreamer yet
Has waked to tell his dream. Men there may be
Who, careless of its worth, toss life away,
A counter in some feverish game of chance,
Or, stranger yet, will sell it day by day
For toys to play with; but a man who knows
The love of life and holds it dear and good,
Prizing each moment, yet will let it go
That others still may keep the precious thing—
He is the truly brave!

                This did Cadieux,
A man who loved the wild and held each day

A gift from Le Bon Dieu to fill with joy
And offer back again to Him who gave.
(See, now, Messieurs, his grave!) We hold it dear
The story you have heard—but no? 'Tis strange,
For we all know the story of Cadieux!
He was a Frenchman born. One of an age
That glitters like a gem in history yet,
The Golden Age of France! 'Twould seem, Messieurs,
That every country has a Golden Age?—
Ah well, ah well!—

             But this Cadieux, he came
No one knew whence, nor cared, indeed, to know.
His simple coming seemed to bring the day,
So strong was he, so gallant and so gay—
A maker of sweet songs; with voice so clear
'Twas like the call of early-soaring bird
Hymning the sunrise; so at least 'twould seem
Mehwatta thought—the slim Algonquin girl
Whose shy black eyes the singer loved to praise.
She taught him all the soft full-throated words
With which the Indian warriors woo their brides,
And he taught her the dainty phrase of France
And made her little songs of love, like this:

         'Fresh is love in May
            When the Spring is yearning,
         Life is but a lay,
            Love is quick in learning.

         'Sweet is love in June:
            All the roses blowing
         Whisper 'neath the moon
            Secrets for love's knowing.

         'Sweet is love alway
            When life burns to embers,
         Hearts keep warm for aye
            With what love remembers!'

Their wigwam rose beside the Calumet
Where the great waters thunder day and night
And dawn chased dawn away in gay content.

Then it so chanced, when many moons were spent,
The brave Cadieux and his brown brothers rose
To gather up their wealth of furs for trade;
And in that moment Fate upraised her hand
And, wantonly, loosed Death upon the trail,
Red death and terrible—the Iroquois!
(Oh, the long cry that rent the startled dawn!)
One way alone remained, if they would live—
The Calumet, the cataract—perchance
The good Saint Anne might help!

    'In God's name, go!
Push off the great canoe, Mehwatta, go!—
Adieu, petite Mehwatta! Keep good cheer.
Say thou a prayer; beseech the good Saint Anne!—
For two must stay behind to hold the way,
And shall thy husband fail in time of need?
And would Mehwatta's eyes behold him shamed?—
Adieu!'—Oh, swift the waters bear them on!
Now the good God be merciful! . . . .

    They stayed,
Cadieux and one Algonquin, and they played
With a bewildered foe, as children play,
Crying 'Lo, here am I!' and then 'Lo, here!' 'Lo, there!'
Their muskets spoke from everywhere at once—
So swift they ran behind the friendly trees,
They seemed a host with Death for General—
And the fierce foe fell back.

    But ere they went
Their wingèd vengeance found the Algonquin's heart.
Cadieux was left alone!

    Ah, now, brave soul,
Began the harder part! To wander through
The waking woods, stern hunger for a guide;
To see new life and know that he must die;
To hear the Spring and know she breathed 'Adieu'! . . .
One wonders what strange songs the forest heard,
What poignant cry rose to the lonely skies
To die in music somewhere far above

Or fall in sweetness back upon the earth—
The requiem of that singer of sweet songs!
They found him—so—with cross upon his heart,
His cold hand fast upon this last Complaint—

'Ends the long trail—at sunset I must die!
I sing no more— O little bird, sing on
And flash bright wing against a brighter sky!

'Sing to my Dear, as once I used to sing;
Say that I guarded love and kept the faith—
Fly to her, little bird, on swifter wing.

'The world slips by, the sun drops down to-night—
Sweet Mary, comfort me, and let it be
Thy arms that hold me when I wake to light!'

[In the early days there came to the region of the Upper Ottawa
—to Allumette and Calumet—a voyager by the name of Cadieux. He
was more than an ordinary adventurer, for not only could he fight
and hunt with the most expert, but he could make sweet songs, words
and music, and sing them, too, in a way that was good to hear. So
thought, at any rate, a pretty Indian maiden of the Algonquin Ottawas,
whom he won for his wife. Their wigwam stood near to the Great
Fall of the Calumet. After the season's hunting, Cadieux and his
Indian friends were preparing to go to Montreal with their accumula-
tion of furs, when, of a sudden, the alarm was given of the approach,
through the woods, of a war party of their deadly enemies, the Iroquois. There was but one means of escape. The canoe was to be
committed to the cataract, while someone remained to hold the Iroquois at bay. Cadieux and a single Algonquin remained. The Iroquois finally withdrew, but not before the Algonquin was killed.
Cadieux, left alone, wandered for a time in the woods until he became
exhausted. Returning at last to Petit-Rocher, and feeling his end
approach, he made for himself a grave, and set up a rustic cross to
sanctify his departure. His friends, returning to search for him,
found him in his grave, partly covered with leaves and branches, the
cross beside him, and his hands closed on his last song, "La Com-
plainte-de Cadieux."

The Lament is still sung by the French-Canadians, and the grave
of Cadieux is still an object of veneration.—Author's Note.]

Tom McInnes

*This remarkable collection of verse 'Lonesome Bar and Other Poems' is the result, one must gather, of much living in the realm of thought and imagination, as well as experience of many lands and people. . . . . There is mystery, fluency, a charm and witchery of word which only lacks in great poetical conviction. . . . . But the best poem is 'The Damozel of Doom,' an eerie, dreamlike, passionate piece, suggested by the teaching of old Tao, who believed that there are regions where dead souls may be awakened by desires so strong that they are drawn outward again to Earth, where, through finer desires, they again pass into Paradise. Then 'the peace of a thousand years may be theirs in Limbo'. . . . The coming of this desire, which shall ultimately free, or banish the soul to ages of 'utter vanishment' is depicted in 'The Damozel of Doom'—a poem worthy of the genius of Poe.—*KATHERINE HALE, *in 'Mail and Empire.'*

THOMAS ROBERT EDWARD McINNES is a son of
the late Hon. T. R. McInnes, M.D., Senator, and subsequently Lieutenant-Governor of British Columbia. He was
born at Dresden, Ontario, Oct. 29th, 1867; was educated
at the public and high Schools, and at University College; and
graduated in 1889 from the University of Toronto, with the
degree of B.A. In December of the latter year, he married
Laura, second daughter of Dr. John Hostetter, Toronto; and
shortly afterwards registered as a student-at-law. He was
called to the Bar, in 1893.

In 1896-7 Mr. McInnes was Secretary of the Behring Sea
Claims Commission; and for the balance of the latter year
was a member of the Yukon special police and customs force
at Skagway. In 1898-1900, he was private secretary to his
father, the Lieutenant-Governor; and in 1901, officiated as
secretary of the British Columbia Salmon Fisheries Commission. In 1907, Mr. McInnes was specially commissioned by
the Dominion Government to investigate 'Anti-Oriental Riots'
in British Columbia, and his secret report was forwarded to
the Imperial Government and acted upon. Two years later,
he was commissioned to make a report on Indian title to land
in Canada. In 1910, he drew up the Canadian Immigration
Act, the Anti-Opium Act, and the Dominion Northwest Water
Power Regulations.

The first book of verse of this brilliant poet, *Lonesome Bar
and Other Poems,* appeared in 1909. His second, *In Amber
Lands,* mostly a reprint of the first book, was issued in 1910.
And his third volume, a work of interesting originality, entitled, *The Rhymes of a Rounder,* was published in 1913.

'Lonesome Bar,' a lengthy poem, is a thrilling description
of tragic life in the Klondyke, in the early days of the rush for
gold.

Originality, constructive imagination, felicitous fancy, and
delightful humour (if sometimes grim), combined with philosophic subtlety, much experience of life, and skilled artistry,
are the outstanding qualities of this poet, so little known to
Canadian readers, so worthy of their appreciation.

The Collected Poems of Tom McInnes will be issued in
1917.

The Damozel of Doom
Part II

THAT dream came not again to me,
  Nor any dream at all;
But well I knew, as the days went past,
  There held me fast in thrall
A something of that shrouded thing
  That wrapped me like a pall.

An aura drear that severed me
  From men and the ways of men;
As some great evil I had done
  My friends did shun me then;
I felt accurst, and kept apart,
  And sought them not again.

But O how chill the World did grow!
  And the Sun, as a thing unreal,
Did glare and glare through the vacant day,
  And never a ray I'd feel
To warm my blood, the light fell thin
  And gray as spectral steel.

A pale disease took hold on me,
  And when the night would come
I had no rest, but sleepless lay
  As stark as clay, and numb;
And could not stir till dawn would break
  Nor gasp, for I was dumb.

And yet were times all faintly tinged
  With a glimmering ecstasy;
Moments that lingered in their flight,
  Trailing a light to me
Elusive and wan as the phosphor foam
  That floats on the midnight sea.

And out of my stricken body then
  My soul would seem to creep,
And over a sheer unfathomed brink
  Of silence sink asleep,

Beyond the shadow and sound of dreams,
   And deeper than Earth is deep.

Yet ever from those slumber spells,
   That seemed like years, I'd start
Sudden awake, bewildered by
   A presence nigh my heart,
As if a soul had stirred in me
   That of me was no part.

And so three seasons passed away,
   And the early summer came;
And still that weird fantasy
   Enshrouded me the same;
But now it seemed as luminous
   With some alchemic flame.

At length in a garden wide and old,
   A garden all my own,
One afternoon I lay at ease
   Under the trees alone,
While the fragrant day fell off in the West
   Like a Titan rose o'erblown.

And lying there I dreamed once more,
   And it seemed that a scarlet bird
Flew out of my heart with a joyous cry,
   To the topmost sky, and I heard
Her song come echoing down to me,
   Yearning word on word:

   'Slow—slow!
O moments—O ages slow!
But love shall be my own again—
   Be it moments or ages slow!'

Illumined

I WOKE in the Land of Night,
  With a dream of Day at my heart;
Its golden outlines vanished,
  But its charm would not depart;

Like music still remaining,
  But its meaning—no man can say
In the Land of Night where they know not
  Of Day, nor the things of Day.

I dwelt in the chiefest city
  Of all the Land of Night;
Where the fires burn ever brighter
  That give the people light;
Where the sky above is darkened,
  And never a star is seen,
And they think it but children's fancy
  That ever a star hath been.

But out from that city early
  I fled by a doubtful way;
And faltering oft and lonely
  I sought my dream of Day;
Till I came at last to a Mountain
  That rose exceeding high,
And I thought I saw on its summit
  A glint as of dawn from the sky.

'Twas midway on that Mountain
  That I found an altar-stone,
Deep-cut with runes forgotten,
  And symbols little known;
And scarce could I read the meaning
  Of the legends carven there,
But I lay me out on that altar,
  Breathing an ancient prayer:

'By the God of the timeless Sky,
  O Saint of the Altar, say
What gift hast thou for me?
  For I have dreamed of Day:
But I seek nor gift nor power,
  I pray for naught but light;
And only for light to lead me
  Out of the Land of Night!'

Long I lay on that altar,
　　Up-gazing fearfully
Through the awful cold and darkness
　　That now encompassed me;
Till it seemed as I were lying drowned
　　Under a lifeless sea.

There shone as a pale blue Star,
　　Intangible—serene—
And I saw a spark from it fall
　　As it were a crystal keen;
And it flashed as it fell and pierced
　　My temples white and cold;
Then round that altar-stone once more
　　The awful darkness rolled.

But there was light on my brow,
　　And a calm that steeled me through,
And I was strong with a strength
　　That never before I knew;
With a strength for the trackless heights,
　　And scorn of the world below—
But I rose not up from that altar-stone,
　　I would not leave it so.

'O Saint of the Altar, say
　　How may this light redeem?
For though on my brow like a jewel
　　Its Star hath left a gleam,
O Saint, 'tis a light too cold and cruel
　　To be the light of my dream!'

Anon 'twas a crimson Star
　　That over the Altar shone,
And there sank as a rose of flame
　　To my heart ere the Star was gone;
And out from the flames thereof
　　A subtle fragrance then
Went stealing down the mountain-side
　　O'er the lowly ways of men.

The Star was gone, but it brought
 To light in its crimson glow
The lovely things forgotten
 I dreamed of long ago;
And gladly then I had given
 My life to all below;
Yet I rose not up from the altar-stone,
 I would not leave it so.

And at last was a golden Star;
 But I scarce know how nor where;
For it melted all around me,
 And the other Stars were there;
And all in one blissful moment
 The light of Day had come;
Then I reeled away from that altar-stone,
 Old, and blind, and dumb.

I dwell again in the city,
 I seek no more for light;
But I go on a mission of silence
 To those who would leave the Night;
And for this—and this thing only,
 Through the evil streets I stray;
I who am free to the timeless Sky
 Illumined forever with Day.

Underground

ON a queer, queer journey
 I heard the queerest sound,—
'Twas the Devil with a banjo
 In a cavern underground,
Where the merry, merry skeletons
 Were waltzing round and round,
While the clicking of their bones kept time.

Through a low, iron door,
 With a huge iron bar,
A door perchance some careless
 Imp had left ajar,

I crept behind a column cut
    All out of Iceland spar,
And the carven angles twinkled frostily.

I was frightened of the Devil,
    And I wouldn't look at him,
But I watched a thousand goblins
    From nook and cranny dim
A-glowering on the skeletons,
    And every goblin grim
And ugly as an old gargoyle.

And bogles played on fiddles
    To help the banjo out,
For 'twas nothing but the music
    Kept alive that crazy rout;
But the big green toads could
    Only hop about
To the rumbling of the bass bassoon.

Behind the Iceland column
    I watched them on the sly,
Above them arched the cavern
    With its roof miles high,
All ribbed with blue rock-crystal, shining
    Bluer than the sky,
And studded with enormous stalactites.

But the lovely floor below,
    With its level crystalline
Splendid surface spreading
    Radiantly green!—
As if a lone, impearlèd lake
    Of waters subterrene
Had frozen to a flawless emerald!

And down, down, down,
    Its moveless depths were clear;
And down, down, down,
    In wonder I did peer
At lost and lovely imagery
    Beneath me far and near,—
Silent there and white forevermore.

But from the sunken beauty
    Of that white imagery
Lissome shadows loosened
    Flame-like and fitfully,
That formed anon to spheres serene
    And mounted airily
And broke in golden bubbles through the floor.

There, bubble-like, they vanished
    Amid the whirling crew,
Yet left a radiance trailing
    Slowly out of view,
That sometimes o'er the skeletons
    Such carnal glamour threw,
It flattered them to human shape again.

How long I watched I know not;
    The weird hours went on,
Lost hours that bring the midnight
    No nearer to the dawn,
When suddenly I felt a clutch,
    And swiftly I was drawn
From out behind that carven block of spar.

My soul!—a skeleton!—
    A rattling little thing,
Twined itself about me
    As close as it could cling!
And in its arms with horror I
    Perforce 'gan circling
Compelled by that fantastic orchestra.

Onward swept the waltzers
    To the wicked tunes they played,
And soon we were amongst them,
    And my rattling partner swayed
Whene'er the golden bubbles broke,
    And trailing lights arrayed
Elusively around its naked bones.

A minute or an hour,—
    Or maybe half a night,—

No matter, for at last
  I was over all my fright,
And the music rippled through me till
  I shivered with delight,
Fascinated like the fat green toads.

And by and by I noticed
  How 'mid that grisly swarm
My clinging little partner
  'Gan strangely to transform,—
I saw the bones as through a mist
  Of something pink and warm,
That quivered and grew firm from top to toe.

Bright copper-coloured hair
  Soon round her did curl,
Her mouth grew sweet with tints
  Of coral and of pearl,
And she looked on me with eyes that seemed
  Of lambent chrysoberyl,
While her body fair as alabaster shone.

A witch she was so lovely,
  To all else I was blind,
And the Devil and the Goblins
  And the Rout we left behind,
In our wild waltz whirling on
  The cool sweet wind
Of the lone lorn caverns underground.

Like rose-leaves strewn
  Upon a crystal tide,
Like thistle-down blown
  By Zephyrs far and wide,
We swept in aimless ecstasy,
  Silent side by side,
Careening through those caverns underground.

A minute or an hour,—
  Or maybe half a night,—
No way have I to measure
  The madness of that flight,

For the loosened zone of witchery
  Made drunk with sheer delight,
Till we sank in happy stupor to the floor.

Nearby there was a grotto
  That opened chapel-wise,
As from a rich cathedral,
  In sacrilegious guise;
On the high Masonic altar were
  Three crystal chalices,
And they held the sweetest poisons Hell can brew.

One was a liquor golden
  That sparkled like the dew,
One was a wine that trembled,
  And blood-red was its hue,
But the last Lethean elixir
  Was dark as night, shot through
With glimmerings of green and violet.

Then rose the witch and muttered,
  'Quick, for the hour is late!
Quick ere the music ceases
  And the locks of the dungeons grate
O'er the host of haunted skeletons
  That here brief revel make!
Come free me by this altar's alchemy!

'Drink thou the golden liquor
  That lights yon jewelled rim,—
That sparkles fair as sunshine
  On curls of seraphim!
Drink for the love I gave thee!
  Or drink for a devil's whim!
But pledge me to the time that yet shall be!

'But the gloomy elixir
  Give me, that I may sleep
With the white wraiths that slumber
  In the dim green deep!
Where the silence of the under-world
  Shall wrap me round and keep
My soul untouched by any dreams of day!'

I drank the cup of sunshine,
  She drank the cup of night,
But the red we spilled between us
  For sacrifice and plight
Of passion that must centre in
  The sphereless Infinite
Ere her sweet life shall mix with mine again.

A moment all her beauty
  Was lightened as with fire,
Her fair voluptuous body
  With its trailing, loose attire,
And her eyes to mine did glow as in
  A sunset of desire,—
Then prone she fell upon the chapel floor.

And the white flesh wasted from her
  As she was falling dead,
Her very bones had crumbled,
  Ere one farewell I said,—
From sight of that dire sorcery
  In wild dismay I fled,
Seeking madly for the low iron door.

Behind the Iceland column
  I found it still ajar,—
Through galleries of darkness
  I travelled swift and far,
Until I reached the upper-world
  And saw the morning star
Paling o'er a meadow by the sea.

From 'Lonesome Bar'

YET oft, to hear the echoes ring and stir
  That vacant valley like a dulcimer,
I flung her name against the naked hills,
And crimsoned all the air with thoughts of her.   .   .   .

Helen M. Merrill

In Picton, Ontario, there lives a very clever Canadian poetess who writes with the mystery of nature around her and the key to its secrets in her heart. Helen M. Merrill was born to the poetic purple. Her gift as a singer is a genuine one. Her work reveals a mind in close sympathy with nature whose subtle influence has moulded and fashioned her highest and holiest dreams. Not always is the thought of poetry born poetry —more frequently is it incarnated in prose, then cradled and clad in the flowers of poetry. The test of true poetry is that it cannot be translated into prose without doing violence to its spirit. Now it will be found that Miss Merrill's poetry measures up to this test. It is thought, born on the mountain top and clad in the most fitting raiment. Miss Merrill has not yet published her poems in book form, but her work has found representation in all recent compilations of Canadian verse. —DR. THOMAS O'HAGAN, in 'Donahoe's Magazine,' 1901.

HELEN M. MERRILL, is a daughter of the late Edwards Merrill, County Court Judge, at Picton, Ontario, and Caroline Wright. She was born at Napanee, Ontario, but was educated in the schools of Picton and at Ottawa Ladies College.

Miss Merrill is of French Huguenot extraction, her first American ancestor having landed on this continent in 1633. He was one of the founders of Newbury Port. The family coat-of-arms has the fleur-de-lis on the shield.

Since 1905 Miss Merrill has resided with her mother in Toronto, and for some years has been a member of the staff of the Ontario Bureau of Archives. In this position her work has been of recognized merit. Having made a special study of New Ontario, she has contributed several series of valuable articles, topographical and relating to colonizing conditions, etc., on our great northlands. And in collaboration with Dr. Wilfred Campbell, of Ottawa, she has for some time been gathering material for a historical and genealogical work on the United Empire Loyalists of Canada.

At the Sir Isaac Brock Centenary Commemoration at Queenston Heights, Ontario, she officiated as honorary secretary, and also went through the ceremony of adoption into the Oneida Band of the Six Nations Indians. She was presented with the tribal totem, and was given the Indian name, *Ka-ya-tonhs*—'a keeper of records.'

Miss Merrill is President of the Canadian Society for the Protection of Birds; Honorary General Secretary of the United Empire Loyalists' Association of Canada; and a Councillor of the Canadian Defence League. And as a great granddaughter of Dr. J. B. Chamberlain, who emigrated from the United States to Canada, before 1791, she has been elected a member of The Chamberlain Association of America and of The Society of Colonial Families, Boston, Massachusetts.

Since the Great War began, Miss Merrill has interested herself much in collecting funds for the Belgians, and has been appointed by Madame Vandervelde, wife of the Belgian Minister of State, as her representative in Canada for further collections.

Bluebirds

O MAGIC music of the Spring,—
  Across the morning's breezy meads
I hear the south wind in the reeds,
I hear the golden bluebirds sing.

O mellow music of the morn,—
Across the fading fields of Time
How many joyous songs are borne
From memory's enchanting clime.

I see the grasses shine with dew,
The cornflowers gleaming in the grain,
And, oh! the bluebirds sing—and you?
We fare together once again.

O haunting music of the dusk,
When silent birds are on the wing
And sweet is scent of pine and musk—
Oh, as we wander hand in hand
Across the shadow-painted land,
I hear the golden bluebirds sing!

Sandpipers

MORNING on the misty highlands,
  On the outer shining islands;
Gulls their grey way seaward winging
  To the blinking zones of blue;
South winds in the shallows singing
  Where I wander far with you,
Little pipers, careless, free,
On the sandlands by the sea.

All day, on the amber edges
Of the pools and silver ledges
Of the sedgelands in the sun,
Restlessly the pipers run—
  Weet, a-weet, a-weet, a-weet!
Sun and wind and sifting sand,

Joy of June on sea and land—
Weet, a-weet, a-weet, weet weet!

Evening on the fading highlands,
On the outer amber islands;
Grey wings folded in the sedges,
In the glimmer of a star
Where the lamps of Algol are
Shining on a world's white edges.

Moonlight on the sombre forelands,
On the outer, silver shorelands;
Peaceful mists that pale and drift
Seaward like a phantom fleet,
Through a sapphire, shadowed rift.

Weet, a-weet, a-weet, weet weet!
Night, and stars, and empty hushes,
Darkness in the purple rushes—
Weet, a-weet, a-weet, weet weet!

When the Gulls Come In

WHEN the gulls come in, and the shallow sings
Fresh to the wind, and the bell-buoy rings,
And a spirit calls the soul from sleep
To follow over the flashing deep;

When the gulls come in from the fields of space,
Vagrants out of a pathless place,
Waifs of the wind that dip and veer
In the gleaming sun where the land lies near,—

Long they have wandered far and free,
Bedouin birds of the desert sea;
God only marked their devious flight,
God only followed them day and night,—

Sailor o' mine, when the gulls come in,
And the shallow sings to the bell-buoy's din,
Look to thy ship and thy gods hard by,
There's a gale in the heart of the golden sky.

In Arcadie

THE sea is green, the sea is grey,
  The tide winds blow, and shallows chime;
Where earth is rife with bloom of May
    The throstle sings of lovers' time,
    Of violet stars in lovers' clime.
Love fares to-day by land and sea,
    On the horizon's utmost hill
    The mystic blue-flower beckons still
Beneath the stars of Arcadie.

Love fares to-day, and deftly builds
    To melodies of wind and leaves;
Castles in Spain yet brightly gilds,
    And song of star and woodbird weaves,
    And flowers, and pearl and purple eves.
With roofs of ever-changing skies
    And fretted walls with time begun,
    Its portals open to the sun,
On dream-held hills a castle lies.

No proud armorial bearings now,
    But God's white seal on every leaf;
No sapphire gleaming on my brow,
    Deep in my heart a dear belief;
    No grey unrest, no pain, no grief.
By day a forest green and fair,
    Where veeries sing in secret bowers
    And lindens blow and little flowers,
And bluebirds cleave the shining air.

By night a quiet wayside grove
    Where Aldebaran lights the gloom,
And silent breezes idly rove
    Above a shadow-painted room
    Builded of many a bough and bloom—
A wafted air of myrrh and musk,
    The music of slow falling streams,
    A whitethroat singing in its dreams,
And thou beside me in the dusk.

A Hill Song

THERE is a little hint of spring,
  A subtle, silent, unseen thing
By shadowed wall and open way,
And I, a gypsy for the day,
Go straying far beneath the sky,
  And far into the windy hills,
Where distant, dim horizons lie,
  And earth with gleams of heaven fills.

My quest is but a singing bird,
Whose voice on uplands lone is heard,
And this my path where none hath been,
And this my tent, an evergreen;
The hills are mine own open way—
  I hate the smother of the town—
I love by breezy hills to stray,
  Where thawing streams come leaping down.

Oh, joy it is and free of care,
With the sun and the wind in my face and my hair,
Alone with the shining clouds which trail
Silently each like a phantom sail,
Over the hills, on the blue of heaven;
  Oh, joy it is to wander here,
Where the wilding heart of the young, sweet year,
  Quickens the earth, and spring is near!

And joy it is, the shorelark's cry—
Full well I know he walketh by;
A sudden winnow of grey wings,
And in the light he soars and sings,
And pausing in his heavenward flight,
A heart-beat, on from height to height,
He trails his silver strains of song
By paths eye may not follow long;
Grey glimpses in the azure fade,
  I only hear sweet sounds in the skies
As if the soul of song had strayed
  Invisible from paradise.

Dr. J. D. Logan

The writer says in his Preface that his work is no better and no worse than what might readily be accomplished by any man of education and literary instincts. Thus it will be seen that Dr. Logan does not claim to be a poet. But what he writes is so essentially national, so strong in spirit, and deals so closely with what is good material for poetry that 'Songs of the Makers of Canada' is the most authentic little book of Canadian poetry that we have this year. . . . . Leaving discussion of Canadian nationalism for the moment to one side, where else can one find poetry which is as fair an attempt to express Niagara, as Dr. Logan's poem, 'The Over-Song of Niagara'? The individual finds at Niagara what he brings there, but this searching out of a mood is far nearer the expression of the indescribable Niagara than the mere exclamations of wonder which precipitate writers generally call the poetry of Niagara.—MARJORIE MACMURCHY in the 'Canadian Courier.'

AN outstanding figure in present-day Canadian literary circles is John Daniel Logan, M.A., Ph.D.,—outstanding as a writer of original and scholarly treatises on academic subjects, as a critic of literature and of music, and as a poet. . Now, Sergeant Logan, of the Nova Scotia Highland Brigade, and 'Brigade Historian and Keeper of the Seals.'

Dr. Logan was born in Antigonish, Nova Scotia, on May 2nd, 1869,—the eldest son of Charles and Elizabeth Gordon (Rankin) Logan. He was educated at Pictou Academy, at Dalhousie University, and at Harvard University. From Dalhousie he graduated with highest honours in Philosophy and with the degree of B.A., in 1893, and was granted his M.A. the following year. While engaged in postgraduate work at Harvard, he had the distinction to win the Derby, Price Greenleaf and Thayer scholarships, and to receive the degrees of A.M. and Ph.D. The latter degree was conferred in 1896.

During the next five years he was a practical educator, holding the Principalship of Hampton Academy, New Hampshire, in 1898, and for the remaining four years, the Professorship of English and Philosophy, in the State University of South Dakota.

Retiring from the teaching profession, he was employed for several years as advertising specialist for Siegel, Cooper & Co., of Chicago and New York.

In 1908-10, he was literary and music critic for the *Sunday World,* Toronto, and later was a member of the staff of the Toronto *Daily News.*

The followng are Dr. Logan's principal publications: *The Structural Principles of Style,* 1900; *Preludes, Sonnets and Other Verses,* 1906; *The Religious Function of Comedy,* 1907; *Quantitative Punctuation,* 1907; *Democracy, Education and the New Dispensation,* 1908; *The Making of the New Ireland,* 1909; *Songs of the Makers of Canada, and Other Homeland Lyrics,* 1911; and *Insulters of Death,* 1916.

Last winter Dr. Logan delivered a series of lectures on Canadian Literature, in Acadia University, Wolfville, N.S., the first of the kind ever delivered in a Canadian University.

The Great War and his enlistment as a soldier have inspired this brilliant author to write a number of new poems, notably 'Timor Mortis' which is striking in conception and treatment and charged with an unusual depth and intensity of feeling.

The Over-Song of Niagara

WHY stand ye, nurslings of Earth, before my gates,
   Mouthing aloud my glory and my thrall?
Are ye alone the playthings of the fates,
   And only ye o'ershadowed with a pall?
Turn from this spectacle of strength unbound—
   This fearful force that spends itself in folly!
Turn ye and hark above the organ-sound
   My Over-song of Melancholy!
      "I rush and roar
      Along my shore,—
         I go sweeping, thundering on;
      Yet my days, O man,
      Are but as a span,
         And soon shall my strength be gone!
      My times are measured
      In whose hand I am treasured,
         (Think not of thy little day!)
      Though I rush and roar
      Along my shore,
         I am passing away—
            Passing away!

      "The sun and the moon
      They too shall soon
         Sink back into eternal Night:
      All earth and the sea
      Shall cease to be,
         And the stars shall melt in their flight!
      Their times are measured
      In whose hand they are treasured,
         (Think not of thy little day!)
      The celestial throng
      Chant my Over-song,—
         'Passing away,—
            Passing away!'"

Then stand not, nurslings of Earth, before my gates,
   Mouthing aloud my glory and my thrall:
Not ye alone are playthings of the fates,

Nor only ye o'ershadowed with a pall!
  But hark to my song
  As I sweep along,
    Thundering my organ-tone—
"O vain is all Life,
O vain is all Strife,
  And fruitless the Years that have flown!
As the Worst; so the Best—
All haste to their rest
  In the void of the Primal Unknown."

Cartier: Dauntless Discoverer
(Sailed Westward, 1534, 1535, 1541)

HAIL, Master Mariner of Sainte Malo!
  Whose name hath been a star for centuries,
Why ventured thou thrice o'er tempestuous seas,
In ships antique and frail? Didst thou then know
The greater issue of thy bold emprise
And trust an unseen providential hand
To guide thee westward to an opulent land
Wherein a mighty nation would arise?

O bold Sea-Rover, instrument of God,
Whose occult purposes were wrought through thee,
A grateful people hail thy name, and laud
Thy dauntless spirit of discovery!
Thy glory sure, rest, Rover, rest, while blow
The winds in requiem round Sainte Malo!

Champlain: First Canadian
(Founded Quebec, 1608)

WISE Colonist who in this storied place,
  With wisdom prescient of thy pregnant deed,
Cast forth the sparsate grains of fruitful seed,
Whence sprang a virile and a patriot race:
Thy aims were not to found a merchantry
Enthralled by vulgar gain; but thy just mind,
Inspired with love of thy benighted kind,
Raised here the throne of Christian empery.

Intrepid, constant, nobly pure and strong,
First citizen of Canada's domain,
Behold, this ancient city is thy fane
And thy compatriots raise thy name in song.
Look downward from thy lofty resting-place
And mark the regnancy of thy just ways.

Laval: Noble Educator
(Founded Quebec Seminary, 1663)

LAVAL, High Priest of Knowledge, who first scanned
The years to come, and saw the pow'rs that lay
Within the docile hearts thy truth should sway,—
Whose work is puissant still upon this land,—
Thou wast the Spirit's patient paragon
In those far, pristine, mercenary days
When thou alone wast master of the ways
That lead into the vale of Avalon.

Lo, now a people learned in all the arts
Greet thee to-day across the distant vale
Of Truth, where dwells obscure the Holy Grail.
And tho they commerce oft upon the marts
Of specious gain, they look beyond the mist
To thee, their first great Educationist.

Brock: Valiant Leader
(Fell at Queenston Heights, 1812)

O VALIANT leader of the little band
That, fearless, forward rushed to victory,
Tho far outnumbered by the enemy,
And, daring death, saved our Canadian land,—
What honours can we pay the noble name
Of one who held as naught th' invaders' art
Of war,—whose glory hath become a part
For evermore of our Canadian fame?

Lo, on the looming crown of that ascent
Where thy life ceased, a loyal host hath reared
To thee—whose patriot heart was pure, nor feared,—

A high commemorative monument!
Still is thy memory green who fell to save,
Still, Brock, art thou the bravest of our brave!

Winifred Waters

WINIFRED WATERS, when I look on you now,—
With the sweet peace of God on your beautiful brow
As you lie lily-white in your lone lethal bed,—
I will conjure your spirit, sit here at your head,
And talk to you, dear, whom I lost, and recall
Our vows when I swooned to the ineffable thrall
Of your eyes that once rivalled the jewels of Night,
Of your kisses that dropped more delicious and light
Than the rose-leaves that perfume the drowsy June air,
Of the glorious gold in your hyacinth hair,
And the treasures of love that we pledged for the days
When our souls should discover Earth's winsomest ways.

O Winifred Waters, mellifluous name
That enamored my soul as rare music, I came
To the wells of Love's wine, and I drank there elate,
Then I joyed daily forth, till an untoward fate
Snapped the cords that enchained us, heart unto heart.
So I passed to the world. You, cloistered apart
In the lonely-celled nunnery of unchanging grief,
Awaited Time's advent with his mortal relief,
Till you drooped like a sun-famished lily, and died.
But I am come, dear, at length, and here by your side
I commune with your spirit while I look on you now,
With the sweet peace of God on your beautiful brow.
Lo, I kiss your cold hands; I warm them with tears
And possess you again after long widowed years.

O Winifred Waters, I re-pledge you above
Your casket, and find there the Treasury of Love.

Wind o' the Sea

O WANDERING minstrel, wild Wind o' the Sea,
That knowest the innermost being of me
Who love thy rude sport with the measureless brine,
And whose spirit is wayward and vagrant as thine,—

O wandering minstrel, sad Wind o' the Sea,
That learnest world-secrets by swift errantry,
Blow hither to me o'er the wide Eastern main
And tell me what meaneth ·the poignant refrain
Of surges that moan like sad souls in their sleep,
And those shuddering shadows that darken the deep.
  Blow, wild Wind o' the Sea!
  Blow, sad Wind o' the Sea!
And speed with thy lay to thy lorn devotee.

Then the Sea-wind sang forth: 'I blow from afar
The ocean's accompaniment to the war
Of the beast and the god that dwell in thy soul,
Forever at strife for the gain of the whole
Of thy manhood's estate, of thy love and desire,
So thou sink to the one; to the other aspire.
And the deep, dark, shuddering shadows,' he shrilled,
'Are the planes of thy life which Destiny willed—
The devilish depths of thy sensual hours
When the beast in thy soul thralls thy senses and pow'rs—
The shadowy heights of thy consecrate days
When the god in thy soul is lord of thy ways.'

Thus ruthlessly sang the wild Wind o' the Sea
That learnest soul-secrets by swift errantry.
  Ah, wild Wind o' the Sea!
  Ah, sad Wind o' the Sea!
That revealest the innermost being of me.

Timor Mortis

'For he to-day that sheds his blood with me
Shall be my brother. .   .   .
And gentlemen in England now abed
Shall think themselves accursed they were not here.'
  King Henry V—Act IV, sc. 3 (King's speech prior to the battle
of Agincourt).

I WEND my ways with one dire dread
Now daily in my heart:
The fear of death obsesses me—
The fear that I may pass
Too soon for my desiring eyes to see

The English camps, and for my feet to tread
The English green-sward grass;
That I, who've heard my God's, my King's, my Country's
     claims
And, though belated, have at length begun
A larger life of holier aims
Than was my wont, may suddenly depart
This shattered world to utter oblivion,
Ere I, in Christian chivalry,
With brave, devoted comrades dauntlessly have stood face to
     the foe
On Flanders' fatal fields and struck a single blow
For man's dear brotherhood and world-wide liberty,
Or ere, upon the blood-steeped slopes
Of France, I've met—mine eyes afront, my soul quite un-
     dismayed—
The Hunnish cannons' fearful fusilade
Or done my share to still the Hunnish hopes,
And thus to leave secure, ev'n if by my poor martyrdom,
A happier heritage to generations yet to come.
Dear God, oh, privilege me the fullest bloom
Of vital-strength, that I may pay the price
For my too selfish, easeful days; spare me to live
That I, if it should be Thy will, may sacrifice
The meagre all I now can give,
And, falling, lie obscurely laid within a nameless tomb.
Perchance, round where mine unknown grave may be,
Unshaded by Canadian maples, unsung by winds from my
     Acadian sea,
I shall in spirit-state revisit foreign slope or plain
On which I fell, and there aloft descry
The Flag of England still flaunting victory to the sky,
'Neath where the hellish holocaust once swept amain,
And I shall know I died not in dishonour nor in vain,
But that I may, at home, in peace, untried, yield up my breath—
This is my direst dread, my fear, of thee, O Death!

Annie Campbell Huestis

*That Annie Campbell Huestis is a true poet must be evi-
dent to any discerning reader of her contributions to this
book, though they are but a few blossoms plucked from her
already fertile muse. . . . . . From childhood she has written verses of high lyrical quality, many of which have been
welcomed to the pages of such publications as 'Harper's Magazine' and the 'New York Independent.' . . . . Her
poems evince a lovely meditativeness, a spirit sensitive to
beauty and to sorrow, consolation, spiritual gladness. They
have spontaneity, originality, distinction: novelty in theme and
turn: clearly springing from a peculiar inspiration. . . . .
Invariably, Miss Huestis employs simple, natural diction, never
straining for preciosity, and never failing to express perfectly
her meaning and designed incantation. Often she pierces the
sense of 'our mortal strife with the immortal woe of life,'
yet always she lifts the listening soul, as does the song sparrow's plaintive refrain, to delight not unaware of immin-
ent tears.—E. W. THOMSON.*

ANNIE CAMPBELL HUESTIS began very early in life to write verse acceptable to magazine editors, for she was but a small child, under her teens, when Charles G. D. Roberts sent her first poem to the *New York Independent.* It was accepted and paid for.

She is the youngest of a family of six, and was born in Halifax, Nova Scotia. Her father is Mr. Martin Bent Huestis, of United Empire Loyalist descent, and her mother, Victoire Ayrton Johnson, a sister of the late George Johnson, Dominion Statistician. Mrs. Huestis is of English and Irish extraction, —one of whose ancestors was a Doctor of Music, so distinguished that he was buried in the cloisters of Westminster Abbey, and another, a Privy Councillor of the United Kingdom.

After attendance at public and high schools, Miss Huestis continued her studies at the Sacred Heart Convent. Since then she has travelled abroad twice, the second time as a writer of descriptive articles for newspapers. She has contributed frequently to magazines. A recent number of *Harper's Weekly* contained 'On the Stair,' and *Harper's Magazine,* of July, 1916, has a story by this author, entitled 'Flannigan.'

The Little White Sun

THE sky had a gray, gray face,
The touch of the mist was chill,
The earth was an eerie place,
For the wind moaned over the hill;
But the brown earth laughed, and the sky turned blue,
When the little white sun came peeping through.

The wet leaves saw it and smiled,
The glad birds gave it a song—
A cry from a heart, glee-wild,
And the echoes laugh it along:
And the wind and I went whistling, too,
When the little white sun came peeping through.

So, welcome the chill of rain
And the world in its dreary guise—
To have it over again,
That moment of sweet surprise,
When the brown earth laughs, and the sky turns blue,
As the little white sun comes peeping through.

The Will-o'-the-Wisp

THE Will-o'-the-Wisp is out on the marsh,
   And all alone he goes;
There's not a sight of his glimmering light
   From break of day to close;
But all night long, from dusk till dawn,
   He drifts where the night wind blows.

The Will-o'-the-Wisp, he has no roof,
   Yet he seeks not hut nor hall;
He will not wait for a friendly foot,
   But starts if a shadow fall;
And never a voice can make him turn,
   But the far off winds that call.

The twilight covers the dreaming hills,
   The evening dews begin;
There's none to care that he wanders there,
   There's none to call him in;
And all the night, with his lonely light,
   He goes where the mists have been.

From firelit window and open doors,
   The roads have golden bars;
And round and round the world is bound
   By a girdle of radiant stars;
But I watch to-night for a fleeting light
   That a moment makes or mars.

Flit, flit, with the hurrying hours,
   In shadow and mist and dew;
Will-o'-the-Wisp, O Will-o'-the-Wisp,
   I would I could follow you,
With your elfin light for a lantern bright
   The bogs and the marshes through!

O Will-o'-the-Wisp, in silver dusk
   Who'd wish for golden dawn?
In purple night, with stars a-light,
   Who'd dream of noontide gone?
Who would not stray by the glimmering way
   Your wandering feet are drawn?

The dawn comes over the silent hills,
And calls to the winds of morn;
The stars grow pale, and the sun cries, 'Hail!'
To the shadowy fields forlorn;
And good-bye, good-bye, to the Will-o'-the-Wisp,
Who dies when the day is born!

Aldaran

ALDARAN, who loved to sing,
Here lieth dead.
All the glory of the Spring,
All its birds and blossoming,
Near his still bed,
Cannot waken him again,
Cannot lure to hill and plain
Aldaran, the singer,
Who is dead.

Homeward through the early dusk
Idly he would stray,
Through the woodland dim and still
Harp in hand and heart athrill,
Singing on his way,—
Singing neath a dark'ning sky
To the birds their lullaby;
To the owls a plaintive note,
Mournful, from his happy throat;
To the brooks, in lighter tone,
Merry music like their own;
To the dreaming fields a tune
Like the wind of afternoon
When it drifts through sunlit spaces
Cooling weary flower faces;
To the wee folk in their beds
Gentle croons for sleepy heads;
And to every timid thing,
Hushed and hidden, he would sing,
Till it crept in wonder sweet,
Fear forgetting, to his feet.
It was so he charmed them, singing,

Bird and beast and man,
Yet no voice can ever waken
Sleeping Aldaran.

Aldaran, who loved to sing,
Here lieth still.
Let the bird upon the bough,
Near where he is sleeping now,
Call if it will.
Never voice of bird or man
Shall awaken Aldaran.
Hushed he lies, whose happy throat
Woke the wood with silver note,
Stirred the slumbering hills, and then
Charmed them all to sleep again.
Hushed he lies, as if content
With the silent way he went,
But the winds come seeking him,
Through the forest to and fro,
In the twilight strange and dim,
Calling, calling as they go.
'Must you lie in silence ever,
Gentle Singer?' cries the river.
And the birds from hill to hill,
Seem to wait and listen still.
'Aldaran, O Aldaran,
Haste thee back, the day is sped!'
So the wind and twilight calleth,
Wild and wistful, near his bed,—
Aldaran, the Singer,
Who is dead!'

It was in the purple dusk
Of a golden day,
Through the woodland that he loved,
Home he made his way.
Here he lay awhile to dream
In the forest dim,
And the bank beside the stream
Was a couch for him;
Kind above him bent the willow,

15

And the low moss was his pillow,
　And his wall the thicket grim.
One by one, the quiet sky
Lit its candles pure and high
Till their light shone swift and far,
Like a smile, from star to star,
And the wind was like a prayer
Chanted in the silence there.
　It was so, while he lay sleeping,
　　Hushed, a weary man,
　Death came through the darkness creeping
　　Unto Aldaran.

Like an enemy it came,
　Through the shade it crept,
With a footstep swift and drear,
In the shadows drawing near,
　Softly, while he slept.
Laid a hand upon his eyes,
　That they might not see the Spring,
Laid a seal upon his lips,
　That they might not sing.

Wept the wind, with voice of fear,
'Wake thee, danger lurketh near!'
Cried the flying owl, 'O follow!'
Hurrying through the silent hollow.
And its shadow weird and grey
Seemed to beckon him away.
So they pled with him, the while
In the woodland that he knew,
Aldaran, with fearless smile,
Lay asleep mid flowers and dew.
What to watch or dread had he,
Who had known no enemy?
Yet, from shadow into light,
Flashed a dagger fierce and bright,
Unto shadow drew again,
False and shamed with crimson stain,
And the grasses trembling near

Felt a step that fled in fear.
Never troubled word he spake,
  Never cry of grief or pain,
But in wonder strove to wake,
  Stirred, and sighed, and slept again.
Flowers in that piteous place
Bent to screen his paling face,
And the dark, with touch that blest,
Hid the wound upon his breast.
  In the friendly wood that knew him,
    Sweet with fern and flower,
  So it was that Death came to him,
    In his trusting hour.

Aldaran who loved to sing
  Here lieth low,
Not again his heart shall spring,
At the time of blossoming.—
  Ah, who can know?
Still at dusk and break of day
Some can hear him on his way,—
Aldaran, the vanished one,
Walking hidden in the sun,
Moving mistlike by the streams
When the early twilight dreams,
Speeding on his quiet way,
Never seen, by night or day,
But in pity drawing near
To the help of those who fear,
To the beds of those who die,
Singing their last lullaby,
Singing still, when they are far
Where the mist and silence are,
Singing softly still, that they
May not fear the unknown way.
  So to those whose day is sped,
    In the hour lone and dread,
  Cometh Aldaran, the Singer,
    Who is dead.

On the Stair

AS I went lonely up the stair
Ah me, the ghost that I saw there!
So bright and near it seemed to be,
It laid a hand with tender touch
On my sad eyes that wept too much,
And bent a wistful face to me,—
It was the friend whose heart I brake
With many a grief for my false sake.

The hand that sought to dry my tears
Had dried her own in earlier years—
The patient tears I made her shed.
The face that bent to comfort me
From the dark hall where none could see
Had smiled on me as she lay dead.
It was the friend I did not spare
Who met me on the lonely stair.

If I could live those years again
And break no trust, and give no pain,
And nobly grieve to see her die,
We could forget that she was dead,
And all the years so strangely fled,
And love this meeting, she and I;
But I was false as friend could be
And she comes back to comfort me.

Alan Sullivan

The charm of his lucid and melodious verse has attracted wide and deep attention in Canada and the United States. A few of the titles are these: 'The Lover,' 'Respice,' 'To Sleep,' 'Suppliant,' 'When in the Speechless Night,' 'The Call,' and 'Came Those who Saw and Loved Her' which is perhaps the poet's greatest achievement. In this poem he has reached a magnificent level. . . . . The apotheosis of honest toil is a golden thread running through much of Alan Sullivan's work. It is the dominant feature of his remarkable poem, 'The City.' . . . . It is the same attitude towards brawn and sinew which we find in his prose sketches, 'The Pilots of the Night,' and 'The Essence of Man.' . . . . He is always paying homage to the native and naked dignity of man. . . . . While he is not in the usual sense a didactic author, he exhibits in his prose work and occasionally in his poetry, some characteristics of the social and moral philosopher.—J. E. WETHERELL, B.A., in 'MacLean's Magazine.'

ALAN SULLIVAN has long had recognition in the United States, through his poems, short stories, and comprehensive articles on various themes, which have frequently appeared in Harper's Magazine, the Atlantic Monthly, and other leading American periodicals; but Canadians are only beginning, it seems to me, to realize his literary genius and fine workmanship. Recently I have read with critical interest most of his output, and am deeply impressed by his keenness of perception, his intellectual grasp, his power of sustained analysis, and by his native sense of the fitness of things. He is not only a distinctive poet, he is a writer of excellent fiction.

Edward Alan Sullivan was born in St. George's Rectory, Montreal, November 29th, 1868. He is the eldest son of the late Bishop of Algoma, the Right Reverend Edward Sullivan, who was of Irish birth, and Frances Mary Renaud, a native of Scotland. In 1869, his father became Rector of Trinity Church, Chicago, and the family was resident there during the terrible conflagration which devastated that city in 1871. In his fifteenth year, he was sent to Loretto, a famous school for boys, in Musselburgh, Scotland, where he remained until his course of studies was completed. On his return to Canada, he attended the School of Practical Science, Toronto, and then engaged in railway exploration work in the West, and later in mining. He was assistant engineer in the Clergue enterprises at Sault Ste. Marie, for a year and a half, before the organization of the Consolidated Lake Superior Company. Subsequently he spent several years as a mining engineer in the Lake of the Woods district, during the period of its gold exploitation.

In December, 1900, Mr. Sullivan married Bessie Salisbury, daughter of Mr. George H. Hees, of Toronto, and their happy and beautiful home in Wychwood Park, Toronto, is now graced with four bright children, two boys and two girls.

In 1903, he became Mechanical Superintendent of Gutta Percha & Rubber, Limited, and held the position for ten years. He is now Secretary-Treasurer of the Canadian Electrical Association, and a Consulting Engineer.

The following are his most important book publications: *I Believe That*, 1912; *The Passing of Oul-I-But and Other Tales*, 1913; and *Blantyre: Alien*, 1914.

Suppliant

GRANT me, dear Lord, the alchemy of toil,
　Clean days of labour, dreamless nights of rest,
And that which shall my weariness assoil,
　The sanctuary of one beloved breast:

Laughter of children, hope and thankful tears,
　Knowledge to yield, with valour to defend,
A faith immutable, and stedfast years
　That move unvexed to their mysterious end.

Prospice

THE ancient and the lovely land
　Is sown with death; across the plain
Ungarnered now the orchards stand,
　The Maxim nestles in the grain,
The shrapnel spreads a stinging flail
　Where pallid nuns the cloister trod,
The airship spills her leaden hail;
　But—after all the battles—God.

Athwart the vineyard's ordered banks,
　Silent the red rent forms recline,
And from their stark and speechless ranks
　There flows a richer, ruddier wine;
While down the lane and through the wall
　The victors writhe upon the sod,
Nor heed the onward bugle call;
　But—after all the bugles—God.

By night the blazing cities flare
　Like mushroom torches in the sky;
The rocking ramparts tremble ere
　The sullen cannon boom reply,
And shattered is the temple spire,
　The vestment trampled on the clod,
And every altar black with fire;
　But—after all the altars—God.

And all the prizes we have won
　Are buried in a deadly dust;

The things we set our hearts upon
    Beneath the stricken earth are thrust;
Again the Savage greets the sun,
    Again his feet, with fury shod,
Across a world in anguish run;
    But—after all the anguish—God.

The grim campaign, the gun, the sword,
    The quick volcano from the sea,
The honour that reveres the word,
    The sacrifice, the agony—
These be our heritage and pride,
    Till the last despot kiss the rod,
And, with man's freedom purified,
    We mark—behind our triumph—God.

The Kite

UPON the liquid tide of air
    It swayed beside a dappled cloud:
It seemed athwart the sun to fare
Full of strong flight, as though endowed
With vibrant life. Buoyed in the sky
It swam, and hardly might the eye
Traverse the fields of ambient light
To scan its heaven aspiring height.
And, like a spider's web, there slipped
A pulsing earthward thread, that dipped
In tenuous line, that throbbed and spoke,
Down through the sunlight and the smoke,
Down to a small and blackened brood
Of puny city waifs that stood,
And—lost to hunger, want or time—
Stared, rigid, through the city's grime
At the far envoy they had given
As hostage to the winds of heaven.

Thus may the Soul to heights elysian
Send argosies of dream and vision:
Send far flung messengers that rise
Strong pinioned, cleaving to the skies,
To float amid the poisèd spheres,

Beyond the tumult of the years,
Till,—down the rare and rainbow line
That earthward trails from fields divine—
Shall pulse the throb of mystic wings,
And faint, sweet, rapturous whisperings
Of incommunicable things.

Came Those Who Saw and Loved Her

CAME those who saw and loved her,
  She was so fair to see!
No whit their homage moved her,
  So proud she was, so free;
But, ah, her soul was turning
With strange and mystic yearning,
With some divine discerning,
  Beyond them all—to me!

As light to lids that quiver
  Throughout a night forlorn,
She came—a royal giver—
  My temple to adorn;
And my soul rose to meet her,
To welcome her, to greet her,
To name, proclaim, her sweeter
  And dearer than the morn:

For her most rare devising
  Was mixed no common clay,
Nor earthly form, disguising
  Its frailty for a day;
But sun and shadow blended,
And fire and love descended
In one creation splendid
  Nor less superb than they.

              .   .   .   .   .

You—of the finer moulding,
 . You—of the clearer light,
Whose spirit life, unfolding,
  Illumed my spirit's night,
Stoop not to end my dreaming,

To stain the vision gleaming,
Or mar that glory, seeming
  Too high for touch or sight.

Dear as the viewless portal
  Of dream embroidered sleep,
Lift me to dreams immortal,
  Till, purified, I leap
To hear the distant thunder
Of dark veils rent asunder,
And lose myself in wonder
  At mysteries so deep.

Till, past the sombre meadows,
  Tearless and unafraid,
Linked even in the shadows,
  Our deathless souls have strayed;
And you, my soul's defender
O valiant one and tender,
Cry out to God's own splendour,
  'Behold the man I made!'

Brébeuf and Lalemant

CAME Jean Brébeuf from Rennes, in Normandy,
    To preach the written word in Sainte Marie—
The Ajax of the Jesuit enterprise:
Huge, dominant and bold—augustly wise.
The zealot's flame deep in the hot brown eyes
That glowed with strange and holy whisperings,
And searched the stars, and caught angelic wings
Beating through visions of mysterious things.
Once, in the sky, a cross and martyr's crown
Hung o'er the squalor of the Huron town.
And spectres, armed with javelin and sword,
Foreshadowed the dread army of the Lord;
But, onward through the forest, to his fate
Marched the great priest, unawed by Huron hate:
In every scourge he glimpsed the sacred Tree
And the dear Master of his embassy.

'Twas in St. Louis, where the Hurons lay,
Screened from the blue sweep of the Georgian Bay,
That the frail brother Lalemant, and Brébeuf,
Built a strange sanctuary, whose trembling wall
Was birchen bark, on whose long, curving roof
Lay tawny skins. A spirit seemed to call
In supplication through the holy place
For some strong mercy on the untamed race
That, naked, sat in this thrice wondrous room;
And, peering through the incense-burdened gloom,
Stared at the altar, where the black-robes bent
O'er the bright vessels of their sacrament.

Till, on the grim and memorable day,
When, to the Host, they bade their converts pray,
There flashed a gasping runner through the wood:
'The Iroquois! The Iroquois!' he cried.
As fire that stings the forest into blood
And drives red gales of ruin far and wide,
So frenzied fear ran riot, in a flood
That surged convulsive. But the great priest stood
Like a strong tower, when fretted billows race
Tumultuously about its massy base:
'Courage, my children, through the flame I see
The dear white Christ, whose long sought sons are ye.'

Then suddenly from out the wood there rose
The shouting of innumerable foes,
And waves of painted warriors from the glade
Swept yelping, through the tottering palisade.
Were devils ere so murderous as men
In whose brown breasts those devils breathed again,
When agony the shuddering sky assailed,
When age and youth in choking anguish wailed?
Torn from the breast, the child was cleft in twain,
The mother shrieked, then fell among the slain;
Age had no power to swerve the dripping knife,
Youth gained but torture as the end of life,
The wounded perished in the bursting flame
That left St. Louis but a woeful name.
But 'midst the dead and dying moved the priest,

Closing dead eyes, speeding the soul released;
'*Absolvo te*'—to trembling lips the word
Descended from the Hurons' new found Lord.
And, ere the night took pity on the dead,
Brébeuf and Lalemant in chains were led;
And one, the giant of Normandy, was bound
To a great stake; when staring boldly round
With ardent gaze, he saw the convert throng
Captive. 'Have courage! It will not be long;
Torture is but salvation's earthly price.
To-day we meet the Christ in Paradise.'

O heart of iron, O strange supernal zeal,
That braves the fire, the torture and the steel!
O torn and shrinking flesh that yet can find
The crown of thorns mysteriously entwined!
O sightless orbs that still their Lord discern,
Howe'er the coals their blackened sockets burn.

Thus sped the Jesuit's triumphant soul.
And Lalemant, ere the rising of the sun,
Achieved through torment his far-shining goal.
And all the Huron missions, one by one,
Were driven by the Iroquois like spray
That strong winds snatch and swiftly whirl away.

Sleep, Lalemant! Brébeuf, a long surcease!
Still moves your martyr's spirit through the glade;
Still mourns the northern forest, when the peace
And benediction of the twilight shade
Awakens in the dark memorial pines
A velvet-footed, cedar-scented breeze,
That whispers where the green and knotted vines
Enmesh the cloistered colonnade of trees.

[There exists no more fascinating record of courage and endurance
than that bequeathed to Canada by the Jesuit Fathers. It excites both
our pride and our wonder. Foremost in the van of these great pioneers
came Brébeuf and Lalemant the first Canadian martyrs. Who can
read without emotion of their dauntless lives, their marvellous and
perilous journeys, and the terrible death that overtook them in 1649,
when captured on the shores of Lake Huron by the merciless Iroquois?—Author's Note.]

Alma Frances McCollum

'*Where Sings the Whippoorwill*' *is for its beauty a strong little etching.*

'*The Angel's Kiss*' *is distinctly high class, and I think Miss McCollum excels in this key.*

'*The Silent Singer*' *is perfect and a beautiful tribute.*

'*Love*' *is grand and Miss McCollum has the true conception.*

'*Little Nellie's Pa*' *is so good that James Whitcomb Riley might have been proud to sign it.*

On the whole my judgment tells me the volume is a valuable addition to our Canadian literature. The only faults are minor ones, and consistent with the writer's youth; and who would have it otherwise? But there is no mawkishness—easy to see what a lovely character is our jeune fille.—DR. W. H. DRUMMOND, in a letter to the Editor, in 1902.

Her poetical compositions, conspicuous for their tender delicacy of sentiment and graceful literary form, constitute a permanent and valued addition to native Canadian literature. —F. R. YOKOME, editor, in the Peterborough 'Examiner.'

ALMA FRANCES McCOLLUM was born in a rural village, near the town of Chatham, Ontario, on the 7th
of December, 1879. She was the youngest of a family of
six. While she was still a child, her father, Edward Lee
McCollum, died, and the family shortly afterwards moved
to Peterborough, Ontario. In this city the mother and three
daughters continued to live until the autumn of 1905, when
they sold their home and purchased one on Delaware Avenue,
Toronto.

Miss Alma had been frail in health for several years before
her short residence in Toronto. In the spring of 1900 she
spent several weeks in a sanitarium at Clifton Springs, where
she was very ill; and it was while her life was almost de-
spaired of there, that she experienced the strange visitation
expressed in that beautiful sonnet, 'The Angel of the Sombre
Cowl.'

Probably the chief object in moving to Toronto was to enable Miss Alma to take lectures in English Literature at
University College; but after a few weeks' attendance, her
health so failed that she had to discontinue her studies.

Her physician believed she had incipient appendicitis and
persuaded her to undergo an operation. This proved fatal, and
she passed away on the 21st of March, 1906.

Miss McCollum inherited her poetical talent from her father,
who, like the elder Lampman, wrote good verse. She began
to make rhymes in early life, and while still in her teens had
written most of the poems which appeared in *Flower Legends
and other Poems,* in 1902. The pretty cover design was
sketched by herself. Besides these accomplishments she sang
sweetly, accompanying herself on a mandolin, and had a rare
gift of mimicry and recitation. To see and hear her recite her
own poems was a pleasure never to be forgotten: her lovely,
expressive face, her graceful movements, her patrician voice
and manners, made up an indescribable charm of personality.

Miss McCollum's parents were both born and brought up
in Ireland; and she was a niece of the late Rev. J. H.
McCollum, of Toronto. Her mother and two sisters are now
residing on the Pacific Coast, in the State of Washington.

THE poems selected and included in the original copy were these: 'Where Sings the Whippoorwill,' 'The Angel's Kiss,' 'The Silent Singer,' 'Love,' The Angel of the Sombre Cowl' and 'Little Nellie's Pa.' But as the consent of the executrix of Miss McCollum's estate could not be obtained the following poems have been substituted. Their inclusion is due to the courtesy of *The Canadian Magazine* and *The Globe*, Toronto.

Miss McCollum, like Isabella Valancy Crawford, spent many happy hours in the beautiful environment of the Kawartha Lakes. She had a pretty summer cottage, "Halcyon," on the north shore of Smith township. It was located about a half-mile from Burleigh Falls where the picturesque view of lake and islands, with a background of thick woods, inspired such poems as 'Forest Sounds' and 'A Song of the Forest.'

Forest Sounds

WHO, in the pines, may hear low voices raised
  To chant in suppliant tone?
They who, in Sorrow's tranquil eyes, have gazed,
  O'ercome, endured alone.

The joyous whispering of lesser trees,
  Who can interpret this?
Awakened souls whose inmost sanctities
  Know Love's revealing kiss.

And lowly vines, the tender clinging things
  That dwell amid the sod?
For pillowed ear, a carillon ne'er rings,
  Unless at peace with God.

A Song of the Forest

The Legend of Love-Sick Lake

WHEN you wander alone through the forest
  And list to the murmuring song,
If your heart be attuned to the music,
  The words will come floating along.
I have listened so oft to the singing
  That when it is plaintive and low
I can hear through the melody's sobbing
  A love tale of long, long ago.
'Nenemoosha! Omemee! Omemee!'
  The waterfalls purl as they flow;
And the echo sighs softly, 'Omemee!
  The sweetheart, the maiden of woe.'
Like a willow wand supple and slender
  Her movements were motions of grace,
And her eyes as the stars of the morning;
  And dusky as twilight her face,
Overshadowed by long silken tresses,
  Which shone with a luminous light,
Like darkness, when daylight appeareth
  Dispersing the shadows of night.

Now the West Wind is dreamily humming
  The love-lays the dusky Braves cooed,
And the brooklet is mocking the laughter
  That silenced each lover who wooed;
But the melody varies and deepens,
  A tenderer message is sighed,
And the brooklet grows fainter and fainter
  To whisper the words which replied.
Oh! this lover was fair as the morning,
  His eyes as the blue of the lake,
And the hair, like its brink sun-illumined,
  And true was the promise he spake:

'Nenemoosha! Omemee! Belovèd!
  The moon is a thin, silver thread;
After, strand over strand, winds it roundly,
  Omemee her lover will wed.'
But the Waterfalls sullenly gurgle
  How, speedily, far from her sight,
With no farewell, her lover was banished,
  Ere moonbeams illumined the night;
How the Braves and the Squaws in derision
  Then pointed the finger of scorn
Harshly laughing, 'Omemee, forsaken,
  The loveless, the maiden forlorn!'

Now the waters roar loudly their anger,
  Till echoing echoes reply;
And the wind wails its anguish of spirit,
  Keyed high to a shrill minor cry;
Then it hushes and sobs how Omemee
  Was dazed with their gibes and her grief,
And afar through the forest went roaming
  To find for her sorrow relief;
How the trees drooped their boughs to caress her,
  The brambles and thorns bent aside,
And the blossoms clung fast to her tresses
  To garland her fair like a bride;
How the Moon rolled its last silver girdle
  And over the maiden shone clear,
Till she startled and shivered enraptured,
  And knew that her lover was near.
From the lakelet she heard his voice calling,
  And following as in a dream,
Where the margin hung high o'er the water,
  She gazed on the moon's sparkling gleam.
For a moment she lingered and hovered,
  Then gliding through quivering light,
Where the Wavelets called softly, 'Omemee,'
  She floated and vanished from sight.

Now the forest is throbbing with music,
   A harmony wondrously blent,
An ecstatic and thrilling emotion,
   Commingled with blissful content;
From the Brooklet a ripple of laughter,
   The Waterfall's note like the dove,
And the Wind in a clear tone of triumph,
   With echoes uniting, sing love.
And though years have rolled decade on decade
   The Forest remembers the song,
And the wraith of Omemee appeareth,
   And flits o'er the water along:
An elusive ethereal vision,
   An eerie and mystical sprite:
Like the vaporous spray of a fountain
   It glides through the silvery light.
And because of this visitant ghostly,
   Which follows the moon's brilliant wake,
And the Waterfall's echoing sighing,
   This region is called 'Love-sick Lake.'

When you wander alone through the forest
   And list to the murmuring song,
If your heart be attuned to the music,
   The words will come floating along.
I have listened so oft to the singing
   That when it is plaintive and low
I can hear through the melodies sobbing
   This love tale of long, long ago.

Peter McArthur

No one who turns over the pages of 'The Prodigal and Other Poems,' or who reads his other printed work, can fail to recognize that Mr. McArthur is the possessor of a genuine lyrical voice. . . . . Perhaps the first thing that strikes the reader of his poetry—and his prose as well, for the matter of that—is that it possesses that rare enough quality,—zest. Mr. McArthur is no mere æsthete, no lackadaisical dilettante, but is alive to his finger tips; and all his writings fairly tingle with life. The next thing one perceives is that a strong human feeling runs through his work. Mr. McArthur is above all things else a human being, and a lover of all things human. But he loves nature, too, and manages to get very close to her: we can fairly smell the good brown earth in every out-of-doors poem of his. Naturalness is another of his qualities. He is ever himself: affectation of all kinds is anathema to him. His work is marked also by a lambent, playful humour, which, however, can become sardonic enough when occasion requires.
—R. H. HATHAWAY.

PETER McARTHUR has recently become one of the most prominent and successful of our Canadian literary men. His 'syndicate' articles pertaining to farm life, which appeared in the Toronto *Globe* and other journals, and which were redolent of humour and wisdom, attracted wide attention; and when the best of them were published in a substantial book, under the alluring title, *In Pastures Green,* the enduring fame of the author was assured. Indeed he has done more than any other writer of his day and generation, to attract attention back to the farm and to popularize its various pursuits. That wholesome poem, 'The Stone,' was found in this notable book, and is reprinted here by kind permission.

His parents were the late Peter and Catherine (McLennan) McArthur, natives of Scotland. He was born at Ekfrid, in the county of Middlesex, Ontario, March 10th, 1866. After he had attended the local public school and worked on his father's farm, until twenty years of age, his higher education was received at the Strathroy Collegiate Institute, and at University College, Toronto. For a short period, he taught in a public school. In 1889, he entered Journalism as a member of the staff of the Toronto *Mail,* and later contributed to *Grip, Detroit Free Press, Saturday Night, New York Sun, Puck, Judge, Life, Harper's Monthly, Atlantic Monthly, Century,* etc. In 1890, he moved to New York. In March, 1895, he became assistant editor of *Truth,* and in the following August, editor-in-chief and art manager. A month later, he was married to Mabel C. Waters, of Niagara Falls, Ontario.

During the years, 1902-4, Mr. McArthur lived in London, England, and contributed to *Punch* and to the *Review of Reviews.* He then returned to New York, and for four years was a member of the firm of 'McArthur and Ryder,' commercial publishers. In 1908, he returned to the old home farm, and has remained ever since.

His chief book publications are: *To Be Taken With Salt: an Essay on Teaching one's Grandmother to Suck Eggs,* 1903; *The Prodigal and Other Poems,* 1907; *In Pastures Green,* 1915; and *The Red Cow and Her Friends,* 1916.

Mr. and Mrs. McArthur have four sons and one daughter. One of the sons is a corporal in the 56th Overseas Battery.

Corn-Planting

THE earth is awake and the birds have come,
  There is life in the beat of the breeze,
And the basswood tops are alive with the hum
  And the flash of the hungry bees;
The frogs in the swale in concert croak,
  And the glow of the spring is here,
When the bursting leaves on the rough old oak
  Are as big as a red squirrel's ear.

From the ridge-pole dry the corn we pluck,
  Ears ripe and yellow and sound,
That were saved apart with the red for luck,
  The best that the huskers found;
We will shell them now, for the Indian folk
  Say, 'Plant your corn without fear
When the bursting leaves on the rough old oak
  Are as big as a red squirrel's ear.'

No crow will pull and no frost will blight,
  Nor grub cut the tender sprout,
No rust will burn and no leaves turn white,
  But the stalks will be tall and stout;
And never a weed will have power to choke,
  Or blasting wind to sear,
The corn that we plant when the leaves of the oak
  Are as big as a red squirrel's ear.

To the Birds

HOW dare you sing such cheerful notes?
  You show a woful lack of taste;
How dare you pour from happy throats
  Such merry songs with raptured haste,
While all our poets wail and weep,
And readers sob themselves to sleep?

'Tis clear to me, you've never read
  The turgid tomes that Ibsen writes,
Or mourned with Tolstoi virtue dead,
  Nor over Howells pored o' nights;

For you are glad with all your power;
For shame! Go study Schopenhauer.

You never sing save when you feel
   The ecstasy of thoughtless joy;
All silent through the boughs you steal
   When storms or fears or pains annoy;
With bards 'tis quite a different thing,
The more they ache the more they sing.

All happiness they sadly shirk,
   And from all pleasure hold aloof,
And are so tearful when they work
   They write on paper waterproof,
And on each page express a yearn
To fill a cinerary urn.

Go, little birds, it gives me pain
   To hear your happy melodies!
My plaudits you can never gain
   With old and worn-out tunes like these;
More up-to-date your songs must be
Ere you can merit praise from me.

An Indian Wind Song

THE wolf of the winter wind is swift,
   And hearts are still and cheeks are pale,
When we hear his howl in the ghostly drift
   As he rushes past on a phantom trail;
And all the night we huddle and fear,
   For we know that his path is the path of Death,
And the flames burn low, when his steps are near,
   And the dim hut reeks with his grave-cold breath.

The fawn of the wind of the spring is shy,
   Her light feet rustle the sere, white grass,
The trees are roused as she races by,
   In the pattering rain we hear her pass;
And the bow unstrung we cast aside,
   While we winnow the golden, hoarded maize,
And the earth awakes with a thrill of pride
   To deck her beauty for festal days.

The hawk of the summer wind is proud,
  She circles high at the throne of the sun;
When the storm is fierce her scream is loud,
  And the scorching glance of her eye we shun;
And often times, when the sun is bright,
  A silence falls on the choirs of song,
And the partridge shrinks in a wild affright,
  Where a searching shadow swings along.

The hound of the autumn wind is slow,
  He loves to bask in the heat and sleep,
When the sun through the drowsy haze bends low,
  And frosts from the hills through the starlight creep;
But oftentimes he starts in his dreams,
  When the howl of the winter wolf draws nigh,
Then lazily rolls in the gold-warm beams,
  While the flocking birds to the south drift by.

Sugar Weather

WHEN snow-balls on the horses' hoofs
  And the wind from the south blows warm,
When the cattle stand where the sunbeams beat
  And the noon has a dreamy charm,
When icicles crash from the dripping eaves
  And the furrows peep black through the snow,
Then I hurry away to the sugar bush,
  For the sap will run, I know.

With auger and axe and spile and trough
  To each tree a visit I pay,
And every boy in the country-side
  Is eager to help to-day.
We roll the backlogs into their place,
  And the kettles between them swing,
Then gather the wood for the roaring fire
  And the sap in pailfuls bring.

A fig for your arches and modern ways,
  A fig for your sheet-iron pan,
I like a smoky old kettle best
  And I stick to the good old plan;
16

We're going to make sugar and taffy to-night
   On the swing pole under the tree,
And the girls and the boys for miles around
   Are all sworn friends to me.

The hens are cackling again in the barn,
   And the cattle beginning to bawl,
And neighbours, who long have been acting cool,
   Now make a forgiving call;
For there's no love-feast like a taffy-pull,
   With its hearty and sticky fun,
And I know the whole world is at peace with me,
   For the sap has commenced to run.

The End of the Drought

LAST night we marked the twinkling stars,
   This morn no dew revived the grass,
And oft across the parching fields
   We see the dusty eddies pass;
The eager hawk forgets to swing
   And scream across the burning sky,
And from the oak's slow-dying crest
   Sends forth a strange and plaintive cry.

The geese on unaccustomed wings
   Flap wildly in ungainly flight,
The peacock's fierce defiant scream
   Scatters the fowls in wild affright,
The crows are barking in the woods,
   The maple leaves their silver show,
The cattle sniff the coming storm,
   Then toss their heads and softly low.

And now along the hazy west
   The swiftly building clouds uprear;
High overhead the winds are loud,
   The thunder rolls and grumbles near;
The housewife trims the leaky eaves,
   The farmer frets of lodging grain,
Till all the world, rejoicing, drinks
   The long-denied, long-prayed-for rain.

The Stone

A MAN! A man! There is a man loose in Canada,
  A man of heroic mould, a 'throwback' of earlier ages,
Vigorous, public-spirited, not afraid of work!
A doer of deeds, not a dreamer and babbler;
A man, simple, direct, unaffected.
Such a one as Walt Whitman would have gloried in,
And made immortal in rugged man-poetry—
Vast polyphloesboean verses such as erstwhile he bellowed
Through roaring storm winds to the bull-mouthed Atlantic.

And yesterday the man passed among us unnoted!
Did his deed and went his way without boasting,
Leaving his act to speak, himself silent!

And I, beholding the marvel, stood for a space astonied,
Then threw up my hat and chortled,
And whooped in dithyrambic exultation.
Hark to my tale!
On the sixteenth sideroad of the township of Ekfrid,
Just south of the second concession line, some rods from the
        corner,
There was a stone, a stone in the road, a stumbling-block;
A jagged tooth of granite dropped from the jaw of a glacier
In an earlier age when the summers were colder;
A rock that horses tripped on, wheels bumped on, and sleigh-
        runners scrunched on,
And no man in all the land had the gumption to dig it out.
Pathmaster after pathmaster, full of his pride of office,
Rode by with haughty brow, and regarded it not,
Seeing only the weeds in the field of the amateur farmer,
And scrawling minatory letters ordering them cut,
But leaving the stone.
Oft in my hot youth I, riding in a lumber waggon,
By that lurking stone was catapulted skyward,
And picked myself up raging and vowing to dig it out—
But dug it not. I didn't have a spade,
Or, if I had a spade, I had a lame back—always an excuse.
And the stone stayed.
As passed the years—good years, bad years,

Years that were wet or dry, lean years and fat years,
Roaring election years (mouthing reforms) ; in short, all years
That oldest inhabitants keep in stock—there grew a tradition
About the stone. Men, it was said, had tried to move it,
But it was a stubborn boulder, deep sunk in the earth,
And could only be moved by dynamite, at vast cost to the
            council;
But every councillor was a watch dog of the treasury,
And the stone stayed.
Since the memory of man runneth the stone was there.
It had stubbed the toe of the Algonquin brave, and haply
Had tripped the ferocious, marauding Iroquois.
It had jolted the slow, wobbling ox-cart of the pioneer;
Jolted the lumber waggons, democrats, buggies, sulkies;
Jolted the pungs, crotches, stoneboats, bobsleighs, cutters;
Upset loads of bolts, staves, cordwood, loads of logs and hay;
Jolted threshing machines, traction engines, automobiles,
Milk waggons, with cans of whey, envied of querulous swine;
It had shattered the dreams of farmers, figuring on crops;
Of drovers planning sharp deals;
Of peddlers, agents, doctors, preachers;
It had jolted lovers into closer embraces, to their bashful
            delight;
But mostly it had shaken men into sinful tempers—
A wicked stone, a disturbing stone, a stumbling-block—
A stone in the middle of the road—
Insolent as a bank, obstructive as a merger!

Year after year the road flowed around it,
Now on the right side, now on the left;
But always on dark nights flowing straight over it,
Jolting the belated traveller into a passion black as midnight,
Making his rocking vocabulary slop over
With all the shorter and uglier words.
Boys grew to manhood and men grew to dotage.
And year after year they did statute-labour
By cutting the thistles and golden-rod, milkweeds and bur-
            docks,
But left the stone untouched.

There is a merry tale that I heard in my childhood,
Standing between my father's knees, before the open fireplace,
Watching the sparks make soldiers on the blazing backlog,
While the shadows danced on the low-beamed ceiling.
A pretty tale, such as children love, and it comes to me now;
Comes with the sharp, crisp smell of wood smoke,
The crackle of flaming cordwood on the dockers,
The dancing shadows and the hand on my tousled head—
A clear memory, a dear memory, and ever the stone
As it lay in my path on the roadway brought back the story—
The loving voice, and, at the close, the laughter.

"Once upon a time there was a king, a mighty ruler,
Deep in the lore of human hearts, wise as a serpent,
Who placed a stone in the road, in the midst of his kingdom,
On the way to his palace, where all men must pass it.
Straightway the people turned aside, turning to right and to
      left of it.
Statesmen, scholars, courtiers, noblemen, merchants,
Beggars, labourers, farmers, soldiers, generals, men of all
      classes,
Passed the stone, and none tried to move it—
To clear the path of the travelling multitude.
But one day came a man, a kindly poor man,
Who thought it a shame that the stone should be there,
A stumbling-block to the nation. Bowing his back
He put his shoulder to it, and behold, a marvel!
The stone was but a shell, hollow as a bowl!
A child might have moved it.
And in the hollow was a purse of gold, and with it a writing:
'Let him who hath the public spirit to move the stone
Keep the purse and buy a courtly robe,
And come to the palace to serve the king as prime minister.'
So the kindly poor man who had public spirit
Became the chief ruler of all the nation.
When the news was told to them, all men rushed to the high-
      ways
And moved away the stones, but found no purse of gold;
But they cleared the roads of stones, and the 'Good Roads
      Movement'

Went through without cost because the king was wise
And well understood our weak human nature."

Ever when passing the stone I remembered this story
And smiled, touched by memories of childhood,
But knew there was no purse under it; there might be an
        angle-worm,
But I was not going fishing—and the stone stayed.

Now mark the sequel, the conclusion of the matter!
Yesterday a man went by—whether a neighbour or stranger,
No man can tell me, though I have questioned widely,
Questioned eagerly, longing to do him honour,
To chant his name in song, or cunningly engrave it
In monumental brass, with dædal phantasies—
To make it a landmark, a beacon to all future ages.
This good man, earnest, public-spirited,
Not fearing work, scorning tradition,
Doing his duty as he saw it, not waiting an order,
Dug out the stone and made it a matter of laughter,
For it was no boulder, deep-rooted, needing dynamite,
But just a little stone, about the size of a milk pail.
A child might have moved it, and yet it had bumped us
For three generations because we lacked public spirit.
I blush with shame as I pass the stone now lying
In the roadside ditch where the good man rolled it,
And left it where all men may see it—a symbol, a portent.

Tremble, ye Oppressors! Quake, ye Financial Pirates!
Your day is at hand, for there is a man loose in Canada!
A man to break through your illegal labyrinths,
A Theseus to cope with your corporate Minotaurs,
A Hercules to clean out your Augean stables of grafters,
A man who moves stones from the path of his fellows!
And makes smooth the Way of the Worker!
And such a man may move you! Tremble, I say!

Marjorie L. C. Pickthall

'The Drift of Pinions' is exquisitely lyrical, with a flawless rhythm and melody. . . . . This poet pays no heed to the headlines of to-day, nor to the rumours of to-morrow, but goes her way in the world of iris-buds and golden fern, hearing and seeing only the things that are most excellent. She possesses that historic imagination to which the world of yesterday is even more real than the thronging events of the present. . . . . It is impossible in comment or quotation to give an idea of the subtle beauty of execution, the ideal spirituality of conception, which make such poems as 'The Lamp of Poor Souls' and 'A Mother in Egypt' poetic achievements of the rarest kind. . . . . To those for whom poetry is a dwelling-place for all sweet sounds and harmonies, these poems will come as new and magic melodies, sung by one of the authentic fellowship. The singer's gifts are splendour and tenderness of colour, sweetness of silvery phrase, and a true poet's unwavering belief in 'the subtle thing called spirit.'—JEAN GRAHAM, in Toronto 'Saturday Night.'

ABOUT the beginning of this century, the attention of many readers was attracted strongly to the remarkable character of the contributions of a seventeen-year-old girl to the 'Young People's Corner' of the *Mail and Empire*. It was evident that a genius of a rare order had appeared in Canadian literature.

The signature was 'Marjorie L. C. Pickthall,' and on enquiry it was found that she was the daughter of English parents—Mr. Arthur C. Pickthall, an electrical engineer, and Helen Mallard—who had emigrated to Toronto in 1890, when their child was about seven years of age. It was also learned that she had been educated in the Bishop Strachan School on College street.

As Miss Marjorie Lowrey Christie Pickthall was born in London, England, the 14th of September, 1883, she achieved fame earlier in life than most poets. For a decade her poems and short stories have appeared in leading periodicals of England, the United States, and Canada; and in the autumn of 1913, the *University Magazine,* Montreal, and John Lane, the Bodley Head, issued a volume of her collected verse, entitled *A Drift of Pinions.*

For once the reviewers and critics generally were of one opinion, that the work was the product of genius undefiled and radiant, dwelling in the realm of pure beauty and singing with perfect naturalness its divine message.

In 1913, Miss Pickthall was assistant librarian in Victoria College, but the close confinement not agreeing with her health, she resigned and went to England to visit relatives. She was there when the Great War broke out, and at once became interested in grey knitting and other matters pertaining to the soldiers.

In 1915, *Little Hearts,* her first novel, was published and was very favorably received by the best critics.

The well-known English writer, Marmaduke Pickthall, is a half-brother of her father.

Miss Pickthall has also a talent for pen-and-ink sketching and for painting small water-colours.

The poems in *A Drift of Pinions* and many others are to be issued shortly by S. B. Gundy, at the Oxford University Press, in a new volume, entitled *The Lamp of Poor Souls.*

The Lamp of Poor Souls

[In many English churches before the Reformation there was kept
a little lamp continually burning, called the Lamp of Poor Souls.
People were reminded thereby to pray for the souls of those dead
whose kinsfolk were too poor to pay for prayers and masses.]

ABOVE my head the shields are stained with rust,
The wind has taken his spoil, the moth his part;
Dust of dead men beneath my knees, and dust,
    Lord, in my heart.

Lay Thou the hand of faith upon my fears;
    The priest has prayed, the silver bell has rung,
But not for him. O unforgotten tears,
    He was so young!

Shine, little lamp, nor let thy light grow dim.
    Into what vast, dread dreams, what lonely lands,
Into what griefs hath death delivered him,
    Far from my hands?

Cradled is he, with half his prayers forgot.
    I cannot learn the level way he goes.
He whom the harvest hath remembered not
    Sleeps with the rose.

Shine, little lamp, fed with sweet oil of prayers.
    Shine, little lamp, as God's own eyes may shine,
When He treads softly down His starry stairs
    And whispers, 'Thou art Mine.'

Shine, little lamp, for love hath fed thy gleam.
    Sleep, little soul, by God's own hands set free.
Cling to His arms and sleep, and sleeping, dream,
    And dreaming, look for me.

The Pool

COME with me, follow me, swift as a moth,
Ere the wood-doves waken.
    Lift the long leaves and look down, look down
Where the light is shaken,
    Amber and brown,

On the woven ivory roots of the reed,
   On a floating flower and a weft of weed
And a feather of froth.

Here in the night all wonders are,
   Lapped in the lift of the ripple's swing,
A silver shell and a shaken star,
   And a white moth's wing.
Here the young moon when the mists unclose
Swims like the bud of a golden rose.

I would live like an elf where the wild grapes cling,
I would chase the thrush
From the red rose-berries.
All the day long I would laugh and swing
With the black choke-cherries.
I would shake the bees from the milkweed blooms,
And cool, O cool,
Night after night I would leap in the pool,
And sleep with the fish in the roots of the rush.
Clear, O clear my dreams should be made
Of emerald light and amber shade,
Of silver shallows and golden glooms.
Sweet, O sweet my dreams should be
As the dark, sweet water enfolding me
Safe as a blind shell under the sea.

The Shepherd Boy

WHEN the red moon hangs over the fold,
      And the cypress shadow is rimmed with gold,
O little sheep, I have laid me low,
My face against the old earth's face,
Where one by one the white moths go,
And the brown bee has his sleeping place.
And then I have whispered, mother, hear,
For the owls are awake and the night is near,
And whether I lay me near or far
   No lip shall kiss me,
   No eye shall miss me,
Saving the eye of a cold white star.

And the old brown woman answers mild,
Rest you safe on my heart, O child.
Many a shepherd, many a king,
I fold them safe from their sorrowing.
Gweniver's heart is bound with dust,
Tristram dreams of the dappled doe,
But the bugle moulders, the blade is rust;
Stilled are the trumpets of Jericho,
And the tired men sleep by the walls of Troy.
   Little and lonely,
   Knowing me only,
Shall I not comfort you, shepherd boy?

When the wind wakes in the apple tree,
And the shy hare feeds on the wild fern stem,
I say my prayers to the Trinity,—
The prayers that are three and the charms that are seven
To the angels guarding the towers of heaven,—
And I lay my head on her raiment's hem,
Where the young grass darkens the strawberry star,
Where the iris buds and the bellworts are.
All night I hear her breath go by
Under the arch of the empty sky.
All night her heart beats under my head,
And I lie as still as the ancient dead,
Warm as the young lambs there with the sheep.
   I and no other
   Close to my Mother,
Fold my hands in her hands, and sleep.

The Bridegroom of Cana

['There was a marriage in Cana of Galilee. . . . . And both
Jesus was called and His disciples, to the marriage.']

VEIL thine eyes, O beloved, my spouse,
   Turn them away,
Lest in their light my life withdrawn
Dies as a star, as a star in the day,
As a dream in the dawn.

Slenderly hang the olive leaves
   Sighing apart;

The rose and silver doves in the eaves
With a murmur of music bind our house.
Honey and wine in thy words are stored,
Thy lips are bright as the edge of a sword
   That hath found my heart,
   That hath found my heart.

Sweet, I have waked from a dream of thee,
And of Him.
He who came when the songs were done.
From the net of thy smiles my heart went free
And the golden lure of thy love grew dim.
I turned to them asking, 'Who is He,
Royal and sad, who comes to the feast
And sits Him down in the place of the least?'
And they said, 'He is Jesus, the carpenter's son.'

Hear how my harp on a single string
Murmurs of love.
Down in the fields the thrushes sing
And the lark is lost in the light above,
Lost in the infinite, glowing whole,
   As I in thy soul,
   As I in thy soul.

Love, I am fain for thy glowing grace
As the pool for the star, as the rain for the rill.
Turn to me, trust to me, mirror me
As the star in the pool, as the cloud in the sea.
Love, I looked awhile in His face
And was still.

The shaft of the dawn strikes clear and sharp;
Hush, my harp.
Hush my harp, for the day is begun,
And the lifting, shimmering flight of the swallow
Breaks in a curve on the brink of morn,
Over the sycamores, over the corn.
Cling to me, cleave to me, prison me
As the mote in the flame, as the shell in the sea,
For the winds of the dawn say, 'Follow, follow
Jesus Bar-Joseph, the carpenter's son.'

A Mother in Egypt

['About midnight will I go out into the midst of Egypt; and all the firstborn in the land of Egypt shall die, from the firstborn of Pharaoh that sitteth upon the throne, even unto the firstborn of the maid-servant that is behind the mill.']

IS the noise of grief in the palace over the river
For this silent one at my side?
There came a hush in the night, and he rose with his hands
      a-quiver
  Like lotus petals adrift on the swing of the tide.
O small soft hands, the day groweth old for sleeping!
  O small still feet, rise up, for the hour is late!
Rise up, my son, for I hear them mourning and weeping
  In the temple down by the gate.

Hushed is the face that was wont to brighten with laughter
  When I sang at the mill,
And silence unbroken shall greet the sorrowful dawns here-
      after,
  The house shall be still.
Voice after voice takes up the burden of wailing,—
  Do you heed, do you hear, in the high-priest's house by the
      wall?
But mine is the grief, and their sorrow is all unavailing.
  Will he wake at their call?

Something I saw of the broad, dim wings half folding
  The passionless brow.
Something I saw of the sword the shadowy hands were hold-
      ing,—
  What matters it now?
I held you close, dear face, as I knelt and harkened
  To the wind that cried last night like a soul in sin,
When the broad, bright stars dropped down and the soft sky
      darkened,
  And the Presence moved therein.

I have heard men speak in the market-place of the city,
  Low voiced, in a breath,

Of a god who is stronger than ours, and who knows not chang-
       ing nor pity,
   Whose anger is death.
Nothing I know of the lords of the outland races,
   But Amun is gentle and Hathor the Mother is mild,
And who would descend from the light of the peaceful places
   To war on a child?

Yet here he lies, with a scarlet pomegranate petal
   Blown down on his cheek.
The slow sun sinks to the sand like a shield of some burnished
       metal,
   But he does not speak.
I have called, I have sung, but he neither will hear nor waken;
   So lightly, so whitely he lies in the curve of my arm,
Like a feather let fall from the bird that the arrow hath taken.
   Who could see him, and harm?

'The swallow flies home to her sleep in the eaves of the altar,
   And the crane to her nest,'
So do we sing o'er the mill, and why, ah, why should I falter,
   Since he goes to his rest?
Does he play in their flowers as he played among these with
       his mother?
   Do the gods smile downward and love him and give him
       their care?
Guard him well, O ye gods, till I come; lest the wrath of that
       Other
   Should reach to him there!

Arthur Stringer

In running the entire gamut of human emotions, in his volume, 'The Woman in the Rain,' Mr. Stringer takes us from the old and ever loved legends of Greece to the intensely modern figure of a city square, leading us from the sensuous beauty of the opening verses, 'The Passing of Aphrodite,' to the grim truth of the title-poem, and displaying at each step boundless sympathy, ready knowledge, serious treatment of his subject, and that philosophic aloofness not usually associated with the lyricist. He never appears to take his work lightly. He is a deep thinker, getting always to the core of things, making sure of his ground before he steps, and then planting his feet firmly, as it were, until he has made a master-stroke with his pen. . . . . 'Sappho in Leucadia' is perhaps the most serious and ambitious effort Mr. Stringer has ever made. The drama, which embodies the conflict between the austere-minded Pittacus and the song and joy loving Sappho, is replete with sensuous movement and melody.
—FLORENCE V. HENDERSON, in the 'Book-News Monthly.'

ARTHUR JOHN STRINGER, poet and novelist, of Cedar Springs, Ontario, has already achieved greatly. His blank-verse drama, 'Sappho in Leucadia,' is an imaginative, passionate, artistic work of surpassing quality. He has published several books of verse, of which *The Woman in the Rain and Other Poems,* 1907, is the most notable. In these, as Arthur E. McFarlane has said, 'there is maintained a standard of beauty, depth of feeling and technical power, which in Canada have had all too little recognition.' His novels and short stories, however, have had a wider vogue and a more lucrative return.

His first novel, *The Silver Poppy,* 1903, a cleverly written romance of passion, brought him prominently into the limelight, and since then he has published many volumes,—*The Wire Tappers,* 1906; *Phantom Wires,* 1906; *The Under Groove,* 1908; *The Gun Runner,* 1909; *The Shadow,* 1913; *The Prairie Wife,* 1915; *The Hand of Peril,* 1915; and *The Door of Dread,* 1916, among the number—all containing vital, gripping work.

Arthur Stringer was born in London, Ontario, February 26th, 1874,—son of Hugh Arbuthnott Stringer. Having passed through public school and collegiate institute, he attended University College, Toronto, and later, for one academic year, the University of Oxford.

For several years he was engaged in editorial work, first, with the Montreal *Herald* and second with the *American Press Association.*

This quotation from McFarlane's 'Appreciation,' in the *Globe Magazine,* will be of interest:

In 1901, Mr. Stringer . . . . threw up his editorial position and its regularity of salary together. It may be said at once that he has never had to regret such apparent rashness. . . . . The variety of Mr. Stringer's work, during recent years, must seem at first a little bewildering. He was getting his inspirations from months of roughing it in the North-West, from cruising the West Indies in fruit steamers, from working a small but highly productive Sabine farm at Cedar Springs, on Lake Erie, and from touring southern Europe and the Mediterranean. . . . . Mr. Stringer has given us poetry as full of beauty as a garden, and prose which affords the same delight as a rapier in the hands of a finished swordsman.

The Lure o' Life

WHEN my life has enough of love, and my spirit enough
of mirth,
When the ocean no longer beckons me, when the roadway
calls no more,
Oh, on the anvil of Thy wrath, remake me, God, that day!

When the lash of the wave bewilders, and I shrink from the
sting of the rain,
When I hate the gloom of Thy steel-gray wastes, and slink
to the lamp-lit shore,
Oh, purge me in Thy primal fires, and fling me on my way!

When I house me close in a twilit inn, where I brood by a
dying fire,
When I kennel and cringe with fat content, where a pillow
and loaf are sure,
Oh, on the anvil of Thy wrath, remake me, God, that day!

When I quail at the snow on the uplands, when I crawl from
the glare of the sun,
When the trails that are lone invite me not, and the halfway
lamps allure,
Oh, purge me in Thy primal fires, and fling me on my way!

When the wine has all ebbed from an April, when the Autumn
of life forgets
The call and the lure of the widening West, the wind in the
straining rope,
Oh, on the anvil of Thy wrath, remake me, God, that day!

When I waken to hear adventures strange throng valiantly
forth by night,
To the sting of the salt-spume, dust of the plain, and width of
the western slope,
Oh, purge me in Thy primal fires, and fling me on my way!

When swarthy and careless and grim they throng out under
my rose-grown sash,
And I—I bide me there by the coals, and I know not heat nor
hope,
Then, on the anvil of Thy wrath, remake me, God, that day!

At the Comedy

LAST night, in snowy gown and glove,
  I saw you watch the play
Where each mock hero won his love
  The old unlifelike way.

(And O were life their little scene
  Where love so smoothly ran,
How different, Dear, this world had been
  Since this old world began!)

For you, who saw them gaily win
  Both hand and heart away,
Knew well where dwelt the mockery in
  That foolish little play.

('If love were all—if love were all,'
  The viols sobbed and cried,
'Then love were best whate'er befall!'
  Low, low the flutes replied.

And you, last night, did you forget,
  So far from me, so near?—
For watching there your eyes were wet
  With just an idle tear!

(And down the great dark curtain fell
  Upon their foolish play,
But you and I knew—oh, too well!—
  Life went another way!)

The Old Garden

I

WHERE the dim paths wind and creep
  Down past dark and ghostly lands
Lost this many a year in sleep,
  Still an ivied sun-dial stands.

Still about the moss-greened urns
  Fall the rose-leaves ghostly white;
Still the sunset flames and burns
  In the basin's ghostly light.

Still the Satyr by its rim
  Holds the marble reed he bore,
And the brazen dolphins swim
  On the fountain's broken floor.

Still afar some evening bell
  Creeps and fails, and sounds and dies,
Where the ghostly shadows dwell
  Here beneath the quiet skies.

Here within the lichened walls
  Sleeps a land forever old,
Where untroubled twilight falls
  On the casements touched with gold.

Here the quiet hours flow,
  And the years take languid breath,
Where the grasses only know
  Dusk and Silence, Sleep and Death.

II

Yet in some remembered June
  When the bird-notes ceased to ring
Down the echoing afternoon,
  Here a woman used to sing.

Once where still the roses climb
  Round her casements framed with green,
Wrapt in thought, O many a time
  From her window she would lean,

And when sun and birds were gone,
  With her cheek still in her hand,
Gazed across this shadowy lawn,
  To a dim-grown valley land,

Where a white road twined and curled
  Through black hills that barred the West,
And the unknown outer world
  Filled her with a strange unrest.

Here she wandered, brooding-eyed,
  Down each pathway fringed with box,
Where the hyacinths still hide,
  Where still flame the hollyhocks.

And across the whispering grass
  Where the ring-doves murmured low,
Oft her singing heart would pass
  In that lyric Long Ago.

Here tuberose and poppy red
  Saw her pause with lingering feet,—
On the sun-dial lean her head,
  Crying out that life was sweet,—

Asking Time, if Spring by Spring,
  When she walked no longer there
Other roses still could swing,
  Other blossoms scent the air?—

Weeping that she needs must leave
  Warmth and beauty, for the grave—
Hush, what ghostly Voices grieve
Where the regal lilies wave?

III

Still it sleeps, this lonely place
  Given o'er to dusk and dreams;
But her sad and tender face
  Never from the casement gleams.

Still the ivied dial shows
  In its old-time wash of light
Noonday open like a rose,
  Though a shadow mark its flight.

Still the blossoms cling and bloom
  Deep about her window-square,
Still the sunlight floods the room,
  Still the tuberose scents the air;

Still it waits, her garden old,
  Still the waning sunlight burns
On the casements tinged with gold,
  On the green and muffled urns.

Still along the tangled walks,
  Though she knows them not again,

Wait the patient rows of phlox,
    Pipes the Satyr in the rain.

Though she comes no more to dream
    Here where she and Youth were one,
Faint and ghostly voices seem,
    Still to frighten back the sun.

IV

Can it be that in some gray
    Twilight She shall swing the gate?—
Where in eager disarray
    Still her asters brood and wait?

Where her wiser poppy knows,
    And her valiant violets
Look and wonder, and the rose
    Round her darkened window frets?

And these things that temporal seem,
    Rapture, Music, Loveliness,
Beauty frail, and passing Gleam,
    Shall outlive the hearts they press?

Since, we trust, each glory strange,
    Each vague hope Regret once gave,
Shall outlive all death and change,
    As earth's love outlasts the grave!

Destiny

HE sat behind his roses and did wake
    With wanton hands those passions grim
That naught but bitter tears and blood can slake,
    And naught but years can dim.

So o'er their wine did Great Ones sit and nod,
    Ordaining War . . . . as it befell:
Men drunk with drum and trumpet mouthed of God
    And reeled down blood-washed roads to Hell!

17

The Keeper

WIDE is the world and wide its open seas,
  Yet I who fare from pole to pole remain
A prisoned Hope that paces ill at ease,
  A captive Fear that fumbles with its chain.

I once for Freedom madly did aspire,
  And stormed His bars in many a burst of rage:
But see, my Keeper with his brands of fire
  Has cowed me quite . . . . and bade me love my cage!

The Seekers

KNOCK, and the Door shall open: ah, we knocked
  And found the unpiteous portals locked.
Waiting, we learned us croons to while along
Those dreary watches—and ye call it Song!

Seek, and thine eyes shall find: oh, we have sought
The Vision of our Dream, yet found it not.
We limn its broken shadow, that our heart
May half remember—and ye call it Art!

War

FROM hill to hill he harried me;
  He stalked me day and night;
He neither knew nor hated me;
  Nor his nor mine the fight.

He killed the man who stood by me,
  For such they made his law;
Then foot by foot I fought to him,
  Who neither knew nor saw.

I trained my rifle on his heart;
  He leapt up in the air.
The screaming ball tore through his breast,
  And lay embedded there.

Lay hot embedded there, and yet
  Hissed home o'er hill and sea
Straight to the aching heart of one
  Who'd wronged not mine nor me.

Morning in the North-West

GREY countries and grim empires pass away,
And all the pomp and glory of citied towers
Goes down to dust, as Youth itself shall age.
But O the splendour of this autumn dawn—
This passes not away! This dew-drenched Range,
This infinite great width of open space,
This cool keen wind that blows like God's own breath
On life's once drowsy coal, and thrills the blood,
This brooding sea of sun-washed solitude,
This virginal vast dome of opal air—
These, these endure, and greater are than grief!
Still there is strength: and life, oh, life is good!
Still the horizon lures, the morrow calls,
Still hearts adventurous seek outward trails,
Still life holds up its tattered hope!

For here
Is goodly air, and God's own greenness spread.
Here youth audacious fronts the coming day
And age on life ne'er mountainously lies.
Here are no huddled cities old in sin,
Where coil in tangled langours all the pale
Envenomed mirths that poisoned men of old,
Where peering out with ever-narrowing eyes
Reptilious Ease unwinds its golden scales
And slimes with ugliness the thing it eats.
Here life takes on a glory and a strength
Of things still primal, and goes plunging on.
And what care I of time-encrusted tombs,
What care I here for all the ceaseless drip
Of tears in countries old in tragedy?
What care I here for all Earth's creeds outworn,
The dreams outlived, the hopes to ashes turned,
In that old East so dark with rain and doubt?
Here life swings glad and free and rude, and I
Shall drink it to the full, and go content!

From 'Sappho in Leucadia'

Phaon (bitterly)

Thus women change—and in their time forget!

Sappho

THERE lies the sorrow—if we *could* forget!
    For one brief hour you gave me all the love
That women ask, and then with cruel hands
Set free the singing voices from the cage,
And tore the glory from the waiting rose;
And through life's empty garden still I dreamed
And called for Love, and walked unsatisfied.
Love! Love! 'Tis we who lose it know it best!
By day a fire and wonder, and by night
A wheeling star that sinks in Mystery.
Love! Love! It is the blue of bluest skies;
The farthest green of waters touched with sun!
It is the calm of moonlight and of leaves,
And yet the troubled music of the Sea!
It is the frail original of faith,
The timorous thing that seems afraid of light,
Yet, loosened, sweeps the world, consuming time
And tinsel empires, grim with blood and war!
It is the voiceless want and loneliness
Of blighted lands made wonderful with rain!
Regret it is, and song, and wistful tears;
The rose upon the tomb of afterthought,
The only wine of life, that on the lip
Of Thirst turns not to ashes! Change and time
And sorrow kneel to it, for at its touch
The world is beautiful, . . . the world is *born!*

The Final Lesson

I HAVE sought beauty through the dust of strife,
    I have sought meaning for the ancient ache,
And music in the grinding wheels of life;
    Long have I sought, and little found as yet
Beyond this truth: that Love alone can make
    Earth beautiful, and life without regret!

Katherine Hale

The writer of 'Grey Knitting' needs no introduction to Canadian readers, as she is a well-known critic and short story writer, and one of the most prominent and best loved of all the band of Canadian women journalists. The name of Katherine Hale is an adornment to the literature of our Dominion, one of which we may be justly proud. Her verse throbs with a sympathetic harmony that cannot fail of an appeal, heightened as it is by a rich poetic beauty that bespeaks a lofty ideal. Those who know Katherine Hale, know her as an idealist who strives ever to visualize for the everyday toiler the haunting visions of beauty that are vouchsafed to the dreamer, and thus she brings the great things of life closer to her readers, ennobling and uplifting their trivial round.—Hamilton 'Spectator.'

Mrs. Garvin's work at its best is delicate, charming, fairy-like, but unusually expressive of emotion and with unusual powers of imagination.—Marjory MacMurchy *in the 'Toronto Daily News.'*

KATHERINE HALE is the pen name of Mrs. John W. Garvin of Toronto, who was formerly Miss Amelia Beers Warnock of Galt, Ontario, the eldest daughter of Mr. and Mrs. James Warnock. She was born in Galt, but her father was a native of Kilmarnock, Scotland, and her mother was Miss Katherine Hale Byard, of Mobile, Alabama.

Major J. B. Hogan, a maternal great-grandfather of Mrs. Garvin, was aide-de-camp to La Fayette, in the State of Alabama, during the latter's tour of the United States in 1824-5.

Miss Warnock was educated in Galt and at Miss Veal's School in Toronto; and later in New York and in Europe.

The work of Katherine Hale is best known in Canada through her connection, as literary critic, with the *Mail and Empire* of Toronto. She has also developed recital and lecture work, which is well and widely known. But it is probably through the medium of poetry that her name has carried farthest up to the present time.

A glance over many criticisms which followed the publication in November, 1914, of *Grey Knitting,* a first and slight book of her verse, brings to one's notice that a number of the most encouraging criticisms were written by English and American reviewers. It is also noticeable that the small brochure ran into four editions of a thousand each, before it had been on the market for six weeks.

Her latest achievement, *The White Comrade,*—a blank verse war poem of thrilling interest, about five hundred lines in length—will be published in 1916.

The study of music has entered largely into the life of this writer, whose youthful ambition was the operatic stage. It was indeed through her graphic articles on Wagnerian opera, sent to the *Mail and Empire* from New York, while she was a student in that city, that led to her appointment as the editor of 'Contemporary Literature.'

Several of her poems have been set to music, notably 'In The Trenches' by the well-known composer, Gena Branscombe. The title of the song is 'Dear Lad o' Mine.'

The portrait is reproduced in part from the life-size painting by Edith Stevenson.

Katherine Hale's love of things lyrical has become so largely a part of her life that its effect is unmistakable in the poems which follow.

At Noon

THOU art my tower in the sun at noon,
  The shaft of shade upon my golden way,
In painted space the healing note of gray,
The undertone in nature's pagan rune;
And like a wave lashed to the dying moon,
When old desire is haunting its old prey,
Thy strength subdues the forces that would slay,
And soft withdrawal brings, all starry-strewn.

So doth the soul return to Truth's strong tower,
Pilgrim secure at last of its abode,
Hearing that voice as beautiful as morn:
'Come to the heart of Silence, O my flower,
Out from the coloured heat, the gleaming road,
Into the place where deathless light is born.'

Grey Knitting

ALL through the country, in the autumn stillness,
  A web of grey spreads strangely, rim to rim;
And you may hear the sound of knitting needles,
  Incessant, gentle,—dim.

A tiny click of little wooden needles,
  Elfin amid the gianthood of war;
Whispers of women, tireless and patient,
  Who weave the web afar.

Whispers of women, tireless and patient—
  'Foolish, inadequate!' we hear you say;
'Grey wool on fields of hell is out of fashion,'
  And yet we weave the web from day to day.

Suppose some soldier dying, gaily dying,
  Under the alien skies, in his last hour,
Should listen, in death's prescience so vivid,
  And hear a fairy sound bloom like a flower—

I like to think that soldiers, gaily dying
  For the white Christ on fields with shame sown deep,
May hear the fairy click of women's needles,
  As they fall fast asleep.

You Who Have Gaily Left Us

YOU who have gaily left us youth-beshorn,
The town is sunless and the roof forlorn;
Dread stands beside the pillow every morn.

But glory is a beacon in the night,
So brilliant that it bathes the world in light,
And lures these slim lads marching out to fight.

Country of mine, so very strong and young,
What of dark banners fast before you flung!
What of the awful battles yet unsung!

No joyous road I ask for you to-day,
I dare not pipe you peace along the way
That leads to Darkness or increasing Day.

For Heaven plays the prelude: drum and fife
Merging the morning into larger life
Challenge the noon of banners and of strife;

Until, within the living crimson flame,
There seems to burn a new-born country's name,
The Friend of Light, and Honour's deathless fame.

When You Return

WHEN you return I see the radiant street,
I hear the rushing of a thousand feet,
I see the ghosts that women come to greet.

I can feel roses, roses all the way,
The fearful gladness that no power can stay,
The joy that glows and grows in ambient ray.

Because slim lads come marching home from war?
Truly, slim lads, home from the Very Far:
From fields as distant as the farthest star.

It will be strange to hear the plaudits roll,
Back from that zone where soul is flung on soul,
Where they go out like sparks to one straight goal.

Where souls go out as moments fly,
Urging their claim on the unbending sky—
Surely it must be wonderful to die!

. . . .

When you return I see the radiant street,
I hear the rushing of a thousand feet—
Living and dead with roses we shall greet.

In the Trenches
(*Christmas, 1914*)

WAR gods have descended:
    The world burns up in fine!
Warm your hands at the trench's fire,
    Dear lad o' mine.

Bullets cease this Christmas night,
    Only songs are heard.
If you feel a phantom step,
    'Twas my heart that stirred.

If you see a dreamy light,
    'Tis the Christ-Child's eyes;
I believe he watches us,
    Wonderful and wise.

Let us keep our Christmas night
    In the camp-light shine;
Warm your hands at the trench's fire—
    They still hold mine.

I Used to Wear a Gown of Green

I USED to wear a gown of green
    And sing a song to May,
When apple blossoms starred the stream
    And Spring came up the way.

I used to run along with Love
    By lanes the world forgets,
To find in an enchanted wood
    The first frail violets.

And ever 'mid the fairy blooms
And murmur of the stream,
We used to hear the pipes of Pan
Call softly through our dream.

But now, in outcry vast, that tune
Fades like some little star
Lost in an anguished judgment day
And scarlet flames of war.

What can it mean that Spring returns
And purple violets bloom,
Save that some gypsy flower may stray
Beside his nameless tomb!

To pagan Earth her gown of green,
Her elfin song to May—
With all my soul I must go on
Into the scarlet day.

To Peter Pan in Winter

['And so it was arranged that Peter Pan should fly back alone to
Fairyland, and that once a year Mrs. Darling would allow Wendy
to go and stay a whole week with him to do his Spring cleaning.']

SPRING house-cleaning in Arcadie,
When every bough is bare;
'If it bring Wendy back to me,
'I wish,' quoth Pan, ' 'twere here.'
For Peter Pan is sometimes sad
In spite of all that's sung;
He has to pipe and dance like mad
To keep this old world young.

And as he pipes the fairies light
A star for every tone.
(Do starry lights burn just as bright
When one is all alone?)
And as he pipes small elfin folk
Foregather from the moon,
And dance, and flash, and fade like smoke
While he plays on and on.

His magic tree-tops shine with ice
　That used to melt in green,
The people creep like small brown mice
　Down in the worlds between.
And Wendy may be well or ill,
　And play or go to school;
But Pan sits high and pipes his fill
　And minds no mortal rule.

O Peter Pan, the winds are cold,
　The snow is deep and high;
The Never-Never Land is gold,
　And yet—perhaps you sigh;
Perhaps you know, though just an elf,
　In your small fairy way,
How wretched one is by himself,
　When Some One Else can't stay!

So pipe your sweetest, Peter Pan,
　And clang the silver bells;
Send all the elfin din you can
　To where the Great One dwells,
Who holds the Spring within His hand,
　That you who wait above,
And we, in this midwinter world,
　May call again—to Love.

The Answer

UNALTERED aisles that wait and wait forever,
　O woods that gleam and stir in liquid gold,
What of your little lover who departed
Before the year grew old?

The leaves are very perfect in the forest,
　This is the perfect hour of summer's wane,
And but last year we watched the blue October,
　Between the parted boughs, as now, Lorane.

We asked of Life the old, eternal questions;
　We asked of God: 'Art Thou not here; and why?

Why never come with heralds of the morning
  Across this blaze of sky?

'Why build Thyself these great and perfect places;
  Why build, and never come to walk therein?'
And only rippling sunshine was the answer,
  Or little pattering footsteps of the rain.

But still we sought Him, in the blue-white winter,
  Or in the rosy spring or shadowy fall;
And faithful winds went forth with us to meet him,
  And all the heaven was one vibrating call.

We sought Him, and our own love seemed the answer;
  We called Him, and the forest smiled us back.
Then we forgot, and only looked for laughter
  Along the wild-wood track.

Yet sometimes, when the moon sang down her cadence
  Through all the forest roof so old and high,
We trembled from the sense of all we knew not—
  The awful incompleteness of the sky.

And all the years we two went forth together
  We never heard that third step on the sod.
I was alone—alone before I felt it,
  And turned, and looked on God.

And God said: 'I am loneliness and sorrow,
  And I am questioning hope, and I am strife;
I am the joy that surges through my forest,
  And I am death in life.

'I am the singing bird, the leaf, the shadow,
  I am the circle of the endless earth;
Out of the infinite of all creation
  I am the silence where the soul finds birth.'

And so, unaltered aisles that wait forever
  And woods that gleam and stir in liquid gold,
You have made answer for the little lover
  Who passed ere you grew old.

Robert Norwood

*Mr. Norwood's is a new voice in Canadian poetry. But
though new, it is a voice already mellowed, whose theme has
been won out of years devoted to scholarship and philosophic
thought; whose music has back of it a technique formed accord-
ing to classical standards. . . . . Those who read Mr.
Norwood's sonnets will note his faculty of choosing right
words, of evolving fresh metaphor, of combining variety with
beauty, of mingling perception and philosophy with musical
skill. . . . . In his 'Dives' the poet sets out to discover
rather than to accept. His text, for the poem has a text goldenly
threaded into the warp and woof of the whole, is concerned
with the mystic union of Christ with mankind. It is a text that
goes down as deep as hell and which soars as high as heaven,
to show that there is no duality, no dualism, no duarchy; that
all things, create and uncreate, are governed from one point,
made of one substance, vitalized by one principle—that Love
is not only the fulfilling but the origin of the Law.*—FANFAN
in the 'Free Press,' London, Ontario.

IT was Emerson who said that the chief event in chronology was the birth of a poet, and the great seer was right. But he meant of course a poet with the keen perception, the intense emotion, the comprehensive mentality and the imaginative vision of genius.

In the Rev. Robert W. Norwood, M.A., Rector of the Memorial Church, London, Ontario, whose first volume of verse, entitled *His Lady of the Sonnets*, appeared in 1915, Canada has, I believe, just such a poet as Emerson had in mind.

This opinion is not based on the sonnet sequence, the title of which was selected as that of his book, brilliant, beautiful and rare as such an achievement is, but rather on the originality of conception, the imaginative reach and the dramatic power of the poet as exemplified in *Dives in Torment,* and in *The Witch of Endor,* a drama (1916; McClelland, Goodchild and Stewart, Toronto) ; on the comprehending sympathy and love and the new philosophic thought as expressed in his two unpublished volumes, *The Modernists* and *Songs of a Little Brother* which will be issued in 1917; and on the many evidences throughout his work of ripe and wide-ranging scholarship.

Mr. Norwood was born in Christ Church Rectory, New Ross, Lunenburg county, Nova Scotia, March 27th, 1874, son of the Rev. Joseph W. Norwood and Edith, daughter of Captain Harding. He was educated at Coaticook Academy, Quebec; at Bishop's College, Lennoxville, Quebec; and at King's College Windsor, Nova Scotia, where he graduated in Arts in 1897. In December of the same year he was ordained deacon in Halifax by Bishop Courtney, and in the following year was ordained priest by the same dignitary.

At King's College, Mr. Norwood had the good fortune to have as his Professor of English Literature, Mr. Charles G. D. Roberts, who detected the poetic gift of the ambitious student, and so taught and encouraged him as to become the most moulding influence in his career.

In 1899, Mr. Norwood was married to Ethel, a daughter of George McKeen, M.D., of Baddeck, C.B., and their two daughters and a son—Aileen, Robert and Jean—make glad the rectory, and inspire their poet father to sing new songs.

His Lady of the Sonnets

(From the Sonnet Sequence)

II

I MEET you in the mystery of the night,
  A dear Dream-Goddess on a crescent moon;
An opalescent splendour, like a noon
Of lilies; and I wonder that the height
Should darken for the depth to give me light;
Light of your face, so lovely that I swoon
With gazing, and then wake to find how soon
Joy of the world fades when you fade from sight.

Beholding you, I am Endymion,
Lost and immortal in Latmian dreams;
With Dian bending down to look upon
Her shepherd, whose æonian slumber seems
A moment, twinkling like a starry gem
Among the jewels of her diadem.

IV

MY love is like a spring among the hills
  Whose brimming waters may not be confined
But pour one torrent through the ways that wind
Down to a garden; there the rose distills
Its nectar; there a tall, white lily fills
Night with anointing of two lovers, blind,
Dumb, deaf, of body, spirit, and of mind
From breathless blending of far-sundered wills.

Long ere my love had reached you, hard I strove
To send its torrent through the barren fields;
I wanted you, the lilied treasure-trove
Of innocence, whose dear possession yields
Immortal gladness to my heart that knows
How you surpass the lily and the rose.

V

LIKE one great opal on the breast of Night,
  Soft and translucent, hangs the orb of June!

I hear wild pipings of a joyous tune
Played on a golden reed for the delight
Of you, my hidden, lovely Eremite—
You by the fountain from the marble hewn—
You silent as in dream, with flowers strewn
About your feet—you goddess, robed in white!

Mute and amazed, I at the broken wall
Lean fearful, lest the sudden, dreadful dawn
For me Diana's awful doom let fall;
And I be cursed with curious Actæon,
Save that you find in me this strong defence—
My adoration of your innocence.

VI

WHEN from the rose mist of creation grew
God's patient waiting in your wide-set eyes,
The morning stars, and all the host that flies
On wings of love, paused at the wondrous blue
With which the Master, mindful of the hue,
Stained first the crystal dome of summer skies;
And afterward the violet that vies
With amethyst, before He fashioned you.

And I have trembled with those ancient stars,
My heart has known the flame-winged seraphs' song;
For no indifferent, dreamy eyelid bars
Me from the blue, nor veils with lashes long
Your love, that to my tender gazing grows
Bold to confess it: I am glad he knows!

IX

LAST night—or was it in the golden morn—
Once more I dreamed that I alone did fare
Forth into spirit-silences; and there
I found you not; my star was set! Forlorn,
I sought the kindred company of worn
And stricken souls—lost, sundered souls, who bear
Old and avoided crosses with each care
Woven together in their crowns of thorn.

Gods of the patient, vain endeavour, these
Claimed me and called me fellow, comrade, friend,
And bade me join in their brave litanies;
Because, though I had failed you, I dared bend
Before you without hope of one reward,
Save that in loving you my soul still soared.

X

LAST night I crossed the spaces to your side,
As you lay sleeping in the sacred room
Of our great moment. Like a lily's bloom,
Fragile and white were you, my spirit-bride,
For pain and loneliness with you abide,
And Death had thought to touch you with his doom,
Until Love stood angelic at the tomb,
Drew sword, smote him, and life's door opened wide.

I looked on you and breathed upon your hair—
Your hair of such soft, brown, translucent gold!
Nor did you know that I knelt down in prayer,
Clasped hands, and worshipped you for the untold
Magnificence of womanhood divine—
God's miracle of Water turned to Wine!

XXIV

I AM all gladness like a little child!
Grief's tragic figure of the veilèd face
Fades from my path, moving with measured pace
Back from the splendour that breaks on the wild,
High hills of sorrow, where the storm-clouds piled
In drift of tears. Lo! with what tender grace
Joy holds the world again in her embrace
Since you came forth, and looked on me, and smiled.

Down in the valley shines a scimiter—
A stream with autumn-gold deep damascened;
And of the bards of day one loiterer
Still lingers at his song, securely screened
By foliage. Dear, what miracle is this,
Transforming void and chaos with a kiss!

XXVIII

COMPANION of the highroad, hail! all hail!
Day on his shoulder flame of sunset bears,
As he goes marching where the autumn flares
A banner to the sky; in russet mail
The trees are trooping hither to assail
Twilight with spears; a rank of coward cares
Creep up, as though to take us unawares,
And find their stratagems of none avail.

Accept the challenge of the royal hills,
And dare adventure as we always dared!
Life with red wine his golden chalice fills,
And bids us drink to all who forward fared—
Those lost, white armies of the host of dream;
Those dauntless, singing pilgrims of the Gleam!

Dives in Torment
(*Latter Half*)

THIS was my failure, who thought that the feast
Rivalled the rapture of bird on the wing;
Rivalled the lily all robed like a priest;
Smoke of the pollen when Rose-censers swing.

This was my folly, who gave for a gown—
Purple and gold, and a bracelet and rings,
Shouts in the streets as I rode through the town—
Life in the love of the kinship of things.

Lazarus, Lazarus, this is my thirst,
Fever from flame of the love I have missed;
Ache of the heart for the friends I have cursed;
Longing for lips that I never have kissed!

Hell is for him who hath never found God
Hid in the bramble that burns by the way;
Findeth Him not in the stone and the clod;
Heareth Him not at the cool of the day.

Hell is for him who hath never found Man.
God and my Brother, I failing to find,
Failed to find me; so my days were a span
Void of the triumph of Spirit and Mind.

Once, I recall, at the table I leaned
Back on the breast of Pomona, my slave,
Saw through the window, with lattice-work screened,
Thee in thy rags, and I laughed! then grew grave:

Up the white street came a Man with a face
Sad with the woe and the pain of the world;
Moving with kingliness, ease, and a grace;
Crowned with wine-coloured hair wavy and curled

Over broad shoulders, so broad that I vowed
Here was Messias—the Samson—the King!
Leaped from the table and joined with the crowd;
Offered my purple, my bracelet, my ring!

Then through the clamour and dust of the street
Words of rebuke were directed to me:
'Lift thou up Lazarus; give him a seat
High among all who are feasting with thee.'

Lift up the beggar! I laughed at Him there—
'Thou and Thy tattered ones take to the street—
I to the palace . . Begone! . . And beware!
Caiaphas comes, and the Sanhedrin meet!

'Go! or I hale Thee to judgment of them;
Go! or Thy God shall avail Thee in vain;
Thou art of Japheth, and I am of Shem,
Lazarus, outcast and cursèd with Cain!

'Needs must there be a division of men;
Hewer of wood is the Gibeonite,
Cutter of stone in the quarries, and then
Slave to the Covenant-Israelite.'

'Nay, all are equal and loved of the Lord,'
Whispered the Stranger. The listening street
Filled with the murmur of those who adored,
Hushed at the sound of His voice that was sweet,

Stirring my heart as a harp in the hall,
Silent for ages, is stirred by the wind
Breathed through the arras; and memories call
Over the summits of spirit and mind.

Yea, for a moment I struggled with Love;
Yearned to embrace thee and pour on thy hair
Oil of anointing, and place thee above
All of the guests who were gathering there—

There in my palace of pleasure and ease,
Builded by Herod, and bought with my gold,
Portaled and curtained with soft tapestries
Woven at looms of the Orient, sold

Down in Damascus. A palm in the sands,
That was my palace; a palm with a soul
Breathing of beauty when each leaf expands
Out to the desert which brims like a bowl—

Brims like a bowl of Falernian wine
Turned to the sun! O my palace and hall!
O sound of the psaltery under the vine
Grown in the garden! O footsteps that fall

Soft as the leaves in a pomegranate grove,
Soft on the pavement of beryl and pearl
Under the moon when my Miriam strove,
Laughing, to dance down the Syrian girl!

These thrust between my compassion and thee—
Beauty that mocked like a maid from her bower—
Beauty that looked through the lattice at me;
Sighed: 'I have tarried, my Love, for this hour!'

Then to the palace all flaming I went,
Flaming with love for Pomona, my pride.
Back like a bow her dear body I bent,
Kissed her and placed her in joy at my side;

Crowned her with myrtle, proclaimed her a queen;
Drank to her eyes and her lips and her hair;
Clasped on her throat of an ivory sheen
Gems of an order kings only might wear.

Oh, how she sparkled and gleamed like a sword!
Oh, how the cymbals and tabours did sound!
Oh, My Pomona, my loved and adored—
Dust of the body is dust of the ground!

.   .   .   .   .

For I forgot Him, and bought with my gold
Houses and lands. Yea, I sought far and wide
Pleasure and ease. Then one day I was old. . . .
Darkness came over the noon . . . and I died!

Dead and companioned in pomp to the grave!
Dead and forgotten in less than a day
Save by Pomona, my mistress and slave
Sold unto Herod! . . Oh, she had a way,

Turn of the head and glance of the eye!
Touch of the hand and a fall of the feet!
Voice that was coo of the dove and a cry
Heard in the night when the seraphim meet!

Sometimes I fancy Gehenna's abyss
Gleams with a light that is love; and I feel
Lips on my lips in the tenderest kiss,
Making hell heaven: as though the appeal

Sent from my soul to Pomona had gained
Heart and the whole of her throned on a star,
Where for an æon of bliss she hath reigned
Lonely for Dives so lost and afar!

Lazarus! Nearer! The light on thy face
Shines through the dark! Oh, what glory is thine!
Nay, not too near lest thou see my disgrace
Naked! behold bruised the image divine!

Lazarus! Pity! Pursue not my soul
Down the last gulf! I am fearful of thee—
Not of Jehovah, Whose thunders may roll
Over my head—Have thou pity on me!

This have I learned in the torment of hell:
Man is the judge of the soul that hath sin;
Man must raise man from the depths where he fell,
Hurled by the hand of his passion. Begin,

Lazarus, Lord of the Light and the dark;
Stand on the cloud that hath bridged the abyss,
Judging my cause; for my spirit is stark
Under thy glance in abandon of bliss!

18

Yea, there is joy in the judgment; a peace
I have not known in an æon of pain;
Joy in the thought that thy love will not cease
Till it hath cleansed all my spirit from stain.

Therefore I hail thee, O Lazarus! cry:
'Hail to the love that restoreth the years
The locusts have eaten! Search me and try
Thought of my heart and tale of my tears!'

Try me and prove me; for I am undone,
Conquered by love of a love that hath sought
Me unto hell! Thou hast triumphed and won,
Lazarus, who for my spirit hath fought.

Yield I the trophies of battle; lay down
All of the pride and the hatred of heart;
Weeping I give thee my sceptre and crown;
Nothing I claim; not a tithe, not a part!

    .   .   .   .

Lazarus, art thou the same that I saw
Begging for crumbs? Thou hast changed, thou hast
       changed!
Through what dominions of wonder and awe,
Beauty and joy, hast thou ranged, hast thou ranged?

Kingly and glorious, mantled with flame,
Lo! in thyself the Messias I see.
Lazarus, thou and the Christ art the same,
Thou art the Christ and the Master of me—

Thou art Messias! . . . . And this Paradise! . . .
There is Pomona! . . . . There Mother who gave
Breast to her babe! . . . . From Gehenna I rise
Cleansed by a love that is mighty to save!

Light, and the sound of a song that is love!
Light, and the freedom of spirit to soar!
Light, and Messias enthronèd above
High where the seraphim bow and adore!

Marian Osborne

*These poems are all graceful and melodious. . . . .
The author tries many metres, both regular and irregular,
. . . . they are well controlled and lend variety to her
muse. For the most part the verses are of love and contemplative moods. . . . . The author's gift of dignified
and harmonious verse is at its best in the sonnets; and there
is a life given briefly and illuminatingly in 'The Professor's
Story,' a little poem in the manner of Browning. . . . .*
—'The Times,' London, England.

*A collection of poems of a high order. . . . . They will
be appreciated by all true lovers of poetry. Mrs. Osborne
proves herself skilled with various measures. The first of
her sonnets is entitled, 'William Osler':—*

> *'The man whose simple human art
> Is to bestow, with generous thought and free,
> On fellow-man, his ever-welcome guest,
> The golden treasures of his mind and heart,
> Of ancient lore, and life's philosophy.' . .*—'Canada.'

[341]

Marian Osborne

MRS. OSBORNE'S mother was a sister of the late Rev. Featherston Osler, M.A., whose sons have won such high distinction, and her father was the late George Grant Francis, of Wales.

Marian Francis was born in the city of Montreal, and was educated at Hellmuth College and at the Collegiate Institute, London, Ontario, and at Trinity College, Toronto. At the age of seventeen she married Mr. Charles Lambert Bath, and lived in Wales for the ensuing five years, until her husband's death. Of this marriage there are two children, a son, who is in the Royal Flying Corps, and a daughter.

In 1902, she married Mr. H. C. Osborne, M.A., barrister, and member of the Toronto Stock Exchange—now Lieutenant-Colonel, attached to the Headquarters Staff, 2nd Division, Ontario.

This promising author has inherited literary talent from both grandfathers—her mother's father particularly having been a noted writer, in his day, on scientific subjects pertaining to medicine. In this connection it is interesting to remember that her cousin, Sir William Osler, as a writer of medical works, has a world-wide reputation.

Mrs. Osborne is also noted in Toronto for her skill in sports, having recently won the championship in fencing, and in ornamental swimming.

Since the publication in England, in 1914, of her book of verse, entitled *Poems,* she has written 'The Song of Israfel,' which appeared in *The University Magazine,* and other poems of merit, and has been occupied in the writing of a novel.

Love's Enchantment

AS when two children, hand clasped fast in hand,
Explore the dimness of a fairy bower
In tremulous encroachment, each one fanned
To ardour by his playmate's fancied power;
Then see with wondering eyes the thing they sought,
Half feared, half hoped for, suddenly in view,
So we on tip-toe came, and dear Love wrought
Enchantments for us, long before we knew

Each other's heart; then led us gaily o'er
The flower-starred meadows, onward, eagerly,
Until we reached at length the open door
Of his domain—for thus it was to be;
There in one brimming kiss soul cried to soul
And found completion 'neath Love's aureole.

Love's Gifts

BELOVED, can I make return to thee
For all the gifts which thy rich heart doth hold,
Gifts that have turned my life's gloom into gold
And opened wisdom's door with magic key.
My eyes enchanted see love's mystery,
And though I fear, yet would I fain be bold,
For thy voice thrills on ears no longer cold
And murmurs wondrous music, tenderly.
And though my hands hold naught, yet would I part
The curtains of my soul to give thee bliss,
Answer thee in the throbbing of my heart
And soothe thy fevered lips with one deep kiss.
Ah! let no shadow fall our souls athwart,
For life holds nothing greater, love,—than this.

Love's Anguish

SHALL I with lethal draughts drowse every thought
And let the days pass by with silent tread;—
Dream that the vanished hour I long have sought
Is once more mine, and you no longer dead?
How shall I grasp the skirts of happy chance
And calm my spirit in adventurous ways,
Like bold Don Quixote hold aloft my lance
Against the world without thy meed of praise?
How can I live through long discordant days,
How cheat despair, or speed Time's lagging feet,
Since I have lost the fragrance of love's ways
That turned life's winter into springtime sweet?
Come to me, Death, come, ere it be too late;
Thy kiss alone can draw the sting of Fate.

Despair

THE darkness of the night bewildering
   Falls on a world of chaos, and alone
I lie, and listen for the single string
Of Hope, with strainèd ears, but hear no moan
Nor any sound, save only the dull beat
Of my starved heart, that totters on the brink
Of abjectness, reason dethroned, her seat
Usurped by folly. Dear God! let me sink
Forever out of sight in nothingness,
As crazed stars fall from heaven. Woe is me!
Is death too merciful for my distress?
Or does my pain mean nothing unto Thee?
Life's stony road I've suffered passing well,
Now its lone sign-post points to my soul's hell.

If I Were Fair

IF only I were fair,
  Or had some charm to bind
In tender loving ways
The passing of the days,
Life would seem less unkind
Less hard at times to bear,
If I were only fair.

If only I were fair
And had blest Beauty's dower,
I should hear flutterings
Of Love's mysterious wings
And feel his kisses shower
On lips and brow and hair,
If I were only fair.

If only I were fair,
A child, whose heart beat free,
Would lay its cheek on mine,
Our arms would intertwine,
Sweetly, caressingly—
A child that I might bear,
If I were only fair.

If only I were fair,
As I passed down the street
Some weary waiting eyes
Might smile in glad surprise,
As though the sun to greet.
How I could banish care,
If I were only fair!

If only I were fair,
I would be generous too;
In my love-laden eyes
Forgiving tears would rise.
And, finding one man true,
I might then all things dare,
If I were only fair.

The Song of Israfel

['And the angel Israfel, whose heart-strings are a lute, and who has the sweetest voice of all God's creatures.'—Koran.]

FAIR Israfel, the sweetest singer of Heaven,
Shook back his burning curls, and from his seven
Stringed lute swept an impassioned prayer
So full of yearning that the very air
Celestial seemed surcharged with pleading love.
Importunate it throbbed and swelled above
Each diamond star-lit crevice of the skies
That oped to hearken, and from shimmering eyes
Let down their tear-spun rainbows for the song.
Eager it sped, and trembling pulsed along
Craving a shelter and a sanctuary
To weave anew on earth Heaven's harmony.

The dying sun had laid his hand of splendour
Upon the watching lake. Burning, yet tender,
His parting kiss enraptured all the night.
A mystic barque seemed in the golden light
Like some pale ghostly moth, that flies away
With fluttering wings out-drooped from circling day.
Onward she came, borne by the music's breath,
Unearthly as an image after death.
Rhythmic she swooned and dreamed,

And ever idly seemed
To float, as lilies float upon a stream
Whose slackened pulses halt awhile to dream.

Then to the soul of those whose eager ears
Were not clay-sealed, came music born of tears,
Far wingèd memories,
Angelic harmonies,
Haunting as dear dead loves for which men mourn,
Sweet as remembered joys to hearts forlorn.
The melody was fraught with dreams of Spring
Poured from uplifted throats of birds who sing
In silvery ecstasy of lover's sighs
And of the pansied darkness in love's eyes,
While over all the azure vaulted height
Of heaven circled a world's delight.

The silences made music. The still air
Breathed incense-laden consecrated prayer,
The grave and cowlèd Night knelt, listening,
And hushed the restless winds, that whispering,
Creep on the borderland of sleep.
Stilled were earth's murmurings deep.
The garrulous waves ceased playing by the shore
In bubbling laughter, and the leaves forbore
Their mirthful dancing, while the rustling grass
Sighed, and was silent, lest the song should pass.
The chords majestic swept the soul. Unrest
Was stilled to peace in fevered hearts distressed.

Wearied of alien ears, and solitude,
The deathless strain soared upwards, to the nude
And silvery sentinel of Paradise,
The patient Moon, that watches o'er the skies.
She turned the song to tears of gentle rain
That washed the earth in loveliness, and Pain
Which like a cold and cruel snake lies curled
In the grim arms of Night, himself unfurled
And sought a refuge in the depths of Hell.
But even there, these tears of Israfel
Found the sad eyes of those whom hope had fled
And as they wept, . . . so were they comforted.

Albert E. S. Smythe

Albert E. S. Smythe might be appropriately called 'The Poet of Theosophy.' All his best verse is tinged or infused with the fundamental beliefs of this all-embracing religion, which, as taught by him, would harmonize and unify all creeds. He is the father of Theosophy in Canada. As a result of his efforts, the Toronto Theosophical Society was chartered and organized, February 16th, 1891. He was elected the first President. . . Let us try to realize the spiritual development of the man who wrote these noble lines:

> *'I know that the Master walked on earth,*
> *For I've heard the tale of His human birth,*
> *And all that He did would I have done*
> *Had He been mortal and I God's Son.'*

> *'And yet, Soul-shiningly, the mist-banks burn*
> *With glory on the hither side of tears.*
> *The out-world phantoms nevermore return:*
> *The world within enfolds the years and spheres.'*

[347]

ALBERT ERNEST STAFFORD SMYTHE was born at Gracehill, a Moravian village, County Antrim, Ireland, December 27th, 1861,—son of Stafford Smythe, whose paternal grandfather had been one of the original settlers in the village about 1760, and Leonora Cary, only surviving child of Lucius Cary, J. P., of Red Castle, County Donegal.

He was educated at local schools and academies, and at the South Kensington Department Science Classes, where he took special prizes in geology, botany and physics. When a young man of eighteen, he was shipwrecked while voyaging to New York, and all his possessions lost. Ten years later, while again crossing the ocean, he met Mary Adelaide Constantine, of Lancashire, and in a few months they were married.

Prior to returning to Ireland and re-crossing in 1889, he had lived for several years in Chicago, employed by a business house. And he came to Toronto in September, 1889, as agent for the Portland Cement Company, and continued in that position for about five years. During this period, his chief interest, apart from business, lay in the Theosophical movement, of which he was the first representative in the Dominion. He joined the American Section of which William Quan Judge was then General Secretary and started propaganda in Ottawa and in Toronto. For several years he edited and published *The Lamp* as a propaganda organ.

Mr. Smythe adheres strictly to the broad platform originally laid down, *which seeks the underlying unity of all religions, and active coöperation for human welfare among all who believe in the brotherhood of man.* Subsequent to Mr. Judge's death in 1906, Mr. Smythe's services as a lecturer were requisitioned and while on several tours in the United States he spoke in a large number of the most important cities. His articles on Theosophic and other themes which have appeared for years in the *Sunday World,* under the heading, 'Crusts and Crumbs,' have been very instructive and illuminating; and these together with his able editorials in the daily *World,* have long been an impelling influence in Canada.

In 1912, Mr. Smythe, a widower since 1906, married the eldest daughter of Thomas Henderson, of 'The Park,' Newtownstewart, Ireland. His only son, by his first marriage, is a commissioned officer at the Front.

The Way of the Master

I KNOW that the Master walked on earth,
For I've heard the tale of His human birth,
And all that He did would I have done
Had he been mortal and I God's Son.

I know that His heart was crushed and wrung,
For I've cherished that which has turned and stung;
And He could not help but love us all
Though some are held in an evil thrall.

And I know that His law was Brotherhood,
And His life was gentle and kind and good,
And all that the sad earth needs this hour
To bring men peace, is to use that power.

I have overtaken many a band
Of pilgrims following Faith's command,
And journeyed awhile where their prophet led,
Then, passing on, found the Path ahead,

With the Master's guide-marks, true and just,
And His foot-prints marked in the clay and dust,
But over-trodden, effaced and blurred,
By those who followed some lesser Word.

I may pass them all in the years, perchance,
And reach new realms of the soul's expanse,
And many may follow where I have gone—
But the Master still will be leading on.

For the best I know of His heart to-day,
When I've bettered that, will have sunk away
In the knowledge gained from my higher place
Of His endless love, of His boundless grace.

O comrade mine, we shall never part
In the living way of the loving heart,
Where the lust of gold and the wanton's guile
And the cup of the curse shall not defile,

For I know the Master walked on earth,
I have heard the tale of his human birth,
And all that He did would I have done
Had He been mortal and I God's Son.

November Sunshine

ONE figure flitting through my dreamland ways
   Holds out dear hands and beckons me to go,
And all the world is sweeter for a phrase
   That dimly whispers when the lights are low.
   Once, leaping through the silences of snow,
Far up the heights, the sky all turned to haze,
   A little rill, escaping, rippled so:
Adventured thus, my dreamland figure strays.

Belated on the spray that afternoon
   The red, unripened bramble-berries hung,
Touched with November sunshine, fading soon—
   A smile, untimely bright, in mockery flung;
   A blackbird, all his summer anthems sung,
Fled with a scream; about our feet lay strewn
   The leafy havoc; and my heart was wrung
To know, too late for life, life's only boon.

They pass, these uninterpretable years,
   A weird, oracular host, abrupt and stern,
Interminably ranked. Time domineers,
   Despoiling us of all the joys we earn;
   And yet, Soul-shiningly, the mist-banks burn
With glory on the hither side of tears.
   The out-world phantoms nevermore return;
The world within enfolds the years and spheres.

By Wave and War

ONCE again the ocean fulness,
   Once again the daring leap,
All my limbs o'er-lapped in coolness,
   All my joy upon the deep—
Arm that urges, wave that surges,
   Foam that flies along the flood,
Over-strive and over-conquer
All the numbness and the nullness
   In the languor of my blood,
And I dash among the breakers, and I overbear their rancour
   Till I feel myself a man in might and mood.
Once again the field of glory,
   Once again the battle-shout,

And my shield is hacked and gory,
  And the foe is bold and stout;
There are rallies, there are sallies,
  There is death in every blow,
But the mood of war grows godlike,
And the young men and the hoary
  Charge with equal hearts aglow,
Till a thrust has pierced their fury—flung them headlong—
      lying clod-like
  They are silent—but they triumph as they go!

Once again the soul's submergence
  Under warring will and sense,
By the Law's almighty urgence
  And the Sun's bright vehemence;
Plunging, diving, onward striving,
  Through the shocks of change and chance—
Through the coils of flesh and passion,
Till the love-compelled convergence
  Towards the Heart of all Romance,
To the Throne of Him who watches in the old victorious
      fashion
  Comes a brother in humanity's advance.

Anastasis

WHAT shall it profit a man
    To gain the world—if he can—
And lose his soul, as they say
In their uninstructed way?

The whole of the world in gain;
The whole of your soul! Too vain
You judge yourself in the cost.
'Tis you—not your soul—is lost.

Your soul! If you only knew
You would reach to the heaven's blue,
To the heartmost centre sink,
Ere you severed the silver link,

To be lost in your petty lust
And scattered in cosmic dust.

For your soul is a Shining Star
Where the Throne and the Angels are.

And after a thousand years
With the salve of his bottled tears
Your soul shall gather again
From the dust of a world of pain

The frame of a slave set free—
The man that you ought to be,
The man you may be to-night
If you turn to the Valley of Light.

The Trysting Path

DEAR little darkened way where we have climbed
    How often and again,
Down to the still, star-shadowed haunt where chimed
    Uncounted hours of peace beyond all pain!—
    There have we lain
And to the leafy whispers of the wood-world rhymed
    The music of our hearts' refrain:
Guard thy rare solitude, and may no sullen feet
    The wedded paces of thy path profane!

And you—so dear that all things else are dear
    That enter your desire—
All that you value, all that I revere
    Transformed in our discourse (as in God's fire
    The starry choir
With life renewed evolves fresh fitness for a higher sphere,)
    With quick interpretings inspire,
Deep inner knowledge, and the need, confessed and sweet,
    Of that Sun-power which holds the worlds entire.

Set in blue darkness, once, through wreathing boughs,
    We saw the Lord's own star,
And breast to breast there sanctified our vows
    Before that throne where all the glories are.
    Not very far
From the bright Kingdom standing then, with radiant brows,
    And love's long kiss that nought can mar,
You sealed our faith, and so, while lives unnumbered fleet,
    As one, we seek th' Eternal Avatar.

L. M. Montgomery

Those familiar with Miss Montgomery's work as novelist are not surprised that she has also written a volume of poetry. One with her joyous outlook on life, vivid imagination, instinct for words and facility in expression, could not help being a poet. More than that, she has lived nearly all her life in Prince Edward Island, where the fairies are said to live. In truth, Miss Montgomery was a poet long before she began to write prose; indeed, it is doubtful if she has ever been anything else, for Anne Shirley is essentially a creature of sentiment, of imagination, and of those qualities of heart and brain which are the products of the poetic mind. Her verse is quite as perfect as her prose, though without its human touch; and her lyrics, especially those dealing with the smiling aspects of her native province, its fragrant fields of red earth and the 'blue sea coming up on every side,' are of rare quality, delicate, lilting and full of music.
—E. J. HATHAWAY.

[353]

IT was in the Fall of 1908 that the editor of this volume read *Anne of Green Gables,* by a new author, L. M. Montgomery. The first edition was just out. The book provided a fresh delight, for Anne had a new and indescribable charm, and it seemed to him that the book must sell in tens of thousands. It has sold in hundreds of thousands, and its immediate successor, *Anne of Avonlea,* 1909, has had almost as phenomenal a sale. Few, however, have known that this brilliant portrayer and interpreter of life in her native island, is a writer of verse of distinctive quality, particularly the poems that picture the sea and the sturdy, ardent fisher folk.

Lucy Maud Montgomery was born at Clifton, Prince Edward Island, but lived from her infancy in Cavendish, of the same province. Her father was Hugh John Montgomery, of Park Corner, P.E.I., a son of the Hon. Donald Montgomery, 'Senator,' and her mother, Clara Woolner Macneill, of Cavendish, a great-granddaughter of the Hon. William Macneill, 'Speaker.' Hector Macneill, the minor Scottish poet, author of the popular lyrics, 'I Lo'ed Ne'er a Laddie but Ane,' 'Saw Ye My Wee Thing,' and 'Come Under My Plaidie,' was a first cousin of her great-great-grandfather.

Until sixteen years of age, she attended the 'district school' in Cavendish, and then went to Prince of Wales College, Charlottetown, for a year, taking the course for a First-Class Teacher's License. Later, she attended for one winter, Dalhousie College, Halifax, taking special courses in English and in languages.

To supply the eager demand, six other books have quickly followed the first two: *Kilmeny of the Orchard,* 1910; *The Story Girl,* 1911; *Chronicles of Avonlea,* 1912; *The Golden Road,* 1913; *Anne of the Island,* 1915; and *The Watchman and Other Poems* (McClelland, Goodchild & Stewart), 1916.

In 1911, Miss Montgomery was married to the Rev. Ewan Macdonald, Presbyterian Minister at Leaskdale, Ontario, and is now the mother of two boys.

Shortly after *Anne of Green Gables* was published, the author received a communication from the secretary of Mark Twain, telling her that the latter had just sent a letter to the actor, Francis Wilson, in which he said: *Anne of Green Gables is the sweetest creation of child life yet written.*

When the Dark Comes Down

WHEN the dark comes down, oh, the wind is on the sea
With lisping laugh and whimper to the red reef's
    threnody,
The boats are sailing homeward now across the harbour bar
With many a jest and many a shout from fishing grounds afar.
So furl your sails and take your rest,
Ye fisher folk so brown,
For task and quest are ended when the dark comes down.

When the dark comes down, oh, the landward valleys fill
Like brimming cups of purple, and on every landmark hill
There shines a star of twilight that is watching evermore
The low, dim-lighted meadows by the long, dim-lighted shore,
For there, where vagrant daisies weave the grass a silver
    crown,
The lads and lassies wander when the dark comes down.

When the dark comes down, oh, the children fall asleep,
And mothers in the fisher huts their happy vigils keep;
There's music in the song they sing and music on the sea,
The loving, lingering echoes of the twilight's litany,
For toil has folded hands to dream, and care has ceased to
    frown,
And every one's a lyric when the dark comes down.

Sunrise Along Shore

ATHWART the harbour lingers yet
The ashen gleam of breaking day,
And where the guardian cliffs are set
The noiseless shadows steal away;
But all the winnowed eastern sky
Is flushed with many a tender hue,
And spears of light are smiting through
The ranks where huddled sea-mists fly.

Across the ocean, wan and gray,
Gay fleets of golden ripples come,
For at the birth hour of the day
The roistering, wayward winds are dumb.

The rocks that stretch to meet the tide
Are smitten with a ruddy glow,
And faint reflections come and go
Where fishing boats at anchor ride.

All life leaps out to greet the light—
The shining sea-gulls dive and soar,
The swallows wheel in dizzy flight,
And sandpeeps flit along the shore.
From every purple landward hill
The banners of the morning fly,
But on the headlands, dim and high,
The fishing hamlets slumber still.

One boat alone beyond the bar
Is sailing outward blithe and free,
To carry sturdy hearts afar
Across those wastes of sparkling sea,
Staunchly to seek what may be won
From out the treasures of the deep,
To toil for those at home who sleep
And be the first to greet the sun.

Off to the Fishing Ground

THERE'S a piping wind from a sunrise shore
    Blowing over a silver sea,
There's a joyous voice in the lapsing tide
That calls enticingly;
The mist of dawn has taken flight
To the dim horizon's bound,
And with wide sails set and eager hearts
We're off to the fishing ground.

Ho, comrades mine, how that brave wind sings
Like a great sea-harp afar!
We whistle its wild notes back to it
As we cross the harbour bar.
Behind us there are the homes we love
And hearts that are fond and true,
And before us beckons a strong young day
On leagues of glorious blue.

Comrades, a song as the fleet goes out,
A song of the orient sea,
We are the heirs of its tingling strife,
Its courage and liberty!
Sing as the white sails cream and fill,
And the foam in our wake is long,
Sing till the headlands black and grim
Echo us back our song!

Oh, 'tis a glad and heartsome thing
To wake ere the night be done
And steer the course that our fathers steered
In the path of the rising sun.
The wind and welkin and wave are ours
Wherever our bourne is found,
And we envy no landsman his dream and sleep
When we're off to the fishing ground!

The Old Man's Grave

MAKE it where the winds may sweep
Through the pine boughs soft and deep,
And the murmur of the sea
Come across the orient lea,
And the falling raindrops sing
Gently to his slumbering.

Make it where the meadows wide
Greenly lie on every side,
Harvest fields he reaped and trod,
Westering slopes of clover sod,
Orchard lands where bloom and blow
Trees he planted long ago.

Make it where the starshine dim
May be always close to him,
And the sunrise glory spread
Lavishly around his bed,
And the dewy grasses creep
Tenderly above his sleep.

Since these things to him were dear
Through full many a well-spent year,
It is surely meet their grace
Should be on his resting-place,
And the murmur of the sea
Be his dirge eternally.

The Old Home Calls

COME back to me, little dancing feet that roam the wide
world o'er,
I long for the lilt of your flying steps in my silent rooms once
more;
Come back to me, little voices gay with laughter and with song,
Come back, little hearts beating high with hopes, I have
missed and mourned you long.

My roses bloom in my garden walks all sweet and wet with
the dew,
My lights shine down on the long hill road the waning twi-
lights through,
The swallows flutter about my eaves as in the years of old,
And close about me their steadfast arms the lisping pine trees
fold.

But I weary for you at morn and eve, O children of my love,
Come back to me from your pilgrim ways, from the seas and
plains ye rove,
Come over the meadows and up the lane to my door set open
wide,
And sit ye down where the red light shines from my welcom-
ing fire-side.

I keep for you all your childhood dreams, your gladness and
delights,
The joy of days in the sun and rain, the sleep of care-free
nights;
All the sweet faiths ye have lost and sought again shall be
your own,
Darlings, come to my empty heart—I am old and still and
alone!

Robert W. Service

The reason of the popularity of this poetry may be summed up almost in a word—it pictures human life. For, after all, nature worship or classic lore, ethics or abstruse philosophy, grow stale and flat when used continually as the basis of literary emotions, but every human being, who has not become a conventionalized fossil, always will be moved by the passions and moods of the surging, restless, primitive, even animal spirit of humanity that permeates Service's poems. . . . . These poems must not be regarded as typically Canadian—they crystallize a phase of Canadian life, but it is a phase which has become Canadian by accident of circumstances. . . . . The rhythm of the poems has an irresistible sweep; no training in the technique of versification is necessary to catch the movement—it carries one away; and the plain, forcible language grips the attention and holds it, while short, vivid, insistent epithets hammer themselves deeply into one's mind.—DONALD G. FRENCH, in the 'Globe Magazine.'

ROBERT W. SERVICE is not a Canadian poet in the truest sense of the term. He was not born in Canada, nor did he arrive in this land in early childhood and grow up in a Canadian environment. He was born in Lancashire, England, in 1876, and when six years of age moved to Scotland with his parents. He was educated in the city of Glasgow, his higher education being received in the Hillhead High School, and in the University of Glasgow.

At the age of twenty, Mr. Service came to Canada and made his way westward from city to city, until he arrived at Victoria, B.C. The next five years he wandered back and forth on the Pacific coast, travelling as far south as Mexico, residing temporarily in every city of importance, and learning by hard, personal experience, some of the deepest lessons of life.

Finally he became a clerk in the Canadian Bank of Commerce at Victoria, and subsequently was stationed at other branches in Vancouver, Kamloops, and White Horse in the Yukon District.

It was in White Horse that most of the poems published in *Songs of a Sourdough* were written. This volume appeared in 1907 and in a few weeks the author was famous. For Canadian poetry the sales were unprecedented, expanding in number in a few months into the tens of thousands.

The same author has given us since, *Ballads of a Cheechako,* 1909; *The Trail of '98,* a novel, 1910; *Rhymes of a Rolling Stone,* 1912; and *The Pretender,* a novel, 1914.

The Montreal *Witness* dubbed Service 'The Kipling of the Arctic World,' and it was soon discovered that Kipling was his favourite author. Said he:

Kipling comes first with me. He is the greatest of modern writers to my mind. In the poem, 'The Law of the Yukon,' they say I've had in mind his 'Red Gods.' I only wish I could write in his class. Of course, there is the Kipling idea, the Kipling method in his poem, and it's a jolly good method.

But as Mr. French also says:

Service is no mere imitator; his themes are his own, and poetic form in any case is governed largely by the subject matter. Even Kipling did not invent the ballad forms—he used what he found.

Service has also made the following interesting references to his poems:

I don't believe in pretty language and verbal felicities, but in

getting as close down as I can to the primal facts of life,—getting down
to the bedrock of things. . . . . My idea of verse writing is
to write something the everyday workingman can read and approve, the
man who, as a rule, fights shy of verse or rhyme. I prefer to write
something that comes within the scope of his own experience and
grips him with a sense of reality.

In recent years, Service has dwelt in Europe—most of the
time in Paris. He was engaged in the second war of the
Balkans, as a correspondent, and shortly after his return
married a French girl, whom he met in a romantic way. He
is now "doing his bit" in the Great War by driving a motor
ambulance, and by the contribution of gripping ballads.

The Call of the Wild

HAVE you gazed on naked grandeur where there's nothing
    else to gaze on,
  Set pieces and drop-curtain scenes galore,
Big mountains heaved to heaven, which the blinding sunsets
    blazon,
  Black canyons where the rapids rip and roar?
Have you swept the visioned valley with the green stream
    streaking through it,
  Searched the Vastness for a something you have lost?
Have you strung your soul to silence? Then for God's sake
    go and do it;
  Hear the challenge, learn the lesson, pay the cost.

Have you wandered in the wilderness, the sage-brush desola-
    tion,
  The bunch-grass levels where the cattle graze?
Have you whistled bits of rag-time at the end of all creation,
  And learned to know the desert's little ways?
Have you camped upon the foothills, have you galloped o'er
    the ranges,
  Have you roamed the arid sun-lands through and through?
Have you chummed up with the mesa? Do you know its
    moods and changes?
  Then listen to the wild—it's calling you.

Have you known the Great White Silence, not a snow-gemmed
    twig aquiver?
  (Eternal truths that shame our soothing lies.)

Have you broken trail on snowshoes? mushed your huskies
        up the river,
    Dared the unknown, led the way, and clutched the prize?
Have you marked the map's void spaces, mingled with the
        mongrel races,
    Felt the savage strength of brute in every thew?
And though grim as hell the worst is, can you round it off
        with curses?
    Then hearken to the wild—it's wanting you.

Have you suffered, starved and triumphed, grovelled down,
        yet grasped at glory,
    Grown bigger in the bigness of the whole?
'Done things' just for the doing, letting babblers tell the story,
    Seeing through the nice veneer the naked soul?
Have you seen God in His splendours, heard the text that
        nature renders?
    (You'll never hear it in the family pew.)
The simple things, the true things, the silent men who do
        things—
    Then listen to the wild—it's calling you.

They have cradled you in custom, they have primed you with
        their preaching,
    They have soaked you in convention through and through;
They have put you in a showcase; you're a credit to their
        teaching—
    But can't you hear the wild?—it's calling you.
Let us probe the silent places, let us seek what luck betide us;
    Let us journey to a lonely land I know.
There's a whisper on the night-wind, there's a star agleam to
        guide us,
    And the wild is calling, calling . . . . let us go.

The Law of the Yukon

THIS is the law of the Yukon, and ever she makes it plain:
    'Send not your foolish and feeble; send me your strong
        and your sane
Strong for the red rage of battle; sane, for I harry them sore;
Send me men girt for the combat, men who are grit to the
        core;

Swift as the panther in triumph, fierce as the bear in defeat,
Sired of a bulldog parent, steeled in the furnace heat.
Send me the best of your breeding, lend me your chosen ones;
Them will I take to my bosom, them will I call my sons;
Them will I gild with my treasure, them will I glut with my
    meat;
But the others—the misfits, the failures—I trample under my
    feet.
Dissolute, damned and despairful, crippled and palsied and
    slain,
Ye would send me the spawn of your gutters—Go! take back
    your spawn again.

'Wild and wide are my borders, stern as death is my sway;
From my ruthless throne I have ruled alone for a million years
    and a day;
Hugging my mighty treasure, waiting for man to come:
Till he swept like a turbid torrent, and after him swept—the
    scum.
The pallid pimp of the dead-line, the enervate of the pen,
One by one I weeded them out, for all that I sought was—Men.
One by one I dismayed them, frighting them sore with my
    glooms;
One by one I betrayed them unto my manifold dooms.
Drowned them like rats in my rivers, starved them like curs
    on my plains,
Rotted the flesh that was left them, poisoned the blood in their
    veins;
Burst with my winter upon them, searing forever their sight,
Lashed them with fungus-white faces, whimpering wild in
    the night;
Staggering blind through the storm-whirl, stumbling mad
    through the snow,
Frozen stiff in the ice pack, brittle and bent like a bow;
Featureless, formless, forsaken, scented by wolves in their
    flight,
Left for the wind to make music through ribs that are glit-
    tering white;
Gnawing the black crust of failure, searching the pit of des-
    pair,

19

Crooking the toe in the trigger, trying to patter a prayer;
Going outside with an escort, raving with lips all afoam;
Writing a cheque for a million, drivelling feebly of home;
Lost like a louse in the burning . . . . or else in the
            tented town
Seeking a drunkard's solace, sinking and sinking down;
Steeped in the slime at the bottom, dead to a decent world,
Lost 'mid the human flotsam, far on the frontier hurled;
In the camp at the bend of the river, with its dozen saloons
            aglare,
Its gambling dens a-riot, its gramophones all ablare;
Crimped with the crimes of a city, sin-ridden and bridled with
            lies,
In the hush of my mountained vastness, in the flush of my
            midnight skies.
Plague-spots, yet tools of my purpose, so natheless I suffer
            them thrive,
Crushing my Weak in their clutches, that only my Strong may
            survive.

'But the others, the men of my mettle, the men who would
            'stablish my fame,
Unto its ultimate issue, winning me honour, not shame;
Searching my uttermost valleys, fighting each step as they go,
Shooting the wrath of my rapids, sealing my ramparts of
            snow;
Ripping the guts of my mountains, looting the beds of my
            creeks,
Them will I take to my bosom, and speak as a mother speaks.
I am the land that listens, I am the land that broods;
Steeped in eternal beauty, crystalline waters and woods.
Long have I waited lonely, shunned as a thing accurst,
Monstrous, moody, pathetic, the last of the lands and the first;
Visioning camp-fires at twilight, sad with a longing forlorn,
Feeling my womb o'er-pregnant with the seed of cities unborn.
Wild and wide are my borders, stern as death is my sway,
And I wait for the men who will win me—and I will not be
            won in a day;
And I will not be won by weaklings, subtile, suave and mild,

But by men with the hearts of vikings and the simple faith of a
    child;
Desperate, strong and resistless, unthrottled by fear or defeat,
Them will I gild with my treasure, them will I glut with my
    meat.

'Lofty I stand from each sister land, patient and wearily wise,
With the weight of a world of sadness in my quiet, passionless
    eyes;
Dreaming alone of a people, dreaming alone of a day,
When men shall not rape my riches, and curse me and go
    away;
Making a bawd of my bounty, fouling the hand that gave—
Till I rise in my wrath and I sweep on their path and I stamp
    them into a grave.
Dreaming of men who will bless me, of women esteeming me
    good,
Of children born in my borders, of radiant motherhood,
Of cities leaping to stature, of fame like a flag unfurled,
As I pour the tide of my riches in the eager lap of the world.'

This is the Law of the Yukon, that only the Strong shall
    thrive;
That surely the Weak shall perish, and only the Fit survive;
Dissolute, damned and despairful, crippled and palsied and
    slain,
This is the Will of the Yukon,—Lo! how she makes it plain!

The Cremation of Sam McGee

THERE are strange things done in the midnight sun
  By the men who moil for gold;
The Arctic trails have their secret tales
  That would make your blood run cold;
The Northern Lights have seen queer sights,
  But the queerest they ever did see
Was that night on the marge of Lake Lebarge
  I cremated Sam McGee.

Now Sam McGee was from Tennessee, where the cotton
    blooms and blows.

Why he left his home in the South to roam round the Pole
    God only knows.
He was always cold, but the land of gold seemed to hold him
    like a spell;
Though he'd often say in his homely way that 'he'd sooner
    live in hell.'

On a Christmas Day we were mushing our way over the
    Dawson trail.
Talk of your cold! through the parka's fold it stabbed like a
    driven nail.
If our eyes we'd close, then the lashes froze, till sometimes
    we couldn't see;
It wasn't much fun, but the only one to whimper was Sam
    McGee.

And that very night as we lay packed tight in our robes be-
    neath the snow,
And the dogs were fed, and the stars o'erhead were dancing
    heel and toe,
He turned to me, and, 'Cap,' says he, 'I'll cash in this trip,
    I guess;
And if I do, I'm asking that you won't refuse my last re-
    quest.'

Well, he seemed so low that I couldn't say no; then he says
    with a sort of moan:
'It's the cursèd cold, and it's got right hold till I'm chilled
    clean through to the bone.
Yet 'taint being dead, it's my awful dread of the icy grave that
    pains;
So I want you to swear that, foul or fair, you'll cremate my
    last remains.'

A pal's last need is a thing to heed, so I swore I would not
    fail;
And we started on at the streak of dawn, but God! he looked
    ghastly pale.
He crouched on the sleigh, and he raved all day of his home
    in Tennessee;

And before nightfall a corpse was all that was left of Sam
    McGee.

There wasn't a breath in that land of death, and I hurried,
    horror driven,
With a corpse half-hid that I couldn't get rid, because of a
    promise given;
It was lashed to the sleigh, and it seemed to say: 'You may
    tax your brawn and brains,
But you promised true, and it's up to you to cremate those
    last remains.'

Now a promise made is a debt unpaid, and the trail has its
    own stern code.
In the days to come, though my lips were dumb, in my heart
    how I cursed that load.
In the long, long night, by the lone fire-light, while the huskies,
    round in a ring,
Howled out their woes to the homeless snows—O God, how
    I loathed that thing!

And every day that quiet clay seemed to heavy and heavier
    grow;
And on I went, though the dogs were spent and the grub was
    getting low;
The trail was bad, and I felt half mad, but I swore I would not
    give in;
And I'd often sing to the hateful thing, and it hearkened with
    a grin.

Till I came to the marge of Lake Lebarge, and a derelict
    there lay;
It was jammed in the ice, but I saw in a trice it was called the
    'Alice May.'
And I looked at it, and I thought a bit, and I looked at my
    frozen chum:
Then, 'Here,' said I, with a sudden cry, 'is my cre-ma-tor-eum.'

Some planks I tore from the cabin floor, and I lit the boiler fire;
Some coal I found that was lying around, and I heaped the
    fuel higher;

The flames just soared, and the furnace roared—such a blaze
you seldom see;
And I burrowed a hole in the glowing coal, and I stuffed in
Sam McGee.

Then I made a hike, for I couldn't like to hear him sizzle so;
And the heavens scowled, and the huskies howled, and the
wind began to blow.
It was icy cold, but the hot sweat rolled down my cheeks, and
I don't know why;
And the greasy smoke in an inky cloak went streaking down
the sky.

I do not know how long in the snow I wrestled with grisly
fear;
But the stars came out and they danced about ere again I
ventured near;
I was sick with dread, but I bravely said: 'I'll just take a peep
inside.
I guess he's cooked, and it's time I looked.' . . . . then
the door I opened wide.

And there sat Sam, looking cool and calm, in the heart of the
furnace roar;
And he wore a smile you could see a mile, and he said: 'Please
close that door.
It's fine in here, but I greatly fear you'll let in the cold and
storm—
Since I left Plumtree, down in Tennessee, it's the first time
I've been warm.'

There are strange things done in the midnight sun
By the men who moil for gold;
The Arctic trails have their secret tales
That would make your blood run cold;
The Northern Lights have seen queer sights,
But the queerest they ever did see
Was that night on the marge of Lake Lebarge
I cremated Sam McGee.

The Lure of Little Voices

THERE'S a cry from out the Loneliness—oh, listen, Honey,
    listen!
Do you hear it, do you fear it, you're a-holding of me so?
You're a sobbing in your sleep, dear, and your lashes, how
        they glisten!
Do you hear the Little Voices all a-begging me to go?

All a-begging me to leave you.   Day and night they're plead-
        ing, praying,
    On the North-wind, on the West-wind, from the peak and
        from the plain;
Night and day they never leave me—do you know what they
        are saying?
    'He was ours before you got him, and we want him once
        again.'

Yes, they're wanting me, they're haunting me, the awful lonely
        places;
    They're whining and they're whimpering as if each had a
        soul;
They're calling from the wilderness, the vast and godlike
        spaces,
    The stark and sullen solitudes that sentinel the Pole.

They miss my little camp-fires, ever brightly, bravely gleaming
    In the womb of desolation where was never man before;
As comradeless I sought them, lion-hearted, loving, dreaming;
    And they hailed me as a comrade, and they loved me ever-
        more.

And now they're all a-crying, and it's no use me denying;
    The spell of them is on me and I'm helpless as a child;
My heart is asking, aching, but I hear them sleeping, waking;
    It's the lure of Little Voices, it's the mandate of the wild.

I'm afraid to tell you, Honey, I can take no bitter leaving;
    But softly in the sleep-time from your love I'll steal away.
Oh, it's cruel, dearie, cruel, and it's God knows how I'm griev-
        ing!
    But His Loneliness is calling and He knows I must obey.

Little Moccasins

COME out, O Little Moccasins, and frolic on the snow!
Come out, O tiny beaded feet, and twinkle in the light!
I'll play the old Red River reel, you used to love it so:
  Awake, O Little Moccasins, and dance for me to-night!

Your hair was all a gleamy gold, your eyes a cornflower blue;
  Your cheeks were pink as tinted shells, you stepped light as
    a fawn;
Your mouth was like a coral bud, with seed pearls peeping
    through;
  As gladdening as Spring you were, as radiant as dawn.

Come out, O Little Moccasins! I'll play so soft and low,
  The songs you loved, the old heart-songs that in my mem'ry
    ring;
O child, I want to hear you now beside the camp-fire glow,
  With all your heart a-throbbing in the simple words you
    sing!

For there were only you and I, and you were all to me;
  And round us were the barren lands, but little did we fear;
Of all God's happy, happy folks the happiest were we. . . .
  (Oh, call her, poor old fiddle mine, and maybe she will
    hear!)

Your mother was a half-breed Cree, but you were white all
    through;
  And I your father was—but, well, that's neither here nor
    there;
I only know, my little Queen, that all my world was you,
  And now that world can end to-night, and I will never care.

For there's a tiny wooden cross that pricks up through the
    snow:
  (Poor Little Moccasins! you're tired, and so you lie at rest.)
And there's a grey-haired, weary man beside the camp-fire
    glow:
  (O fiddle mine! the tears to-night are drumming on your
    breast.)

Florence Randal Livesay

(Kilmeny)

*We ought to be proud that the foreign folk among us
have found a sympathetic voice singing in our language
the songs of their fatherland. Mrs. Livesay composes as
easily as William Morris. She has the lyric gift, and she has
the feeling for these people that gives her verse vitality.* . .

*Her verses have the singing quality and the true feeling.
. . . . In her translations Mrs. Livesay has certainly entered into the spirit of the original, reproducing the passion,
the patriotism, and the very song itself. . . . . 'The
Young Recruits' is a genuine dramatic lyric. Read it twice
and you will read it three times. . . . .*

*She has surely captured throughout the number and variety
of her translations,—love-songs, war cries, heart-break, dance
—the peculiar wit and wisdom of the Ukrainian nation, the
twist of the national temperament. She has given to them
again their claim to poetry, and has retained 'the tang of race.'*
—The Bookman, in the 'Manitoba Free Press.'

FLORENCE RANDAL LIVESAY, daughter of Stephen and Mary Louisa Randal, was born at Compton, P.Q., and educated at Compton Ladies' College, now King's Hall. She taught for one year in a private school in New York, and subsequently for seven years was a member of the staff of the *Evening Journal,* Ottawa,—editor of the Woman's Page.

In 1902, the Hon. Joseph Chamberlain requested Canada to send some teachers to the Boer Concentration Camps, and Miss Randal, offering her services, was one of the forty chosen. She remained for one year and then returned to Canada, locating at Winnipeg. She joined the staff of the Winnipeg *Telegram*, and three years later, that of the *Manitoba Free Press*. For several years she edited the Children's Department of the latter, but now writes as a 'free lance,'

In 1908, she married Mr. J. Fred. B. Livesay, of Winnipeg, Manager and Secretary of the Western Associated Press, Limited, and is now the mother of two girls.

Of recent years, Mrs. Livesay has contributed poems, short stories and articles to Canadian and American magazines and journals, and a volume of her verse, entitled *Songs of Ukraina,* is now being published by J. M. Dent & Sons.

Mrs. Livesay's folk songs translated from the Ruthenian are unusual and notable, but her poetical gift is quite as discernible in her other poems. She has the imagination and the practised touch of the artist.

Immortality

I DIED once, but I came to life
With pain that stabbed me like a knife;

And once again I know I died—
Afraid! And yet that shell flew wide.

A singing bullet cut the air;
I said a catch of a childish prayer—

'If I should die before I wake
I pray the Lord my soul to take.

'Before I wake—'

The Young Recruits
(Cossack Song)

ALONG the hills lies the snow,
But the streams they melt and flow;
By the road the poppies blow—
Poppies? Nay, scarlet though they glow,
These are no flowers—the young recruits!
  They are the young recruits!

  To Krym, to Krym they ride,
  The soldiers, side by side—
  And over the country wide
  Sounds the beat of the horse's stride.

One calls to her soldier son:
'Return, O careless one!
Of scrubbing wilt have none?
Let me wash thy head—then run!'

'Nay, mother, wash thine own,
Or make my sister groan.
Leave thou thy son alone!
Too swift the time has flown.

'My head the fine spring rain
Will soon wash clean again,
And stout thorns will be fain
To comb what rough has lain.

'The sun will make it dry,
Wind-parted it will lie—
So, mother mine, good-bye!'

      .   .   .   .   .

He could not hear her cry.

Song of the Cossack
(Ruthenian Folk Song)

HEAVILY hangs the rye
Bent to the trampled ground;
While brave men fighting die
  Through blood the horses bound.

Under the white-stemmed tree
    A Cossack bold is slain—
They lift him tenderly
    Into the ruined grain.

Some one has borne him there,
    Someone has put in place
A scarlet cloth, with prayer,
    Over the up-turned face.

Softly a girl has come—
    Dove-like she looks; all gray—
Stares at the soldier dumb
    And, crying, goes away.

Then, swift, another maid—
    Ah, how unlike she is!—
With grief and passion swayed
    Gives him her farewell kiss.

The third one does not cry,
    Caresses none has she:
'Three girls thy love flung by—
    Death rightly came to thee!'

Khustina—The Kerchief

(From the Ukrainian of Fedkovich)

[It is the custom among Ukrainian maidens to embroider such a
kerchief for the betrothal, and then it is bound upon the arm or
worn in some noticeable way on the man's person.]

THE sun was drowning in the ocean's brim
    Red, red as blood;
    And in the crimson flood
A young girl sewed a handkerchief with gold.

Embroidering in gold with stitches fine—
    Like lilies white
    Her cheeks will look to-night,
Like pure-white lilies washed with tears.

And as she sewed she pressed it to her heart;
    Then, weeping sore,
    She opened wide the door:
'Strong wind, my Eagle, take this on your wings!'

'Strong as the Dunai swiftly onward flows,
   O Wind so free
   Deliver this for me
Where now he serves, yea, where the heart well knows!
'He in the Uhlans' ranks is fighting now—
   Go, Golden One,
   From sun to sun
Float on the wind until that place you find!
'And, Golden One, when you shall hear one call
   Even as a dove,
   Rest, for my love,
My loved one will be waiting there below!
'He has a bay horse, and his weapons are
   Shining as gold.
   Wind, free and bold,
Fall to his heart as the rose petals fall!
'If sleeping, wake him not; and if—O God!—
   If slain he lie,
   For your good-bye
O Golden One, cover his sweet dead face!'

At Vieille Chapelle

"At Vieille Chapelle there was a furious encounter in a cemetery."

*BURYING, burying . . .
   Clods are we, clods we toss.
The children weave flower garlands in the sun
For this or that dead one
   Or make a cross,
While we are burying.*

Listening, listening,
   The dead men heard the battle overhead.
The gravestones fell in ruins to the ground—
   Beneath, more dead we found.
Fighting on, fighting on,
   The rest passed by—or halted here—
We buried two, up in the graveyard there.
   German and French they were.
Pitiless, merciless,
   But well-matched, too, they cut and thrust,

Until they reached that little cottage door—
They never came out more.

Lying so—buried so—
I sometimes think, at night, of how they must
Hate still, and struggle to arise
Death-fury in their eyes.

Side by side, side by side,
Surely they would not, think you, rest in peace?
Too near was dug each grave.
Eh bien, they both were brave!

The Bride of the Sea
(The Titanic)

DECKED as a bride with charms
She left her ancient isle
To come unto my arms—
I waited, mile on mile.

A maiden ship, all gay
With gilt and 'broidery,
She sang, upon her way,
'Neptune, I come to thee!'

But all the journey long
Spite of her revelry,
I heard her undersong,
'Nay, but I would be free!'

Then I sent curtseying hosts
To greet her as she came—
Soundless and white as ghosts
And terrible as flame.

They drew her to my side,
Fair in her wedding dress,
Where every lapping tide
Shall give her my caress.

.   .   .   .   .

'God of all souls forlorn,'—
The cry comes piteously
From hearts by anguish torn—
'Restore my dead to me!'

Theodore Goodridge Roberts

For recognition as a poet Theodore Goodridge Roberts has had to stand comparison with the high achievements of his distinguished brother. Yet, as poets, he and Charles G. D. differ widely. Charles began on Pierus, but wandered off into the more practical realm of prose, where, apart from occasional diversions, he has remained. Theodore, on the other hand, attacked the novel at the beginning of his literary career, and it is on the novel that he has had to depend for most of his reputation. . . . As yet a book of his poems has not appeared. Nevertheless, the results of his muse so far, though vagrant, are sufficient to display a quality which, if not peculiar to the author, is at least vigorous and refreshing. And there are touches, even some fine conceits, in such poems as 'The Blind Sailor,' 'Private North,' and 'The Lost Shipmate' that seem to distinguish him from other poets, and to make him a man's poet. And it is on his achievements as a man's poet, and not as a novelist, that Theodore Roberts undoubtedly will stake his final reputation.

—NEWTON MACTAVISH, editor of the 'Canadian Magazine.'

[377]

THEODORE GOODRIDGE ROBERTS, as a poet and novelist, is not the least great of a distinguished family. His poetry has strength and originality and should develop into lyrics, ballads and epics very much worth while.

It has been pointed out that he is a man's poet; he is also a man's novelist. His many novels of adventure and romance have wide popularity in English-speaking lands. These are a few of the best known: *Hemming, the Adventurer,* 1904; *Brothers of Peril,* 1905; *The Red Feathers,* 1907; *A Cavalier of Virginia,* 1910; *A Captain of Raleigh's,* 1911; *The Wasp,* 1913; and *The Toll of the Tides,* 1914.

Mr. Roberts was born in Fredericton, New Brunswick, July 7th, 1877. He is the youngest of four brothers of which Charles G. D. Roberts (*q.v.*) is the eldest. His education was received at the Fredericton Collegiate School, and at the University of New Brunswick, but, like his sister, he did not complete the University course.

In November, 1903, he married Frances Seymore Allen, daughter of the Rev. Thomas Allen. Since their marriage they have lived in Barbados, England, France, and much of the time in and near Fredericton, N.B. They have three children living, a boy and two girls.

Captain Theodore Goodridge Roberts is now at the Front, serving as 'Assistant Canadian Eye-Witness.'

The Maid

THUNDER of riotous hoofs over the quaking sod;
Clash of reeking squadrons, steel-capped, iron-shod;
The White Maid, and the white horse, and the flapping banner
        of God.

Black hearts riding for money; red hearts riding for fame;
The maid who rides for France and the king who rides for
        shame.
Gentlemen, fools and a saint, riding in Christ's high name!

Dust to dust it is written! Wind-scattered are lance and bow.
Dust, the Cross of St. George; dust, the banner of snow.

The bones of the king are crumbled and rotted the shafts
    of the foe.

Forgotten, the young knight's valour. Forgotten, the captain's
    skill.
Forgotten, the fear and the hate and the mailed hands raised
    to kill.
Forgotten, the shields that clashed and the arrows that cried
    so shrill.

Like a story from some old book, that battle of Long Ago!
Shadows, the poor French King and the might of his English
    Foe:
Shadows, the charging nobles and the archers kneeling a-row—
But a flame in my heart and my eyes, the Maid with the banner
    of snow.

The Blind Sailor

'STRIKE me blind!' we swore.
    God, and I was stricken!
I have seen the morning fade
And noonday thicken.

Be merciful, O God, that I have named in vain.
I am blind in the eyes; but spare the gleam in my brain.
Though my footsteps falter, let my soul still sight
The things that were my life before you hid the light.

Little things were they, Lord, too small to be denied:
The green of roadstead waters, where the tired ships ride,
Bark and brig and barkentine, blown from near and far,
Safe inside the spouting reef and the sobbing bar.

Leave to me my pictures, Lord, leave my memories bright:
The twisted palms are clashing, and the sand is white.
The shore-boats crowd around us, the skipper's gig is manned,
The nutmegs spice the little wind that baffles off the land.

The negro girls are singing in the fields of cane,
The lizards dart on that white path I'll not walk again,

The opal blinds melt up at dawn, the crimson blinds flare down,
And white against the mountains flash the street-lamps of the
     town.

Leave to me my pictures, Lord, spare my mind to see
The shimmer of the water and the shadow of the tree,
The cables roaring down, the gray sails swiftly furled,
A riding-light ablink in some far corner of the world.

Leave to me my pictures, Lord: the islands and the main,
The little things a sailorman must out to see again;
The beggars in the market-place, the oxen in the streets,
The bitter, black tobacco and the women selling sweets.

I have fed my vision, Lord; now I pray to hold
The blue and gray and silver, the green and brown and gold.
I have filled my heart, Lord; now I pray to keep
The laughter and the colour through this unlifting sleep.

> 'Strike me blind!' we swore.
> God, and I am blind!
> But leave me still, O Lord,
> The pictures in the mind!

Private North

HUNCHED in his greatcoat, there he stands,
Sullen of face and rough of hands,
Ready to fight, unready to drill,
Willing to suffer and ready to kill.

He isn't our best; he isn't our worst;
He won't be the last, and he wasn't the first.

What does he offer to you, O king?
Himself—an humble and uncouth thing.
What does he offer you fit to take?
A life to spend, a body to break.

His brow is sullen, his ways are rough;
But his heart, I'll warrant, is true enough.

I've seen his shack, low-set and gray,
In the black woods thousands of miles away
Where he lived, from the mad, loud world removed,
Masterless, eager, and greatly loved.

Hunched in his greatcoat, there he stands,
Offering all with his heart and hands.

He offers his life to your needs, O King!—
A sullen, humble, and untrained thing—
And with it, for chance to spare or take,
A woman's spirit to wring and break.

The Lost Shipmate

SOMEWHERE he failed me, somewhere he slipped away—
Youth, in his ignorant faith and his bright array.
The tides go out; the tides come flooding in;
Still the old years die and the new begin;
But youth?—
Somewhere we lost each other, last year or yesterday.

Somewhere he failed me. Down at the harbour-side
I waited for him a-little, where the anchored argosies ride.
I thought he came—the steady 'trade' blew free—
I thought he came—'twas but the shadow of me!
And Youth?—
Somewhere he turned and left me, about the turn of the tide.

Perhaps I shall find him. It may be he waits for me,
Sipping those wines we knew, beside some tropic sea;
The tides still serve, and I am out and away
To search the spicy harbours of yesterday
For Youth,
Where the lamps of the town are yellow beyond the lamps on
          the quay.

Somwhere he failed me, somewhere he slipped away—
Youth, in his ignorant heart and his bright array.
Was it in Bados? God, I would pay to know!

Was it on Spanish Hill, where the roses blow?
Ah, Youth!
Shall I hear your laughter to-morrow, in painted Olivio?

Somewhere I failed him.　Somewhere I let him depart—
Youth, who would only sleep for the morn's fresh start.
The tides slipped out, the tides washed out and in,
And Youth and I rejoiced in their wastrel din.
Ah, Youth!
Shall I find you south of the Gulf?—or are you dead in my
　　heart?

The Reckoning

YE who reckon with England—
　Ye who sweep the seas
Of the flag that Rodney nailed aloft
　And Nelson flung to the breeze—
Count well your ships and your men,
　Count well your horse and your guns,
For they who reckon with England
　Must reckon with England's sons.

Ye who would challenge England—
　Ye who would break the might
Of the little isle in the foggy sea
　And the lion-heart in the fight—
Count well your horse and your swords,
　Weigh well your valour and guns,
For they who would ride against England
　Must sabre her million sons.

Ye who would roll to warfare
　Your hordes of peasants and slaves,
To crush the pride of an empire
　And sink her fame in the waves—
Test well your blood and your mettle,
　Count well your troops and your guns,
For they who battle with England
　Must war with a Mother's sons.

Grace Blackburn

Miss Blackburn, under the nom de plume, 'Fanfan,' has for years been giving us articles in the London Free Press that place her in the fore-front, if not at the head, of the writers upon literary topics, in the daily press of Canada.—'Catholic Record,' London, Ontario.

Miss Blackburn is well known throughout Western Ontario, under the nom de plume, 'Fanfan,' and in the New York theatrical world, is considered one of the best dramatic critics in Canada.—'Hamilton Herald.'

*A writer with a large brain and a big, warm heart: a twentieth century thinker, with the individuality of original thought and expression: a poet just beginning to realize her gift, and its underlying responsibility: one of the best equipped of our literary and dramatic critics, and with the faculty of logical and comprehensive interpretation—altogether, a distinct force in the intellectual life of the Dominion, of whom much may be expected.—*The Editor.

GRACE BLACKBURN is the fifth daughter of the late Josiah Blackburn, of London, Ontario, proprietor and editor, for nearly forty years, of the *Free Press,* and one of the ablest and most influential of the earlier newspaper men of Canada. Her mother's maiden name was Emma Delemere. Her paternal grandfather was the Rev. John Blackburn, a Congregationalist pastor of London, England, and for many years editor of the official organ of that denomination. He was also a writer of prominence on matters literary and archeological.

Miss Grace was educated in the public and high schools of her native city, and later in Hellmuth College, then the Diocesan School of Huron. Since graduation, she has been engaged chiefly in educational and journalistic work. She taught English for two years in the Bishop Whipple Schools, Faribault, Minnesota, and for one year was acting Principal of the Diocesan School of Northern Indiana, at Indianapolis. In 1900, she returned to Canada to join the staff of the *Free Press,* as literary and dramatic critic, etc., and has held the position ever since. Three of those years were spent in New York, in the interests of the paper, and four in Europe, where she journeyed entensively and wrote many fascinating travel articles. Besides her regular newspaper work, she is now giving considerable time and attention to poetic achievement, and to the writing of a novel, with a basic motive arising out of the Great War.

Miss Blackburn is not a 'club woman' as that term is ordinarily understood, but she has long been much interested in 'The Association of Canadian Clubs,' and in 1913, was elected to the official position of Literary Correspondent, and reëlected the ensuing year.

The Evening Star

ABOVE the sunset's many-tinted bar,
Where light on light, a smiling iris gnar,
Mellows to mystery of near and far,
Swings passionately pale the Evening Star!
Queen of the twilight—from a conquered sky
She smiles to see the Day grow faint and die.

Epic of the Yser

'DEAD with his face to the foe!'
From Hastings to Yser
Our men have died so.
The lad is a hero—
Great Canada's pride:
We sent him with glory,
For glory he died—
So ring out the church-bells! Float the flag high!

.　　.　　.　　.

Then I heard at my elbow a fierce mother-cry.

.　　.　　.　　.

On the desolate plain
Where the dark Yser flows
They'll bury him, maybe,
Our Child of the Snows:
The message we sent them
Through fire and through flood
He signed it and sealed it
To-day with his blood—
United we stand! Our Empire is One!

.　　.　　.　　.

But this woman beside me? . . . The boy was her son.

Sing Ho for the Herring

ALONG the sea shore, surf-beaten and brown,
The Fisher-Lass hastes to the Fishing-Town,
In kirtle of blue and bodice of red,
The sun at its nooning over her head,
And braw is the salt wind blowing—
Then sing, sing ho for the Herring,
The shimmering, sliddery Herring!

Along the sea shore the Fisher-Lads sigh
For the daffing mouth and the daunting eye,
And they sue and they woo, Rubin, Lubin and Bill,
But she taunts and she flaunts as a Fisher-Lass will;
And sleek is the water flowing—
Then sing, sing ho for the Herring,
The gleeking, glamourish Herring!

20

Along the sea shore she shadeth her eyes
To where on the wave his white sails rise,
For it seems there's a wraith in the midst of the glare,
And a voice that she loves calls shrilly and rare;
Ah, sly is the under-towing—
Then sing, sing ho for the Herring,
The spectral, the silver-hued Herring.

Along the sea shore in the teeth of the gale,
In its rage and its roar, its swash and its swale,
With faltering steps and staggering tread
They bear him up softly the stark, stark, Dead;
Oh, lang and dour is the knowing—
Then sing, sing ho for the Herring,
The life-giving, death-dealing Herring!

If Winter Come

DISDAINFUL, Earth!
Hooded in clouds and snowdrifts—
Great gray Earth,
That shivers and gathers her garments!
Just for a space you lower your eyelids,
Just for a moment you turn me the cold of your shoulder.
There! There! Already!—
Now I have caught you—
A turquoise rift in the rack,
That was relenting!
And back of the pine-trees a flash like a smile,
That, O earth, was your promise!

Below the depth of the frost
Is the warmth of your bosom.
The ice in your veins
Is troth to the rain and the runnel.
The catch in the call of the wind
Is your lip at my ear—
Your whisper of breezes,
Of breezes and blossom—
Of summer—of sweetness—of love!

The Cypress-Tree

OUT of the clod of earth
    That holds me to this melancholy place,
As ancient servitors
Held flambeaux for their lords
In draughty corridors,
I leap into the sky.

I am a torch with an inherent blaze,
No winter bears me or my verdure down:
The whirling snow and ice
Fall on me to their peril, not to mine:
The swift and sudden wind
Deflects but can not quench
My everlasting fire,
My fire that mounts out of the cerecloth of the dead
And draws its essence from mortality,
Transmuting dissolution and despair
Into aspiring form—
A shape that is a symbol—
A pose prophetic!
I am the Cypress-Tree men plant on graves,
And on their graves—I flame!

The Chant of the Woman

CLASH the cymbals!
    String the harp and sound it—
Cymbals and harp, there, you Makers of Music!

I will chant to my Comrade the chant of my being,
Woman to Man will I chant it.

I am as old as any. I too have a lineage.
I have come up by forms and through æons;
Forms of manifold fashion, æons of infinite dream.

I, too, am projected of Poets, offspring of the Singers:
I have lain in the womb of the World and incarnate its
            wonder—
I have played with the Child of the ages and captured its glee—
I have been kissed with the kisses of Kings—
Great Lovers have whispered their lore for my learning.

Then and now and always, wide away and the length of a span,
I gather that I must gather, by impulse, election:
In me only is attraction,
It alone could attract me,
So am I myself, and none other,
Myself—a mystery! a mouthpiece!

Myself and yet yourself, we two inexplicably one—
Flesh in its consummation, Soul in its incompleteness—
And because of the incompleteness of Soul,
Woman to man,
I chant you the chant of my being.

I cannot live on the crumbs that fall from a Table:
I must be lifted,
Lifted level with my love and with my Lover.
I must be clothed with the purple, made free of the signet—
I must put my hand in his dish, my head on his bosom—
Eye to eye must we lean, loquacious together.

So, and so only
Can I give him to drink of the wine of my winning,
My strange new wine that seethes and bubbles.
So and so only
Can I kiss on his lips the message of Kings—
Whisper the wonder of Life,
The laugh of the Child—
The lore of the Lovers.

Level! Level! Level!
Level with your lips and your eyes my Comrade,
Swing to the height of your heart,
Caught in your soul and kept there
Pervading and peerless!

So, and so only, your Lover, your Servant:
Every passionate pulse-beat
Under the blue veins in my white wrist
Your Servant and Lover—
I cannot live on the crumbs that fall from a Table!

George A. Mackenzie

Mr. Mackenzie belongs to that rare company of cultured, refined, modest minds who regard poetry as dainty messages of the spirit for appreciation by souls akin to themselves. . . . . He is, above all things, an artist in versification. Technically viewed his sonnets are superb. They are much more than this in beauty of thought and spiritual appeal. . . . . 'In That New World Which Is The Old' is remarkable for a novel simile in the octette. . . . . 'Magellan' is rhythmically as fine as Joaquin Miller's celebrated 'Columbus,' and in quiet dignity much more satisfying. . . . . 'Malcolm' is a narrative poem, finely, movingly signalizing the function of the tragedy of Love in the Restoration of Faith. Written in blank verse, iambic pentameter, the beauty of the poem, apart from its high spiritual dignity, lies in its refined diction and in its extraordinary imagery, whenever the poet wishes to enhance a sentiment or a vivid picture of reality. It has many fine lines and memorable metaphors.—DR. J. D. LOGAN, in a letter to The Flaneur, of the 'Mail and Empire.'

WHEN the Fenians raided Upper Canada in 1866, George Allan Mackenzie, a lad in his 17th year, who had enlisted as a private in the 13th Battalion of Hamilton, took part in the affair of Ridgeway, and was wounded by the enemy, suffering a compound fracture of an arm.

Mr. Mackenzie was born in Toronto, July 20th, 1849, the eldest son of the Rev. John George Delhoste Mackenzie,— first Rector of St. Paul's, Toronto, and also first Master of Arts of Trinity University—and Catharine Eliza, eldest daughter of Mr. Marcus Crombie, Head Master of the Toronto Grammar School. His grandfather, Captain John Mackenzie, served as an officer in the Peninsula, under Wellington, and later fought in the battle of New Orleans.

He was educated at his father's private Grammar School in Hamilton, and later at Trinity College, Toronto, entering the latter in the autumn of 1866 and, after a brilliant record, graduating in 1869 with first-class honours in classics and with the much coveted Prince of Wales Prize. Mr. Mackenzie chose law as a profession and was called to the Bar in 1873. For a time he served as legal secretary to Hon. (afterwards Sir) Oliver Mowat, then Attorney-General of Ontario, and then entered into partnership with Jones Bros., barristers, etc., Toronto. This firm, 'Jones Bros. & Mackenzie,' became afterwards, 'Jones, Mackenzie & Leonard.' Failing health induced him to retire from active practice about 1900.

In 1886, Mr. Mackenzie married Miss Ella Therese Demuth, daughter of Mr. Lawrence I. Demuth, of Philadelphia. Of this marriage, a daughter, is at present engaged in voluntary service in a military hospital at Folkestone, England, and a son, Lieutenant G. L. B. Mackenzie of the 3rd Battalion, Toronto, was killed in action in Flanders, in 1916. Mrs. Mackenzie died in 1899. His brothers, E. C. Mackenzie and J. B. Mackenzie, are well-known practising lawyers in Toronto.

In June of 1915 our poet went to England, and is temporarily resident at Folkestone.

His poems appeared in book form in 1914, entitled 'In that New World Which is the Old.' They are the artistic expression of a scholarly mind, imbued with deep religious conviction and the nobler purposes of life.

In that New World which Is the Old

ONCE, like the Arab with his shifting tent
　　To some new shade of palms each day addrest,
My soul, a homeless wanderer, unblest,
　　Roamed all the realm of change, in purpose bent
To find a happier world, with banishment
　　Of that dull pain which drove away its rest.
　　Through fruitless years my soul pursued its quest,
Until with longing I was well-nigh spent.

And then I found God's Presence; and the ray
　　Of that mysterious dayspring, clear and sweet,
Touched all the common things of every day,
　　And there in house, and field, and in the street
　　From childhood trodden by my heedless feet,
The long-sought world in dewy freshness lay.

To a Humming-Bird

THOU vagrant melody, light crown
　　Of rainbow mist above the flower,
Rifler, with touch like thistledown,
　　Of blooms that meekly yield their dower
Of sweets to thy soft and yet imperious power,

Gay, flashing, flickering, fairy thing,
　　Embodied zephyr, shimmering sound,
Whence hast thou come on gauzy wing
　　To my straight plot of city ground?
Whence hast thou come and whither art thou bound?

Hast thou been where the Northern wave
　　Breaks half the year on coasts of snow?
Hast thou flashed on the dreary cave
　　Of the squat, stolid Eskimo
With the keen splendour of thy tropic glow?

And now, thy merry summer jaunt
　　Completed, dost thou wisely fare
Homeward, to some safe jungle haunt,
　　Whither 'mid close-locked boughs repair
Strange feathered things of plumage rich and rare?

I marvel at thy countless leagues
    Of travel; how, secure from harm,
Thou bravest perils and fatigues;
    I marvel how thy tiny form
Weathers the drenching rain, the driving storm.

Thou art fled! my garden seems bereft
    Of all its beauty! yet some sense
Of joy and blessing thou hast left
    Behind thee, as a recompense,
Which shall remain when thou art flown far hence.

A sense of joy, that He whose hand
    Shaped thee and all things sweet and fair,
Hath pleasure in the thing He planned;
    A sense of trust, in Him whose care
Pilots thy course through the uncharted air.

Magellan

THERE is no change upon the deep:
    To-day they see the prospect wide
Of yesterday; the same waves leap;
    The same pale clouds the distance hide,
    Or shaped to mountain-peaks their hopes of land deride.

On and still on the soft winds bear
    The rocking vessel, and the main
That is so pitiless and so fair,
    Seems like a billowy, boundless plain
    Where one might sail, and sail, and ever sail in vain.

Famine is there with haggard cheek,
    And fever stares from hollow eyes;
And sullen murmurs rise, that speak
    Curses on him whose mad emprise
    Has lured men from their homes to die 'neath alien skies.

But he, the captain, he is calm;
    His glance compels the mutineer;
In fainting hearts he pours the balm
    Of sympathy, and lofty cheer:
    'Courage! a few more leagues will prove the earth a sphere.

'The world *is* round: there is an end;
  We do not vainly toil and roam;
The kiss of wife, the clasp of friend,
  The fountains and the vines of home,
  Wait us beyond the cloud, beyond the edge of foam.'

My Baby Sleeps

THE wind is loud in the west to-night,
    But Baby sleeps;
The wild wind blows with all its might,
    But Baby sleeps;
My Baby sleeps, and he does not hear
The noise of the storm in the pine trees near.

The snow is drifting high to-night,
    But Baby sleeps;
The bitter world is cold and white,
    But Baby sleeps;
My Baby sleeps, so fast, so fast,
That he does not heed the wintry blast.

The cold snows drift, and the wild winds rave,
    But Baby sleeps;
And a white cross stands by his little grave,
    While Baby sleeps;
And the storm is loud in the rocking pine,
But its moan is not so deep as mine.

The Sleep that Flits on Baby's Eyes

A paraphrase of Rabindranath Tagore's prose translation

THE sleep that flits on baby's eyes,
    Whence does it come? Can you surmise?

Yes! in a cool, deep forest glade,
Where glowworms dimly light the shade,
They tell of a fairy village shy,
Where two enchanted buds hang high;
Thence, borne by fairy fingers, flies
The sleep that kisses baby's eyes.

The smile in his sleep, that will twinkle and go—
Where was it born? Pray, do you know?

Yes! for a rumour floats about—
A rumour—its truth I dare not doubt—

That a crescent moon, with a pale, young ray
Touched a cloudlet's edge, ere it melted away,
And there, in the dream of a dew-washed morn,
Baby's flickering smile was born.

And where was it hidden—that soft, fresh glow
On baby's limbs? Does any one know?

Yes! in a day that is long since fled,
Ere baby's mother was grown and wed,
With the first sweet dawning of love, it stole
Into the depths of her dreaming soul,
And there lay hidden—the soft, fresh rose
That now on the limbs of baby glows.

'Compel Them to Come In'

I WAS a beggar of most evil fame,
　Uncleanly, ragged, full of sores and scars:
Steeped in deceits and sunk in shame,
　The hedge my bed and husks my daily bread,
Never a baser thing crept under Heaven's stars.

Before the palace of the King I strayed,
　And saw the splendid casements filled with light.
A feast for the King's Son was made.
　With sordid hate, I cursed their royal state,
Lifting my impious hands, out there in the black night.

A marvel then! I saw the doors wide swung,
　And in a burst of light and joyous press
Of music on the darkness flung,
　Straight to my place, with swift, composèd pace,
The royal servants came, swift and with strong duress.

With strong duress unto the palace gate
　They dragged my unwilling feet and held me fast.
Lo! there the Prince Himself did wait.
　On my distress and ragged nakedness
He looked, and His gold-broidered cloke about me cast.

O dear compassion! Heavenly ruth! O true
　And knightly deed that won my callous breast
To shame and love! In that high retinue
　I stood with lowered brow. But the King said, 'Thou
Hast honour of my Son: henceforward be My guest!'

Gertrude Bartlett

This fine artist in words whose poems have appeared in the 'Atlantic Monthly,' the 'Metropolitan,' the 'Windsor' and other leading periodicals, is Mrs. John W. C. Taylor, of Montreal. She was born in New Haven, Oswego County, N.Y. Her father was the late William Cheever Bartlett, of New Haven, a veteran of the Civil War, and a descendant of Lieutenant George Bartlett, one of the founders of Guilford, in Connecticut, in 1639; and her mother, Mary Moulton, also a native of the Empire State. . . . . After studying in public schools and under private tutors, until seventeen years of age, Miss Bartlett came to Toronto and secured employment in the law offices of Macdonald & Marsh, of which firm Sir John A. Macdonald was the senior partner. In 1891, she married the young English artist who has since become President of a Lithographing Company, and shortly afterwards had the advantage of a year in England, visiting Cathedral towns, birth-places of poets, and 'unfrequented by-ways and villages of pure English charm.' Mr. and Mrs. Taylor have one child, a daughter.—The Editor.

[395]

The Gunners

WHO may the victors be, not yet we know;
  Our care, all sights set true, the shell in place,
The flame outleaping, sending death apace
To check the rush of the oncoming foe.
And then, as sounds of thund'rous hoof-beats grow,
With grind of wheels 'neath allies' guns at race,
We hear a shriek the air brings nigh, and face
Our instant doom.   Then tumults cease; and lo!—

The shining dead men, rank on rank, appear,
Their voices raised in one great cry, to hail
The gunners prone, for whom reveille clear
Their silver bugles blow in morning pale.
Your battle, God! to make men great; and here,
In that cause, dead, unvanquished, we prevail.

Put by the Flute

O LOVE, put by the flute.
    Too slight the tender, liquid strain
We heard amid the April rain
    Of wild white blooms, to voice the spell
      Whereof our lips are mute.
    Let organ diapasons tell
The music of the waves which roll
From that unfathomed Sea, the Soul.
      So, Love, put by the flute.

    The flute, O Love, put by;
For we unto the wonder-strand
Are come, from out the valley land
    Upon the Great Adventure bound.
      Here river reed notes die
    Within the larger pulse of sound.
Lest list'ning for the luring call
We lose the greater rhythm's fall,
      The flute, dear Love, put by.

    Put by the flute, O Love.
And yet, so piercing keen the tone

Once heard in yon far vale, wind-blown
  Down that bright stream, whose brim we twain
    With laughter leaned above,
  The joy thereof do we retain
Among our mighty chords, that so
How sweet is youth all men may know—
    Put by the flute, O Love.

Ballade of Barren Roses

THERE sounds his step receding on the stair,
  The bridegroom's, that my love could not detain;
For whose captivity the woman's snare
  Of veilèd brows was woven all in vain.
A rose I held he keeps with tender care.
  Tell him, dear Jesu, that no blossom blows
For its own beauty, howsoever rare.
  The Lord of Life loves not a barren rose.

The destiny of roses is to bear
  Their scarlet fruit through drear autumnal rain;
To hold upon the crystal drifting air
  Of winter days the cups that pour again
New springtime loveliness for earth to wear,
  When all the verdure now her bounds enclose
Is gone forever, lily with the tare.
  For this our Lord loves not a barren rose.

What thought of his is left for me to share
  Aroused from that rapt dream in which we twain
Lighted our little lamps of joy, to flare
  Along a single path to Love's domain?
Will he, in that mysterious region where
  The ruby chalice on his vision glows,
Exceeding all the stars, remembrance spare
  To one his Lord loves not, a barren rose?

Envoy

O Mystic Rose, the heart of Jesu, fair
  Creative source from which all beauty flows,
Ever transfusing Love, hear now my prayer:
  Resume for Love's own sake one barren rose.

Ballade of Tristram's Last Harping

THE end that Love doth seek, what bard can say,
  In that fair season when the tender green
Of opening leaves doth roof the woods of May,
  And sweet wild buds from out their places lean
To touch the dainty feet that heedless stray
  Among them, with a youth in knight's attire?
His lady's will capricious to obey,
  This is the end of dawning Love's desire.

And when amid the summer's bright array
  Of blossoms, are the crimson roses seen,
And one young maid, fairer than any spray
  In perfect bloom, wanders their lines between,
What blessëd solace can the lover pray
  Of her compassion, for his heart of fire?
With kisses on her mouth all words to stay—
  This is the end of eager Love's desire.

With driven clouds the lowering sky is grey;
  The winds above the frozen hills are keen,
And all fair buds have fallen in decay;
  What joy hath now the true knight of his Queen?
No rapture less exultant can allay
  His need, than softly craves this faulty lyre:
To answer all his pleading with sweet 'Yea'—
  This is the end of yearning Love's desire.

Envoy

Beloved, now is done our life's brief day;
  Not with the day howe'er doth Love expire.
Within thine arms the night to dream away—
  This is the end of Love's supreme desire.

William E. Marshall

To be remembered—to have your name engraven not on some pompous marble, but in the fleshly tables of a loving heart—to have a gentle light ever burning before the inner shrine of a human memory, is the measure of fame the wise man covets. . . Here is a poem of twenty-five Spenserians celebrating with simple earnestness an unknown man, unknown even to his contemporaries. No such poem has appeared in Canada since Roberts' 'Ave!' In dignity and depth of feeling, 'Ave,' DeMille's 'Behind the Veil' and 'Brookfield' stand together—a noble trio. . . That in these noisy self-advertising days there should be men like Marshall quietly doing their duty in their narrow spheres, but reaching out to the stars through Literature and Art, makes for the nation's moral health. . . Perhaps the technique of the poem is not flawless; but its heart is right. Through it shines a faith in man and God, a love of the simple, eternal, unchanging things, and above all, the devotion of a sacred memory. These rare qualities make 'Brookfield' an event in Canadian literature.— Prof. A. M. MacMechan, Ph.D.. in the Montreal 'Standard.'

[399]

WILLIAM E. MARSHALL was born in Liverpool, Nova Scotia, April 1st, 1859,—the youngest of a family of three. His father was the late James Noble Shannon Marshall, and his mother, Adelaide Amelia Allison. He was educated at the County Academy, and at Mt. Allison Collegiate Academy, Sackville, New Brunswick. In September, 1876, he entered his father's law office, as an articled student, and in January, 1881, was admitted to the Bar. For the ensuing years he practised law, chiefly at Bridgewater, Nova Scotia, until appointed in March, 1898, Registrar of Deeds for Lunenburg District.

Mr. Marshall was married in Liverpool, N.S., the 27th of December, 1883, to Margaret Jane Bingay Campbell, the third daughter of Archibald John Campbell and his wife, Sarah Budd Moody. They have a son and a daughter, both married.

In January, 1909, he published a collection of his poems, entitled *A book of Verse,* which was put on the local market only. It contains some fine poetry.

'Brookfield,' the poem that has brought this author extended fame, was first published in the April number of the University Magazine, Montreal, 1914. It is unquestionably a threnody of rare excellence—beautiful, noble, sweet. It was inspired by Marshall's love of his friend, Robert R. McLeod, a Nova Scotian graduate of Harvard University, in Divinity, who died in 1909. In a letter to Dr. Andrew McPhail, editor of the University Magazine, he says of him:

As to what the man himself really was, and what he accomplished along the way, besides getting a living—He was first and always a Minister of the tidings of God revealed to him in the ways of nature and freedom of thought. To me he was an interpreter of the truth and beauty of Life, a teacher who sought to save souls alive, a power for good and an example of greatness unto the people. His delightful 'Nature Studies,' his symphony of prose and poetry in 'Pinehurst,' 'Markland,' and his other multifarious writings, have enlarged Nova Scotia. Personally, he was very kind and helpful to me: many radiant days and nights I spent with him and his family in their idyllic Brookfield home. And that my love is more than Art I know full well. . . .

The explanatory notes accompanying the poem were supplied by the author.

Brookfield

R. R. M.

NOW hath a wonder lit the saddened eyes
Long misted by a grievous winter clime;
And now the dull heart leaps with love's surprise,
And sings its joy. For 'tis the happy time;
And all the brooding earth is full of chime;
And all the hosts of sleepers under ground
Have burst out suddenly in glorious prime;
And all the airy spirits now have found
Their wonted shrines with life and love entwinèd 'round.

And now I no more sorrow for the dead,
The friend I love hath pain of death no more,
He hath mortality forever shed,
He is of happiness the spirit's core.
And my heart's memory brims, yea, runneth o'er,
With lavish bounty of his teeming worth;
(What times he did his garnered wealth outpour,
In wisdom's word and deed and pleasure's mirth)
Wherefore my soul hath joy in life's great freedom-birth.

And so, I mount the richest sunset hill,
Singing the wandering echo of a fame
That shall forever have its roaming will
In love-awakened hearts where dwells the name
Of him whose genius, burning to high flame,
Was reared within these woods with spark divine.
Brookfield! Thy beauty slept, until he came
To wake thee up to visions that were thine
Hadst thou but dreamed what lay beyond the rule and line.

Hadst thou but dreamed! Ah, dreamers 'neath the blue
Of day, the dreamers in the starry night,
Pillowed on stone and kissed by sun and dew!
On ye, the ardours of the Infinite
Descend in wingèd raptures, and the light
Of Heav'n stirreth to bliss each mortal pain,
Wide opening dreaming eyes in spirit sight!—
Alas! how many waken up again,
Singing their ecstasy unto the wind and rain.
Behold, one cometh in the spirit now!—*

*McPherson.

A wraith of tender, melancholy song—
The once familiar friend of bird, and bough,
And flower, and brook, and meadow. Not for long
He wandered with the meagre, vagrant throng'
Of shepherds piping in the early day.
Death mocked his young heart-ease; and soon among
Forgotten things a woeful shepherd lay:
And soon the melody grew faint and died away.

On yonder hill, close to a great high road,
Made by the pioneers from sea to sea,
The Poet lay, unheeded;—and the load
Upon his broken heart sank heavily
With cattle's tread, and withered grew the tree
That bent o'er him, and dwindled to a path
The great highway that was so wide and free;—
Only a chance-hewn stone of poorest worth
Clung like a widowed love to his dead, buried earth.

We know his fellow-shepherds cried to Heaven,
And thrilled the winds with their melodious loss;
And doubtless, some late-straying sheep were driven,
By that rude, wailing music's urge, to cross
The moonlit stream and crop the golden moss;
And evermore were changed from sheep to man,
And evermore cared not for wordly dross,
And evermore heard call of Spring, and ran
Into the joyous woods to follow after Pan.

And He, our freedom's guide, our Spirit's friend,
Had more than loving word for that lone grave,
Where homing neighbour never came to lend
It presence. His warm heart was moved to save,
From utter, last neglect, a name that gave
The grace of life in songs now little read,
Since other ease of heart we most do crave.
Dear Friend! Whose love our weak remembrance fed,
Thou gav'st our silent bard a home among the dead.*

Among the mounds of love—no more alone—
With charity of marble at his head,
And, clinging to his feet, that poor, chance stone,

*McLeod collected money and had McPherson's remains trans-
ferred to North Brookfield churchyard, and a monument erected.

Now, in the churchyard, rests the long lost dead.
What though his coming was unheralded
With pomp and praise, he hath his meed of earth;
And on his grave the flowers he loved are spread,
And many a kindly eye will read his worth,
And sometimes there the heart of love be pourèd forth.

Lo! now, another comes to swell the praise:†
He bringeth far-off memory of the sea,
And of the pathless woods' alluring maze,
And of the ringing ax, and crashing tree,
And first log hut, and brush fire setting free
The age-imprisoned soil to ease the needs
That crown the pioneer's hard destiny.
Haply, the warring world no braver breeds,
Than he who turns a forest into waving meads.

Yet still we sing: *Saul hath his thousands slain,
And David tens of thousands!* As of old,
We make great holiday of bloodiest gain,
And wreathe the shining victor's head with gold,
And bless his gory trophies, and unfold
Them in Love's sacred temple, and outpour
Loud gratitude to God—that didst uphold
Our hands to kill our brother man in war.
Ah! Christ is dead,—and we the Roman Guard adore.

But see this happy village festival,‡
Where all the country folk are gathered round
Responsive to the clear, vibrating call
Of one uplifted voice,—whose echoes sound
Above the hill-tops now. This toil-won ground
Is holy; here the burning bush flamed high
One hundred years ago, when faith was crowned
In the first settler's log hut built near by,
And love, in that rude home, was blessed with children's cry.

Not that the Venturer grew rich or great,
Or seemed a hero or was honoured more
By those who followed him to conquer fate

†William Burke, first settler in Brookfield.

‡The Burke Centennial Festival, the proceeds of which we used for a Burke monument of red granite. McLeod was the originator and had charge of all these proceedings.

In the far wilderness; nor that he bore
Himself as one who paid for other's score;
But that among the forest immigrants,
He was the first life-bringer to explore
These hills, where the shy Indian had his haunts,
And prove the settler's worth, beyond the body's wants.

And it was well the body's wants were few,
To those who made the homes here—day by day
Toiling and sweating while they hacked and slew
The forest, burned the brush, and cleared away
For garden patch and grain, and flax and hay,—
But ah! the wives in rudest suffering strong!
Little of rest there was for such as they,
Little save care, ev'n in the baby song
They crooned, in midst of work for all the household throng.

And yet they were not sad—these pioneers:
(Tales have been told of humour all their own,
And of their wit that crackled unawares,
And of their sturdy way, and look, and tone,
And high assurance when their work was done.)
Surely, for them, the thrush at evening sang,
The Pleiades and great Orion shone,
And the life-giving sun in splendour sprang,
And the glad harvest moon her golden lamp did hang.

Long years ago, they went to take their rest
Beneath the spreading trees on yonder hill—
The field they cleared for use at God's behest,
And where the quiet tenants of his will
Are undisturbed of any joy or ill.
And here and there, white stones with carven name
Tell who lies covered up, forever still:
But the First Settler has a shaft of flame
Reared by the villagers unto his worth and fame.

Since then the years have flown, flown like the wind
That passeth o'er this hill, laden with life.
This is the hill where I was sure to find
My friend in days of old. Here, I am rife
In freedom—not from the surcease of strife
Of God with man (Lord, Lord, cease not with me!)
But from the bloodless Fate with hidden knife,

Shearing the heart aspiring to be free
Of lust and greed and self, whate'er the prize may be.

I will lift up mine eyes unto the hills,
Whence cometh help! My help is in the Lord!
Behold, O man, what is it that He wills
Of thee! But to do justice in accord,
And to love mercy better than the sword,
And to walk humbly in the sight of Him:
Thus, is the olden vision still outpoured
Upon the hills, for all whose eyes are dim
With seeking in the places where the bale-fires swim.

Thus, am I in the spirit with my friend,
Here in the village which he glorified;
And unto which his heart would always wend,—
Impatient of the world of human tide—
When Spring began to call him to her side
With robin's song and the arbutus trail,
And all the lure of freedom undenied,
And all the wistful life of hill and dale,
And river, lake, and stream, and love that would not fail.

And as he roamed the shores and woods and clears,—
Seeking, for aye, the bloom of yesterdays—
The mayflowers smiled and lent their sweetest airs,
And violets curtsied from the road-side ways;
The red-veined slippers of the elves and fays
Were hanging near the rose and eglantine,
And mystic trilliums still did heavenward gaze;
The blue flags waved, and lilies gan to shine;
The golden-rods and asters thronged the steep incline.

And something of that bloom was shown for me,
One eager day, when the Rhodora flamed
Her leafless beauty on us suddenly
Down in an old-time pasture road, and claimed
A first love's privilege, and was not shamed:
My friend had fondest greeting for the flower,
And gentlest love-speech ever poet framed;*
And all my vagrant heart was stayed, with power
Of love I never knew, until I shared his dower.

*This actually occurred. McLeod recited *Rhodora*.

Ah, he was richly dowered of the earth!
The grain of sand, the daisy in the sod,
Awoke his heart; and early he went forth,
Through field and wood, with young eyes all abroad;
And saw the nesting birds, and beck and nod
Of little creatures running wild and free,
Which know not that they know, yet are of God!
And kept his youth, and grew in sympathy,
And loved his fellows more, and had love's victory.

To such as heard, he was an answerer
Of things that lay outside the rule and line.
To those who loved, the follower of a star
That led him on and on with heavenly sign,
And lit his soul, and made his utterance shine;
So he went forth to many in his day:
And when he passed beyond at Sun's decline,
Some who had never seen him caught the ray;
And some came then to praise who could have cheered his way.

There is the little cabin in the tree,†
Where sometimes he would go for solitude,
And ease of heart, and thoughtful reverie,
And rain upon the roof, and dreamy mood,
And light the world hath never understood.
Ah me! the door is broken now, and wide:
And yet, I feel as if it might intrude
Upon a resting soul to look inside;—
Such is the quietness and lack of earthly pride.

O Friend! who so didst joy of knowledge use,
That men look up and brighten at thy name,
And speak of genius, and put by the news
To tell some good of one death cannot claim,
Nor life require to read in sculptured fame.
The wind upon the hill hath sweetest hush;
The day is melting into tenderest flame;
And from the valley, where the waters rush,
Comes up the evensong of the lone hermit-thrush.

†McLeod built it himself, in a great pine tree back of his house.

Norah M. Holland

Linked close by ties of blood to Ireland, where the veil is thin between the earth and the spirit world, and the fairy rings upon the grass attest the fairy revels, Norah Holland must have early glimpsed the vision of the Unseen things and known them for the Real, and been made free of the country which lies behind the gates of gold and ivory where the fairy folk welcome the children, and their elders who keep a childlike heart. . . . . But this singer of Canadian birth and nurturing has tender care also for the little things of earth, and her dog's devotion and the dancing feet of Kitty O'Neil are dear to her. . . . . Her verses show that she has encountered sorrow and met the trials of a toiling world, but these have never checked the play of humour, which dances irrepressibly among them, nor clouded a clarity of judgment as shrewd and guileless as a child's. The hand of Materialism has never touched her, and there is none of the soil of sordidness upon her garments.—CECILIA MARY WHITE, *of 'The Globe,' Toronto.*

[407]

HOW interesting to know that among Canada's women
poets is a cousin of W. B. Yeats,—Miss Norah Mary
Holland, a native Canadian, born at Collingwood, Ontario,
and, since 1889, a resident of Toronto.

Miss Holland's mother (deceased), née Elizabeth Yeats, was
a first cousin of the Irish poet, and her eldest daughter's lyrical
gift is akin to that of the distinguished relative. From her
father, Mr. John H. Holland, she also inherits poetic talent,
as he is a nephew of the late Chief Justice Hagarty.

Miss Holland was educated in the public school and the
collegiate institute of Port Dover, and in the Parkdale collegiate of Toronto.

Until recently she was for eight years employed as a reader
by the Dominion Press Clipping Bureau, but is now on the
staff of *The Daily News,* Toronto.

In 1904, she toured on foot the whole of the south and
west of Ireland, and a considerable portion of England; and
while she was a guest of the father of W. B. Yeats, he made
the crayon sketch reproduced on the preceding page.

The old homes of both families from which she has sprung
are in Sligo County, Ireland.

'Home Thoughts from Abroad' comes from the heart, as
Miss Holland has two brothers at the Front.

To W. B. Yeats

A WIND of dreams comes singing over sea,
     From where the white waves kiss the coasts of home,
Bringing upon its rainbow wings to me
     Glimpses of days gone by,
Of wastes of water, where the sea-gulls cry
     Above the sounding foam.

Or through the mists do Finn and Usheen ride
     With all their men along some faery shore,
While Bran and Sgeolan follow at their side,
     Adown the shadowy track,
Till in the sunset Caoilte's hair blows back,
     And Niamh calls once more.

Or the brown bees hum through the drowsy day
     In glades of Inisfree, where sunlight gleams,

The bean-flower scents again the dear old way,
  Once more the turf fire burns,
The memory of the long dead past returns
  Borne on that wind of dreams.

The Unchristened Child

ALANNA! Alanna! Within the churchyard's round
  There's many graves of childer there; they lie in holy
    ground.
But yours is on the mountain side beneath the hawthorn tree,
O sweet one, my fleet one, that's gone so far from me.

Alanna! Alanna! When that small mound was made
No mass was sung, no bell was rung, no priest above it prayed;
Unchristened childer's souls they say may ne'er see Heaven's
    light—
O lone one, my own one, where strays your soul to-night?

Alanna! Alanna! This life's a weary one,
And there's little time for thinkin' when the hours of work
    are done,
And the others have forgotten, but there's times I sit apart,
O fair one, my dear one, and hold you in my heart.

Alanna! Alanna! If I were Mary mild
And heard outside the gates of Heaven a little cryin' child,
What though its brow the chrisom lacked, I'd lift the golden
    pin,
O bright one, my white one, and bid you enter in.

Alanna! Alanna! The mountain side is bare,
And the winds they do be blowing and the snows be lying
    there,
And unchristened childer's souls, they say, may ne'er see
    Heaven's light,
O lone one, my own one, where strays your soul to-night?

The King of Erin's Daughter

THE King of Erin's Daughter had wind-blown hair and
  bright,
The King of Erin's Daughter, her eyes were like the sea;

21

(O Rose of all the roses, have you forgotten quite
The story of the days of old that once you told to me?)

The King of Erin's Daughter went up the mountain side
And who but she was singing as she went upon her way,
'O somewhere waits a King's Son and I shall be his bride,
And tall he is and fair he is and none shall say him nay.'

The King of Erin's Daughter—O fair was she and sweet—
Went laughing up the mountain without a look behind,
Till on the lofty summit that lay beneath her feet
She found a King's Son waiting there, his brows with poppies
       twined.

O tall was he and fair was he. He looked into her face
And whispered in her ear a word un-named of mortal breath,
And very still she rested, clasped close in his embrace,
The King of Erin's Daughter, for the bridegroom's name was
       Death.

My Dog and I

MY dog and I, the hills we know
Where the first faint wild roses blow,
  We know the shadowy paths and cool
That wind across the woodland dim,
And where the water beetles swim
  Upon the surface of the pool.

My dog and I, our feet brush through
Full oft the fragrant morning dew,
  Or when the summer sun is high
We linger where the river flows,
Chattering and chuckling as it goes,
  Two happy tramps, my dog and I.

Or, when the winter snows are deep,
Into some fire-lit nook we creep
  And, while the north wind howls outside,
See castles in the dancing blaze,
Or, dozing, dream of summer days
  And woodland stretches, wild and wide.

My dog and I are friends till death,
And when the chill, dark angel's breath
  Shall call him from me, still I know

Somewhere within the shadowy land
Waiting his master he will stand
  Until my summons comes to go.

And, in that life so strange and new,
We'll tramp the fields of heaven through,
  Loiter the crystal river by,
Together walk the hills of God
As when the hills of earth we trod,
  Forever friends, my dog and I.

Cradle Song

LITTLE brown feet, that have grown so weary
  Plodding on through the heat of day,
Mother will hold you, mother will fold you
Safe to her breast; little feet, rest;
  Now is the time to cease from play.

Little brown hands, that through day's long hours
  Never rested, be still at last;
Mother will rest you; come, then, and nest you
Here by her side, nestle and hide;
  Creep to her heart and hold it fast.

Little brown head, on my shoulder lying,
  Night is falling and day is dead;
Mother will sing you songs that shall bring you
Childhood's soft sleep, quiet and deep;
  Sweet be your dreams, O dear brown head!

Home Thoughts from Abroad

APRIL in England—daffodils are growing
  By every wayside, golden, tall and fair;
April—and all the little winds are blowing
  The scents of springtime through the sunny air.
April in England—God, that we were there!

April in England—and her sons are lying
  On these red fields, and dreaming of her shore;
April—we hear the thrushes' songs replying
  Each unto each, above the cannons' roar;
April in England—shall we see it more?

April in England—there's the cuckoo calling
  Down in her meadows where the cowslip gleams;
April—and little showers are softly falling,
  Dimpling the surface of her babbling streams;
April in England—how the shrapnel screams!

April in England—blood and dust and smother,
  Screaming of horses, men in agony.
April—full many of thy sons, O Mother,
  Never again those dewy dawns shall see.
April in England—God, keep England free!

Sea Song

I WILL go down to the sea again, to the waste of waters,
    wild and wide;
I am tired—so tired—of hill and plain and the dull tame face
    of the country-side.

I will go out across the bar, with a swoop like the flight of
    a sea-bird's wings,
To where the winds and the waters are, with their multitudin-
    ous thunderings.

My prow shall furrow the whitening sea, out into the teeth of
    the lashing wind,
Where a thousand billows snarl and flee and break in a smother
    of foam behind.

O strong and terrible Mother Sea, let me lie once more on
    your cool white breast,
Your winds have blown through the heart of me and called me
    back from the land's dull rest.

For night by night they blow through my sleep, the voice of
    waves through my slumber rings,
I feel the spell of the steadfast deep; I hear its tramplings
    and triumphings.

And at last when my hours of life are sped let them make me
    no grave by hill or plain,
Thy waves, O Mother, shall guard my head; I will go down to
    my sea again.

Father Dollard

In all Father Dollard's poetry there is a wealth of beauty and a perfection of skill, seldom met with outside the pages of great composers. To this beauty and skill are added a refinement of lofty thought and an aptitude and delicacy of expression that, at once, charm and delight the reader. But it is when he sings of his own native land—of Ireland—that the voice of his song touches the core of our hearts. Here, in his moments of highest inspiration, his paths are in the land.—The Very Rev. W. R. Harris, LL.D.

The poems of Father Dollard have long been appreciated for their high literary quality, spirituality and Celtic insight. To the scholarly touch of the classicist he adds the magic and vision of the true Celt. Born under the shadow of Slieve-na-mon, dreamful of mystical lore, Father Dollard was early inspired by the beauty and charm and tender melancholy of his native land. Though with a versatile pen he touches many themes, his supreme gift is that of an Irish lyrist.—Lindsay Crawford, in 'The Globe,' Toronto.

[413]

THE Rev. James B. Dollard is Parish Priest of St. Monica's church, North Toronto. He was born at Mooncoin, County Kilkenny, Ireland, August 30th, 1872, the youngest son in a large family, whose parents were Michael and Anastasia (Quinn) Dollard.

After taking the course in Classics at Kilkenny College, he sailed in 1890 for New Brunswick, where his brother, the Rev. William Dollard, was Parish Priest of St. Stephen, and his maternal uncle, the Rev. James Quinn, was Vicar-General of the Diocese of St. John. Another relative, the late Archbishop Walsh, was then in Toronto and young Dollard decided to study for the priesthood in his Archdiocese. He took the course in Philosophy and Theology at the Grand Seminary of Montreal and received from Laval University the degrees of Bachelor of Theology and Bachelor of Canon Law. The same University conferred on him in 1916, the honorary degree of Litt.D.

Father Dollard was ordained to the priesthood in December, 1896. He served as a curate in St. Helen's Church, and St. Mary's Church, Toronto, and prior to his present charge, was, for nine years, Parish Priest of Uptergrove, Ontario, where he built a new church and presbytery.

His first book of verse, *Irish Mist and Sunshine,* was published in 1902, and his second, entitled *Poems,* in 1910. And he has now ready for publication, a third and larger volume, written in the last five years and containing his most mature and artistic work. This includes a lengthy drama, *Clontarf,* the theme of which is the Danish overthrow in Ireland.

In a lecture on "The War and the Poets," delivered in Toronto, 1916, Mr. Joyce Kilmer, poetry editor of the *Literary Digest,* declared that Father Dollard's sonnet was the best poem that had appeared on the death of Rupert Brooke.

Father Dollard is also author of a volume of short stories, entitled *The Gaels of Moondharrig.*

The Dollards are descended from an old Norman family who went to England with William, the Conqueror, and later to Ireland with the first English invaders. A grand-uncle of our poet, the Right Rev. William Dollard, was the first Roman Catholic Bishop of New Brunswick.

Rupert Brooke

SLAIN by the arrows of Apollo, lo,
The well-belovèd of the Muses lies
On Lemnos' Isle 'neath blue and classic skies,
And hears th' Ægean waters ebb and flow!
How strange his beauteous soul should choose to go
Out from its body in this hallowed place,
Where Poesy and Art's undying grace
Still breathe, and pipes of Pan still murmur low!

Here shall he rest untroubled, knowing well
That faithful hearts shall hold his memory dear,
Moved to affection weak words cannot tell
By his short, splendid life that knew no fear;
Belovèd of the gods, the gods have ta'en
Their Ganymede, by bright Apollo slain!

The Haunted Hazel

ADOWN a quiet glen where the gowan-berries glisten
And the linnet, shyest bird of all, his wild note warbles
    free;
Where the scented woodbine-blossoms, o'er the brooklet, bend
    to listen,
There stands upon a mossy bank, a white-hazel tree.

Oh! fair it is to view, when the zephyr rustles lightly,
And warm sunlight glances back from polished bole and
    branch;
For then like wavelets on a rill the pendent leaves flash
    brightly,
And daisies nod in concert, round the column straight and
    staunch.

But when the day is ended, and the solemn moon is shining,
And shadows grim and ghostly, fall on grove and glen and lea,
Then godless elves their fairy paths with glow-worm lamps
    are lining,
And potent spells of magic bind this white-hazel tree!

For from their gorgeous palaces the fairy bands come stealing,
To dance in sportive circles on the never bending moss;
And the velvet-soft caressing of their finger-touches healing,
Brings to the sere white-hazel bark again its youthful gloss.

And round and round they skip and glide, in strange fantastic
          measure,
To weird, unhallowed melodies of fairy minstrelsy,
Yet mortal ear may never hear those sounds of elfin pleasure,
And no whisper of its secrets gives the white-hazel tree!

But should the peasant wander nigh that baleful bower, un-
          thinking,
And sudden feel the chilling of the haunted hazel's shade,
A nameless horror seizes on his spirit, bowed and shrinking,
And making oft the Holy Sign, he hurries home dismayed.

For maid that treads the path of doom beneath the hazel's
          shadow,
Shall be the bride of Death, they say, before a month has flown;
And laughing swain, in pride of strength, who crossed at eve
          the meadow,
Shall moulder 'neath the matted moss, e'er yet that mead is
          mown!

So, in the solemn hours of night the fairies dance unharmed,
Till thro' gray dawn the haggard moon her waning span doth
          dree,
Then from the blessèd sunbeam flies the evil power that
          charmed,
And fairy spell is lifted from the white-hazel tree!

The Fairy Harpers

AS I walked the heights of Meelin on a tranquil autumn
          day,
The fairy host came stealing o'er the distant moorland gray.
     I heard like sweet bells ringing,
     Or a grove of linnets singing,
And the haunting, wailful music that the fairy harpers play!

Like thunder of deep waters when vast-heaving billows break,
Like soughing of the forest when ten thousand branches shake,
     Like moaning of the wind,
     When the night falls bleak and blind,
So wild and weird the melodies the fairy minstrels make.

The sunbeams flecked the valley, and the cloud-shades ranged
the hill,
The thistle-down scarce drifted in the air so calm and still.
But along the slopes of Meelin
Came the ghostly music pealing,
With sad and fitful cadences that set my soul a-thrill!

Then wan and wistful grew the sky o'er Meelin's summit lone,
And weeping for the days gone by, my heart grew cold as
stone,
For I heard loved voices calling
Beyond the sunlight falling
On Meelin's mournful mountain where the magic harps make
moan!

At Dead o' the Night, Alanna

AT dead o' the night, alanna, I wake and see you there,
Your little head on the pillow, with tossed and tangled
hair;
I am your mother, acushla, and you are my heart's own boy,
And wealth o' the world I'd barter to shield you from annoy.

At dead o' the night, alanna, the heart o' the world is still,
But sobbing o' fairy music comes down the haunted hill;
The march o' the fairy armies troubles the peace o' the air,
Blest angels shelter my darling for power of a mother's pray'r!

At dead o' the night, alanna, the sleepless Banshee moans,
Wailing for sin and sorrow, by the Cairn's crumbling stones,
At dead o' the night, alanna, I ask of our God above,
To shield you from sin and sorrow, and cherish you in His
love.

At dead o' the night, alanna, I wonder o'er and o'er,
Shall you part from our holy Ireland, to die on a stranger
shore?
You'll break my heart in the leaving like many a mother I
know—
Just God look down upon Erin and lift her at last from woe!

At dead o' the night, alanna, I see you in future years,
Grand in your strength, and noble, facing the wide world fears;

Though down in the mossy churchyard my bones be under the
    sod,
My spirit shall watch you, darling, till you come to your rest
    in God!

Ballad of the Banshee

BACK thro' the hills I hurried home,
  Ever my boding soul would say:
'Mother and sister bid thee come,
  Long, too long has been thy stay.'

Stars shone out, but the moon was pale,
  Touched by a black cloud's ragged rim,
Sudden I heard the Banshee's wail
  Where Malmor's war-tower rises grim.

Quickly I strode across the slope,
  Passed the grove and the Fairy Mound
(Gloomy the moat where blind owls mope)
  Scarcely breathing, I glanced around.

Mother of mercy! there she sat,
  A woman clad in a snow-white shroud,
Streamed her hair to the damp moss-mat,
  White the face on her bosom bowed!

'Spirit of Woe' I eager cried,
  'Tell me none that I love has gone,
Cold is the grave'—my accents died—
  The Banshee lifted her face so wan.

Pale and wan as the waning moon,
  Seen when the sun-spears herald dawn.
Ceased all sudden her dreary croon,
  Full on my own her wild eyes shone,

Burned and seared my inmost soul.
  (When shall sorrow depart from me?)
Black-winged terror upon me stole,
  Blindly gaping, I turned to flee!

Back by the grove and haunted mound,
  O'er the lone road I know not how,

Hearkened afar my baying hound
    Home at last at the low hill's brow!

Lone the cottage—the door flung wide,
Four lights burned—oh, sight of dread!
Breathing a prayer, I rushed inside,
    'Mercy, God!' 'twas my mother, dead!

Dead and white as the fallen leaf,
    (Kneeling, my sister prayed near by),
Wild as I wrestled with my grief,
    Far and faint came the Banshee's cry!

The Passing of the Sidhe

THERE is weeping on Cnoc-Aulin and on hoary Slieve-na-
    mon,
There's a weary wind careering over haggard Knocknaree;
    By the broken mound of Almhin
    Sad as death the voices calling,
Calling ever, wailing ever, for the passing of the Sidhe.

Where the hunting-call of Ossian waked the woods of Glen-na
    mar,
Where the Fianna's hoarse cheering silenced noisy Assaroe,
    Like the homing swallows meeting,
    Like a beaten host retreating,
Hear them sobbing as they hurry from the hills they used to
    know!

There's a haunted hazel standing on a grim and gloomy scaur,
Tossing ceaselessly its branches like a keener o'er the dead;
    Deep around it press the masses
    Of the Sluagh-shee* that passes
To the moan of fairy music timing well their muffled tread.

Came a wail of mortal anguish o'er the night-enshrouded sea,
Sudden death o'ertook the agèd while the infant cried in fear,
    And the dreamers on their pillows
    Heard the beat of bursting billows,
And the rumble and the rhythm of an army passing near.

* Pronounced Slua Shee—The Fairy Army.

They have left the unbelieving—past and gone their gentle
        sway,
Lonely now the rath enchanted, eerie glen and wild crannoge;
        But the sad winds, unforgetting,
            Call them back with poignant fretting,
Snatching songs of elfin sorrow from the streams of Tir-na-
        n'Og.

Ould Kilkinny

I'M sick o' New York City an' the roarin' o' the thrains
That rowl above the blessèd roofs an' undernaith the dhrains;
Wid dust an' smoke an' divilmint I'm moidhered head an'
        brains,
    An' I thinkin' o' the skies of ould Kilkinny!

Bad luck to Owen Morahan that sint the passage-note
'Tis he's the cause, the omadhaun, I ever tuk the boat;
'Tis he's the cause I'm weepin' here, a dhrayman on a float,
    When I should be savin' hay in ould Kilkinny!

The sorra bit o' grassy field from morn till night I see,
Nor e'er a lark or linnet—not to mind a weeshy bee!
Och! an' honest Irish mountain now would lift the heart o'
        me,—
    Will I ever see the hills of ould Kilkinny?

The rattle on the pavement-blocks is fit to make you cry,
A hundhert snortin' carriages like fire an' brimstone fly;
Tin thousant people tearin' wild, black sthrangers pass me by,
    An' to think I left me frinds in ould Kilkinny!

'Tis well me lovin' parents all are in their coffin-shrouds,
'Twould break their hearts to see their boy half-smothered in
        these crowds,
Wid buildin's all around that high they're berrid in the clouds,
    When the little cot would suit him in Kilkinny!

Bad luck to Owen Morahan, if I'd the passage back,
'Tis shortly I'd be home agin across the ocean thrack;
I'd not delay in Queenstown, an' I'd fly through Ballyhack,
    For to greet the neighbours kind in ould Kilkinny!

Laura E. McCully

*Miss McCully's poetry is enriched by classical illustrations,
and expressed in forceful and melodious language. Her imagination relates us to the universe and to humanity. Wordsworth found new lessons in the fields and woods, and taught
them; Lanier made trees, flowers and clouds our intimate
friends; when we read Miss McCully's nature poems we are
not conscious of the moralizing of the poet, we are in the glens
ourselves listening to the bird-songs or pine psalms, or on
the hill-top looking at the afterglow, with the purity, the glory,
the growth spirit and the transforming beauty of nature flowing into our lives. In a few flaming lines her stories reveal
the love, the despair and the ultimately triumphant faith of
humanity. With tender pathos she unveils the evils of social
and industrial conditions, and in clear tones arouses each soul,
and makes it conscious of the splendour of the better conditions ahead, and thrills it with the determination to achieve
for justice, freedom and truth.—JAMES L. HUGHES, LL.D.*

IN a very real sense Miss Laura Elizabeth McCully, M.A., is a Toronto writer, as, with the exception of one academic year in the United States, and a few months in Ottawa, she has lived all her life in this city.

She is a grand niece of the late Hon. John McCully, of Truro, Nova Scotia, one of the Fathers of Confederation; and is the daughter of Samuel Edward McCully, M.D., and Helen (Fitzgibbon) McCully. Her father is of Manx descent, and her mother is a descendant of the late James McBride, of Halton county, Ontario, magistrate, who was one of the pioneers of this province, and who heroically cleared off forest and left to his heirs, one thousand acres of valuable farm lands.

Miss McCully was educated at Deer Park Public School, Jarvis Collegiate, and University College. Throughout her University course she stood high in the class lists, and graduated in 1909 with first-class honours in English, History, French and German. She was and is particularly attracted to the ancient Anglo-Saxon language and her written theses on this branch of study, together with the recommendation of her teacher, Professor David Keyes, M.A., procured for her a Fellowship in Yale College. In this Institution she studied for an academic year (1909-10) under the well-known author of text-books in Anglo-Saxon, Dr. Albert S. Cooke.

Miss McCully is proficient in athletics; and is an ardent advocate of the rights of women, political, professional and industrial. She has firm belief that this century will fully establish equality of sex and of racial responsibility.

She began her poetical career by winning in her teens several prizes offered by the Young People's Corner of the *Mail and Empire*.

Her first book of verse, *Mary Magdalene and Other Poems,* was published in 1914. It contains fifty poems of such quality that one feels, after several readings, that this young poet must yet climb far up the heights of poetic achievement.

Besides labouring in a munitions factory in 1916, to aid the cause of the Allies, Miss McCully has been engaged in writing a metrical translation of the epic of Beowulf, the most precious of Old English literary relics. This is important work for which she is admirably qualified.

Our Little Sister

WEEP, little shrinking spirits of the woods,
    Hang down your fair, green faces, all ye leaves,
And dews be heavy on the year's firstborn,—
Yea, weep as rain, all ye that breathe of spring,
To-day I passed her in the city streets!

Surely the kind brown earth must pity her,
Nursing its young so safely at the breast,
All the great winds that no man may defile
Compassionate her, and the bending trees
Happy in fruitfulness and blest with song!

But where her feet are set of all God made
No stone remains; and wearing childhood's face
Fixed in an awful lethargy and calm,
Defiled, defiling, yet accusing not,
Avenged upon her race, she passes on.

The Troubadour's Lyre

SING low, my precious lyre, low in each string,
    Thou wast not framed for exaltation's burst,
Or chant sustained, straining thy golden chords,
Sing low, sing low, thou constant friend, my lyre!

For now we two may wander forth in peace,
Shattered our shackles are and stricken from us,
And we shall rise and steal out into the world,
Singing all day, on every way, my lyre.
Like Orpheus have we two sojourned through hell,
And with our eyes seen evil, nor availed
To wrest their treasure from the envious shades.
Therefore come forth, leave to the Gods their world!

If we should find that orchard lamped with gold
Of heart's desire, fasting will we pass on,
Nor rifle one small, new-blown wayside flower,
But bless its beauty, pass, and passing, sing.

Thus shall we travel light of foot and free,
And call the world our garden and the woods

Our house, and hear the great winds call to us,
And sometimes feel the dripping of the dews
In lonely places. Come, for we are free.
O lyre, heart of my heart, formed for the wind
That is God's breath, and not for human hands
Jangling amid the strings, come, let us go!

Canoe Song at Twilight

DOWN in the west the shadows rest,
Little grey wave, sing low, sing low!
With a rhythmic sweep o'er the gloomy deep
    Into the dusk of the night we go,
        And the paddles dip and lift and slip,
        And the drops fall back with a pattering drip;
The wigwams deep of the spirits of sleep
Are pitched in the gloom on the headland steep.
    Wake not their silence as you go,
    Little grey wave, sing low, sing low!

From your porch on high where the clouds go by,
    Little white moon, look down, look down!
'Neath night's shut lid the stars are hid,
    And the last late bird to his nest has flown.
        The slow waves glide and sink and slide
        And rise in ripples along the side;
The loons call low in the marsh below,
Night weaves about us her magic slow,—
    Ere the last faint gleam in our wake be gone,
    Little white moon, look down, look down!

A Ballad of the Lakes

MY love she went a-sailing
Ere yet the day was done,
And a wind blew up, and a wind blew up,
    Straight out of the setting sun.

I sat on a rock a-fishing
    Where flashes the bronze-black fin
And the eddies swirl and suck and curl
    When the river tide comes in.

She hailed me from the headland
  And I saw the brown sail swing
Till the rope ran tight and it lifted light
  As the sweep of a wild duck's wing.

'O where go ye a-sailing,
  For the day will soon be done,
And see the shroud of shifting cloud
  That's following up the sun?'

'It's off I am to the eastward,
  To the rim of the world away,
Ply sail and oar for the far-off shore
  And none shall bid me stay.'

So she sailed away to the eastward
  To the far horizon's rim,
Where rosy kissed through a veil of mist
  The line of the shore lay dim.

And the sun sank down the marshes,
  In a field of flame he rolled,
The heaving track from the boat slipped back
  Like a path of molten gold.

Each little wave seemed smiling,
  Lips curled in a rosy bow,
Like a babe asleep on the breast of the deep
  That rocked it to and fro.

And I sat on my rock a-fishing
  While further down the west
The sun sank slow to his bed below
  In the marshes' swaying breast.

Sudden a white owl hooted
  From his nest in the pine hard by,
And a whip-poor-will sent an answer shrill
  From the depths of the flaming sky.

I looked away to the westward
  And there I saw it stand,
A cloud pure white and small and bright
  As the palm of an opened hand.

One leap to the jutting headland,—
  Like a blow it stung my face,
The cap of wind with the threat behind
  Of the squall that comes apace.

Out on the lake there widened
  A wreathing ring of black,
And the spreading cloud like an out-flung shroud
  Promised the coming wrack.

The waves rose white and frothing,
  With a hiss like a rattlesnake
That glides at night past the lantern's light
  On the path through a slimy brake.

Have you seen the inland waters
  When the black squall rides the wave?
For it comes like light and there is no flight,
  And you call on God to save,

As I, one breath, 'Save, save her!'
  And I plunged in the driving roar,
For my light canoe pierced through and through
  Lay high on the rocky shore.

Clean stroke, long breath, poised body,
  They laugh at your manhood's pride,
The billows that seethe and drive in your teeth
  When the breath cramps in your side.

A quarter-mile to the headland?
  Ten miles of boiling hell!
Blind, choked and stung, bruised, tossed and flung
  In a world that heaved and fell.

But once, from the crest of a comber
  The gleam of a distant sail,
As slight a thing as a butterfly's wing
  Tossed into the teeth of the gale.

On, on! Is your blood turned water?
  Shall a straining muscle's pain,
Though it snap like tow, speak louder now
  Than the cry of heart and brain?

In my ears the roar of thunder,
    In my eyes a spray blood-red,
But once I sank, lost wind and drank,
    And something snapped in my head.

Do you know the way of the waters
    When their sudden wrath is o'er?
Rubbish and wrack they cast safe back,
    And they cast me on the shore.

Do you know the way of the waters,
    The hungry, restless wave?
They take for toll a living soul
    And no man knows the grave.

Then search no more by the marshes
    Where the moon stands up so white,
Has never a bird through the silence stirred
    All the long, bright summer night.

Then seek no more by the river
    Where the water lilies gleam,
So pale and still, so ghostly chill
    Like a dead face in a dream,

For the eyes may ache with seeking,
    They may search till they see no more,
And the heart grow old and the pulse beat cold
    Ere my love comes back to shore.

Mary Magdalene Soliloquizes

On Love

SING, heart of spring, along the winter ways,
 Go lightly feet, 'twas here His footsteps fell,
The birds sing of Him for he counted them
And knew them all, the little wingèd loves
Like happy thoughts! Yea, every leaf that kissed
Him passing in the garden hath such life
As puts our immortality to shame.
The winds are pregnant with His message now,
The universal, all-uniting winds

That know no limitation, like the spirit
Of mighty truths, sweeping creation's bounds,
Disdaining man-made barriers, change and time.

Yea, since He came, sing resurrected soul,
As nature sings, through winter unto spring!
For now the ancient curse is past away,
The simple way and straight made plain to man
And love exalted, love revealed, proclaimed.
Not love that self has sought for selfish ends,
Nor love possessing or possessed, but love
Creating, sacrificing, binding all,
Conceiving good but as the good of all,
Laying down life that life may be fulfilled
In the new life that springs a thousandfold
More rich for sacrifice. O perfect bliss
Which man alone of all creation failed
To grasp, to comprehend! See how the earth
Meekly and sweetly, with a sure content,
Lays down the old year's leaves, yields to the wind
Her precious, garnered seeds, nor makes complaint,
But in her heart, all lowly, sings of spring;
See her emerge from tempest, recreate,
Instinct with life, noble and large and calm,
At peace with the infinite purposes of God!

Sing, heart of spring, along the wintry way
His blessèd feet made glad. Weep not for Him,
Nor for the world, nor for thy human pain.
Cound'st thou have died as He did, who could rend
That place from thee? Most perfect was His part,
But thou hast thine, to succour, heal and teach,
Even as He, perchance to die as He
For man. Sing, happy heart, along life's way
For joy and love are met in thee and life
Wells new within thee, sing for spring is here,
Sing, for thine eyes have seen the Risen Lord!

Lloyd Roberts

Mr. Roberts as a poet is fundamentally a word-painter, a nature colourist, rather than a lilter or verbal musician. By this it is not meant that his verse does not appeal by its rhythmic swing and vowel music, consonance, assonance and alliteration. As a verbal musician his rhythms are limited, quite conventional, though not artificial; he employs rhythms suited to his subjects, and he is adept in the use of pure terminal rhymes, assonance, and alliteration, gifted in this respect, somewhat like Swinburne. But essentially Mr. Roberts shows distinction as a colourist, using words with the same beauty and power that a master-painter in oils uses pigments. He is a master of vivid colourful diction and phrase. . . . . Mr. Lloyd Roberts is a genuine poet because he sings with the poet's chief inspiration, namely: ecstasy of delight in the magic and mystery of earth, and in the lust of life. He is a poet of exceeding great promise.—J. D. LOGAN, PH.D., in the Montreal 'Herald.'

BECAUSE of the warm place held in the hearts of Canadian readers, by Charles G. D. Roberts, a first volume of poems from the pen of his eldest living son, Mr. Lloyd Roberts, was a matter of national interest.

This volume, *England Over Seas,* published in the spring of 1914, at once attracted wide attention. It was soon discovered that the son is as true a poet as the father, possessing the same unerring vision and sureness of touch in nature description, and the same fine mastery of words and of rhythmic effects.

In an excellent review in the Halifax *Herald,* appears this passage:

> It is the simplicity of statement, the lyric charm and the spontaneous joy of its utterance which make Mr. Roberts' work such a pleasure and a profit to read. This simplicity is obviously Mr. Roberts' ideal, and with such an ideal held steadily before him, there is no distance he may not travel and no height he may not climb to deliver his message to the world. . . . . Lloyd Roberts comes upon the scene as a writer of true lyric poetry, singing the song of his native land, and with each successive poem fulfilling the promise of becoming one of the way-marks of Canadian literature.

Mr. Roberts was born in Fredericton, N.B., October 31st, 1884. He was educated in the schools of his native city and subsequently at Windsor, N.S. When eighteen years of age, he broke away from the class-room and began his career of self-directed effort. In 1904 he joined the staff of *Outing Magazine,* New York, as assistant editor; and later became an editorial writer for 'The National Encyclopædia of American Biography.' Since then he has done newspaper work in British Columbia and in Ontario, and is now occupied in the Department of the Interior, at Ottawa, as editor of immigration literature.

Mr. Roberts has been twice married,—in 1908, to Helen Hope Farquhar Balmain, of England, to whom his first volume is dedicated, and who died in 1912, leaving him with one little daughter, Patricia—and in 1914, to Lila White, of New York State.

The readers of *England Over Seas* will learn with very real pleasure that Mr. Roberts' second book of verse is ready for the press.

The Fruit-Rancher

H E sees the rosy apples cling like flowers to the bough:
He plucks the purple plums and spills the cherries on
the grass;
He wanted peace and silence,—God gives him plenty now—
His feet upon the mountain and his shadow on the pass.

He built himself a cabin from red cedars of his own;
He blasted out the stumps and twitched the boulders from
the soil;
And with an axe and chisel he fashioned out a throne
Where he might dine in grandeur off the first fruits of his
toil.

His orchard is a treasure-house alive with song and sun,
Where currants ripe as rubies gleam and golden pippins
glow;
His servants are the wind and rain whose work is never done,
Till winter rends the scarlet roof and banks the halls with
snow.

He shouts across the valley, and the ranges answer back;
His brushwood smoke at evening lifts a column to the moon;
And dim beyond the distance where the Kootenai snakes black,
He hears the silence shattered by the laughter of the loon.

Miss Pixie

D ID you ever meet Miss Pixie of the Spruces?
Did you ever glimpse her mocking elfin face?
*Did you ever hear her calling while the whip-poor-wills were
calling,*
And slipped your pack and taken up the chase?

Her feet are clad in moccasins and beads.
Her dress? Oh, next to nothing! Though undressed,
Her slender arms are circled round with vine
And dusky locks cling close about her breast.

Red berries droop below each pointed ear;
Her nut-brown legs are criss-crossed white with scratches;
Her merry laughter sifts among the pines;
Her eager face gleams pale from milk-weed patches.

22

And though I never yet have reached her hand—
  God knows I've tried with all my heart's desire;—
One morning just at dawn she caught me sleeping
  And with her soft lips touched my soul with fire.

And once when camping near a foaming rip,
  Lying wide-eyed beneath the milky stars,
Sudden I heard her voice ring sweet and clear,
  Calling my soul beyond the river bars.

Dear, dancing Pixie of the wind and weather,
  Aglow with love and merriment and sun,
I chase thee down my dreams, but catch thee never—
  God grant I catch thee ere the trail is done!

Did you ever meet Miss Pixie of the Thickets,
  Where the scarlet leaves leap tinkling from your feet?
Have you ever heard her calling while a million feet were
    falling,
  And a million lights were crowding all the street?

England's Fields

ENGLAND'S cliffs are white like milk,
  But England's fields are green;
The grey fogs creep across the moors,
  But warm suns stand between.
And not so far from London town, beyond the brimming
    street,
A thousand little summer winds are singing in the wheat.

  Red-lipped poppies stand and burn,
    The hedges are aglow;
  The daisies climb the windy hills
    Till all grow white like snow.
And when the slim, pale moon slides down, and dreamy night
    is near,
There's a whisper in the beeches for lonely hearts to hear.

  Poppies burn in Italy,
    And suns grow round and high;
  The black pines of Posilipo
    Are gaunt upon the sky—

And yet I know an English elm beside an English lane
That calls me through the twilight and the miles of misty rain.

Tell me why the meadow-lands
    Become so warm in June;
Why the tangled roses breathe
    So softly to the moon;
And when the sunset bars come down to pass the feet of day,
Why the singing thrushes slide between the sprigs of May?

Weary, we have wandered back—
    And we have travelled far—
Above the storms and over seas
    Gleamed ever one bright star—
O England! when our feet grow cold and will no longer roam,
We see beyond your milk-white cliffs the round, green fields
    of home.

Husbands Over Seas

EACH morning they sit down to their little bites of bread,
  To six warm bowls of porridge and a broken mug or two.
And each simple soul is happy and each hungry mouth is fed—
    Then why should she be smiling as the weary-hearted do?

All day the house has echoed to their tiny, treble laughter
  (Six little rose-faced cherubs who trip shouting through the
    day),
Till the candle lights the cradle and runs dark along the
    rafter—
    Then why should she be watching while the long night
    wastes away?

She tells them how their daddy has sailed out across the seas,
  And they'll be going after when the May begins to bloom.
Oh, they clap their hands together as they cluster round her
    knees—
    Then why should she be weeping as they tumble from the
    room?

The May has bloomed and withered and the haws are cling-
    ing red,

The winter winds are talking in the dead ranks of the trees;
And still she tells of daddy as she tucks each tot in bed—
God pity all dear women who have husbands over seas!

The Winter Harvest

BETWEEN the blackened curbs lie stacked the harvest of
the skies,
Long lines of frozen, grimy cocks befouled by city feet;
On either side the racing throngs, the crowding cliffs, the cries,
And ceaseless winds that eddy down to whip the iron street.

The wagons whine beneath their loads, the raw-boned horses
strain;
A hundred sullen shovels claw and heave the sodden mass—
There lifts no dust of scented moats, no cheery call of swain,
Nor birds that pipe from border brush across the yellow
grass.

No cow-bells honk from upland fields, no sunset thrushes call
To swarthy, bare-limbed harvesters beyond the stubble
roads;
But flanges grind on frosted steel, the weary snow-picks fall,
And twisted, toiling backs are bent to pile the bitter loads.

No shouting from the intervales, no singing from the hill,
No scent of trodden tansy weeds among the golden grain—
Only the silent, cringing forms beneath the aching chill.
Only the hungry eyes of want in haggard cheeks of pain.

Come Quietly, Britain!

COME quietly, Britain, all together, come!
It is time!
We have waited, weighed, and wondered
Who had blundered;
Stared askance at one another
As our brother slew our brother,
And went about our business,
Saying: 'It will all be right—some day.
Let the soldiers do the killing—

If they're willing—
Let the sailors do the manning,
Let the Cabinets do the planning,
Let the bankers do the paying,
And the clergy do the praying.
The Empire is a fixture—
Walled and welded by five oceans,
And a little blood won't move it,
Nor a flood-tide of emotions.'

Well, now we know the truth
And the facts of all this fighting;
How 'tis not for England's glory
But for all a wide world's righting;
Not for George nor party power,
Not for conquest nor for dower,
Not for fear of our last hour,
But the lone star of liberty and light.
What the Puritans left England for,
What the Irish their green isle;
What Adolphus pledged his life to,
And Orange took from Spain—
The Spain that Grenville throttled,
And Frankie broke in twain—
What Washington starved and strove for
In the long winter night;
Lincoln wept for, died for—
Do we doubt if *he* were right?

Ah! It is time, if the soul of these is ours—
Time to put an end to reason
And take the field for right.
They will lead us, never fear it,
They will lead us through the night.
They will steel the soul and sinew
Of the legions of the land;
They will pilot up the Dreadnoughts
With the tillers in their hand—
Howard and Frobisher and Drake—
And who would fear to follow

When Nelson sets the course?
And who would turn his eyes away
From Wellington's white horse?

Not one, I warrant, now—
Not one at home to-day;
In England? In Scotland?
In the Green Isle 'cross the way?
No, nor far away to westward
Beyond the leagues of foam—
They are coming, they are coming,
Their feet are turning home.
In Canada they're singing,
And love lies like a flame
About their hearts this morning
That sea-winds cannot tame.
Africa? Australia?
Aye, a million throats proclaim
That their Motherland is Mother still
In something more than name!

It is time! Come, all together, come!
Not to the fife's call, not to the drum;
Right needs you; Truth claims you—
That's a call indeed
One must heed!
Not for the weeping
(God knows there is weeping!);
Not for the horrors
That are blotting out the page;
Not for our comrades
(How many now are sleeping!)
Nor for the pity nor the rage,
But for the sake of simple goodness
And His laws,
We shall sacrifice our all
For The Cause!

Beatrice Redpath

*When a poet belongs to no clique or côterie, nor has estab-
lished a reputation, opinions come uneasily. Beatrice Redpath
in 'Drawn Shutters' can be commonplace in the noble contemplation of essential life: a virtue in poetry. She comes down
at times to the minor level of 'The Dancer.' But 'To One Lying
Dead' is a poem of true loveliness, elegiac without dullness,
eloquent without gush. . . Beatrice Redpath feels the passions of rebellion and indignation. But to her they imply more
than mere dissatisfaction and chafing. Indeed, one might make
the quality of those passions the supreme test of character, certainly of poetic power. . . There is evidence in the volume
of life lived at first hand, of the discipline of actuality that
forces people either to a calm, strong normality, or to hectic
agony, and disquietness of spirit. And it is because the poet
soul rises to the reality of experience that her poems will not
depress. Of her brief songs it may be said that they come
like sunshine amid clouds, themselves noble and impressive.*
—T. P.'s WEEKLY.

BEATRICE REDPATH is the youngest of a family of three, the daughters and the son of the late Alexander Peterson, C.E., and his wife whose maiden surname was Langlois. Both parents were native Canadians; and their daughter, Beatrice, was born in Montreal.

Alexander Peterson, C.E., was very distinguished in his profession. He was the engineer of the C.P.R. bridge, built in 1886, across the St. Lawrence, at Lachine; and was Chief Engineer of the Canadian Pacific Railway, when the Ste. Anne and Vaudreuil bridges were constructed, and the great bridge at Sault Ste. Marie. The New York *Times* declared that he was 'one of the best railway engineers in the world.'

Beatrice Peterson was educated in private schools in her native city, until she was seventeen years old, when she moved to Goderich, Ontario, and lived there for five years. In April, 1910, she married Mr. William Redpath, of Montreal. They have one little boy.

Drawn Shutters, her first book, was published in 1914, and capable critics were quick to discern the clear vision and fine artistry of the poet.

Earth Love

GOD, in Thy Heaven hast Thou ever known
Toil, when the heart and hand were fused in one,
The sweet bruised scent of grasses newly mown,
The sharp delight to see each dawn the sun
Rising above the margent of the seas?
And hast Thou ever felt within Thy breast
That strange delight in dim uncertainties
With every day's apparellings unguessed?
Ah, hast Thou lain with wide entrancèd eyes
Wrapped in the purple veilings of the night
Beneath the fretted splendour of the skies
And seen them tressed with coronal of light,
Yearning to push their silvern fringe apart
And so adventure to Eternity?
God, I have strangely felt it in my heart
Walking upon the earth to pity Thee.

To One Lying Dead

STRANGE that thou liest so, void of all will
For loving; so content with thy long sleep
That neither word nor sound may stir the still
Calm quiet of the dream that thou dost keep.

Pale now the cherished contour of thy face,
Thy lids lie heavy 'gainst the ache of light,
And hold in their wan stillness ne'er a trace
Of waking from the shadow of thy night.

Languid thy tender feet unsandalled rest,
Wearied of passage o'er the furrowed earth;
They say thou art gone forth upon thy quest
Seeking a greater fullness of rebirth.

Yet all that I have ever known of thee
Lies here. What has gone out from thee this hour
That leaveth thee, unstirred by word from me,
Low lying, like a fallen scentless flower?

Hadst thou a soul which through the drifting years
My earth-bound vision was too dull to see?
And didst thou know the weight of unshed tears?
Hadst thou a spirit straining to be free?

A heart that knew regret and all desire,
And envy and that malice men call hate,
And saw with fear the slow consuming fire
Of life, and learned to be compassionate?

Then all of this was what I knew not of,
Thou wert but loveliness made manifest,
And wore the garment fashioned of my love
So fittingly that I ignored the rest.

Shall all of thee that I have ever known
Become as dust the sun shines not upon?
I did not know thy soul so strangely flown,
So may not find thee where thou now art gone.

Then let me kneel thus worshipping and see—
Thee whom I love, still lying as thou art,
That I may ever keep long dreams of thee
And hold thine image close within my heart.

So shall I look upon thy face so fair,
And thy sealed lids which sleep doth seem to please,
Thy mouth's pale blossom and thy fallen hair,
Where heavy shadows lie at pleasant ease.

Rebellion

THE earth lay wrapped in pale low hanging mist,
As some white tomb all ready for its dead
I thought, and shudderingly forward pressed
Into that shadowed house where night still hung
Darkly, as though it yet were loath to leave
While he lay there so still within the room.

. . . . .

There was a garden once where the rose trees
Were heavy with white globes of scented bloom,
There the bright-shafted arrows of the moon
Fell down the amethystine ways of night,
And silence hung so heavy on the air
We scarcely dared to fret the night with speech.

. . . . .

Ah, how the scent of that rose garden now
Drifts back, and for a moment lulls my pain,
But then more poignant seems my heart's sharp ache,
For he lies dead, silent and all alone.

How strange it is to be the first time here,
And pass by every room where he has been
Which now are empty as a disused frame.
Along these halls his feet have often trod
Unto the sound of Her voice calling him,
So careful of Her pleasure as his wont. . .
Ah, how the shadows of these empty halls
Seem pressing on my throat to stifle me,
Until I feel I may not reach that room. . .
I thought my heart acquainted well with grief,
But oh, I had not known there was such woe
In all the world as this, O God as this,
To stand and look on my belovèd dead.
O Death, I did not know thou wert so still

And so remote from all this troubled world;
Thou takest from me what was never mine,
And yet all mine the loss, all mine to bear
The hungry emptiness of aching days.

For oh, Belovèd, though so far from thee
Yet thy love warmed me as the distant sun
Lightens a planet in a further space,
And so I was not wholly comfortless.
Now is the light gone out across the world,
Yet earth reels always purposelessly round.
Ah, I would scream aloud unto the stars
That thou art dead, what need have they to shine,
What need have moons to drift across the skies,
Or suns to flare above a barren earth?

Belovèd, now thou art beyond the world
And art no longer bound to cherish Her,
But now shalt love me as thy spirit wouldst.
Ah, shall repression be our single creed?
All Thou hast made, God, Thou hast fashioned free,
But man would place a bridle on it all,
Chain the glad golden lightnings to his need,
Stem the bright rivers eager from the hills,
And burden earth with palaces of steel;
So would he place his rule above our hearts
And stifle love with a remorseless law.

But now, Belovèd, dust thou not have grief
And know regret because of wasted years
That knew no profiting but only loss?
Surely thou seest now how vain are laws,
How greatly God in Heaven esteemeth love.
There was a garden once where the rose-trees
Were heavy with white globes of scented bloom. . .
Ah, dear, canst thou not hold thine arms again
More wide for me, I am so tired with tears,
And resting even now within thine arms
I might forget a little while to weep.

The Daughter of Jairus

I HAVE fashioned soft raiment for her to wear
   And have laid her embroidered sandals in her room,
I have said I would braid and bind her heavy hair,
But she has gone out to the orchard to gather bloom.

Last night she lay in the dusk with her eyes adream,
And I questioned of what were her dreams as I touched her
      hand,
But she looked at me with a smile in her eyes' dark gleam,
What word might she use to make me understand?

So she spoke instead of the earth all bathed in light,
Of the moon as a lily when the leaves unfold,
Of the trees like silver plumes to deck the night,
Of the starry skies as a blazoned script unrolled.

She has no praise for all she had cherished before,
And has given away her beads of yellow gold,
Strange she seems, yet more kind than heretofore,
And I marvel much at the dreams she must withhold.

She has spoken no word about her curious sleep,
And the light in her eyes we have vainly essayed to read,
The secret of her dream she must hidden keep,
For her lips are framed but to an earthly need.

She has left her sandals lying upon the floor
And all untasted her goblet of amber wine,
She has gone out to the sun beyond the door
To sit in the cool green gloom of the hanging vine.

My Thoughts

MY thoughts are as a flock of sheep
   Upon a windy wold,
At eventide they homeward creep
To shelter from the cold;
And when I lay me down to sleep
They rest within the fold.

Alfred Gordon

Mr. Alfred Gordon, who for some years has been residing in Montreal, is a young English poet whose work reveals extraordinary genius and distinction. No praise can be too high for some of the poems in this most promising volume of initial verse. . . . . The changes that have come over English poetry, largely on account of the war, are seen faithfully reflected in this book, and these changes make for greater manliness, greater nobility and greater austerity of thought. . . . . It is in the poems that make up the first section of this remarkable book that the young poet's genius shines out in all its mature and austere nobility. The 'Vision,' 'Easter Ode' and the 'Ode for Dominion Day,' with the poems 'England to France,' 'The Little Church,' 'At Evening Prayer' and 'On a Dead Modern Poet,' contain some of the finest and most exalted writing that has been done in the field of modern English poetry.—REV. JAMES B. DOLLARD, in 'The Globe,' Toronto.

TO meet unexpectedly a new poet of originality and power, and to feel for a few minutes the charm of his frank, sincere and warm-blooded personality, was my privilege in a Yonge Street bookstore, one fortunate day in January, 1916. The poet was Mr. Alfred Gordon of Montreal, and my attention had just been drawn by Mr. Albert Britnell to Father Dollard's appreciative critique, when in walked Mr. Gordon with a volume of his *Poems* under his arm.

Mr. Gordon was born in London, England, in 1888. He was educated in a private school, and at Finsbury Technical College, where he studied for three years and graduated with a certificate in Mechanical Engineering. Shortly after graduation he was employed by the Underfeed Stoker Company, and in connection with this company, first saw Canada in 1908, when he came out on the Allan Line steamer, Corinthian, assisting in boiler tests to determine the relative efficiency of mechanical stoking as against hand-firing.

This was the voyage on which the Corinthian came into collision with the Malin Head, and Mr. Gordon was stranded with the rest for a fortnight at Levis. Through a misunderstanding the steamer continued homeward without him, and he was left alone and penniless.

Eventually he got back to England, but not finding congenial employment of a permanent nature, he decided, in June, 1910, to cross the ocean again, this time to settle in Canada. He came first to Toronto where he says,

I was engaged in almost unbelievably humble work, before I went to Lachine and entered the employ of The Dominion Bridge Company as a structural draughtsman.

Mr. Gordon stuck to draughting, 'eventually making good,' and was with The St. Lawrence Bridge Company when the Great War broke out, unsettling industrial conditions and causing loss of employment to himself and others.

The drudgery—to him—of a clerkship in an insurance office provided a livelihood for a time, when he resigned to become Managing Editor of *The Canadian Spectator and Bookman,* a new journalistic venture with headquarters in Montreal. In this city Mr. Gordon resides with his mother, to whose devotion and guidance he ascribes whatever attainment and success he has achieved.

Dedication

THERE was a time in boyhood, ere life ceased
   To hold a miracle in every hour,
We saw a City shining in the East
   That drew us towards it with a magic power.

I saw its spires in glittering array,
   And called you to me, while, with shaded sight,
We looked and wondered how far off it lay.
   And looked again along the roadway white.

I told you how right fair it was, and you,
   Half-willing only, placed your hand in mine—
'T was but a mirage—aye, that all men knew,
   But yet none mortal ever might divine.

And now the whole width of the Atlantic main
   Divides the fortune of our temporal ways;
Perhaps we shall not meet on earth again
   Except in memories of those bygone days.

With strengthened vision you, maybe, have wrought
   The consummation of that early dream,
Whilst I, too certain in Youth's pride, am brought
   To cry the passing of its transient gleam.

Indeed, I think now that I did not see
   The Eternal City of man's endless quest—
'T was Art, not Life, that first awakened me,
   Though, once awakened, I might never rest.

I saw the beauty, first, of Form alone;
   To Knowledge, not to Wisdom, I aspired:
But hardly even God to Youth makes known
   The things 'more excellent' of Him required.

Who were the captains of my early song?
   Swinburne and Dowson, Symons, Oscar Wilde:
Sensuous or violent, but seldom strong;
   By them unconsciously I was beguiled.

Yet it was natural I should mistake
   Their loves and lutes and towers of ivory
For that Adventure which the soul must make
   Or else for ever ignominious be.

And, at the root, the difference is not great;
  'T is but a strangeness more profound I seek:
The Boy's romance, to him, is filled with Fate,
  Although his elders of it lightly speak.

So here, inversely, and from time to time,
  Is told, dear friend, my pilgrimage since then—
From decoration and embroidered rhyme
  To some poor reading of the minds of men.

I sometimes ponder if each soul that wins
  An entrance to the far-off gates thereof,
May make atonement for a spirit's sins,
  If once it dwelt with it, on earth, in love.

I wonder if those hours, though so long past,
  When we in word and deed went hand in hand,
Will be a sacrament, and, at the last,
  Together in that City we shall stand?

Easter Ode, 1915

O SPRING! To whom the Poets of all time
    Have made sweet rhyme;
And unto Lovers, above all, most dear!
How shall they hymn thee in this latter year,
When Death, not Life, doth ripen to his prime?
What pulse shall quicken, or what eye grow bright,
With Love's delight,
Now sleepeth not the bridegroom with the bride?
What flowers shall cover, or what grasses hide
The miles of mounds that thrust upon our sight?

April's light showers, that made the sun more sweet,
Seem now to beat
In constant boding of the nations' tears:
Across the pastures, to each mother's ears,
The lambs and ewes more piteously bleat.
The fledglings fallen from the nest awake,
In hearts that break,
A new compassion for their fluttering:
The brown soft eyes of every furry thing
Seem doubly tender for our sorrow's sake.

Pity, through Terror, hath touched every heart;
None stand apart,
In blunted sense or in the spirit's pride:
The base and gross are cleansed and purified;
Life to the lettered grows more great than Art.
Terror, of Tragedy the nether pole,
Hath purged the soul;
The priest and prophet cry not now alone:
Blood and burnt-offerings, that we thought outgrown,
Now seem the centre of a cosmic whole.

On every hill, blood stains the melting snow,—
The rivers flow
Crimson and swollen with the unburied dead;
Through vale and meadow like a silver thread
The streams wind not as but a year ago.
The stolid ploughman as a rite or prayer
Doth drive his share,
But Plague and Famine in the furrows stalk;
While, in the cities, our distracted talk
Betrays the fever of a constant care.

Nay! It is Autumn, surely, and not Spring,
That we should sing?
Autumn whose breath makes every leaf forlorn!
'Put in thy sickle on the standing corn!
The sheaves are ready for the garnering!'
But, like a trumpet, even as we doubt,
A Voice rings out
Above the shrill of the increasing strife:
Lo, it is Easter! And there dawns such life,
The very stars, in exultation, shout!

Before the glory of the seraphim
Earth's hosts grow dim;
The Rights of Nations and man's empires fade:
No more from God each seeks peculiar aid;
In equal penitence all turn to Him.
And though the quickening of the countless slain
We plead in vain,
Life, and not Death, shall reap this harvest-tide:

Love in the Pit shall seal the Prince of Pride;
The Peace we mocked, in triumph shall obtain.

Caught up in vision, lo, I dare to pen
Patmos again:
'Behold! The kingdoms of this world shall be
Those of our Lord, and of His Christ; and He
Shall reign for ever and for evermore.'   Amen.

England to France

A paraphrase of Mr. Clutton-Brock's prose tribute, 'France'

O FRANCE! On this dire anniversary
    After what fashion should we sing to thee?
Or should we sing?
Or if one sang in such an hour, should we?
For, in times past, how often have we said
But vanity and folly crowned thy head,
And that in thee there was no stable thing?

Yet thou didst judge us with like jaundiced eyes—
A people gloomy as their own grey skies,
Whom neither love
Nor hate nor fear nor death might agonise:
That never new a lifetime in one kiss;
Deaf to all rhapsody of woe or bliss,
Of Hell beneath them, or of Heaven above.

For perfidy we were to thee a name,
As thou to us for all licentious shame,
Until that day
All such loose folly was consumed with flame:
But now, howe'er the tide of battle run,
This year for us an era has begun
Which shall not soon or lightly pass away.

As lovers' quarrels now stand forth revealed
The petty wrangles that we kept unhealed
In jealous pride,
But now for ever and for ever sealed;
Only the wasted past shall we now rue,
The love unowned which yet at heart we knew,
And which from now shall never be denied.

As Sidney hailed thee in thy fame gone by,
'France, that sweet enemy!' So now we cry,
'France, that sweet friend!'
Yet, as of old, a Queen; with fame more high.
Sweet friend for ever, yet on this high day
A Queen in meet and glorious array
To whom in homage all the nations bend.

O France! Fair land of sunlight and the vine,
To whom illusion and romance were wine,
By what new light,
High o'er the conflict, doth thy spirit shine?
We have grown old and outlived dangerous dreams,
While through thy veins the fire of youth yet streams—
How shall *we* praise thy calm restraint aright?

Girt by the sea, howe'er so greatly pressed,
Always secure we had one place of rest,
And well we doubt
If we or any had endured thy test:
Wherefore we praise thee as none else before,
And in our hearts a memory of thee store
That shall not fade till all the stars die out.

For thou not merely hast survived thine hour,
Not, in thy trial, but preserved thy power;
But hast come forth
From thine affliction with yet richer dower:
A strange, new strength thy spirit doth endue,
A strength unknown of nations hitherto—
Far from the fury of this day of wrath.

As of fair women purged by bitter ruth,
Who have outlived the passions of their youth
And find at length
Peace in the quiet sanctuaries of truth;
Who smile where once they laughed, and yet are seen
More beautiful than they have ever been
In any triumph of their former strength,

Who walk in ways so gracious and so still,
Whose mien so calm a majesty doth fill,
Their purpose seems

Not theirs, but part of the eternal will:
So thou, O France, before the world dost fight
Not for thyself alone, but that great light
In which the very flood of freedom streams.

That light indeed which always lighted thee,
Howe'er disguised or fitful it might be—
Aye, even when
The holiest things thou mad'st but mockery:
Falsehood for truth, in error, thou hast deemed,
But never the idea of truth blasphemed—
So that great light thou guardest once again.

There is no God, thou saidst, but never said
Thyself wast God, and power unlimited
Thy right divine,
That all the earth should tremble at thy tread:
Aye, with what laughter, sweetly terrible,
Voltaire had hurled this Anti-Christ to Hell,
Cleaving him shrewdly to the very chine.

How thine immortal soul in him had flamed
To see thy temples ruined and defamed;
What thing more crude
The lightning laughter of his scorn had claimed?
For though destruction overtake thy fanes,
Yet indestructible the faith remains,
Purged of its dross, and strengthened and renewed.

Barbarian hordes that have but one recourse,
How shall thy foes, O France, assail the source
Of that hid life,
Who think to slay the spirit by brute force?
Upon the glory of the past they war,
But, 't is the future that thou fightest for,
And that great glory which shall crown thy strife,

For lo! Whatever wounds are this day thine,
More clear through suffering doth thy spirit shine,
Made once again
For all mankind a standard and a sign:
Aye, as of old, o'er Terror and o'er Wrath,
The clarion cry of Liberty goes forth,
And, as of old, it doth not cry in vain!

Virna Sheard

A study of 'The Miracle and Other Poems' shows at once that the author is not merely a Canadian poet; her outlook and her range know little of time or place; she belongs to the readers of poetry at large. . . . Though Mrs. Sheard's poems are by no means of uniform quality, there are enough of the best to ensure her a high place in Canadian poetry. Her tender sympathy with small or helpless things, her interpretation of the music of nature, her spiritual quality and her rendering of reverent Biblical subjects reflect the mind of an idealist, and are the inspired lines of one deeply moved. Often there is a touch of sadness or of the whimsical, but never a suggestion of triviality or flippancy. There is little of incident or action: most of the poems are pure lyrics. In many cases there is a strong appeal to the æsthetic.—M. O. HAMMOND, in 'The Globe,' Toronto.

The attention of the reader is directed very specially to the sublime figure of the 'Slumber Angel,' 'As down the dusk he steps, from star to star.'—The Editor.

[451]

VIRNA SHEARD was born in Cobourg, Ontario, a
daughter of the late Eldridge Stanton, and is of United
Empire Loyalist descent. Her grandmother was a first cousin
of the famous American abolitionist, Wendell Phillips. She
was educated in Cobourg, and in the city of Toronto.

In 1885, she married Dr. Charles Sheard, of Toronto, and
for years devoted most of her time and energy to domestic and
social duties.

Mrs. Sheard is the mother of four stalwart, talented sons,
one of whom is serving as a lieutenant at the Front, and
another is in training.

In 1898, poems and short stories by 'Virna Sheard' began
to appear in magazines and journals and since then she has
published four novels: *Trevelyan's Little Daughters,* 1898; *A
Maid of Many Moods,* 1902; *By the Queen's Grace,* 1904; and
The Man at Lone Lake, 1912.

The novels have merit and were well received, but Mrs.
Sheard's fame will likely rest in greater measure on her
exquisite lyrics. A collection of these was published in book
form in the fall of 1913, under the title, *The Miracle and Other
Poems.* Of these, 'In Egypt,' the longest and greatest poem in
the book, is too lengthy for quotation in full. It is based on the
biblical story of Pharaoh and his obstinate refusal to deliver
the Israelites from bondage, and its dramatic spirit is so well
sustained throughout, that we should like to see more poems
from this author's pen, with mythical and historical themes.

The Slumber Angel

WHEN day is ended, and grey twilight flies
  On silent wings across the tired land,
The slumber angel cometh from the skies—
The slumber angel of the peaceful eyes,
  And with the scarlet poppies in his hand.

His robes are dappled like the moonlit seas,
  His hair in waves of silver floats afar;
He weareth lotus-bloom and sweet heartsease,
With tassels of the rustling green fir trees,
  As down the dusk he steps, from star to star.

Above the world he swings his curfew bell,
   And sleep falls soft on golden heads and white;
The daisies curl their leaves beneath his spell,
The prisoner who wearies in his cell
   Forgets awhile, and dreams throughout the night.

Even so, in peace, comes that great Lord of rest
   Who crowneth men with amaranthine flowers;
Who telleth them the truths they have but guessed,
Who giveth them the things they love the best,
   Beyond this restless, rocking world of ours.

Dreams

KEEP thou thy dreams—though joy should pass thee by;
   Hold to the rainbow beauty of thy thought;
It is for dreams that men will oft-times die
   And count the passing pain of death as nought.

Keep thou thy dreams, though faith should faint and fail,
   And time should loose thy fingers from the creeds,
The vision of the Christ will still avail
   To lead thee on to truth and tender deeds.

Keep thou thy dreams through all the winter's cold,
   When weeds are withered, and the garden grey,
Dream thou of roses with their hearts of gold,
   Beckon to summers that are on their way.

Keep thou thy dreams—the tissue of all wings
   Is woven first of them; from dreams are made
The precious and imperishable things
   Whose loveliness lives on, and does not fade.

Keep thou thy dreams, intangible and dear
   As the blue ether of the utmost sky—
A dream may lift thy spirit past all fear,
   And with the great may set thy feet on high.

In Solitude

HE is not desolate whose ship is sailing
    Over the mystery of an unknown sea,
For some great love with faithfulness unfailing
    Will light the stars to bear him company.

Out in the silence of the mountain passes,
    The heart makes peace and liberty its own—
The wind that blows across the scented grasses
    Bringing the balm of sleep—comes not alone.

Beneath the vast illimitable spaces
    Where God has set His jewels in array,
A man may pitch his tent in desert places
    Yet know that heaven is not so far away.

But in the city—in the lighted city—
    Where gilded spires point toward the sky,
And fluttering rags and hunger ask for pity,
    Grey Loneliness in cloth-of-gold, goes by.

The Daisy

AN angel found a daisy where it lay
    On Heaven's highroad of transparent gold,
And, turning to one near, he said, 'I pray,
    Tell me what manner of strange bloom I hold.
You came a long, long way—perchance you know
In what far country such fair flowers blow?'

Then spoke the other: 'Turn thy radiant face
And gaze with me down purple depth of space.
See, where the stars lie spilled upon the night,
Like amber beads that hold a yellow light.
Note one that burns with faint yet steady glow;
It is the Earth—and there these blossoms grow.
Some little child from that dear, distant land
Hath borne this hither in his dimpled hand.'
Still gazed he down. 'Ah, friend,' he said, 'I, too,
Oft crossed the fields at home where daisies grew.'

The Lily Pond

ON this little pool where the sunbeams lie,
This tawny gold ring where the shadows die,
God doth enamel the blue of His sky.

Through the scented dark when the night wind sighs,
He mirrors His stars where the ripples rise,
Till they glitter like prisoned fireflies.

'Tis here that the beryl-green leaves uncurl,
And here the lilies uplift and unfurl
Their golden-lined goblets of carven pearl.

When the grey of the eastern sky turns pink,
Through the silver edge at the pond's low brink
The little lone field-mouse creeps down to drink.

And creatures to whom only God is kind,
The loveless small things, the slow, and the blind,
Soft steal through the rushes, and comfort find.

Oh, restless the river, restless the sea,
Where the great ships go, and the dead men be!
The lily-pond giveth but peace to me.

The Harp

ACROSS the wind-swept spaces of the sky
The harp of all the world is hung on high,
And through its shining strings the swallows fly.

The little silver fingers of the rain
Oft touch it softly to a low refrain,
That all day long comes o'er and o'er again.

And when the storms of God above it roll,
The mighty wind awakes its sleeping soul
To songs of wild delight or bitter dole.

And through the quiet night, as faint and far
As melody down-drifted from a star,
Trembles strange music where those harp-strings are.

But only flying words of joy and woe,
Caught from the restless earth-bound souls below,
Over the vibrant wires ebb and flow.

And in the cities that men call their own,
And in the unnamed places, waste and lone,
This harp forever sounds Life's undertone.

The Lonely Road

WE used to fear the lonely road
    That twisted round the hill;
It dipped down to the river-way,
    And passed the haunted mill,
And then crept on, until it reached
    The churchyard, green and still.

No pipers ever took that road,
    No gipsies, brown and gay;
No shepherds with the gentle flocks,
    No loads of scented hay;
No market-waggons jingled by
    On any Saturday.

The dogwood there flung wide its stars,
    In April, silvery sweet;
The squirrels crossed that path all day
    On tiny flying feet;
The wild, brown rabbits knew each turn,
    Each shadowy safe retreat.

And there the golden-belted bee
    Sang his sweet summer song,
The crickets chirped there to the moon
    With steady note and strong;
Till cold and silence wrapped them round
    When autumn nights grew long.

But, oh! they brought the lonely dead
    Along that quiet way,
With strange procession, dark and slow,
    On sunny days and grey;
We used to watch them, wonder-eyed,
    Nor cared again to play.

And we forgot each merry jest;
    The birds on bush and tree

Silenced the song within their throats
    And with us watched to see,
The soft, slow passing out of sight
    Of that dark mystery.

.   .   .   .   .

We fear no more the lonely road
    That winds around the hill;
Far from the busy world's highway
    And the gods' slow-grinding mill;
It only seems a peaceful path,
    Pleasant, and green, and still.

From 'In Egypt'

O WHEN the desert blossomed like a mystic silver rose,
    And the moon shone on the palace, deep guarded to the
        gate,
And softly touched the lowly homes fast barred against their
        foes,
    And lit the faces hewn of stone, that seemed to watch and
        wait—

There came a cry—a rending cry—upon the quivering air,
    The sudden wild lamenting of a nation in its pain,
For the first-born sons of Egypt, the young, the strong, the
        fair,
    Had fallen into dreamless sleep—and would not wake again.

And within the palace tower the little prince slept well,
    His head upon his mother's heart, that knew no more
        alarms;
For at the midnight hour—O most sweet and strange to tell—
    She too slept deeply as the child close folded in her arms.

Hard through the city rode the king, unarmed, unhelmeted,
    Toward the land he loaned his bondsmen, the country kept
        in peace;
He swayed upon his saddle, and he looked as looked the dead—
    The people stared and wondered though their weeping did
        not cease.

On did he ride to Goshen, and he called 'Arise! Arise!
Thou leader of the Israelites, 'tis I who bid you go!
Take thou these people hence, before the sun hath lit the
skies ;—
Get thee beyond the border of this land of death and woe!'

Across the plains of Egypt through the shadows of the night
Came the sound as of an army moving onward steadily.
And their leader read his way by the stars' eternal light
While all the legions followed on their journey to the sea.

. . . .

The moon that shineth overhead once saw these mysteries—
And then the world was young, that hath these many years
been old;
If Egypt drank her bitter cup down even to the lees
Who careth now? 'Tis but an ancient tale that hath been
told.

Yet still we hear the footsteps—as he goeth to and fro—
Of Azrael, the Angel, that the Lord God sent below,
To Egypt—long ago.

From ' The Temple '

HERE is the perfume of the leaves, the incense of the
pines—
The magic scent that hath been pent
Within the tangled vines :
No censer filled with spices rare
E'er swung such sweetness on the air.

And all the golden gloom of it holdeth no haunting fear
For it is blessed, and giveth rest
To those who enter here—
Here in the evening—who can know
But God Himself walks to and fro!

And music past all mastering within the chancel rings;
None could desire a sweeter choir
Than this—that soars and sings,
Till far the scented shadows creep—
And quiet darkness bringeth sleep.

J. Edgar Middleton

Jesse Edgar Middleton was born, November 3rd, 1872, in the township of Pilkington, Wellington county, Ontario. His father, Rev. E. Middleton, is of English birth, and his mother, Margaret Agar, was born and brought up at Newton Brook, near Toronto. The future poet and humourist had the advantage of the Methodist Itinerancy in becoming acquainted with many types of humanity. He was educated at the Strathroy Collegiate Institute, and at Dutton High School. For three years he was a public school teacher, then he entered a publishing house in Cleveland, Ohio, as a proof-reader. After three years of this, he entered Journalism in Quebec city. Later, he came to Toronto as music critic of the 'Mail and Empire,' but since 1904, he has been on the staff of 'The News.' Mr. Middleton is choirmaster of Centennial Methodist Church, and a member of the Mendelssohn Choir. He was married in 1899, to Bessie A. Jackson, of London, Ontario, and has one son. Some excellent war verse from his pen has appeared in his widely-read column, 'On The Side.'—The Editor.

The Colonial

I NEVER saw the cliffs of snow,
  The Channel billows tipped with cream,
The swirling tides which ebb and flow
  About the Island of my dream.
I never saw the English downs
  Upon an April day,
The quiet old Cathedral towns,
  The hedgerows white with may.

  And still the name of England
    Which faithless tyrants scorn
  Can thrill my soul. It is to me
    A very bugle-horn.

A thousand leagues from Albion's shore
  In newer lands I saw the light,
I never heard the cannon's roar,
  Nor saw a mark of Britain's might,
Save that my people lived in peace
  And blessed the harvest sun,
And thought that tyranny would cease,
  And battle-days be done.

  And still the flag of England
    Was rippling in the breeze
  And twice two hundred ships of war
    Were surging through the seas.

I heard Polonius declaim
  About the new, the golden age,
When Force was but the mark of shame,
  When men would curb their hellish rage.
'Beat out your swords to pruning hooks,'
  He shouted to the throng,
But I—I read my History-books
  And wondered at the song.

  For it was glorious England,
    The guardian of the free,
  Who loosed those foolish tongues—but kept
    Her cruisers on the sea.

And liberty was ours to love,
  To raise a brood of lusty sons,

To worship Him who reigns above,
  And ah!—we never saw the guns,
The search-lights sweeping o'er the sky,
  The seamen stern and bold,
Our only thought, to live and die,
  And comb the earth for gold.

But it was glorious England
  Who scanned the threatening morn,
And ah, the very name of her
  Is like a bugle-horn!

Off Heligoland

GHOSTLY ships in a ghostly sea,—
  Here's to Drake in the Spanish main!—
Hark to the turbines, running free,
  Oil-cups full and the orders plain.
Plunging into the misty night,
  Surging into the rolling brine,
Never a word, and never a light,—
  This for England, that love of mine!

Look! a gleam on the starboard bow,—
  Here's to the *Fighting Temeraire!*—
Quartermaster, be ready now,
  Two points over, and keep her there.
Ghostly ships—let the foemen grieve.
  Yon's the Admiral, tight and trim,
And one more—with an empty sleeve—
  Standing a little aft of him!

Slender, young, in a coat of blue,—
  Here's to the *Agamemnon's* pride!—
Out of the mists that long he knew,
  Out of the *Victory*, where he died,
Here, to the battle-front he came.
  See, he smiles in his gallant way!
Ghostly ships in a ghostly game,
  Roaring guns on a ghostly day!

There in his white silk smalls he stands,—
  Here's to Nelson, with three times three!—

Coming out of the misty lands
  Far, far over the misty sea.
Now the Foe is a crippled wreck,
  Limping out of the deadly fight.
Smiling yond, on the quarterdeck
  Stands the Spirit, all silver-bright.

Hell's Half Acre

SIX years of life in the reek of things
  Where love is a fay unknown;
A wolfish boy on the crowded street
  Who stoops for the cruel stone;
No laughter-light in his infant eyes,
  No joy and no baby shame.
'Tis Hell's Half Acre has made him thus
  And we are the ones to blame.

Oh, look you well at the rosy lad
  Who sits on your knee to-night,
His arms entwining about your neck,
  His big round eyes alight.
Oh, list you well to his silver laugh
  Which echoes on Heaven's street,
Till the angels smile as they pause to hear
  The sound so glad and sweet.

Your boy is filled with the joy of love;
  He knows your protecting hand.
It keeps him out of the Lake of Lies
  'Mid the hills of Hopeless Land.
And yet his brother, a child of woe,
  Is living in black despair
In Hell's Half Acre, and you and I
  Are willing to leave him there.

God help the child of a devil's home
  With his broken-hearted sigh.
He cringes low in his filthy rags,
  A curse for his lullaby.
Six years of life in the reek of things
  Where God is an empty name.
'Tis Hell's Half Acre, beside our doors,
  And we are the ones to blame.

Arthur S. Bourinot

The name Bourinot stands for a good deal in Canadian letters, and it is gratifying to observe that the mantle of a gifted father gives promise, in this little volume of poems, of worthily descending to a literary son. . . . . There is a good deal of promise in 'Laurentian Lyrics and Other Poems.' The meaning throughout the poems is always clear, and there is no straining after effect. The poetic conception is, however, yet lacking in that strength which comes from a higher vision and deeper realization of life, for as yet, using the words of Tennyson, 'Sorrow has not ruled our author's life. Divine dissatisfaction and suffering are the altar stairs whereby genius develops and bears goodly fruit.'—'The Globe,' Toronto.

The sonnet 'To the Memory of Rupert Brooke' is an admirable piece of work.—'The Literary Digest.'

There is a delicacy and fragrance about them; they breathe the love of nature's wide spaces.— 'The Evening Telegram,' Toronto.

MR. ARTHUR STANLEY BOURINOT, B.A., was born in Ottawa, Oct. 3rd, 1893, of native Canadian parents, —his father, the late Sir John Bourinot, K.C.M.G., Clerk of the House of Commons and an author of repute, and his mother, Isabelle Cameron, a daughter of the late Mr. John Cameron, of Toronto—and his education was received in the public school, in the Ottawa Collegiate Institute, and in University College, Toronto.

After graduation in 1915, he became a civil servant in the Department of Indian Affairs at Ottawa, but in a few months was granted leave of absence to accept a commission as lieutenant in the 77th Overseas Battalion.

Lady Bourinot resides in Ottawa.

In reply to a question or two, Mr. Bourinot writes:

I never went in much for sports but always did a lot of walking. Most of my summers have been spent camping at Kingsmere in the Laurentians, whence I got the title of my book.

Laurentian Lyrics and Other Poems was published in December, 1915. It contains but twenty-four short lyrics— not much in quantity—but the quality is that of a true singer, piping his first notes with a sure instinct and with the joy of creation.

To the Memory of Rupert Brooke

HE loved to live his life with laughing lips,
And ever with gold sunlight on his eyes,
To dream on flowered uplands as they rise,
O'er which the moon like burnished metal slips;
To hear the gypsy song in sails of ships,
And wander o'er the waves 'neath azure skies,
Seeing the splendour of tired day which dies
And into lone oblivion slowly dips.

But suddenly his country clashed in arms,
And peace was crushed and trampled like pale bloom,
Beneath the careless feet of man and beast,—
The world was turmoil, stirred from west to east,
And song and gladness had no longer room,
For drum and bugle called with loud alarms.

Autumn Silence

HOW still the quiet fields this autumn day,
The piled up sheaves no more retain their gold,
And ploughmen drive their horses o'er the mould,
While up into the hills and far away
The white road winds to where the sun's last ray
  Mantles the heavens in a scarlet fold
  Of glorious colour, of radiance untold,
And then the twilight turns the red to gray.

How still the quiet fields this autumn eve;
  And yet we know that here, in other lands,
Red war still causes mothers' hearts to grieve,
  And lives are spent as countless as the sands.
O God, we ask that Thou wilt put to flight
The shadows of this quiet autumn night!

A Flower in the City Street

I FOUND a flower in the city street,
Crumpled and crushed it lay,
Trodden down by the careless feet
Of all who passed that way.

Its colour was not o' the fairy green,
Grey was its gypsy face,
But still it wore a wisp o' sheen
The world could not efface.

It fell like a gem from a woman's breast,
Loosed like a frightened thing,
And I recalled the haunting rest
Of meadows in the spring.

I found a flower in the city street,
With red heart crushed to grey,
And life to me seemed sweet, so sweet,
Bright as the break of day.

Returning

I CAME once more 'midst the Laurentian Hills,
Where love and I with laughter used to stray,
And wandered o'er green uplands where life stills
And fauns and fairies dance at dying day.
The pallid trilliums nodded fast asleep,
With pale, white faces peering through the gloom;
A sweet and subtle incense seemed to creep
Across the silence of the world's broad room;

And breath o' dusk was sweet in lilac time
And dark, brown throated birds burst forth in song,
While through the valley rang the evening chime,
And little stars flowered the skies ere long;
Dreaming, I trod the shadowed, dusty way;
Alas, with dawn, my dreams were dimmed and grey!

The Harvest Wind

LAST night the wind swept swiftly o'er the fields,
Where late the wheat swayed golden in the sun,
And where no more the singing reaper wields
His scythe, for now the harvest toil is done.

The wind stole quietly, but with chilling breath,
And voice as seeking, seeking without end,
And low, its murmur said, 'I bring not Death
But only sleep, the lover and the friend.'

The wind swept past and onward o'er the hills,
With restless pace, unwearying in its quest,
And in my heart I felt the fear that stills,
For swift I heard its beating in my breast.

The whispering of strange voices filled the night;
I dreamed the dead were drifting on the wind,
Returning to their land with hastening flight;
And still I hear the words the wind's voice dinned.

Index

PAGE

Bartlett, Gertrude 395
The Gunners 396
Put by the Flute 396
Ballade of Barren Roses. 397
Ballade of Tristram's Last
  Harping 398

Blackburn, Grace 383
The Evening Star 384
Epic of the Yser 385
Sing Ho for the Herring 385
If Winter Come 386
The Cypress-Tree 387
The Chant of the Woman. 387

Blewett, Jean 189
Chore Time 191
For He Was Scotch, and
  So Was She 192
The Passage 193
Quebec 194
What Time the Morning
  Stars Arise 194
The Usurer 196

Bourinot, Arthur S. ... 463
To the Memory of Rupert
  Brooke 464
Autumn Silence 465
A Flower in the City Street 465
Returning 466
The Harvest Wind 466

Cameron, Geo. Frederick 101
Ah, Me! the Mighty Love 102
Standing on Tiptoe 103
The Way of the World... 103
I Am Young 104
What Matters It? 104
To the West Wind 105
An Answer 106
Wisdom 107

PAGE

Amoris Finis 107
In After Days 107

Campbell, Wilfred 87
England 89
The Children of the Foam 91
The Dreamers 93
Stella Flammarum 95
The Mother 96
The Last Prayer 99

Carman, Bliss 109
Earth Voices 111
A Mountain Gateway 113
Garden Shadows 114
The Tent of Noon 115
Spring's Saraband 116
Low Tide on Grand-Pré. 117
Threnody for a Poet 118
At the Making of Man ... 119

Coleman, Helena 205
More Lovely Grows the
  Earth 206
To a Bluebell 207
Indian Summer 208
Prairie Winds 209
Enlargement 211
Day and Night 211
Beyond the Violet Rays.. 212
As Day Begins to Wane.. 212

Crawford, Isabella Valancy 33
Songs of the Soldiers 35
  His Mother 35
  His Wife and Baby ... 36
  His Sweetheart 37
From Malcolm's Katie ... 38
From 'The Helot' 43
The Mother's Soul 44
The Rose 46

[467]

PAGE

Dollard, Rev. James B. . 413
Rupert Brooke 415
The Haunted Hazel 415
The Fairy Harpers 416
At Dead o' the Night,
Alanna 417
Ballad of the Banshee .. 418
The Passing of the Sidhe 419
Ould Kilkinny 420

Drummond, Wm. Henry 177
The Wreck of the 'Julie
Plante' 179
Little Bateese 180
Johnnie Courteau 182
De Nice Leetle Canadienne 184
Madeleine Vercheres 185

Eaton, Arthur W. H. .. 197
The Phantom Light of the
Baie Des Chaleurs 199
The Lotus of the Nile.. 200
I Watch the Ships 201
L'Ile Sainte Croix 202
The Bridge 203

Gordon, Alfred 443
Dedication 445
Easter Ode, 1915 446
England to France 448

Hale, Katherine 323
At Noon 325
Grey Knitting 325
You Who Have Gaily Left
Us 326
When You Return 326
In The Trenches 327
I Used to Wear a Gown of
Green 327
To Peter Pan in Winter.. 328
The Answer 329

Harrison, S. Frances .. 123
Gatineau Point 125
The Voyageur 125
Danger 126
Les Chantiers 126

PAGE

Petite Ste. Rosalie 127
St. Jean B'ptiste 128
Catharine Plouffe 129
Benedict Brosse 129
In March 130

Holland, Norah M. 407
To W. B. Yeats 408
The Unchristened Child.. 409
The King of Erin's
Daughter 409
My Dog and I 410
Cradle Song 411
Home Thoughts From
Abroad 411
Sea Song 412

Huestis, Annie Campbell 273
The Little White Sun .. 274
The Will-o'-the-Wisp 275
Aldaran 276
On the Stair 280

Johnson, E. Pauline.... 145
In the Shadows 147
As Red Men Die 149
The Song My Paddle Sings 150
The Lost Lagoon 152
The Pilot of the Plains... 152
The Songster 154
The Riders of the Plains. 155

Lampman, Archibald .. 61
April in the Hills 63
The Truth 64
Morning on the Lievre .. 65
Heat 66
A January Morning 67
After Rain 68
Winter Evening 69
In March 69
The Railway Station 70
War 70
April Night 73
The Largest Life 73

Livesay, Florence Randal 371
Immortality 372

PAGE

The Young Recruits 373
Song of the Cossack 373
Khustina—The Kerchief.. 374
At Vieille Chapelle 375
The Bride of the Sea 376

Logan, John Daniel ... 265
The Over-Song of Niagara 267
Cartier: Dauntless Dis-
coverer 268
Champlain: First Canadian 268
Laval: Noble Educator... 269
Brock: Valiant Leader ... 269
Winifred Waters 270
Wind o' the Sea 270
Timor Mortis 271

MacDonald, E. Roberts. 221
Voices 223
The Spell of the Forest.. 223
The House Among the Firs 223
The Fire of the Frost.... 224
White Magic 225
The Signal-Smokes 225
Dreamhurst 226

Mackay, Isabel E. 237
The Mother 239
Out of Babylon 239
Marguerite de Roberval.. 240
The Passing of Cadieux.. 243

Mackenzie, George A. . 389
In That New World Which
Is the Old 391
To a Humming-Bird 391
Magellan 392
My Baby Sleeps 393
The Sleep That Flits on
Baby's Eyes 393
Compel Them to Come In 394

Mair, Charles 19
The Last Bison 21
From 'Tecumseh' 26
Tecumseh to General Har-
rison 29

PAGE

Enter General Brock and
Lefroy 30

Marshall, William E. . 399
Brookfield 401

McArthur, Peter 295
Corn-Planting 297
To the Birds 297
An Indian Wind Song.... 298
Sugar Weather 299
The End of the Drought 300
The Stone 301

McCollum, Alma Frances 289
Where Sings the Whip-
poorwill 291
The Angel's Kiss 291
The Silent Singer 292
Love 292
The Angel of the Sombre
Cowl 292
Little Nellie's Pa 293

McCully, Laura E. ... 421
Our Little Sister 423
The Troubadour's Lyre.. 423
Canoe Song at Twilight.. 424
A Ballad of the Lakes .. 424
Mary Magdalene Solilo-
quizes (On Love) 427

McInnes, Tom 247
The Damozel of Doom... 249
Illumined 250
Underground 253

Merrill, Helen M. 259
Bluebirds 261
Sandpipers 261
When the Gulls Come In 262
In Arcadie 263
A Hill Song 264

Middleton, J. Edgar... 459
The Colonial 460
Off Heligoland 461
Hell's Half Acre 462

PAGE

Montgomery, L. M. 353
When the Dark Comes
Down 355
Sunrise Along Shore 355
Off to the Fishing Ground 356
The Old Man's Grave ... 357
The Old Home Calls 358

Norwood, Robert 331
His Lady of the Sonnets. 333
Dives in Torment 336

O'Hagan, Thomas 213
An Idyl of the Farm 215
The Old Brindle Cow 216
The Dance at McDougall's 217
The Song My Mother
Sings 218
Ripened Fruit 219
The Bugle Call 219
The Chrism of Kings 220

Osborne, Marian 341
Love's Enchantment 342
Love's Gifts 343
Love's Anguish 343
Despair 344
If I Were Fair 344
The Song of Israfel 345

Pickthall, Marjorie L. C. 305
The Lamp of Poor Souls 307
The Pool 307
The Shepherd Boy 308
The Bridegroom of Cana 309
A Mother in Egypt 311

Redpath, Beatrice 437
Earth Love 438
To One Lying Dead 439
Rebellion 440
The Daughter of Jairus .. 442
My Thoughts 442

Roberts, Charles G. D. .. 47
The Solitary Woodsman . 49
Kinship 50
The Succour of Gluscâp . 52

PAGE

Two Spheres 53
Earth's Complines 54
Introductory 55
The Flight of the Geese 55
The Furrow 56
The Sower 56
The Mowing 57
Where the Cattle Come to
Drink 57
The Pumpkins in the Corn 58
A Nocturne of Conse-
cration 58

Roberts, Lloyd 429
The Fruit-Rancher 431
Miss Pixie 431
England's Fields 432
Husbands Over Seas 433
The Winter Harvest ... 434
Come Quietly, Britain 434

Roberts, Theo. Goodridge 377
The Maid 378
The Blind Sailor 379
Private North 380
The Lost Shipmate 381
The Reckoning 382

Sangster, Charles 9
Sonnet 10
Lyric to the Isles 11
The Soldiers of the Plough 12
Harvest Hymn 13
The Rapid 14
The Wine of Song 15
Brock 16
The Plains of Abraham .. 17

Scott, Frederick George 75
The Feud 77
Samson 78
Dawn 80
The River 81
The Storm 82
In the Winter Woods ... 83
The Unnamed Lake 84
The Burden of Time 85

PAGE

Scott, Duncan Campbell 133
  At the Cedars 135
  The Forgers 137
  The Voice and the Dusk.. 138
  The Sea by the Wood ... 139
  The Wood by the Sea ... 140
  The Builder 141
  The Half-Breed Girl 142
  From 'Lines in Memory of
    Edmund Morris' 143

Service, Robert W. 359
  The Call of the Wild..... 361
  The Law of the Yukon .. 362
  The Cremation of Sam
    McGee 365
  The Lure of Little Voices 369
  Little Moccasins 370

Sheard, Virna 451
  The Slumber Angel...... 452
  Dreams 453
  In Solitude 454
  The Daisy 454
  The Lily Pond 455
  The Harp 455
  The Lonely Road 456
  From 'In Egypt' 457
  From 'The Temple' 458

Smythe, Albert E. S. .. 347
  The Way of the Master.. 349
  November Sunshine 350
  By Wave and War 350
  Anastasis 351
  The Trysting Path 352

Stringer, Arthur 313
  The Lure o' Life 315
  At the Comedy 316
  The Old Garden 316
  Destiny 319
  The Keeper 320
  The Seekers 320
  War 320
  Morning in the North-
    West 321
  From 'Sappho in Leucadia' 322
  The Final Lesson 322

PAGE

Sullivan, Alan 281
  Suppliant 283
  Prospice 283
  The Kite 284
  Came Those Who Saw
    and Loved Her 285
  Brébeuf and Lalemant.... 286

Thomson, Edward Wm. 157
  Thundercloud's Lament .. 159
  The Mandan Priest 161
  The Canadian Rossignol
    (In May) 163
  The Canadian Rossignol
    (In June) 164
  From 'Peter Ottawa' 166

Watson, Albert D. 227
  Dream-Valley 229
  From 'Love and the Uni-
    verse' 229
  Breeze and Billow 230
  The Comet 231
  The Sacrament 232
  The Lily 232
  God and Man 233
  A Prayer 233
  From 'The Hills of Life'. 234
  Cromwell 235
  Usury 236

Wetherald, Ethelwyn .. 167
  The House of the Trees .. 169
  The Screech-Owl 169
  My Orders 170
  If One Might Live 170
  Legacies 171
  The Hay Field 171
  The Followers 172
  The Wind of Death 172
  The Indigo Bird 173
  At Waking 174
  The Song Sparrow's Nest 174
  Earth's Silences 175
  Mother and Child 175
  Prodigal Yet 176
  Pluck 176

Warwick Bro's & Rutter, Limited, Printers and Bookbinders, Toronto, Canada.